Thought Forms

Volume III of the Introduction to Magic series

Bob Makransky

ISBN 9780967731582

Library of Congress Catalog Card Number 00-90021

Makransky, Bob
Thought forms / by Bob Makransky. – 2nd ed.
p. cm. -- (Introduction to Magic ; part 3)
Includes bibliographical references

1. Magic--Handbooks, manuals, etc.
2. Astrology--Handbooks, manuals, etc.
3. Consciousness. I. Title.
BF1566.M35 2000   133.3'4
QBI00-229

Published by Dear Brutus Press

"All that we are is the result of what we have thought: it is founded on our thoughts, it is made up of our thoughts"

— *The Dhammapada*

Table of Contents

Frontispiece – An Astrological Map of Consciousness
Preface 1
An Introduction to the Astrology of Consciousness .. 5

What are Thought Forms?

Part I: The Doorway to Happiness 20
Part II: The Stuff That Dreams are Made Of 27
Part III: Importance 33
Part IV: Active Imagination 38
Part V: Homunculi of Cognition 46
Part VI: The General Theory of Thought Forms .. 49
Part VII: Dreaming and Waking 57

Chapter I: The Synodic Cycle of Mercury

Introduction 69
   The Astronomical Basis of
       Mercury's Synodic Cycle 78
   The Conjunctions 87
      Inferior Conjunction (IC) 94
      Superior Conjunction (SC) 97
   The Elongations 99
      Greatest Western Elongation (GWE) 104
      Greatest Eastern Elongaton (GEE) 104
   The Stations 105
      Stationary Direct (SD) 107
      Stationary Retrograde (SR) 108
   The Retrograde Phases 109
      Phase 1: IC to SD 111
      Phase 6: SR to IC 112
   The Standard Phases 113
      Phase 3: GWE to SC 113
      Phase 4: SC to GEE 114
   The Balanced Phases 116
      Phase 2: SD to GWE 118
      Phase 5: GEE to SR 118

Chapter II: Waking Mind

Society Teaches Us to Deny our Senses 120
Society Teaches Us to Deny our Sexuality 131
Society Teaches Us to be Irresponsible 140
Society Teaches Us to be Phony
    and to Hate Ourselves 144
How, Then, Can We Know Our True Feelings? 150

Chapter III: Dream Mind

The Theory of Light Fibers 162
Personal History and Future 172
A Brief History of Consciousness
    (with Future Prospects) 196

Chapter IV: Active Imagination

Examples of Active Imagination 238
Banishing Thought Forms 249
Light Fiber Techniques:
    Creative Visualization 253
    Defeating Black Magicians 261
    Casting Out Demons 272
    Tree Spirits 277

Summary 285
Glossary 291

Appendix 1: The Progressed Mercury Cycle ... 294
    Table of Day Numbers 297
    Progressed Conjunctions 298
    Progressed Elongations 301
    Progressed Stations 303

Appendix 2: The Transiting Mercury Cycle 307

Books by Bob Makransky 315

Appendix 3: Instructions for Determining
               Birth Types 325

Tables of Mercury's Synodic Cycle 1900 – 2050 327

An Astrological Map of Consciousness:

Symbol	Principle (skandha)	Manifestation in everyday life:	Conditioned by: (the three enemies of wisdom)	Aspect of Separatedness emphasized: (the three conditions of suffering)	Potential source of:
Sun	Intent (vinnana)	Decision			Purpose
Mercury	Mind (sankhara)	Attitude (thought forms)	Importance	Isolation	Creativity
Moon	Memory (sanna)	Mood (feeling – past)	Familiarity	Forgetting	Joy
Venus	Desire (vedana)	Concern (feeling – future)	Expectation	Doubt	Worth

Two Great Inventions in the History of Consciousness:

Mitosis = The invention of the sensory thought form (dream consciousness)

Meiosis = The invention of the conceptual thought form (waking consciousness)

Preface

All of us, deep in our inmost hearts, know that we are phony; and that all our pride and glory are just masks we wear for other people, so they won't see that we are actually ashamed of ourselves.

What we don't all know is that everyone else also feels the same way; and that in fact it is our society which imposes this burden of shame and silence upon us. Precisely why society does this to us, and what we can do about it – how we can overcome our guilt and "helplessness" and build a true self-esteem in line with our true feelings – will be the subject of this book.

What we will be talking about here are our feelings; and feelings are extraordinarily difficult to talk about. How, for example, could we describe the feelings of e.g. hunger, or sadness, or orgasm to someone who has never experienced them, in such a way that he or she would truly understand them? Feelings can be shared directly, but they cannot be comprehended intellectually nor communicated verbally (except in poetry).

This book is not a poem; but neither is it a presentation of ideas which can be developed in a linear, discursive fashion. In the four chapters of this book we will discuss the theory of thought forms from four very different points of view (astrological, psychological, metaphysical, and magical); and it must be borne in mind that we are not changing the definition of the term "thought form" as we go along. Rather, just as the elephant appeared quite different to each of the six blind men who touched different parts of its body, so too will our idea of what a thought form is depend upon how we approach it. Thus the following exposition should be regarded as a highly metaphorical account of what mind is and how it functions – i.e. as an intellectual model which can help us to get a handle on what we are truly feeling inside – rather than as a scientific or academic treatise.

Two further volumes in the present series are in preparation: one about the moon (the principle of memory), and the other about Venus (the principle of desire). Certain techniques mentioned en passant in this book (past life and probable reality regressions, recapitulation, and lucid dreaming) will be fully expounded in the companion volumes. The present series of books represents an attempt to build a bridge between Sigmund Freud and Carl Jung on the one hand, and Carlos Castaneda on the other – that is to say, between the psychotherapy of the twentieth century and the psychotherapy of the twenty-first. The practice of magic must indeed be viewed as a form of psychotherapy: it is founded on the proposition that what we call the world or reality is in fact the creation of each individual, influenced by his or her social training. There is no objective, factual reality out there – what we perceive to be reality is but a collection of thought forms inculcated into us by our parents and society. Hence, by changing our individual perceptions of the world, we can indeed change the world.

At the present time mainstream society's stand on magic is about the same as its stand on sex during Freud's time: it pretends that magic doesn't exist, and that only weird or evil people indulge in it or discuss the issue openly. But just as Freud didn't invent sex, neither did Castaneda invent magic. Rather, these two revolutionaries merely pointed out society's hypocrisy on these issues – and for that temerity they were both vilified.

Magic – particularly black magic – is what everyone is doing all the time and pretending they're not doing it. Just as until recently the society we live in forced us to repress our sexual feelings (e.g. pretend we aren't masturbating, pretend we are disgusted by oral sex, pretend that we men aren't casting furtive and predatory glances at the breasts, legs, buttocks, etc. of practically every woman we lay eyes on, etc., etc.), so too does it force us to pretend that magic doesn't exist; that we aren't actually bewitching and cursing one another, and engaging in all sorts of evil sorcery, beneath a superficial veneer of social niceties. Our society is, at root, evil; and it has a vested interest in keeping us – its individual members – as dissatisfied, angry, and fearful as possible in order to control us and keep us quiescent. What makes this issue so tricky is that our personal unhappiness and our ability to think and reason are inextricably intertwined. We are the only thinking species of animal on this earth, and we are the only truly miserable and self-destructive animal on this earth; and this is not a coincidence but rather cause and effect, as will be explained in these pages.

What we will be describing in the present series of books is an astrological map of consciousness. Freud's theory of the id, ego, and super-ego constitutes a simple map of consciousness; similarly, Castaneda's theory of the body of light fibers and the assemblage point constitutes another map of consciousness – rather more encompassing and far-reaching than Freud's. The astrological map of consciousness described in the present books falls somewhere between these two in both scope and complexity. However, it must be remembered that a model is only a model – it is not reality. It is merely a means of orienting ourselves intellectually, since understanding is necessary to pave the way for will to follow. Mind is the scout of intent.

Except for the astrological chapter, most of the material in this book was channeled. Some of the ideas discussed here derive from Castaneda, but a different nomenclature is employed. For example, the terms *waking consciousness*, *dream consciousness*, and *dreamless sleep* are used instead of *first attention*, *second attention*, and *third attention*; the terms *customary moods* and *customary concerns* are used instead of *human form*; and the term *demons* is used instead of *flyers*. Also, we will employ the terms *God* or *The Spirit* rather than the more accurate appellation *The source of light fiber emanations*.

The approach here is astrological, but no previous knowledge of astrology is required of the reader to understand and apply the astrological techniques. Technical information that would only interest a practicing astrologer is relegated to the appendices.

Much of the material in Chapter IV originally appeared in *Diamond Fire* magazine, and thanks are due to Joseph Polansky for permission to republish it here. I would also like to thank Fiona Percy for doing the drawings; Jonathon Bouchard for doing the cover; and Karen Collins, Milly Hernandez, Ed Lee, Janeen Simon, and Bob Wachtel for their perceptive critique and suggestions.

– B. M.

Note to 2nd (2010) edition: the essay *What are Thought Forms?* has been added to the text. This is an overview of the subject, which repeats some of the information given later on in the book.

If your only interest is astrology, then it suggested that you read only Chapter I and the Appendices, and skip the rest.

If your only interest is magic, then it is suggested that you read only Chapters III and IV, and skip the rest.

If your only interest is cognitive psychology, then it is suggested that you read only *What are Thought Forms?* and Chapters II and IV, and skip the rest.

Note to 3rd (2019) edition: the essay *An Introduction to the Astrology of Consciousness*, which originally appeared in *AA Journal*, has been added at the beginning.

An Introduction to the Astrology of Consciousness

"For now we see through a glass darkly; but then face to face: now I know in part; but then shall I know even as also I am known." – Corinthians I:13

"If the doors of perception were cleansed every thing would appear to man as it is, Infinite. For man has closed himself up, till he sees all things thro' narrow chinks of his cavern." – William Blake, *The Marriage of Heaven and Hell*

Mystics aver that humans' original (infant) awareness of the world is purer than that of adults, whose social training has obscured the true perception of what is actually going on "out there" by overlaying it with distorting interpretations. Evidently this distortion has survival value, inasmuch as adults are clearly abler than are infants; but on the other hand, according to the mystics, it also is the cause of all their unhappiness. In the words of Chögyam Trungpa [with the corresponding astrological archetype in brackets], *"The process that takes place here takes place in a fraction of a second of consciousness, that lasts something like a five-hundredth of a second. First you have an impression of something* [sun]. *It is blank, nothing definite. Then you try to relate to it as something and all the names that you have been taught come back to you and you put a label on that thing* [Mercury]. *You brand it with that label and then you know your relationship to it* [Venus]. *You like it or you dislike it, depending on your association of it with the past. ... Then you immediately send your message back to Memory, to the associations you have been taught.* [moon]*"*

These overlaying "filters" which modify moment-to-moment perception in order to make it "digestible" – i.e. which make the everyday world seem familiar and sensible (as opposed to utterly ineffable, which is how infants perceive it) – are termed *skandhas* in Buddhist philosophy. These *skandhas* carry meanings similar to that of the inner planets in astrology: the sun can be thought of as *vinnana* (Attention); Mercury *sankhara* (Mind); Venus *vedana* (Desire); and moon *sanna* (Memory). Consider, for example, the "life cycle" of a sensation: first there is pure awareness [sun] – the background or canvas upon which the sensation is painted. Then comes arousal [Venus] – the initial phase of the sensation, e.g. the first pulse of an orgasm or smell of a rose or spoonful of tiramisu, which is exquisitely intense and sublime. Subsequent pulses or smells or tastes lose that initial purity and immediacy as the "=>**I!**<= **am experiencing this sensation**" [Mercury] takes over (the sense of a detached self observing itself from a distance), and consequently the feeling dulls, becomes more remote, more separated from the true (original) sensation. In the final phase [moon] the sensation becomes a Memory, receding into the past. Actually, each individual sensation – pulse, smell, taste, whatever – goes through all of these phases in an instant; it's just that it's easier to see the progression it if you consider several happening in a row.

A similar categorization is described by Carlos Castaneda (quoted in Armando Torres' *Encounters With The Nagual*), who uses the term "Eagle's emanations" in place of "pure awareness": *"Imagine that at this moment you witness a group of the Eagle's emanations* [sun]. *Automatically, you transform it into something sensorial, with characteristics like brightness, sound, movement, etc.* [Venus]. *Then memory intervenes, which is under the obligation to give everything meaning, and you recognize it, for example, as another person* [moon]. *Lastly, your social inventory classifies it, by comparing the person with those you know; that classification allows you to identify him* [Mercury]. *Already, you are a good distance away from the real fact, which is indescribable, because it is unique."*

So, what is this real fact – the way infants apprehend the world? And what does it mean to get back to it? Mystical experiences, such as religious ecstasy (usually induced by spirits such as Jesus, Krishna, Buddha), as well as psychedelic tripping, are ways to peel back some of these layers and deconstruct adult consciousness; or at least allow us a glimpse of how the pieces fit together (by slowing the process down so that it becomes readily visible). For example, if you go out in the rain naked while tripping, you can feel (are consciously aware of) every individual drop of water as it hits your skin, as a discrete event. On the other hand you can't balance a checkbook while tripping because you can't think – there's too much going on to be able to focus that much Attention. The point is that adult consciousness is a matter of focus; whereas infant consciousness is a matter of awareness; focus and awareness work inversely (as one goes down the other goes up).

Infant perception consists of a flood of random, staccato impressions which bombard the Attention [sun] willy-nilly. This cavalcade of impressions consists largely of primary sensations [action of Venus] – not merely physical sensations (sights, sounds, smells) but also feelings. Venus thus acts as a kind of scout which saccades the Attention from thing to thing from moment to moment to take in what's out there, like a hungry animal sniffing out prey. Thus Venus is the planet of Desire: it is like a javelin which hurls Attention forward through time to reach out to a future. Actually, it is this hurling, this looking forward and outward (striving), which creates the "future"; thus we give Venus the keyword Expectation. The action of Venus is what animates Attention, which left unto itself has no preferences or direction but merely abides and takes everything in indiscriminately. Note that Desire is not Desire *for* something – Desire is a movement for its own sake: awareness naturally hungers for focus, and focus for awareness; and Desire is what moves Attention back and forth between the two. This dynamic – like a snake devouring its own tail – is what keeps the whole kit and caboodle in motion; and it is the cessation of this striving (by stilling Desire) that produces the state of ecstasy sought by mystics.

Which sensation to pay primary Attention to (to give the most Importance at any given moment) is the action of Mercury. It is Mercury which creates a separated "self" out of the sensations apprehended by Venus. For example, when you listen to sounds, particularly when you are very relaxed, sleepy, or tripping, you can distinguish between two phenomena: "sounds" and "listener listening to sounds." "Sounds" is when you are hearing all sounds indiscriminately, like a tape recorder does; when all sounds are impacting on your awareness with equal vividness [action of Venus]. This is how an infant perceives aurally. On the other hand, "listener listening to sounds" [action of Mercury] is when you are focusing on one specific sound, and the other sounds are in the background of your Attention; when one particular sound is more Important than the other sounds, and there is a =>YOU<= there who is listening to it.

In order to be able to focus upon one thing at a time (by separating it out from its background) it is necessary to create an artificial sense of a detached perceiver who is perceiving – i.e., a separation between perceiver and the object being perceived. This is the action of Mercury (Mind). Thus we can say that the difference between infant and adult consciousness is that the latter is focused through an artificial *self*. That is, the very act of focusing Attention on one thing at a time (instead of everything at once) creates a "self" – a separated =>I<= there in the midst of things – who is doing the focusing. Infants have no such sense of an =>I<=, a detached perceiver perceiving. All the *skandhas* (symbolized by the inner planets) are different filters which narrow this focus of Attention begun on the level of *sankhara* – Mind; and they enable the creation and sustenance of a (false, because impermanent) sense of a unique =>ME!<= in the midst of things which must be delimited and defended.

What sustains this detached perceiver perceiving from moment to moment – i.e., what endows this self with its (false) sense of continuity and permanence – is the action of the moon (Memory). Perhaps you have noticed (upon awakening) that in dreams which refer to events which supposedly occurred earlier in the same dream, the "previous events" are improvised ad hoc, on the fly; i.e. there were no "previous events" in that same dream. The so-called "previous events" which you (falsely) remember in the dream carry a gloss of Familiarity, which makes it seem "reasonable" (action of Mercury) that this credible (albeit non-existent) backstory in fact happened. Déjà vu is another example (taken from waking consciousness) of how Memory can make sensory impressions seem Familiar, even when no such events actually occurred. It is Memory which creates the illusion that the separated self had a personal history which led up to the present moment, just as it is Desire which creates the illusion that this separated self is moving forward through time to some probable future.

The problem is that sustaining this separated self (i.e., maintaining focus on a separated self with its personal history and probable future from moment-to-moment), requires a great deal of energy and discipline. In truth, it demands a continual clenching up of the Attention, what psychologists term "emotional repression", which is quite painful and exhausting. This is why infants find it necessarily to sleep so much of the time, to temporarily relieve the stress of the alien adult consciousness which is being imposed upon them from without (as Freud pointed out, this clenching up Attention to create a sense of a discrete, continuing self in the midst of things is completed by toilet training: that's the Great Divide, the capstone on the process of focusing Attention which separates infant from adult consciousness).

Adults' ongoing sense of a "self" – their feeling that they are discrete, continuing beings at the center of a world which is stable and real (instead of incomprehensible and overwhelming) – is achieved by their clinging frenetically to their "sanity" – their sense of having a separated self there – every moment they are awake. Adults have to be constantly wary, vigilant, and uptight – live their everyday lives in a state of unremitting anguish and suffering (albeit most adults have learned strategies of denial to pretend that this is "normal", inasmuch as everyone around them is upholding the selfsame lie; or else alleviate their pain by casting it onto other people) – in order to keep their "self" functioning. Otherwise, they'd go insane – lose their grip on their focus, so that everything dissolves back into pure awareness and they return to the state of helpless, vulnerable infants.

Of course, this "insanity" is precisely the state of ecstasy which mystics seek. However, mystics don't pursue this state as their permanent, everyday consciousness, since they too have to lead lives in the so-called real world; and religious ecstasy is not a particularly effective approach to addressing everyday concerns. Rather, what mystics seek to do is to bring the experience of religious ecstasy (self-lessness) to bear upon their quotidian lives and relationships just by being more *aware*; i.e., unfocusing (relaxing their tight grip on their "self") just enough to make themselves comfortable, but without losing their focus entirely.

For example, a basic level of religious ecstasy (of increased awareness) which practically everyone has experienced is called *flow*. This occurs when people's Attention is so caught up in an activity (e.g. listening to music, playing sports, making love) that they temporarily lose their sense of a separated self and thus become one with what is going on in the world around them. The point is that without focus there is no self – so the goal of spiritual training is to keep just enough focus going to lighten up, but without completely losing one's marbles. This is accomplished by obtaining volitional control over Mind, Desire, and Memory by paying Attention in the now moment, rather than reflexively ceding command to the automatic pilots of Importance, Expectation, and Familiarity.

Let's look at how the action of the inner planets defines the *self* in the horoscope; i.e., how different types of people maintain the illusion that they are separated, abiding entities going about their unique lives in a relatively stable environment:

Planet	Principle (*skandha*)	How focuses / traps Attention:	How delimits / defends the self
Sun	Attention (*vinnana*)		
Venus	Desire (*vedana*)	Expectation	What they deserve
Mercury	Mind (*sankhara*)	Importance	How they know they're right
Moon	Memory (*sanna*)	Familiarity	Where they fit in / belong

In a natal horoscope, conjunction of an inner planet with the sun symbolizes *focus* (behavior which is socially conditioned or constrained); whereas elongation from the sun symbolizes *awareness* (a more individualistic expression of that planetary energy). That is to say, the sun – which symbolizes pure awareness in infant sentience – in adults comes to symbolize societal conditioning. The place that pure awareness (joy) occupies in infant consciousness, becomes anxiety over how the person is thought of and treated by other people in adult consciousness.

Conjunction with the sun means that everything is seen through the lens of the self instead of perceiving what is actually out there. There is little objectivity, detachment, perspective; rather, the things that happen are seen as happening to a ME! whose reactions are predetermined by parental and societal training. On the other hand, when there is some distance between a planet and the sun, then that planet's activity is freer, more effective, not as constrained by conditioned defenses and pre-scripted agendas, and therefore better able to act effectively in the moment according to what a situation or other people actually require.

Conjunction with the sun creates a feeling of *self-consciousness*: as though all eyes are on the person (in that respect), hence these people keep themselves under tight control at all times. On the other hand, elongation from the sun – being as far away from the sun as a planet can get – means that these people are relatively uninhibited / uninfluenced by parental / societal fiat in making their choices (at least insofar as this planetary activity is concerned): they do their own thing and don't give as much of a damn about what other people think of them.

Mercury's relationship with the sun shows ways that different types of people establish their taken-for-granted assumptions – the peculiar varieties of logic which they bring into play to make and defend their decisions. Mercury indicates how and why people think they are *right* – doing the *right* thing and making the *right* choices. Mercury conjunction sun natives think that they are right because it is overwhelmingly Important to them to mechanically uphold the beliefs and standards which have been inculcated into them by their parents and society, rather than question them or take too close a look at their own motives in defending them. On the other hand, Mercury elongation natives know that they are right precisely because they haven't bought into what they were taught, but rather have ruminated endlessly to think things through and figure out all the angles for themselves.

Venus' relationship with the sun shows what people feel that they *deserve*. Venus conjunction sun natives feel they are undeserving unless they can be or do more than is humanly possible. They defer gratification of their Desires indefinitely in order to keep their hungry, striving self going on an endless treadmill. They Expect that if they play the game (whatever game they've been taught) by the strictest of rules, then their Desire will be fulfilled no matter how much bending themselves and other people out of whack this seems to require. On the other hand, Venus elongation natives believe they deserve whatever they can grab – they unhesitatingly reach out to take and enjoy whatever the smorgasbord of life offers them, and don't work up such a sweat (take it as a personal rejection / defeat) when they are thwarted.

The moon's relationship with the sun shows where people feel they *belong*: new moon people secure / Familiarize their selves by immersing themselves in a group, playing to an audience, enlisting supporters; thus always trying to be one up on other people and life itself. They underuse Memory by tending to drift along rather than "get down to it" and make a stand in life. By contrast, full moon people are thoroughly alienated, belong nowhere, and revel in their status (in their own eyes) as sojourners or outcasts; they learn to accustom themselves to the feeling of a permanent state of insecurity (unFamiliarity) in which everything around them is in flux.

Mercury conjunct sun natives tend to operate on instant, gut-level impressions and responses rather than on thinking things through. They possess powerful concentration and focus: once they have made up their Minds about something, they are indomitable. They have great personal force because they stand by their decisions and opinions come hell or high water; and standing by one's decisions is indeed the key to all personal power and success in life. However, the problem with Mercury conjunction is that the decisions they stand by are usually not their own, and therefore are not necessarily in their best interests. They hew very closely to the training their parents and society inculcated into them, with very little reflection or questioning. They were "good" and obedient children; and later on become "good" and obedient citizens who keep their mouths shut and do as they are told (and expect the people they have power over – children, spouse, employees – to do the same). Mercury conjunction natives are the backbone of society. Actually, what we are saying here about Mercury conjunction natives is true of everyone to one degree or another; the conjunction just represents the extreme case. No one ever escapes societal conditioning; however, greater separation between Mercury and the sun permits greater freedom of choice.

Mercury conjunct sun people don't examine their motives or reasons but rather charge ahead in the sure and certain knowledge that "God" – their parent and society – is on their side. Thus their decisions have great power and force of will behind them but evince little objectivity, discernment, or depth of understanding. They tend to be closed-minded and emotionally repressed individuals, with blinders which only permit them to see what they want to see, and they are critical and disapproving of anyone who doesn't measure up to their own prejudices. They don't permit other people the space to have feelings of their own: i.e., to disagree with them. This is why their intimate relationships so often turn into power struggles; and they can never see their own role in creating this reality for themselves. In spite of their lack of self-awareness, these natives nonetheless achieve a certain depth and delicacy of feeling because of the mythic terms in which they cast their lives – seeing themselves as bulwarks of righteousness and truth. Their noble (if grossly naïve and self-serving) idealism seeks to encompass all of the pathos of the human condition, and as such endows them with a principled moral rectitude.

Mercury elongation sun people have Mind developed to a high degree of refinement, embellishment, and decadence. Instead of relying upon gut-level instinct, they must puzzle everything through, and convince themselves (and other people) through logic and reasoned argument. Where the conjunctions sweat and bleed to stand their ground and defend their beliefs and opinions, the elongations are wholly creatures of practicality and expedience, flitting here and there like hummingbirds. Where the conjunction may be considered to be an underuse of Mind – that is, a refusal to take intelligent responsibility for the choices of everyday existence by operating on automatic pilot, the elongation may be considered an overuse of Mind – a refusal to act on the pure promptings of the heart without first thoroughly rationalizing them. Where the conjunction types are hamstrung by their societal training – utterly committed to upholding it to the death – the elongation types use their training as a springboard for further investigation. They can pick and choose behavior patterns, likes and dislikes, to a greater degree than the Mercury conjunction types (who fear change). On the other hand, these natives have more self-doubt than the conjunction types because their Mind is further removed from the ultimate source of self-assurance [sun]. Where the Mercury conjunctions rarely share their thoughts and feelings (indeed, they have a horror of sharing their thoughts and feelings, and thereby making themselves vulnerable); elongation natives, by contrast, tend to think out loud. They are generally quite frank and forthcoming about what's on their Minds. Where conjunction types clearly sense that all power in life comes from standing by one's already-made decisions (their problem being that the decisions they stand by are not their own, but those made for them by their parents and society), elongation natives stand by no decisions at all, hence they have less power over their lives no matter how clever and incisive they may be. The question that Mercury conjunction natives never ask themselves – which elongation natives never stop asking themselves – is: "Suppose I'm wrong?" These people are able to see everyone else's point of view, as well as the pros and cons of their own viewpoint; but this facility necessarily weakens their decisiveness (their willingness to make a commitment or take a firm stand). Where Mercury conjunction natives rely on immediate, knee-jerk responses; or immediate dismissal of new ideas to oblivion (once they've decided something, their Minds are made up forever); Mercury elongation sun natives rely on continual self-analysis, sifting and refining their thinking, over and over and over. The conjunction operates on blind faith; the elongation on lack of faith. What the elongation needs is a good dose of humility and a little less self-delight. There is a call here for a bit less cleverness and a bit more wisdom.

Venus conjunct sun people fancy themselves to be emotionally independent individuals, projecting a façade of blasé insouciance; but in truth this is but a defense to protect themselves precisely because they feel so vulnerable and susceptible to hurt. At root they are a good-natured souls, with benevolent impulses and a great deal of love to give; nevertheless they feel uncomfortable accepting expressions of love in return. They tend to brim with brooding frustration and bitter pride. In spite of their self-sufficient exteriors they take everything which happens very much to heart (though they try not to show it). They turn inward, hide their feelings, plow a lonely furrow (feeling put upon and unfairly judged);

and as a result, they tend to seek out / attract cold, unsympathetic intimates (who will put upon them and judge them unfairly). In their stubborn, even wrong-headed pride, these natives may make light of their shortcomings and failures; but they obsess over them and let things fester inside them. Their self-esteem is wrapped up in what they believe is Expected of them, thus they often feel trapped by circumstances, forced to do more than is necessary to acquit themselves with honor (and then feel unfairly used). They have a poorly developed sense of personal space – their own, and other people's. They find it difficult to just relax and be themselves in relationships – they must be constantly vigilant, guarded, picking at other people (and themselves), messing around with this and messing around with that, trying to make everything perfect, instead of enjoying and letting be. While outwardly they may affect a bluff bravado, inwardly they cringe and shrink from confrontation, preferring to suffer the slings and arrows of outrageous fortune, rather than take arms against a sea of troubles, and by opposing perhaps get beyond their depth (lose control). On the positive side, the fact that these natives are so overburdened with neurotic guilt makes them scrupulous in their personal conduct. They will always go more than halfway to meet and make peace with other people, and their naiveté and wishful thinking are undeniably part of their charm.

Venus elongation sun natives (for dates when Venus reaches both its conjunctions and its elongations, see http://www.astro.com/swisseph/ae/venus1600.pdf) are unapologetic and even a bit brazen in reaching out to take whatever life offers, with no shame or hesitation. They exalt in their own competence and freedom of action. They take a matter-of-fact (perfunctory) approach to everyday life and relationships. They are optimistic and adaptable, able to take setbacks in stride; and they refuse to let themselves be bent out of whack by the push and shove of everyday society. Thus they are able to capitalize on whatever opportunities arise, and patiently outwait obstacles without getting themselves into a twist. They don't regard rejection and frustration as a direct attack upon the foundations of their being because they have a strong sense of inner self-worth. They remain unswayed by the opinions of other people and the vagaries of circumstances: because they don't take the things which happen to them so personally, they are able to just shrug disappointments off and pick up where they left off (in contrast to the Venus conjunction natives, who are truly cut to the bone by rejection and hug their failures to the bosom). These natives tend to avoid relationships which they cannot dominate, and conflicts which they cannot win. For the most part, such adverse power positions are easily avoidable in life, except for people (e.g. Venus conjunction natives) who are deliberately seeking them. This is not to suggest that the Venus elongation natives shrink from combat when it comes their way: but they are out to win, not to indulge their sense of drama (like the histrionic Venus conjunction natives do). Venus elongation natives keep themselves aloof and unaffected – they are low-key and maintain an even keel, which on the negative side can make them difficult to reach or influence. On the positive side their ability to take things in stride without pother makes them cool in crises – they are realists who don't lose their heads or wring their hands helplessly, so they are the sort of people others look up to in times of doubt and confusion.

Moon conjunct sun natives seek to be looked up to and respected, and they are energetic, resolute, and daring, with an adventurous spirit which drives them forward. They may cultivate some area of expertise and competence at which they are undisputed masters in order to lend themselves a voice of authority, and to inspire the admiration of others. They seek out the unusual, the path less traveled, and they are constantly in motion. They possess a can-do willingness to follow their impulses, and they like to push the envelope, and be on the forefront. They possess a spirited freshness and spontaneity, and a jaunty individualism which enjoys holding the limelight. They are brash (brusque and bumptious) and outspoken (presumptuous), with an impatient bravado which doesn't suffer fools gladly. They just leap blindly ahead, and they have an infectious (reckless) optimism and sense of fun, living in the moment with little perspective or regard for consequences. Because they are direct, naïve, and credulous, they have a tendency to take things and other people at face value, and to turn their Attention and energy elsewhere if relationships get sticky or bog down, or if their fond imaginings don't pan out immediately. They have a nervous, restless energy that must be constantly on the move, and they try at all times to keep themselves loose and fancy-free; ergo, they have little staying power or stick-to-itiveness, and they are not very good at picking up undercurrents or warning signals since their focus is on whatever impression they are making right now. They are nonplussed by subtleties and possess little capacity for guile, preferring "open covenants openly arrived at"; and they are unable to take criticism or rejection because they are incapable of seeing their own personal motives, or anyone else's point of view, objectively. They are deaf to anything they don't want to hear and they will not be pinned down but slither off in some new direction. They are constantly on the run. They don't know how to hold their own – their wrong-headed obstinacy is but a pose, a last defense, since they never truly feel themselves to be standing on firm ground, which seems to be always shifting beneath their feet. Rather, they improvise and contrive expedients as need be, sweeping unsettling problems under the rug when they can, or else turning their Attention to something more pleasant. As a result, they don't learn much from their experience since they inevitably try to cover their butts and make lame excuses when they are caught with their hands in the cookie jar. On the other hand, they provide levity and hope when the going gets tough.

Moon opposition sun natives are more steadfast and grave than are the flighty new moon people. Where new moon instinctively gravitates towards groups, full moon instinctively pulls away and watches from the outside. These natives withdraw from others to do their own thing with little concern for issues of approval or rejection; and they depend on no one else for support or succor. They are independent and resolute, and they dig in their heels and tough it out as their first, middle, and last recourse. Where the new moon people are light and irrepressible, full moon natives are staunch and unconquerable. They actually prefer isolation and seclusion to human society since they feel little security that there is anything that can be depended on outside themselves. They prefer solitude to collaboration; or at least to any sort compromise unless it places them in a position of undisputed control. They possess infinite patience and are capable of beating a strategic retreat when necessary, willing to wait for a favorable turn of events rather than expose themselves unnecessarily. Because they are so wary and suspicious, and try to take into account all factors that must be reckoned with, they are far more alert to the possible ramifications and repercussions of their actions, and to other people's feelings (at least intellectually / strategically), than new moon natives are. However, they are by no means warm or sympathetic people – rather they are emotionally distant ("cold fish" is a good description – in comparison with the conjunction which is charismatic). They may make responsible spouses, parents, and citizens, but this is more a response to their own concept of where their duty lies, and to their (extreme) sense of personal honor – their fitness as human beings – than it is a spontaneous outpouring of affection, or a sense of real concern for the welfare of their family or society. Guided by their own abstract philosophy of what is moral and dignified, these natives are immoveable. They don't belong to any group, really; their acute awareness of what everyone around them is taking for granted makes them perennial outsiders. In all events they keep their own counsel, and share nothing of what they are truly feeling inside with anybody. In spite of their seeming self-sufficiency, full moon natives are often torn with self-doubt precisely because they are too distrustful of others to accept any feedback: they become huffy, feisty, and obtuse as a defense when their plans go awry and they are called to account, or when their considerable poise and élan fail them. Since they care not a fig for what others think of them, they are basically a law unto themselves, and recognize no authority but their own.

What Are Thought Forms?

The following series of articles originally ran in Bob Makransky's quarterly astro-magical ezine *Magical Almanac*, (http://groups.yahoo.com/group/MagicalAlmanac), and they repeat some of the information given in the main body of *Thought Forms*, and extend and elaborate on it. The purpose of magical training is to liberate ourselves from our social conditioning by learning how to operate on intent – direct knowing and acting – rather than by thought. To do this requires, first of all, analyzing exactly what thoughts we are thinking in our own moment-to-moment, day-to-day lives; and then controlling or rejecting these thoughts volitionally instead of being their mindless slaves.

This is what the theory of thought forms is all about: it gives us an intellectual handle on the magical process so that we can talk about it and describe it to other people. At the same time, the theory of thought forms dovetails quite well with current theories of consciousness being propounded by certain schools of materialistic cognitive psychology and philosophy; so we can see clearly where magical and materialistic thought coincide, and where they differ.

Part I: The Doorway to Happiness

There *is* a doorway to happiness; moreover, it's not that difficult to open it and step through. The doorway to happiness is sensory thought forms – what cognitive philosophers term *qualia*. Qualia are usually defined as the affective content of sensory perceptions. In the magical view, by contrast, sensory thought forms are regarded as an intermediate evolutionary stage between feeling and thinking (= conceptual thought forms).

In the present series of seven articles we will look at sensory and conceptual thought forms from different points of view – descriptive, practical, and theoretical. In this article we will describe, by example, what is meant by the term "sensory thought form". In the next six articles we will attempt to place sensory thought forms (qualia) and conceptual thought forms (variously termed memes, agents, schema control units, etc. in different materialistic theories of cognition) within a theoretical framework of alternative (non-materialistic) cognitive philosophy.

What is unique about magic as a religion (here the term "magic" is taken to subsume paganism, witchcraft, shamanism, etc. – as compared to e.g. the Abrahamic religions or the materialistic pseudo-science practiced in academia) – is that magic is a cognitive system rather than a belief system: it is a matter of direct knowing rather than idle speculation and validation by mutual back-patting. That is to say, unlike the Abrahamic religions and Rationalistic Materialism, magic is a matter of operating on sensory thought forms rather than conceptual thought forms.

Sensory thought forms are not only the doorway to happiness; they are the *only* doorway to happiness. Conceptual thought forms – that is to say, our socially-conditioned beliefs which lead us to pursue monetary wealth, social success and acceptance, or the love of Mr. or Ms. Right – are decidedly *not* the doorway to happiness but rather the doorway to slavery. Undoing our social conditioning and reconditioning ourselves is thus a matter of dethroning the power of our conceptual thought forms – the incessant, moment-to-moment yak-yak which occupies our attention most of the time we are awake – and substituting sensory thought forms (mindfulness, paying attention to the now moment) in their stead.

In the present article we will seek to answer the questions of what sensory thought forms are, and why are they the doorway to happiness, by example. Instead of trying to explain what sensory thought forms are (i.e. qualia – the affective content of sensory perceptions), we will let Thomas Wolfe explain it by example in the story which follows. Note that operating on sensory thought forms – being mindful, present in the now moment and experiencing "suchness" or "thusness" – is the doorway to happiness not only for Wolfe's narrator, but also for the two Negro boys who appear in the course of the story.

Circus at Dawn

By Thomas Wolfe

There were times in early autumn – in September – when the greater circuses would come to town – the Ringling Brothers, Robinson's, and Barnum and Bailey shows, and when I was a route-boy on the morning paper, on those mornings when the circus would be coming in I would rush madly through my route in the cool and thrilling darkness that comes just before break of day, and then I would go back home and get my brother out of bed.

Talking in low excited voices we would walk rapidly back toward town under the rustle of September leaves in cool streets just grayed now with that still, that unearthly and magical first light of day which seems suddenly to re-discover the great earth out of darkness, so that the earth emerges with an awful, a glorious sculptural stillness, and one looks out with a feeling of joy and disbelief, as the first men on this earth must have done, for to see this happen is one of the things that men will remember out of life forever and think of as they die.

At the sculptural still square where at one corner, just emerging into light, my father's shabby little marble shop stood with a ghostly strangeness and familiarity, my brother and I would "catch" the first street-car of the day bound for the "depot" where the circus was – or sometimes we would meet some one we knew, who would give us a lift in his automobile.

Then, having reached the dingy, grimy, and rickety depot section, we would get out, and walk rapidly across the tracks of the station yard, where we could see great flares and steamings from the engines, and hear the crash and bump of shifting freight cars, the swift sporadic thunders of a shifting engine, the tolling of bells, the sounds of great trains on the rails.

And to all these familiar sounds, filled with their exultant prophecies of flight, the voyage, morning, and the shining cities – to all the sharp and thrilling odors of the trains – the smell of cinders, acrid smoke, of musty, rusty freight cars, the clean pine-board of crated produce, and the smells of fresh stored food – oranges, coffee, tangerines and bacon, ham and flour and beef – there would be added now, with an unforgettable magic and familiarity, all the strange sounds and smells of the coming circus.

The gay yellow sumptuous-looking cars in which the star performers lived and slept, still dark and silent, heavily and powerfully still, would be drawn up in long strings upon the tracks. And all around them the sounds of the unloading circus would go on furiously in the darkness. The receding gulf of lilac and departing night would be filled with the savage roar of the lions, the murderously sudden snarling of great jungle cats, the trumpeting of the elephants, the stamp of the horses, and with the musty, pungent, unfamiliar odor of the jungle animals: the tawny camel smells, and the smells of panthers, zebras, tigers, elephants, and bears.

Then, along the tracks, beside the circus trains, there would be the sharp cries and oaths of the circus men, the magical swinging dance of lanterns in the darkness, the sudden heavy rumble of the loaded vans and wagons as they were pulled along the flats and gondolas, and down the runways to the ground. And everywhere, in the thrilling mystery of darkness and awakening light, there would be the tremendous conflict of a confused, hurried, and yet orderly movement.

The great iron-gray horses, four and six to a team, would be plodding along the road of thick white dust to a rattling of chains and traces and the harsh cries of their drivers. The men would drive the animals to the river which flowed by beyond the tracks, and to water them; and as first light came one could see the elephants wallowing in the familiar river and the big horses going slowly and carefully down to drink.

Then, on the circus grounds, the tents were going up already with the magic speed of dreams. All over the place (which was near the tracks and the only space of flat land in the town that was big enough to hold a circus) there would be this fierce, savagely hurried, and yet orderly confusion. Great flares of gaseous circus light would blaze down on the seared and battered faces of the circus toughs as, with the rhythmic precision of a single animal – a human riveting machine – they swung their sledges at the stakes, driving a stake into the earth with the incredible instancy of accelerated figures in a motion picture. And everywhere, as light came, and the sun appeared, there would be a scene of magic, order, and of violence. The drivers would curse and talk their special language to their teams, there would be the loud, gasping and uneven labor of a gasoline engine, the shouts and curses of the bosses, the wooden riveting of driven stakes, and the rattle of heavy chains.

Already in an immense cleared space of dusty beaten earth, the stakes were being driven for the main exhibition tent. And an elephant would lurch ponderously to the field, slowly lower his great swinging head at the command of a man who sat perched upon his skull, flourish his gray wrinkled snout a time or two, and then solemnly wrap it around a tent pole big as the mast of a racing schooner. Then the elephant would back slowly away, dragging the great pole with him as if it were a stick of match-wood.

And when this happened, my brother would break into his great "whah-whah" of exuberant laughter, and prod me in the ribs with his clumsy fingers. And further on, two town darkeys, who had watched the elephant's performance with bulging eyes, would turn to each other with ape-like grins, bend double as they slapped their knees and howled with swart rich nigger-laughter, saying to each other in a kind of rhythmical chorus of question and reply: "He don't play with it, do he?"

"No, suh! He don't send no boy!"

"He don't say 'Wait a minute,' do he?"

"No, suh ! He say, 'Come with me!' That's what he say!"

"He go boogety – boogety!" said one, suiting the words with a prowling movement of his black face toward the earth.

"He go rootin' faw it!" said the other, making a rooting movement with his head.

"He say 'Ar-rumpf!'" said one.

"He say 'Big boy, we is on ouah way!'", the other answered.

"Har! Har! Har! Har! Har!" – and they choked and screamed with their rich laughter, slapping their thighs with a solid smack as they described to each other the elephant's prowess.

Meanwhile, the circus food-tent – a huge canvas top without concealing sides – had already been put up, and now we could see the performers seated at long trestled tables underneath the tent, as they ate breakfast. And the savor of the food they ate – mixed as it was with our strong excitement, with the powerful but wholesome smells of the animals, and with all the joy, sweetness, mystery, jubilant magic and glory of the morning and the coming of the circus – seemed to us to be of the most maddening and appetizing succulence of any food that we had ever known or eaten.

We could see the circus performers eating tremendous breakfasts, with all the savage relish of their power and strength: they ate big fried steaks, pork chops, rashers of bacon, a half dozen eggs, great slabs of fried ham and great stacks of wheat-cakes which a cook kept flipping in the air with the skill of a juggler, and which a husky-looking waitress kept rushing to their tables on loaded trays held high and balanced marvelously on the fingers of a brawny hand. And above all the maddening odors of the wholesome and succulent food, there brooded forever the sultry and delicious fragrance – that somehow seemed to add a zest and sharpness to all the powerful and thrilling life of morning – of strong boiling coffee, which we could see sending off clouds of steam from an enormous polished urn, and which the circus performers gulped down, cup after cup,

And the circus men and women themselves – these star performers – were such fine-looking people, strong and handsome, yet speaking and moving with an almost stern dignity and decorum, that their lives seemed to us to be as splendid and wonderful as any lives on earth could be. There was never anything loose, rowdy, or tough in their comportment, nor did the circus women look like painted whores, or behave indecently with the men.

Rather, these people in an astonishing way seemed to have created an established community which lived an ordered existence on wheels, and to observe with a stern fidelity unknown in towns and cities the decencies of family life. There would be a powerful young man, a handsome and magnificent young woman with blonde hair and the figure of an Amazon, and a powerfully-built, thick-set man of middle age, who had a stern, lined, responsible-looking face and a bald head. They were probably the members of a trapeze team – the young man and woman would leap through space like projectiles, meeting the grip of the older man and hurling back again upon their narrow perches, catching the swing of their trapeze in midair, and whirling thrice before they caught it, in a perilous and beautiful exhibition of human balance and precision.

But when they came into the breakfast tent, they would speak gravely yet courteously to other performers, and seat themselves in a family group at one of the long tables, eating their tremendous breakfasts with an earnest concentration, seldom speaking to one another, and then gravely, seriously and briefly.

And my brother and I would look at them with fascinated eyes: my brother would watch the man with the bald head for a while and then turn toward me, whispering:

"D-d-do you see that f-f-fellow there with the bald head? W-w-well he's the heavy man," he whispered knowingly. "He's the one that c-c-c-catches them! That f -f -f fellow's got to know his business! You know what happens if he m-m-misses, don't you?" said my brother.

"What?" I would say in a fascinated tone. My brother snapped his fingers in the air.

"Over!" he said. "D-d-done for! W-w-why, they'd be d-d-d-dead before they knew what happened. Sure!" he said, nodding vigorously. "It's a f-f-f-fact! If he ever m-m-m-misses it's all over! That boy has g-g-g-got to know his s-s-s-stuff!" my brother said. "W-w-w-why," he went on in a low tone of solemn conviction, "it w-w-w-wouldn't surprise me at all if they p-p-p-pay him s-s-seventy-five or a hundred dollars a week! It's a fact!" my brother cried vigorously.

And we would turn our fascinated stares again upon these splendid and romantic creatures, whose lives were so different from our own, and whom we seemed to know with such familiar and affectionate intimacy. And at length, reluctantly, with full light come and the sun up, we would leave the circus grounds and start for home.

And somehow the memory of all we had seen and heard that glorious morning, and the memory of the food-tent with its wonderful smells, would waken in us the pangs of such a ravenous hunger that we could not wait until we got home to eat. We would stop off in town at lunchrooms and, seated on tall stools before the counter, we would devour ham-and-egg sandwiches, hot hamburgers red and pungent at their cores with coarse spicy sanguinary beef, coffee, glasses of foaming milk and doughnuts, and then go home to eat up everything in sight upon the breakfast table.

(Copyright 1935 by Thomas Wolfe)

Part II: The Stuff That Dreams are Made Of

Sensory thought forms are the stuff that dreams are made of. In the previous article we described what sensory thought forms are by example. Sensory thought forms are similar to what cognitive philosophers term qualia (the affective content of sensory perceptions). The chief difference between the ideas of qualia and sensory thought forms is that the qualia of the materialistic model are regarded as adventitious tassels on sensory perceptions (the feeling that a sight, sound, smell, taste, or touch evokes); whereas in the sensory thought form model the aroused feelings are considered to be the real McCoy – what's really happening – and the sense perceptions associated with them are the mere tassels, the pale reflection, the dance of shadows in Plato's cave, added as an afterthought (at a later stage of temporal evolution).

Any time that we are feeling feelings in the now moment, we are operating on sensory thought forms. Although we operate on sensory thought forms at times while awake, basically sensory thought forms are the stuff of dreams. The true distinction between waking and dreaming is not between whether our bodies are active versus dormant, but rather between whether we are operating on conceptual versus sensory thought forms (mindlessly or mindfully, respectively).

Dreaming came first evolutionarily (dreaming is the consciousness of one-celled beings); and waking is an outgrowth of dreaming which arose at the time multi-cellular life evolved. Any time that we are feeling feelings such as pleasure, pain, humor, sadness, hunger, orgasm, etc. we are basically dreaming. We are "awake" only when we're thinking (paying attention to something other than what is happening here and now). Since thinking and feeling cannot take place at the same time; and since we are thinking most of the time we are awake; and moreover since we have everyone around us in the waking world patting us on the back and corroborating the same distortion; it seems to us that waking (conceptual) consciousness is reality, and dreaming (sensory) conscious-ness is a kind of nebulous nonsense.

The reason why dreaming seems to be nonsensical as compared to waking is precisely the same reason that your non-dominant hand is clunky as compared to your dominant hand: your social training has led you to withdraw importance (focus) from your dreaming / non-dominant hand so as to specialize your attention on your waking / dominant hand. Indeed, these distinctions (dreaming vs. waking and handedness) arose at about the same time, when agriculture was invented.

Thinking – which enables us to sharpen our focus in waking – is a recent invention in human history, not even 12,000 years old. Ancient humans didn't think about what they would do next – they didn't make decisions based on reason – rather they *felt* what to do next. They just knew what to do, and they did it. This is a more functional mode of operation for a hunter-gatherer, who has to make a lot of quick decisions in the here-and-now; whereas the thinking mode is more functional for agriculture, trade, etc. where the concern is more for the past and future than for the now moment. Sensory awareness is closer to ancient humans' perception of the world than is our conceptual awareness.

According to the magical model, the experiences we have while dreaming are symbols for feelings – in dreaming, we feel our feelings by reacting to "objective" events (sensory thought forms). However it is actually our feelings which create the sensory thought form symbols, not the other way around. We are not feeling feelings in reaction to objective events, but rather the "objective events" are being called up by our feelings. This is why in the sensory thought form (as opposed to materialistic qualia) model the feelings are taken to be primary, and the sensory perceptions secondary: a sym-bolic reflection or projection of the feelings.

The manner in which feelings create sensory perceptions is easiest to see and understand when we are just dropping off to sleep, but are still awake enough to objectively discern the process (hypnagogic imagery) by which dreaming kicks in. At such times it is obvious that we are creating our own dream experiences, even if we are not consciously controlling or directing the process. In waking consciousness we operate on sensory thought forms whenever our thinking stops – either because we are very relaxed, or else because we are overcome by some powerful feeling (terror, awe, hilarity, etc.) so that our thinking is momentarily numbed or suspended.

According to the magical model, our senses are not input devices, but rather output devices; they don't perceive reality, they create it (project it outwards), using whatever programs society has installed in their thought form computer. This is what is meant by "you create your own reality." From the magical point of view what we call reality – or waking mind – is but a highly specialized form of dreaming, which we as a human society have learned to define and uphold together, and to pass along in turn to our children.

Infants are basically dreaming as their normal state of mind. They learn how to "be awake" from the adults around them. The point is that if we want to recapture that feeling of joy in being alive which we felt when we were infants – and that we still feel when we are dreaming – then we have to relearn how to operate on sensory thought forms in our waking lives, in a sustained moment-to-moment fashion (not merely now and then haphazardly, as when making love or listening to music). This is what insight meditation is all about. Another good way to begin making this shift is by going out to nature – particularly to trees – every single day without fail. Also, the "Following Feelings" chapter of my book *Magical Living* gives a complete explanation of a technique for easily learning how to make the shift to operating on sensory awareness in a sustained and deliberate fashion.

To briefly summarize this technique: go out alone to a place in nature away from people. You *can* go with someone else, but the tendency then is to try to slough the responsibility off onto the other person. You're going to die alone, so you might as well try to learn to live alone. It's best to do this technique at night at first, while you're still learning the technique, after you've already had a few hours' sleep. Once you master the technique, however, you can make the shift in awareness yourself any time, day or night. But the learning should be done at night because feelings are stronger at night. That is why people are afraid of the dark in conceptual awareness – it symbolizes feeling. In the state of sensory awareness the night isn't scary, but invigorating.

Take off all your clothes. If there's very rough ground or a real danger of cutting your feet, you may leave your shoes on; otherwise, go barefoot. The reason you go naked is to more easily feel the forces around you – the earth, wind, etc. – which are dulled by clothing. Also, if there's any chance of your being discovered, going naked helps to keep you alert. If it's cold or rainy, so much the better. Comfort is the enemy of feeling. To feel the world, you have to be raw and naked and vulnerable. Being "comfortable" is another one of those hoaxes – like being "secure" – which the capitalists have fooled you into buying, in order to sell their useless products.

Face east. It is helpful to be able to read the cardinal directions from the stars; but if you can't do this, or if it's cloudy, wear a compass around your neck. At all times and places you should always know where the cardinal directions lie. Now, see if you can feel a "pull" or "tug" in one direction. If not, turn slowly to your right until you feel a pull in one direction. You can use your eyes to help out: scan the area in front of you as you turn, to see if some one direction "looks" right. It's difficult to explain what this pull is supposed to feel or look like; if you just go out there and try it, you'll find that doing it is a lot easier than thinking about it or trying to describe it. Once you've done it once or twice, you'll have the idea; there's nothing abstruse about it whatsoever. In fact, we've all operated in sensory awareness when we were babies, so it's not as if we're conjuring up some alien state of consciousness from scratch.

If you feel silly out there in the wilderness in the middle of the night; or if you feel bemused or fretful about what you're supposed to be doing; know that this is just your self-importance trying to assert itself by copping out of taking responsibility for being here now. Following feelings must be done by feeling, not thinking. Wondering "Am I doing this right?" is an absurd (albeit natural) question – absurd, because the very asking of it is "wrong". Such a question makes sense in conceptual awareness because there feelings don't matter much – the important thing is the impression we're making on other people, and the little reward we get from them for salivating when the bell rings. In conceptual awareness the question "Am I doing this right?" is not only sensible, it is the very crux. But in sensory awareness you are following your own feelings, so there's no way to refer judgments to anyone else – no one but you can feel your feelings.

If you feel fearful, that's okay. It's normal for people to feel fearful when their self-importance is under attack. Take a few deep breaths, sit down, and relax. Look around; listen to the sounds; feel the night.

Now, when you feel that one direction is the "right" one, start walking in that direction. Take care not to have any preconceived ideas, because things can change at any moment. If a moment before you felt that you should go a certain way, but now you feel you should go a different way, by all means drop the earlier idea and go with how you feel now. You can't flip on an automatic pilot in sensory awareness – that just flips you back into conceptual awareness. You have to be constantly alert to the feeling of what direction you should be going in. If you're in doubt, just face east again and start over. If two different directions seem to pull you, switch from one to the other – scan one and then the other – to see which one feels stronger.

If all else fails, spin around in a clockwise direction faster and faster until you get dizzy and collapse on the ground. Whatever direction you are facing (or your head is pointing) when you fall is the direction you should go in.

In general, you should avoid depressions (low spots) in the land since they're energy depleting. You can feel how depressions have low vibrations: sounds become lower, and you feel as though you are walking through something viscous. On a "high" way things are cleaner and clearer: you are more alert and joyous. When following your feelings at night you must keep especially alert to smells, since these can help guide you as much in the dark as sight does in the daytime. There are smells that indicate danger, others that mean protection, happiness, etc. You pick up this kind of information as you go along, without really having to think about it.

Following feelings means following feelings. Fear of being lost is not a feeling; it's thinking. You can only be lost in the future, because in the now moment you're always right there, where you're standing. So if you indulge in worrying about whether you're getting lost, you've shifted out of sensory awareness and are back in conceptual awareness. In sensory awareness you know that by relaxing and following your feelings you'll always arrive at the place where you're supposed to be. If you don't have this conviction – this calm certainty – then you've shifted out of sensory awareness.

Whenever you feel as though you've gotten off the track or have lost the thread, you get back on the track by starting from right where you are, and following your feelings from there. Face east, etc., or spin around until you get dizzy and fall. Because operating on sensory thought forms bypasses the thinking level, there's really no way to block it – you can't help but succeed. To be running around naked in the wilderness in the middle of the night is to be operating on sensory thought forms. If you're out there at all, you're doing it right.

Part III: Importance

There are two basic types of thought forms: sensory thought forms and conceptual thought forms. Sensory thought forms were described in the two previous articles in this series. Sensory thought forms are thought forms of mindfulness: they are what we experience when we are paying attention to what is happening here and now. These thought forms consist of sensory and extrasensory perceptions of the now moment: sights, sounds, smells, tastes, and feelings (both physical and nonphysical). Sensory thought forms have a high proportion of feeling to them, such as the sight of a beautiful woman; the smell of roses; the roar of the ocean; the feel of slime. Sensory thought forms are innately joyous, and any true joy in our lives derives from our operating on sensory thought forms (rather than conceptual thought forms).

Conceptual thought forms are thought forms of mindlessness, and operate when we are on automatic pilot (lost in thought, paying attention to something other than the now moment). For example, when we are driving our automobiles, most of the time we are not paying particular attention to the act of driving but have our minds elsewhere, and this entails operating on conceptual thought forms. But if we spot an accident up ahead, we snap-to and start paying attention to our driving; and this is operating on sensory thought forms.

We deliberately remember conceptual thought forms by making them important to us, and we do this by means of repetition. For example, if we want to remember a telephone number, we repeat it over and over to ourselves until we have made the conceptual thought form of that telephone number (its importance covering) strong enough to take its place in the inventory of remembered thought forms. Remembered thought forms hang around at the fringes of conscious attention, ready to spring into action to take over conscious attention in response to the remembered stimulus.

All thinking consists of conceptual thought forms. We cannot think and pay attention to the now moment at the same time. In order to think, we must conceive something (whatever we are thinking about) to be more important than paying attention to the now moment. Thus we can say that the difference between sensory and conceptual thought forms is that the latter have a covering, or gloss, of *importance*.

Importance may be defined as a screen of inattention: when we operate on sensory thought forms we pay attention to what is happening in the now moment; however, when we operate on conceptual thought forms, we pay attention to something other than what is happening right now by screening out (forgetting) what is happening right now; and this is accomplished by feeling that something else is more important (more urgent) to pay attention to than what is happening right now. In order to think, we have to stop paying attention to what is happening right now and focus our attention on something else, and it is importance which allows us to focus our attention by disregarding (screening out) what we are experiencing in the now moment.

Sensory Thought Forms = AWARENESS
Conceptual Thought Forms = FOCUS

Just as most of the thought forms of dreaming are sensory thought forms, most of the thought forms of wakefulness are conceptual thought forms. Indeed, conceptual thought forms are a specialized form (an evolutionary outgrowth) of sensory thought forms, just as waking consciousness is a specialized form (an evolutionary outgrowth) of dream consciousness. The reason why the dream state is so mutable (as compared to waking) is that there is little sense of importance to it. It is importance which stabilizes attention; the attention we have in dreams has little importance to it, thus we can't control what we will pay attention to (what will happen next) as well as we can in wakefulness.

The effect of psychedelic substances is to substantially lower importance (focus). For example, if we take a shower while tripping, we can feel (are consciously aware of) every individual drop of water as it hits our skin, as a discrete event. On the other hand we can't balance a checkbook while tripping because we can't focus that much attention – there's too much going on to be able to focus. To operate on conceptual thought forms – to be able to focus upon one thing at a time by separating it out from its background – is to create importance.

Importance, then, is a screen of inattention, a criterion for selecting just one of the innumerable possibilities of where attention will be placed at any given moment in order to bring just one piece of the overall picture into high focus. The feeling that something is important is sufficient of and by itself to bring that thing into focus and to disjoin it from its surroundings. It's magic: to feel something is important is to be able to separate it from its background and hold it in place.

Different cultures have historically inculcated importance in different ways. In our decadent, materialistic society we rally importance through shamelessness. We are taught to feel the validation of our conceptual thought forms by other people as glory; and to feel the beckoning of our own true feelings as shame. We are taught to seek the one and to hide the other: to deny our senses and true feelings, and to substitute instead a false distinction which other people will applaud. It is an endless loop because glory cannot be arrived at without shame: to seek glory is to seek a lie, and lies bring about feelings of shame because we know in our hearts that we are not what we claim to be – more important than anything else.

If you have ever stopped for a moment and objectively analyzed your constant thinking – your continual, moment-to-moment, all-day-long inner dialogue – you have probably realized that it consists mostly of thoughts about your past and thoughts about your future. When you think thoughts about your past, you feel feelings of shame and embarrassment: hatred of your looks, your actions, and your desires – particularly your sexual desires – which you try to hide from other people. On the other hand, when you think thoughts about your future, you fantasize scenes of glory in which you have absolute power and control (fantasies of sex and romance fall into this category); and other people dote on you with their approval, approbation, or regret for having done you wrong. Note that, as Freud pointed out a century ago, both the shame and glory manifestations of importance tend to attach to conceptual thought forms of sex.

Hiding shame from other people and seeking glory in their eyes is the chain which binds us to our unhappiness. In other words, conceptual thought forms are the stick and carrot which our society uses to enslave us. In order for us to be able to feel good about ourselves right now, in the present moment (i.e., to operate on sensory thought forms), obviously we first have to overcome our feelings of shame from our past and our fantasies of glory in some future that will never come (dethrone the importance of our conceptual thought forms).

There's no reason on earth why we shouldn't feel completely content all the time, perfectly at peace with ourselves and the world around us. The reason why most of us don't feel this way is because our conceptual thought forms are at war with our true feelings (our intent); we're too busy telling ourselves why we're not happy to allow a moment's pause to *be* happy. Our habitual thoughts drive us relentlessly, never allowing us a space in which to reflect objectively upon what we're doing, much less to consciously direct or control our reactions.

Importance is our sense of being trapped by life. Whatever is important to us – whatever areas of life we have chosen to be important to us in this lifetime – is what makes us feel trapped and helpless. For example, if we believe that money is important, then we'll always feel trapped by money – either trapped by our belief that we lack money, or trapped by our fear of losing it. No matter how much money we have or don't have, we are trapped by our obsessive concern over money. Clearly, money doesn't have anything to do with our "money problems"; money is just a conceptual thought form we use to symbolize our decision to be worried and jealous and unhappy.

The key point of magical training is to learn how to change the focus of where we place our moment-to-moment attention. This requires volition. We have to somehow make a space for ourselves away from compulsively indulging our customary conceptual thought forms of shame and glory, and instead pay attention to the world around us in the now moment (i.e. operate on sensory thought forms). Note that the goal of magical training is not to stop thinking altogether (which some critics of magical science – particularly materialistic academics – seem to want to believe); but rather to dethrone the moment-to-moment compulsion to think: to be able to turn thinking on when it is needed (e.g., for problem-solving), and then turn it off at will and pay attention to the now moment the rest of the time. This facility is also known as "enlightenment".

This is what the coming transformation in consciousness is all about: when our unsustainable materialistic society inevitably collapses (towards the end of the present century), the surviving remnant of the human race will have to redeploy importance from hiding shame and seeking glory (inflating self-importance) to following true feelings – working for the good of our mother earth and the human race as a whole. Or better said: only those who have accomplished such a redeployment, and who are able to follow their true feelings and seize the now moment instead of obeying the importance coverings on their conceptual thought forms (their shame and glory), have a chance of surviving the coming collapse.

Part IV: Active Imagination

Importance is not itself a thought form, but rather a thought form covering. It is a feeling of urgency created by the denial of a true feeling (telling oneself some sort of lie in order to fulfill society's expectations). Importance coverings are casings, like sausage casings, into which feelings can be stuffed; and they are controlled by the conceptual thought forms which created them. In a manner of speaking, import-ance coverings are our conceptual thought forms' thought forms. Like the Spirit does for us, we give our conceptual thought forms a certain amount of independence. Actually, about all we can do is to create them and destroy them; other than that, they roll their own. And not only are we subject to our conceptual thought forms, but we are also subject to our conceptual thought forms' thought forms – the energy which we gave our conceptual thought forms originally, which they have in turn bestowed upon their importance coverings.

This is to say that most of what we have been trained to consider "our" feelings such as jealousy, envy, greed, etc., are not actually "our" feelings at all, but rather are importance coverings on conceptual thought forms learned from our parents and society. These sorts of importance coverings are our conceptual thought forms' feelings; and as such they differ considerably from society to society (e.g. sexual jealousy is not as important in Eskimo or Yanomami culture as it is in ours). In fact we can define "society" to be the set of conceptual thought forms which are common to a particular milieu at a particular time. The way to distinguish between true feelings and importance coverings within ourselves is that we are born with our true feelings, whereas we learn importance coverings from the people around us.

The importance coverings on our conceptual thought forms assure that we will keep thinking the same thoughts over and over and over all the time. When those thoughts happen to be negative thoughts, then they tend to conjure up negative emotions such as jealousy, anger, lust, self-pity, etc. When we feel these negative emotions, we release emotional "darts" – we feel something like a clenching up / letting go of that emotion – from our tummies. The actual "physical" feeling of releasing a dart of negative energy varies from person to person; but if you pay close attention when you release such a dart, you'll notice that it stems from your solar plexus.

Demons, who subsist upon negative energy, work hand-in-hand with the importance coverings on our thought forms to generate food for themselves. They hover around us constantly waiting for us to think a negative thought and release a dart of negative energy; and then they snap it up. Therefore, to liberate ourselves from slavery to demons, it is not only necessary to cast out any demons which might be possessing us, but it is also sine qua non to stop thinking negative thoughts – i.e. to get rid of the importance coverings on our thought forms. This is done by banishing the thought forms – one at a time – and thereafter by rejecting those thoughts as they arise (which is the purpose of the active imagination exercises in Chapter IV). This is equivalent to the nagual Julian's Method I:

"For the nagual Julian, self-importance was a monster that had three thousand heads. And one could face up to it and destroy it in any of three ways. The first way was to sever each head one at a time; the second way was to reach that mysterious state of being called the place of no pity, which destroyed self-importance by slowly starving it; and the third was to pay for the instantaneous annihilation of the three-thousand-headed monster with one's symbolic death."
– Carlos Castaneda, *The Power of Silence.*

Basically, then, the goal of magical training is losing importance: reaching the conviction that this or that "terribly important" thing – particularly the things we are afraid of or angry at – just isn't that important. It's only when we lose our importance that true spiritual growth becomes possible. Without importance we are content to let things unfold all in good time, without pushing-pushing-pushing to get our way or else cringing and whining helplessly in self-pity. Without importance we can turn our compulsion to think every minute we are awake OFF and listen to sounds, or feel the breeze caress our face.

But just as it takes money to make money, so too does it take losing (LOTS) of importance to understand the advantage of losing importance. It is importance which blinds us to the truth; and the truth is that nothing is important. It is our social training which makes us believe and act as though this and that and the other thing are important. Conventional thought form religions are full of that kind of crap: if you believe this, that, or the other; if you pat your head while rubbing your tummy on odd-numbered Tuesdays, Thursdays, and Saturdays; then you will go to heaven when you die. But the truth is that belief, especially religious belief, is irrelevant. Belief is what blinds us to the truth: that only by losing importance can we see the truth, since the truth is not something which can be apprehended by an intellectual process. It can only be intuited by intent – by direct knowing – not by getting a little pat on the head from other people or from "God".

The only way to lose importance is to look at things from the Spirit's point of view. The Spirit says, "You are NOT IMPORTANT!" Obviously. If you were important, if you mattered in the least to the Spirit, it wouldn't make you die, would it? Death is the Spirit's way of cluing you in as to how unimportant you really are in the cosmic scheme of things.

The process of losing importance is very painful – don't let anyone tell you that it isn't. If you find the spiritual path enjoyable, you're not on it. Losing all your expectations, your images, your fantasies; having your sense of importance – your feeling that you are better than other people; or that God gives the slightest damn about you and that you are something more elevated than Purina worm chow – stomped into the mud and rubbed in your face (which is basically what the spiritual path entails) … ain't much fun. That's why so few people even attempt it; and of those that do, very, very few succeed. It's just so much, much easier to run away from yourself, especially in a superficial society like ours which provides so much mindless diversion, and so much phony "spirituality" for people who want to lie to themselves.

To deliberately follow the magician's path requires the utmost courage and determination: an importance of purpose which is strong enough to overcome the hypnotically obsessive importance of everyday life (a counterweight to it). Fundamentally, becoming a magician entails fighting against the current of the past 12,000 years of human evolution. It's taken the human race all that time to stabilize waking consciousness into the hard, unyielding substance it has become. Importance has to be durable – otherwise we go "insane" (lose the ability to keep dreaming and waking separated). For a single practitioner to turn back this evolutionary tide is well-nigh impossible; it will be easier to lose importance in the future, as society's impending collapse calls up magicians who will work together at the task (just as people today prop up each other's importance by mutual back-patting).

In don Juan's (Carlos Castaneda's teacher's) heurism, the student deliberately seeks a merciless son of a bitch to stomp his or her sense of self-esteem and self-worth into the mud (see the "Petty Tyrants" chapter of Carlos Castaneda's *The Fire from Within*). The point is that losing importance is the only way to clear out your social conditioning (conceptual thought forms of expectation) to allow your intent (direct knowing) to operate. Losing importance really does require being pushed beyond your limits – way, way beyond anything you thought you could endure – and stripping away everything, but everything, to which you cling. Going that extra mile – or being forced to go that extra mile – when you already thought you couldn't stand any more, is how you really lose oodles of importance. Thus, in the case of the human race as a whole, it will probably take some very unpleasant consequences of the forthcoming collapse of society to bring off the much-vaunted coming transformation of consciousness. People aren't going to give up their selfish materialism and comfortable, smug stupidity voluntarily. And those who are left standing (if there are any) will be those who have had all their importance (self-pity) completely stripped away.

You lose importance by stopping caring about the things you most care about – by becoming accustomed to (accepting) your fate instead of whining and complaining about your plight, and running around like a chicken with its head cut off to try to improve matters. You lose importance every time you "give up the ghost" – surrender something you were expecting or clinging to. Usually this is due to complete defeat. The process can be speeded along by going to tree or nature spirits every day; but really, there's no substitute for having all your dreams and illusions stomped into the mud, and having everything you live for destroyed.

The ultimate goal is to be calm and relaxed in your heart; to be able to confront everyday life and other people with complete equanimity; even if there is a maelstrom swirling around you. And magicians aver, that there's no other way in which you could possibly learn how to do this except in a maelstrom. This is how the coming collapse of society will usher in a transformation of consciousness for the survivors.

The stages or steps of losing importance vary from person to person, of course. Chögyam Trungpa gives a good description of the process (of shifting from conceptual to sensory awareness) in his book *Shambhala*:

"Discovering real goodness comes from appreciating very simple experiences. ... We experience glimpses of goodness all the time, but we often fail to acknowledge them. When we see a bright color, we are witnessing our own inherent goodness. When we hear a beautiful sound, we are hearing our own basic goodness. When we step out of the shower, we feel fresh and clean, and when we walk out of a stuffy room, we appreciate the sudden whiff of fresh air. These events take a fraction of a second, but they are real experiences of goodness. They happen to us all the time, but usually we ignore them as mundane or purely coincidental. ...

"We should feel that it is wonderful to be in this world. How wonderful it is to see red and yellow, blue and green, purple and black! All of these colors are provided for us. We feel hot and cold; we taste sweet and sour. We have these sensations and we deserve them. They are good."

Where Chögyam Trungpa put it on the vibrancy of colors and sensations, for me it's more the way that things look – like Andrew Wyeth when I'm out in the country, and like Giorgio de Chirico when I'm in town. Also, for me it's more the motion of the leaves of the plants in the wind, and the flash of the sun in dewdrops on the grass and in ripples on the river; and the stark contrast between sounds and silence when I'm out in nature.

In my case, after years and years of resorting to tree and nature spirits, the first thing I noticed was that when I awoke in the morning, instead of an automatic blah-blah-blah-blah-blah starting up in my brain, instead I would be confronted with >BLANK<.

The next noticeable change in my wonted mentation, a few years later, occurred after being forced to make a highly unpalatable life decision – a tremendous defeat and the crash of a lifetime's dream, actually – after which I began to notice that my customary self-hatred and great-I-am (shame and glory) litanies had diminished; and also that my rancor fantasies had decreased markedly (most of my fantasy life traditionally revolved around fantasies of violence, vengeance, murder of my enemies, etc. Most of my internal dialogue consisted of thoughts of rancor and violence – in contrast to most people, whose inner dialogue consists mostly of thoughts of worry, depression, futility, hopelessness, uselessness). It's not that I no longer think rancorous thoughts; but rather that when such a thought pops up now, I can and do automatically reject it. It's also true, as the nagual Julian claimed, that my own process of losing importance was greatly speeded after the second time I reached the Place of No Pity. This happened in the middle, between when the >BLANK< feeling first began and the big defeat occurred.

Anyway, after this big defeat I began to feel the >BLANK< feeling all day long. The immediate upshot of this event was a general de-stressing of my life: little things that used to put me uptight previously ceased to do so; I began to be able to take things more in stride. It was kind of weird at first – like always being "on" (operating on sensory awareness), paying attention to everything every minute – instead of being lost in la-la land most of the time. It's a strange sensation, and it's accompanied by a strange indifference. This indifference isn't so much a listlessness per se, as it is a disinclination to become involved if you can possibly avoid it. And, because you are uninvolved, you can see all the ego games which everyone around you is playing with crystal clarity. And when you do have to act, then you act with a cold, hard detachment which is kind of scary. It's like someone else is acting.

The other noticeable thing with the >BLANK< feeling is an everyday equilibrium mindset of devil-may-care élan, and a sense that you can handle the things that happen okay. You get a moment-to-moment cushion of well-being: a feeling that (most of the time, anyway) things are fine just as they are now – exactly as Thomas Wolfe described it in *Circus at Dawn*. My book *What is Magic?* kept repeating the same mantra over and over, "The self is self-pity"; but you have to lose lots of self-pity (importance) before you truly understand this point: that things don't happen "to you"; they just happen, period.

It is important for the aspirant to always keep in mind that importance is not lost little-by-little as you go along; it's lost in big chunks in relatively short periods of time, after years and years and years and years of a Dark Night of the Soul. As don Juan told Carlos Castaneda, "A warrior is waiting, and he knows what he is waiting for." The point is not to become discouraged when years and decades go by and it seems to you that you've made no spiritual progress whatsoever. This is the norm. Read your Saint John of the Cross. Just keep on keeping on – going to tree or nature spirits every day, doing whatever your spiritual practice is, and doing what you must do to keep the faith. When importance finally runs out, it runs out all at once – and when that happens, it takes your breath away.

Importance can be felt in the body as a heavy, viscous substance which exerts uncomfortable pressure, particularly in the regions of the heart and solar plexus: that "wad of dough in the tummy" feeling when we are frightened or angry. Most people deny this feeling by venting their importance through self-pity thought forms of whining and complaining; or else by projecting conceptual thought forms of anger, fear, jealousy, etc. onto other people. To lose importance it is necessary to confront the yucky, depressing, bodily feeling of importance directly rather than to deny it by disguising it behind conceptual thought forms or hurling it as darts at other people.

Losing importance – the goal of magical training – is exactly the opposite of what our materialistic society trains us to do. Our society trains us to clench ourselves up and repress our ability to feel; and then to preen and prance and vaunt our phoniness and shamelessness like the naked emperor; and to vomit our self-hatred onto others (blame other people for our own stupidity).

How can we lose importance? The same way we obtained it. Conceptual thought forms are cut off from their importance coverings the same way they were attached in the first place: through repetition. We first banish the thought forms (make a firm decision to destroy them), and then we continually reject those thoughts as they arise, as the importance coverings attempt to reconstruct their banished conceptual thought forms. Eventually, by refusing those thoughts, we sever them altogether from the importance coverings to which they were attached – we lose that importance. Note, however, that this can (and usually does) take years and years of inner work, particularly the daily resort to trees or other nature spirits. This is because the importance coverings on our conceptual thought forms are necessarily quite durable (as mentioned previously, if they weren't so durable we'd go "insane" – be unable to keep waking and dreaming separated).

Carl Jung devised a technique for obtaining information from conceptual thought forms which he called active imagination. A magical adaptation of this technique will be presented in the last chapter of this book.

Part V: Homunculi of Cognition

To simplify our discussion we will postulate monads or homunculi of cognition termed *thought forms*. There is no question here of whether thought forms actually "exist" or not: this is all just a manner of speaking. In truth, "existence" doesn't "exist" (waking consciousness is no more "real" in any objective sense than is dreaming).

We will say that when we are being mindful – i.e., paying attention to what we are doing – then we are operating on sensory thought forms; and when we are acting mindlessly – thinking about something else – then we are operating on conceptual thought forms.

Both sensory (mindful) and conceptual (mindless) thought forms can be considered to be momentary awarenesses. Whether we are awake or dreaming, we possess moment-to-moment awareness; and the content of each moment's awareness is a thought form (sensory when we are being mindful and conceptual when we are acting mindlessly). Although we believe that we are self-existent entities which persist in time (i.e., we believe we are continuous from moment-to-moment), in fact this is an illusion. All "we" are, is a baton being passed from one thought form to another, from one moment to the next. It is our own inattention which covers the breaks (and thereby creates the illusion that we are abiding individuals embedded in a flow of linear time).

Thought forms are like a language in which the quotidian self couches its decisions as to what to pay attention to. The content of dreamless sleep is formless; thought forms give dreamless sleep a semblance of form – a gloss which appears to be "reality." The reason why it is impossible to define dreamless sleep is because only thought forms can be defined, and there are no thought forms in dreamless sleep (which is why we can't consciously remember what transpires there as we can in normal dreaming, except when we have prophetic or precognitive dreams, or dream wars with other people).

Whether we are awake or we are dreaming, "things" seem to happen to "us". The "things" which happen to "us" are thought forms. In order for there to be cognition, there have to be both "things" there, and also an "us" to whom those things are happening (separation between that which is happening and the being which is experiencing it). This is a distinction which most definitely does not exist in dreamless sleep. In dreamless sleep all is one, and separatedness is illusory. This is why sensory or conceptual thought forms (mentation) are like a gloss – they're not really what's going on, at all. They can be considered a shorthand record of, or a symbol for, what is really going on, on a level of feeling.

Various homunculi theories have been posited by cognitive theorists <see Daniel Dennet, *Consciousness Explained*, Penguin London 1991 pp 260-1>. The most popular of these homunculi theories is the theory of memes proposed by Richard Dawkins <*The Selfish Gene*, Oxford NYC 1976 p 192 ff; and Dennet op. cit., p 200 ff>. In fact the idea of memes is very close to that of conceptual thought forms described here, in the sense that ....

"In homunculus theories, the serious content is in the claims about how the posited homunculi interact, develop, form coalitions or hierarchies, and so forth. ... Bureaucratic theories ... organize homunculi into predesigned hierarchies. There are no featherbedding or disruptive homunculi, and competition between homunculi is as tightly regulated as major league baseball. Pandemonium theories, in contrast, posit lots of duplication of effort, waste motion, interference, periods of chaos, and layabouts with no fixed job description" <Dennet, op. cit. p 261>

Sensory thought forms are a pandemonium model, whereas conceptual thought forms are a bureaucratic model. Conceptual thought forms are distinguished from sensory thought forms in that they carry an importance covering – like an index value – which correlates with where in the bureaucratic hierarchy of importance that thought form fits in. Obviously, this index value varies from moment to moment. For example, the "hot stove" conceptual thought form carries a powerful importance covering ("Do Not Touch!"), whose importance index shoots up in proximity to a hot stove, and drops off with decreasing propinquity. Another example:

when we are about to dial a phone number, the digits of that phone number spring to mind in advance; i.e., the importance index of the conceptual thought form of that phone number goes way up momentarily, until the phone call is made, and then drops back to zero afterwards.

The magical theory of conceptual thought forms is a homunculus theory of the bureaucratic type, with importance (based, ultimately, on hiding shame and seeking glory) serving as the arbiter of status in the attentional hierarchy. The first decision made in response to a given type of situation is the bottom-level decision – the conceptual thought form which will automatically take control in the future in response to similar situations unless a subsequent decision to unseat the foregoing bottom-level decision has been made. However, if the bottom-level decision is forgotten, or is being "overlooked", then it can never be unseated. Most people simply "overlook" their bottom-level decision conceptual thought forms by taking them completely for granted – i.e., by assuming that that's just the way things are; by obediently and mindlessly fulfilling their parents' and society's expectations and never questioning them.

The materialistic cognitive theory which comes closest to the theory of conceptual thought forms presented here is that of schema control units, which was proposed by Donald Norman and Tim Shallice, and which is fundamentally a bureaucratic theory (with what Norman and Shallice term "contention scheduling" taking the place of importance). Their paper *Attention to Action: Willed And Automatic Control of Behavior* (in Davidson, Schwartz, and Shapiro's *Consciousness and Self-Regulation*, vm. 4, 1986, pp 1 – 18) begins by defining the goal to be "to account for the role of attention in action, both when performance is automatic and when it is under deliberate conscious control." The distinction is made between deliberate, conscious control of activity (= sensory, mindful) versus automatic response (= conceptual, mindless). Per Norman, the chief difference between schema control units and Dawkins' memes is that the former are homunculi of decision whereas the latter are homunculi of memory. In the magical model, conceptual thought forms possess features of both intent and memory: these two faculties are regarded as intertwined (this is not true, but for present purposes will serve).

Homunculus theories are not popular in orthodox cognitive theory because they don't lead to statistically testable propositions. The magical theory of thought forms – in its general implications – does produce testable propositions, for example that personality disorders (absence of shame) will correlate positively with early toilet training and the planet Mercury in the natal horoscope near the sun; and neuroses (excess of shame) will correlate positively with late toilet training and natal Mercury relatively removed from the sun. However the specifically homunculus aspects of the theory do not yield testable propositions per se.

On the other hand, testability is not the point in a magical model, since magic is more interested in *how* things work rather than *why* things work (regarding this inquiry as futile – answers just leading to more questions). When we are talking about thought forms – particularly conceptual thought forms – we are discussing something which we can manipulate magically, as spirits are manipulated: thought forms can be addressed and interrogated by means of channeling (what Carl Jung termed "active imagination"); and they can be banished when they are no longer of use to the individual. Conceptual thought forms can be channeled in the same way that spirits are channeled: in trance (altered states), by automatic writing, and by internal dialogue (conversation in the mind). And they can be banished in the same way that demons are banished, by using intent to cast them out.

Part VI: The General Theory of Thought Forms

"... a branch of science we have invented and for which a crying need is generally experienced." – Alfred Jarry

Abstract: There is no space or time; there are only familiarity and importance.

There are two basic types of thought forms: sensory thought forms (aka qualia, in the jargon of materialistic cognitive philosophy) and conceptual thought forms (aka memes, agents, schema control units, etc., in materialistic cognitive philosophy. See Richard Dawkins' *The Selfish Gene*, Oxford NYC 1976 p 192 ff, and Daniel Dennet's *Consciousness Explained*, Penguin London 1991 p 200 ff; cf. Michael Gazzaniga-Richard Ivry-George Mangun, *Cognitive Neuroscience*, Norton NYC 1998 p 458 ff).

Sensory thought forms are thought forms of mindfulness: they are what we experience when we are paying attention to what is happening here and now. These thought forms consist of sensory perceptions: sights, sounds, smells, tastes, and feelings (both physical and nonphysical); together with the feelings which sensory perceptions evoke.

Sensory thought forms are similar to what materialistic cognitive philosophers term *qualia*. However, in the materialistic view qualia are conceived of as affective adjuncts of sensory perceptions. The sensory perceptions are considered primary or causal. By contrast, in the magical view sensory thought forms are considered to be basically feelings (i.e. the affective part), and the associated sensory perceptions are but symbols for the feelings. In this view, feelings are considered to be the basic stuff of the universe, and sensory perceptions arose later evolutionarily (with mitosis, when life on earth began) as a gloss of order on what is fundamentally chaos (aka *Shunyata*).

Sensory thought forms are the interface between waking and dreaming – and also the doorway into altered states. This doorway entails feeling with the senses instead of perceiving with the senses. For example, the feeling (qualia) associated with the sound thought form which a two-year old makes banging on a drum is very different from the feeling of the sound thought form which a military band makes banging on a drum. The first is joyous and light and the second is hard and harsh. When you can feel the sensory thought forms (as everyone does now and then when e.g. listening to music; or when the breeze blows on their faces and they feel a rush of joy) then that is enlightenment. That's all enlightenment means: feeling the world instead of conceptualizing it.

In other words, in the materialistic model sensory perceptions are considered to be primary, and qualia are considered to be adjuncts or properties of perceptions. By contrast, in the magical model the feelings are primary and the sensory thought forms associated with them are merely symbols or projections of the feelings – i.e. the "qualia" are a residue of the underlying feelings rather than adventitious tassels on the sensory perceptions (as in the materialistic view).*

When we listen to sounds, particularly when we are very relaxed or tripping, we can distinguish between two phenomena: "sounds" and "listener listening to sounds." "Sounds" is when we are hearing all sounds indiscriminately, like a tape recorder does; when all sounds are impacting on our awareness with equal vividness. This is sensory awareness, which is basically "dreaming" (mindfulness) whether we are nominally awake or not.

"Listener listening to sounds", or mindlessness, is when we are focusing on one specific sound, and the other sounds are in the background of our attention; when one particular sound is more important than the other sounds. Importance can be defined as one-thing-at-a-time awareness instead of everything-at-once awareness (adults' awareness vs. infants' awareness). Importance, the momentary feeling that something is important, not only enables waking consciousness by distinguishing it from dreaming and emphasizing its "realness" and continuity (as opposed to the "bizarreness" and disjunctiveness of dreaming); importance also provides the matrix for our sense of linear time (which is so much sharper – more inexorable – in wakefulness than it is in dreaming). Linear time is really nothing more than our sense of importance, and it ceases when we lose our importance (e.g. go into altered states; or die). Linear time is a consequence of one-at-a-time awareness, i.e. focus upon one thing at a time. One-thing-at-a-time implies one-thing-after-another, i.e. sequence, hence linearity. Our linear thinking does the rest (fills in any gaps).

Ancient hunter-gatherers had a very different sense of time than we moderns do: they didn't have the same itinerary of importance categories "first I'll do this, then I'll do that, then I'll do the other thing", that we have. Their moment-to-moment decisions about what to do next were made much more on instinct, like those of a baby. However unlike a baby, an adult hunter-gatherer had been trained to hunt and gather; he or she went about daily life purposefully, but without thinking. Where our equilibrium state when we are not engaged in purposeful thought is feeling angry about the past or worrying or fantasizing about the future, the hunter-gatherer's equilibrium state was relaxing, looking around, listening to sounds, feeling the world.

"Altered states" can be defined as when time seems to slow down. If we slow linear time down even further, it turns into a strobe light perception of the flow of thought forms (at which point the interstices between thought forms become quite visible). Conversely, at the moment of death (according to people who have died and been revived) we see all the thought forms of our lives pass by our window in no time at all.

Sensory thought forms are monads of perception. At the interface of intent (feeling) and perception (for example, in hypnagogic imagery – the jumble of visual images which flood the mind as one is dropping off to sleep) feeling breaks into "droplets" – the homunculi of perception which are sensory thought forms – and these have a covering or gloss of *familiarity*. The individual perceptions are familiar, recognizable. Sensory thought forms are propped up by familiarity in the exact same way that conceptual thought forms are propped up by importance. Without a gloss of familiarity, everything that is perceived would be thoroughly unrecognizable (which is how it appears to a newborn).

In meditation or altered states we sometimes experience sensations for which we have no reference, which we interpret as feeling as though e.g. our body is tilted, or upside down, or being compressed or expanded. It is familiarity which immediately attempts to fit such sensations into something which can be recognized. Familiarity stabilizes our sense of being embedded in space, just as importance stabilizes our sense of being embedded in time.

Feeling is spatial; that is, what we call space is merely the sense of having feelings and what we call time is the sense of having thoughts – hence everyone's need for their own personal space (or right to their own feelings), and their own time to make up their minds. Physical, three-dimensional space is a symbol for feelings, just as time is a symbol for thoughts; hence space still exists in the dream state, but time doesn't (certainly not in the same sense in which it exists in the waking state). Our sense of personal continuity in the dream state is not based upon a linear, sequential, unfolding of events, as it is in the waking state

Linear time is really nothing more than importance; when nothing is important, when we lose our sense of control, time slows way down. For example, in altered states of consciousness, such as while having an automobile accident, or during a big earthquake, we can see everything that is happening in great detail, as it if were unfolding in slow motion. Similarly, space is really nothing more than our innate sense of familiarity: when nothing is familiar we feel as though we are plummeting through emptiness. Lack of familiarity is the sensation of falling – the startle response, most notable in infants.

Mind and linear time arise together. This is the magical view of what our waking consciousness does: it imposes a flow of time on ineffable feelings to be able to make some sort of sense out of them, just as dream consciousness imposes an orientation in space on unbounded feeling in order to make it seem familiar.

What are thought forms made of? Sensory thought forms are made of familiarity and conceptual thought forms are made of importance. Or at least familiarity and importance are the canvases upon which sensory thought forms and conceptual thought forms, respectively, are painted. What, then, are familiarity and importance made of? Importance is made of familiarity – i.e. it is a sharper, more evolved and focused form of familiarity. But familiarity isn't made of anything per se – it is what W. B. Yeats termed "Deception" or desire, which is not a desire for anything but is merely an action unto itself. Like the whirling that creates a vortex, it just whirls, that's all. What we're doing here is descriptive, not (as in the materialistic model) explanatory, since nothing can be explained. It can't really be described, either, and the best magicians have no need of either explanations or descriptions – they just plunge ahead. But some of us like to have intellectual guideposts even though we know that our intellectual models are descriptive of nothing.

Magical practitioners deliberately seek altered states (which minimize importance and familiarity) since it is only by bringing a mood of timelessness and novelty to bear upon our everyday waking experience that we can live our everyday lives more effectively – in a detached and sober mood rather than in mindless, helter-skelter fashion. However, altered states are not as functional in performing all the routine tasks of everyday life as is normal, unaltered, linear-time consciousness. Or better said, mindfulness is more useful in hunting-gathering, and mindlessness is more useful in post-agricultural society. Our hunter-gatherer ancestors were doing what we would consider to be dreaming as their everyday frame of mind.

With the coming collapse of our decadent society everyone, willy-nilly, will once again be thrust into a NOW moment consciousness similar to hunting-gathering (just trying to survive from day to day), instead of the present shame-glory, past-future (trying to decide what to buy next to impress other people) materialistic type of consciousness. So it behooves us, if we wish to survive as a species and to save our mother earth, to learn how to turn the importance switch off and on at will.

Importance is a specialization of forgetting which separates waking consciousness from dreaming. The obvious division line between waking and dreaming is the forgetfulness as one passes from one level to another (dreamless sleep and dreaming are not separated so much by a barrier of forgetfulness as by a dearth of thought forms in the state of dreamless sleep – which is pure intent or feeling – so that there is nothing to consciously remember. Or to put it another way, there is no time in dreamless sleep, no before or after, so everything is always completely new and unrecognizable. Nonetheless things can be known, and decisions can be made. Really, there is no point in talking about dreamless sleep since there is nothing there to talk about).

It might be asked, why do we forget our dreams when we are awake and our waking while we are dreaming? The mechanism is the same and is exactly as Freud described it: *"Freud's famous explanation was that dream forgetting was an active function of repression. We have instead attributed this prominent failure of recall to a state dependent amnesia caused by aminergic demodulation of the sleeping brain."* <Hobson, Pace-Schott, and Stickgold, *Dreaming and the Brain: towards a cognitive neuroscience of conscious states*, Cambridge 2003, page 13>. (Yeah. Right).

The magical model agrees with Freud that the same mechanism which enables people to "forget" (repress) socially-forbidden sexual desires is also the mechanism which erases memories across the boundary of waking and dreaming – which makes waking seem more "real" than dreaming, and hence stabilizes it. The waking world seems "real" to us because we're all uptight about it; and what makes us so uptight is repressing our true feelings – particularly our true sexual desires (e.g. homosexual desires, which are pretty much universal but are stringently repressed in our society).

Without such a separative mechanism as forgetting, the focus (importance, urgency) which props up waking consciousness dissolves into the ineffability of dreaming. Much of magical practice is designed to erase this distinction, to blend the two states, to make waking more dreamlike and dreaming more rational (lucid dreaming). This makes it easier to reduce one's compulsive grasp on the "on" switch.

In the magical view, Freud was right on the button: the sharp focus and delineation of waking experience as compared to the ineffability (bizarreness) of dreaming is precisely due to the barrier of forgetfulness which separates the two states. The bizarreness of dreaming per se does not distinguish it from waking, because bizarreness is a matter of opinion. Waking is equally bizarre, but people don't consider it so because they've accustomed themselves to living their daily lives in a society which is completely insane. A primitive tribesman dropped into the middle of Manhattan Island would feel as though he was dreaming; and even a Philadelphian such as myself tends to find New York City pretty bizarre. Things can only be considered sensible or bizarre in retrospect, when measured against some other standard of reality. And, ultimately, there is no objective standard of reality – "reality" just a matter of popular opinion.

The two states of waking and dreaming are not as distinct to a newborn, who has not yet learned to repress his emotions and sexuality (this is the function of toilet training). It is precisely the emotional repression which, as Freud noted, is learned through toilet training, that creates the forgetfulness barrier between waking and dreaming and sharpens the sense of importance ("realness") of the former at the expense of the latter.

We forget the memories of our infancy and early childhood precisely because they were based upon sensory awareness (feeling the world) rather than conceptual awareness (thinking about a past or future). Forgetting is like right- or left- handedness: it is an evolutionarily successful specialization on waking at the expense of dreaming, which enables waking to have a sharper focus and functionality, achieved at the cost of our forgetting (repressing) our true feelings.

The borderland between waking and dreaming (hypnagogic imagery) is the place where the interface between intent and perception – between light fibers (feelings) and sensory thought forms – is most visible. In fact, that interface is present all day – and all night – long, every day; but we can't see it as clearly as we do in hypnagogic hallucination, because we are stupidly convinced that what we are experiencing is "real".

---

*The centrality of the qualia question is acknowledged by the materialists in their futile attempts to sweep this whole issue under the rug: *"The functionalist approach is challenged by many because it ignores subjective experience, or qualia as it is sometimes called. When this issue is put to leading proponents of functionalism, such as Daniel Dennett, they maintain that we are worried over nothing. When the cognitive neuroscience of intelligence, language, feelings, memory, attention, and perception are explained, qualia will come along free. It too will be understood."* <Gazzaniga, Ivry, Mangun, *Cognitive Neuroscience*, W.W. Norton 1998, p529-30>. Yeah. Right.

Part VII: Dreaming and Waking

"The primary evolutionary context for considering the possible adaptive function of dream consciousness is the prehistoric Pleistocene environment in which humans and their ancestors lived as hunter-gatherers for hundreds of thousands of years. If dream consciousness is biologically functional, it should have adaptive value at least in that original environment, under the conditions in which human ancestral populations lived. Whatever the adaptive role of dream consciousness might have been in that long-gone original context, there is no guarantee that the average dreaming brain today, facing a completely different environment than the one in which it evolved, should fulfill any functions that we recognize as adaptive in the present environment."

– Antti Revonsuo <*The Reinterpretation of Dreams: An Evolutionary Hypothesis of the Function of Dreaming*, in Pace-Schott et. al, *Sleep and Dreaming*, Cambridge 2003 p 90>

In contrast to the foregoing materialistic view of dream consciousness, the magical view holds that waking consciousness only arose (or better said: became primary, since waking consciousness has existed ever since the evolution of meiosis) in the Upper Paleolithic, i.e. since just before humans invented agriculture. Before that time humans' normal, everyday state of mind was what we today would consider to be dreaming.

Let us make a thought experiment. Let us imagine what consciousness is like for a one-celled being. One-celled beings do not die – they live forever in the consciousness of all of their ramifications – their antecedents and descendants. A one-celled being is instantaneously aware of any changes taking place in the environments and bodies of any of its ramifications; but it has no way of laying these events out in temporal sequence. Thus although experience is episodic (things happen), the events do not take place in linear time, nor are they especially focused – they are felt more than perceived in a sensory fashion. One-celled beings are quite capable of responding to events, but these responses are pretty basic chemical reactions rather than reasoned decisions. They can access a surfeit of information, so have no way of compartmentalizing what they are experiencing (laying it out in linear fashion so as to be able to focus on one-thing-at-a-time).

Forgetting is the basis of the evolution of consciousness. When there is too much information available, action becomes impossible. Everything-at-once is too much. Everything-at-once consciousness is rather like how one-celled beings experience the world. There is no sense of time, everything is happening at once, and while events take place (such as individual ramifications dividing and dying) the overall consciousness of the thing is too NOW, too intense, for much focus or reflection to take place.

Carlos Castaneda describes a two-things-at-a-time aware-ness, which he terms "silent knowledge", and which he implies was the everyday awareness of our ancient hunter-gatherer forebears. This sort of telepathic awareness would be especially functional in a hunting / gathering environment to allow a hunter to project his awareness into his prey, so as to anticipate the prey's actions (as Castaneda himself experienced once in pursuing a jaguar); or to permit a gatherer to find food (as Castaneda himself was taught how to find plants outside his field of vision by tuning into the plants' awareness. Even my naturopath ex-wife could do that). Just as humans developed handedness in order to achieve greater manual skill by focusing attention ("smarts") on one (usually the right) hand at the expense of the other; so too did humans suppress their dream selves at the time agriculture was invented in order to be able to achieve a higher degree of focus and skill in their waking selves – which duality was the basis of primordial silent knowledge (being able to operate with both selves at will).

In *The Power of Silence* Castaneda described his teacher don Juan's first experience of this double awareness as follows: *"He could be thoroughly one or the other. Or he could be both at the same time. When he was both, things became fuzzy and neither being was effective, so he abandoned that alternative. But being one or the other opened up inconceivable possibilities for him. ... He established that one of his beings* [i.e., the dream self] *was more flexible than the other and could cover distances in the blink of an eye and find food or the best place to hide."* Castaneda's teacher explained that silent knowledge was the original consciousness of human beings; and that only recently (presumably since the invention of agriculture, which requires a greater consciousness of past and future than hunting / gathering does) has one-at-a-time awareness been the vogue.

The traditional tripartite division of quotidian consciousness into dreamless sleep, dreaming, and waking is misleading. It can be more fruitful to consider the true distinction to be that between intent (feeling), sensation (mindfulness), and conceptualizing (mindlessness). The difference between these three states is a matter of increasingly sharper focus from one state of attention to the next, rather than a hard and fast division. In like manner it can be more useful in describing consciousness to take as base concepts familiarity and importance in place of space and time, respectively.

Nonetheless, it can be convenient, as a starting point for discussion, to follow tradition and divide our quotidian experience into the three categories: waking consciousness, dream consciousness, and dreamless sleep. Magicians, more than most other people, are quite aware that these categories are arbitrary, since they have had experiences themselves which don't fit neatly into any of the three categories. The materialistic model also distinguishes between these three states of consciousness: dream consciousness is termed REM sleep (for "Rapid Eye Movement") and dreamless sleep is termed Non-REM sleep.

Current research suggests that while dreaming can occur in Non-REM; and REM can occur without dreaming; <Solms, *Dreaming and REM sleep are controlled by different mechanisms, S&D* p51ff>, nonetheless *"NREM reports are far more likely than REM reports to be short, dull, and undreamlike"* and the *"distinction (is made) between NREM dreaming as a simpler and REM dreaming as a more complex state of consciousness."* <Hobson et. al. *S&D* p 12>. This conclusion is congruent with the magical view that dreamless sleep is pure feeling, thus contains few thought forms (mentation), and therefore doesn't provide as much material to consciously remember as do dreaming and waking.

This triune division of consciousness is also found in Carlos Castaneda, who terms the division the first, second, and third attentions: *"Seers say that there are three types of attention. ... But the three are not just types of attention, they are rather three levels of attainment. They are the first, second, and third attention, each of them an independent domain, complete in itself. ...*

"The first attention in man is animal awareness, which has been developed, through the process of experience, into a complex, intricate, and extremely fragile faculty that takes care of the day-to-day world in all it innumerable aspects. In

other words, everything that one can think about is part of the first attention. ...

"The second attention, on the other hand, is a more complex and specialized state of the glow of awareness. It has to do with the unknown. ... Having a dream is the forerunner of the second attention.

"The third attention is attained when the glow of awareness turns into the fire from within. ... At the moment of dying all human beings enter into the unknowable and some of them do attain the third attention, but altogether too briefly."

– Carlos Castaneda, *The Fire from Within*

Contrary to popular opinion, there is not really that much difference between waking and dream consciousness; and there are many intermediate states. Psychedelic tripping and shamanic journeying combine features of both wakefulness and dreaming, although the person is undeniably awake. Similarly, lucid and prophetic dreaming combine features of the two states, although one is undeniably asleep. Thus it is clear that these three categories are not exclusive, but rather shade into one another. However unless we draw distinctions where distinctions don't in fact exist, we have nothing to talk about.

Dreamless sleep consists of pure feeling (affect). By "feeling" is meant precisely what is understood by that term in everyday speech. The basic stuff of the universe is feeling. The universe is not made of matter, but rather of awareness. Awareness and feeling are the same thing; mind and intelligence are a subset, or outgrowth, or later evolutionary adaptation, of awareness and feeling.

Dreamless sleep is happening whether we are awake or asleep. In both dreaming and waking we are connected to dreamless sleep whenever we are feeling feelings. In the state of orgasm we are especially close to dreamless sleep because there is very little separatedness in orgasm. Orgasm is the matrix of all sensory thought forms – that is to say, all sensory thought forms are "made of" – or are an evolutionary outgrowth of – orgasm. Orgasm is what dreamless sleep is made of, just as sensory thought forms are what dreams are made of and conceptual thought forms are what waking "reality" is made of.

To psychic vision, feelings can be perceived as fibers of living light which permeate everything and sparkle and glow. Feelings can be perceived visually as fibers of living light; but they can also be perceived aurally as rhythmic sounds (or better said: rhythmic pulses or emanations). These primordial sensory impressions are the matrices of the sensory thought forms of vision and hearing. That is to say, in the scheme of temporal evolution the senses of vision and hearing arose before there was anything to be seen or heard, or anyone to see or hear it. This is why we say that the eyes and ears are output devices, not input devices. They don't perceive reality, they create it using whatever software society has installed in their thought form computer.

These light fibers of awareness tend to agglomerate or agglutinate at certain points, and when they do a sentient being is born:

"Your perception unfolded its wings when something in you realized your true nature. You are a cluster. ... The nagual is the unspeakable. All the possible feelings and beings and selves float in it like barges, peaceful, unaltered, forever. Then the glue of life binds some of them together. ... When the glue of life binds those feelings together a being is created, a being that loses the sense of its true nature and becomes blinded by the glare and clamor of the area where beings hover, the tonal. ... As soon as the force of life leaves the body all those single awarenesses disintegrate and go back again to where they came from, the nagual."

– Carlos Castaneda, *Tales of Power*

Dreamless sleep is intent (affect), or pure feeling. It is the executive (decision-making) part of our quotidian self. Intent can be described as the canvas upon which dreaming and waking life are painted. The things which happen to us when we are awake or dreaming are a projection, or symbol, of decisions made in dreamless sleep. Without the decisions exercised in dreamless sleep there would be stasis. All change, all striving (all "Deception", in W. B. Yeats' nomenclature), ultimately arises on the level of dreamless sleep. Dreamless sleep is eternal; or better said, pre-temporal. It encompasses a form of cognition in which time does not exist – an eternal now moment in which everything which ever was and ever will be is happening all at once. Linear time is a way of getting a grip on something that is actually timeless; of providing an orientation for something which is utterly disorienting; of finding a point of reference in complete chaos.

In the magical view there is no need to provide further definition of dreamless sleep than this. Where the materialistic view sees purpose, order, and its concomitant – intelligence – as the end result of evolution, the magical model – like the Christian model – sees intent as the cause of evolution. However, unlike the Christian model, the magical view sees no reason or purpose in anything.

One difference between the magical and the materialistic points of view is that the former is merely descriptive, asking only the question "how"; whereas the latter asks the question "why". Materialism seeks reasons why, whereas magic ultimately does not, regarding this inquiry as futile (running around in circles, with answers just giving rise to more questions). At the interface between dreaming and waking – between light fibers and thought forms – for example, in the flood of hypnagogic images which arise as one is dropping off to sleep, there are no reasons why. Actually, there really are no reasons why in everyday society, either. All reasons why have to be conjured up after the fact, to justify the fait accompli.

In the materialistic view *"there is only one sort of stuff, namely matter – the physical stuff of physics, chemistry, and physiology – and the mind is somehow nothing but a physical phenomenon. In short, the mind is the brain."* <Daniel Dennet, op. cit. page 33> *"For us, the cognition production system is the brain."* <Hobson et. al. p 12>. By contrast the magical view does not locate consciousness within the brain, which – together with the body of which it is a part – is considered merely a thought form. The physical body, like the body we have while we are dreaming, is just a projection of the mind. The magical view is not predicated upon the linearity of time, hence post hoc does not necessarily imply propter hoc. The fact that e.g. certain types of aphasia arise together with lesions in certain areas of the brain does not imply that the latter cause the former. Or that blood flow in the anterior cingulate increases when novel action must be taken and decreases when the action ceases to be novel. <Gazzinaga, Ivry, Mangun, *Cognitive Neuroscience*, Norton NYC 1998, p 460 column 2>. Rather, the magical model holds that all causality arises in dreamless sleep. According to the magical view there is indeed a connection between what happens in the physical brain and what happens in consciousness, but that connection is not a causal connection per se. Or if one is conceived of as causing the other, then changes in consciousness are reflected as changes in the brain; the changes in consciousness come "first" (are primary to) the changes in the physical brain.

The so-called physical brain is like the scoreboard at an athletic contest. The scoreboard reflects what is happening on the field, but it doesn't create it. Similarly, the brain reflects decisions that are being made on a feeling level, but it certainly doesn't create anything. It doesn't even apprehend anything. It just keeps count, keeps score, keeps tabs on what is really going on. A body – whether in dreaming or waking – is merely a counter: first this happens to it, then that happens to it, then the other happens to it, then it dies.

It's wrong to place the seat of consciousness in the brain. According to Castaneda, it's located outside the physical body above the right shoulder blade. The point is that it's useless to seek a mechanism for consciousness, a link between consciousness and the physical brain, because *there is no such mechanism*. Not in the sense in which the materialists want to believe. Moreover, since they are hobbled by the notion of linear time, they will always be looking at what causality there may be backwards (post hoc, ergo propter hoc).

In hypnagogic hallucination we can view the process by which we create our own dream reality; our waking reality is created analogously. In waking life, as in hypnagogic hallucination, there is no reason why this image or situation is chosen and not that one. Reasons why things are have to be cobbled together in retrospect, to provide a post-hoc justification for why things are the way they are. Although causes do give rise to effects, and these effects are even predictable at times, there is in truth no reason why this and not that. In other probable realities it came out that and not this.

Anyone who discerns any purpose in the outworkings of the universe – whether this purpose is conceived of as the will of God, or survival of the fittest and most prolific reproducers, or the selfishness of genes – is looking at things backwards. Both Christianity and materialism are projecting images which aren't there. Like the cabalistic Gematria which finds hidden connections in every biblical name and phrase; or like a paranoid who detects sinister plots against him in every chance occurrence; Christianity and materialism project meaning and purpose onto complete chaos. There is no purpose to anything except as in retrospect it can be argued that things are the way they are because that is how they were meant to be. But this is an illusion, the old post-hoc-ergo-propter-hoc fallacy, which in turn is predicated on the fallacy of linear time. What we call linear, well-ordered time is an illusion (and thus the mathematical real number system has no actual model in nature). The universe is not continuous, but rather explodes into being and dissolves into nothingness with every passing instant of "time". There is no space, there is no time, and there is no reason for anything.

Chance viewed in retrospect appears to be reasonable. But nothing in the universe is reasonable. In the magical view evolution does not favor the individuals and species with the greatest reproductive success, but rather the luckiest individuals and species – the ones who just happened to make all the cuts. The question of why they made the cuts and other individuals and species didn't is relevant only as long as you are considering one line of probable realities, but says nothing about the future. Actually, it doesn't say that much about the past, either. It's all just a matter of opinion.

The question of there being any meaning or purpose in evolution is clearly tied up with the question of self-importance. It is difficult for a certain type of intellect (let it be uncharacterized) to abide the notion that humans (and themselves in particular) are not the pinnacle of the evolutionary process, who stand in God's presence with the privilege of naming each species; or, in the sociobiological version, that humans are not the sole possessors of consciousness.

In the practice of magic (as in dreaming) we do not make this mistake because we never ask that question – whether anything has a purpose. We just accept things as given and try to deal with them; we don't question why this or why that. This question can in fact be considered the definitive difference between dreaming and waking: only when we are awake do we ask: Why? What is the purpose of this? And then we futilely struggle to try to provide and prove an answer. It is not God's will, or reproductive success via adaptation to scarcity of resources, which revolves the wheel of birth and death that is waking consciousness. Rather it is the "Deception" (in William Butler Yeats' nomenclature) of trying to find some sort of purpose in existence:

"Without this continual Discord through Deception there would be no conscience, no activity; Deception is a technical term of my teachers and may be substituted for 'desire'."
– William Butler Yeats, *A Vision*

Magic assumes that it's *okay* if certain matters are beyond human comprehension, ineffable, sacred. The materialistic view, in its insufferable hubris and contempt, rejects the idea that the human mind cannot penetrate to the bottom of the mystery of consciousness: *"If dualism is the best we can do, then we can't understand human consciousness. Some people are convinced that we can't in any case. Such defeatism, today, in the midst of a cornucopia of scientific advances ready to be exploited, strikes me as ludicrous, even pathetic."* <Daniel Dennet op. cit. page 40>. Note that the magical model is no more dualistic (making a distinction between body and mind) than the materialistic model. In the materialistic model mind is considered merely an adjunct of the body (the brain); whereas in the magical model the body is considered merely a projection of the mind (a thought form, just as the body we have while we are dreaming is a thought form).

In the scheme of temporal evolution, dreaming arose together with mitosis and waking arose with meiosis. In other words, in the beginning there was dreamless sleep. Dreaming is the quotidian consciousness of single-celled organisms; waking consciousness arose when multi-celled life appeared: *"REM arousal mechanisms, and hence presumably the rudiments of dreaming, are more ancient in brain evolution than the waking circuits of the Extended Reticulo Thalamic Activating System (ERTAS). ... The epicenter for REM sleep is slightly more caudal in brainstem tissues than the epicenter for waking."* <Jaak Panksepp, *The dream of reason creates monsters*, Sleep and Dreaming, Cambridge U. Press 2003, p201>. *"REM arousal may reflect an ancient form of waking arousal that was devoted largely to activating genetically ingrained emotional subroutines, which guided behavioral actions in ancestral species long before the behavioral flexibility provided by higher cerebral evolution. Those ancient, value-coding processes may still provide background operations that help higher brain mechanisms sift and integrate fundamental survival concerns from the Niagara of cognitive information flowing in from newly evolved forebrain regions."* < Panksepp, op. cit., p 201>

Note that from both the magical and materialistic points of view all life on the earth descended from one primordial cell; thus all life on earth can be considered to be a single organism. The consciousness of this single organism is dreamless sleep. As this organism ramified into individual cells its consciousness ramified into a multitude of individual dreamers who are separated in space. When it further ramified into multicellular beings its consciousness ramified into a multitude of awake individuals who believe that they are important beings living their unique lives in linear time.

Unfortunately, this is just not true; nor is any belief system, such as Christianity or Rationalistic Materialism, which is based upon this assumption, true.

Chapter I: The Synodic Cycle of Mercury

*"You get born and you try this and you don't know why
only you keep on trying it and you are born at the same time
with a lot of other people, all mixed up with them, like trying
to, having to, move your arms and legs with strings only the
same strings are hitched to all the other arms and legs and the
others all trying and they don't know why either except that
the strings are all in one another's way like five or six people
all trying to make a rug on the same loom only each one wants
to weave his own pattern into the rug ..."*
  – William Faulkner, *Absalom, Absalom!*

Introduction

We begin with some technical definitions; not because this
is a scientific treatise, but because that way we have
something concrete to refer back to. What we are trying to do
here is to explain the inexplicable: what's *really* going on out
there in the universe is not anything we can even conceive of,
much less talk about. However, we do have to start
somewhere. Therefore, don't worry too much about
understanding these definitions – in the pages that follow we'll
be going back over it all again and again.

The basic unit of mind is called a *thought form*. A thought
form is an observer / observed duality: the observer and the
thing being observed arise together. If a tree falls in a forest
where no being can hear it, it does *not* make a sound thought
form. There can only be a sound thought form if some being
is hearing it. Although we believe that we are separated from
what we are observing (seeing, hearing, smelling, etc.), the
fact is that this is indeed merely a belief.

This is actually a very difficult point to grasp – that things
don't happen outside of us, as seems to be the case, but rather
we and the things that happen to us are but two sides of the
same coin. It's like that optical illusion which can be viewed
as either a vase, or else as two people facing each other.
Which is it: a vase, or two people? In the same fashion, there

is no world outside of ourselves, but merely a belief we have that there is an outside world there impacting on us. Things don't happen *to* us; rather, the things that happen *are* us. This is what is meant by the astrological axiom, "Character is destiny"; or the New Age watchword, "You create your own reality."

This is easier to understand with regard to dreaming. While we are dreaming we believe that what is happening to us is real; but when we wake up, we realize that it was just our projection, no matter how real it appeared to be while we were asleep. Similarly, the world we experience when we are awake is also just our projection, and it is only our belief that it is real which makes it seem real.

Whether we are awake or we are dreaming, things seem to happen to us. The "things" which happen to "us" are thought forms; in order for mind to operate there has to be both "things" there, and also an "us" to which those things are happening (separation between that which is happening and the being which is experiencing it).

There are two basic types of thought forms: *sensory thought forms* and *conceptual thought forms*. Sensory thought forms are known in materialistic cognitive philosophy as "qualia"; and conceptual thought forms have also been termed "memes", "agents", "schema control units", etc. Sensory thought forms are thought forms of mindfulness: they are what we experience when we are paying attention to what is happening here and now. These thought forms consist of sensory and extrasensory perceptions of the now moment: sights, sounds, smells, tastes, and feelings (both physical and nonphysical). Sensory thought forms have a high proportion of feeling to them, such as the sight of a beautiful woman; the smell of roses; the roar of the ocean; the feel of slime.

In fact, sensory thought forms are symbols for feelings. This is easier to see in dreaming, which consists mostly of sensory thought forms. The experiences we have while dreaming are symbols for feelings – in dreaming, we feel our feelings by reacting to "objective" events (sensory thought forms). However it is actually our feelings which create the sensory thought form symbols, not the other way around. We are not feeling feelings in reaction to objective events, but rather the "objective events" are being called up by our feelings. This is easiest to see when we are just dropping off to sleep, but are still awake enough to objectively discern the process (hypnagogic imagery) by which dreaming kicks in. At such times it is obvious that we are creating our own dream experiences, even if we are not consciously controlling or directing the process. In waking consciousness we operate on sensory thought forms whenever our thinking stops – either because we are very relaxed, or else because we are overcome by some powerful feeling (terror, awe, hilarity, etc.) so that our thinking is momentarily numbed or suspended.

In contrast to sensory thought forms, conceptual thought forms, are thought forms of mindlessness and consist mainly of thoughts about the past or future. Actually, the distinction between sensory and conceptual thought forms is not all that clear-cut. For example, the technique of creative visualization (discussed in Chapter IV) may be considered to consist of sensory thought forms of the future; and the technique of recapitulation (discussed in the companion volume *The Great Wheel*) may be considered to consist of sensory thought forms of the past. The sensory / conceptual distinction correlates roughly with the right and left hemispheres of the brain.

When we are thinking, we are operating with conceptual thought forms. For example, when we are driving our automobiles, most of the time we are operating on automatic pilot – not paying attention to our driving – and this is operating on conceptual thought forms. But if we spot an accident up ahead, we snap to and start paying attention to our driving; and this is operating on sensory thought forms. Just as most of the thought forms of dreaming are sensory thought forms, most of the thought forms of wakefulness are conceptual thought forms. Indeed, conceptual thought forms are a specialized form (an outgrowth) of sensory thought forms, just as waking consciousness is a specialized form (an outgrowth) of dream consciousness.

Dreamless sleep consists mostly of Feelings;
Dreaming consists mostly of Sensory T.F.'s (sights,
sounds, sensations);
Wakefulness consists mostly of Conceptual T.F.'s
(thoughts).

When we are conversing with someone but not looking them in the eye; or if we are looking them in the eye but not actually paying attention to them; then we are operating on conceptual thought forms. But if we are looking them in the eye and feeling what they are feeling (paying attention to them), then we are operating on sensory thought forms. In what follows the simple term "thought forms" will usually mean "conceptual thought forms".

All thinking consists of conceptual thought forms. We cannot think and pay attention to the now moment at the same time. In order to think, we must conceive something (whatever we are thinking about) to be more important than paying attention to the now moment. Thus we can say that the difference between sensory and conceptual thought forms is that the latter have a covering, or gloss, of *importance*. Importance may be defined as a screen of inattention: when we operate on sensory thought forms we pay attention to what is happening in the now moment; however, when we operate on conceptual thought forms, we pay attention to something other than what is happening right now by screening out what is happening right now; and this is accomplished by feeling that something else is more important than what is happening right now. In order to think, we have to stop paying attention to what is happening right now and focus our attention on something else, and it is importance which allows us to focus our attention by disregarding (screening out) what we are experiencing in the now moment.

An example of how importance turns a sensory thought form into a conceptual thought form is: "Pain!" is a sensory thought form; but "MY Pain!" ("Ouch!") is a conceptual thought form. The latter thought form has a gloss of importance that the former lacks. It has often been observed that lunatics appear insensible to pain and cold. However, this is not correct: they feel exactly what anyone else would feel in that situation, but because they have a different schedule of importance priorities than most people, they don't put importance on "their" pain or "their" cold – they just feel the sensation (sensory thought form) of pain or cold without attaching importance to it (interposing an "I" gloss over the raw sensation in order to dull it – i.e., turning it into a conceptual thought form).

Importance is the arrangement of thought forms in a hierarchy: for example when we are driving our automobiles, our attention is placed primarily on whatever we are thinking about; secondarily on the act of driving, what our eyes are seeing outside the car and inside it; the song on the radio; our destination and how to get there; what we have to do this afternoon and tomorrow; etc. etc. Importance is the arrangement of all these various thought forms in a scheme of decreasing emphasis, from the forefront of our attention to the background. What "we" are, then, is a collection of thought forms at any given moment arranged into a hierarchy of importance categories. Without importance, "we" would cease to exist – everything that we see, hear, smell, touch etc. in the same moment would impact our attention with equal vividness, and we would lose our mind – our sense of there being a detached observer observing.

At the same time that mind is clicking out thought forms there are also feelings being felt; however, these don't fit in anywhere along the continuum of mind. Feelings underlie mind (although every now and then, like volcanic eruptions, they break through to the surface of conscious attention). Since in our society we have been trained to give our primary attention to our thought forms and to ignore our feelings, most of the time our feelings just churn around down below the level of conscious mind, unacknowledged and unappreciated.

This is an unfortunate loss since, in truth, it is our feelings and not our thought forms, which are directing the entire process. Feelings are the projectionist in the booth, selecting the general tenor of the next moment, which mind will then have to picture with a thought form. Feelings are manifestations of intent (symbolized by the sun) which is entertaining itself with its thought form movie (symbolized by Mercury).

Most of the thought forms which mind creates simply drift off into oblivion when the attention moves on to the next form. However, when the same thought form keeps popping up before conscious mind, it becomes possible for conscious mind to recognize it and remember it – i.e., to make it part of a history / future inventory that each new thought form carries with it. Thus memory may be considered a species of networking between thought forms: from any given thought form it is possible to go next to any other thought form in its memory inventory.

The sum total of our remembered thought forms is what we call our personalities. From the magical point of view we are not unitary personalities but rather multiple personalities (like Eve, Sybil, and Truddi), whose behavior is the product of now one, now another, of our thought forms. Thought forms are the wall of self-consciousness which we erect between ourselves and the world outside of us; indeed, they are what make the world seem to be "outside" of us.

We can deliberately remember thought forms by means of repetition. For example, if we want to remember a telephone number, we repeat it over and over to ourselves until we have made the thought form of that telephone number strong enough to take its place in the inventory of remembered thought forms. Remembered thought forms hang around at the fringes of conscious attention, ready to spring into action to take over conscious mind in response to the remembered stimulus. A remembered thought form is a record of a decision we once made – an automatic pilot which will always make the same decision in response to the same stimulus. This is the magical view of all learned behavior – why, in the example of our driving, we can drive our automobiles across town without having to think for even a moment about what we are doing. Our conditioned "chauffeur" thought forms are doing the driving for us, and they only relinquish control to our conscious attention (switch from conceptual to sensory) when they encounter a dangerous or unfamiliar situation which they haven't been programmed to handle. The aim of our thought forms is to reduce all of life to a set of mindless routines, to thereby bypass the need for conscious decision-making altogether.

The interplay between mind and intent could be, and indeed should be, a joyous activity. There's no reason on earth why we shouldn't feel completely content all the time, perfectly at peace with ourselves and the world around us. The reason why most of us don't feel this way is because our thought forms are at war with our feelings (our intent); we're too busy telling ourselves why we're not happy to allow a moment's pause to *be* happy. Our habitual thoughts drive us relentlessly, never allowing us a space in which to reflect objectively upon what we're doing, much less to consciously direct or control our reactions.

To be mindful of what we're doing requires balance. To operate on pure intent is to live entirely in the now moment, on instinct and gut-level intuition, and thus to be incapable of planning, organizing, and directing our experience. This is how our ancient hunter forebears operated and how we still operate in dreams. On the other hand, to operate purely on conceptual thought forms is to make our experience so routinized and compartmentalized that there isn't much satisfaction or depth left in it. This is pretty much how we modern humans operate.

Intent, which is symbolized by the sun in astrology, has been called different things in different philosophies: Tao, the Will of God, Impeccability, etc.; but here we will use the term "true feelings" to describe what we are truly feeling in our inmost hearts at any moment. Our true feelings know what we really want; they know right from wrong; they know what is good or bad for us; they know whom we can trust and whom we should avoid. Our true feelings are capable of making the most apropos response in any situation. However, we modern humans rarely act on our true feelings, but rather on our thought forms, or social conditioning, which is symbolized by Mercury. At about the time agriculture was invented, the human race en masse decided that each individual should repress his or her true feelings in order to enable the race as a whole to develop a more complex and intricate social organization than that which had existed before. Thus intent plays a very small part in modern society (as compared to hunting societies); nonetheless, everyone acts on their true feelings now and then, as when they fly with their gut-level intuition, or stand up for what they know is right in the face of societal opposition.

Mind, which is symbolized by the planet Mercury in astrology, is the same thing as attitude. Attitude is a matter of feeling rather than thinking, but it originates and tends to perpetuate itself in our thinking. It isn't our thoughts which control our experience but rather our intent (feelings); nonetheless, our feelings are controlled by our thoughts, though they do have a momentum of their own. For example, when something heart-breaking happens to us, it takes us some time to get over it. That is to say, it takes some time for our feelings to respond to the commands issued by our thoughts, which is why consistency and decision are needed to move our feelings and to turn the wheel of fortune.

The fundamental manifestation of intent in everyday life is decision: every time we make a decision, large or small, we are manifesting the principle of intent. Every single decision we make creates the universe – or at least *a* universe, in which that particular decision was made. Every one of our acts is nothing more nor less than an act of God. If it wasn't an act of God, by definition, it wouldn't have happened. Since it did happen; and since we are the ones who made it happen; we are one with God in every single decision we make. Decisions are animated by desire and preserved in memory, but they are actually made by mind. Mind calls all the shots – directs intent and thus creates reality.

The fundamental manifestation of mind in everyday life is attitude, which is to say slant or point of view (what we choose to focus on). We tend to keep making the same decisions over and over to perpetuate our basic attitude; and our basic attitude keeps making the same decisions. What is symbolized by the synodic cycle of Mercury (its cycle of revolution around the sun as observed from the earth) are the different ways in which different types of people rationally underpin their decision-making. Just as in mathematics certain postulates are assumed and everything else is derived from them by rules of logic, so too is every one of us a mathematician of sorts, who makes certain assumptions about life in order to prove that he or she is making the correct decisions. The Mercury cycle shows the different ways different types of people establish their taken-for-granted assumptions and the peculiar varieties of logic which they bring into play to make and defend their decisions; it shows how and why people think they are *right* – doing the *right* thing and making the *right* choices.

The sun represents our true feelings – who we really are in our hearts; the reason we were born. Mercury represents thought forms – who we think we are (our images), and what our parents and society have trained us to believe and want. When assisting our true feelings Mercury is the planet of calmness, sobriety, reason, judgment, detachment, objectivity. When obstructing our true feelings Mercury is the planet of pretense, seeking approval, phoniness, self-justification, making excuses, acting shamelessly.

The Mercury cycle is a symbolic description of the different ways in which people create and manage their thought forms – different ways in which they reconcile within themselves the competing demands of mind and intent; different ways in which they assign relative emphasis to the activities of mind and the activities of intent. What the Mercury cycle reveals is thus more a matter of a person's character than his or her intelligence.

Whenever intent (the sun) is the more emphasized of the two principles, the natives (the subjects whose horoscopes are being analyzed) place primary reliance upon their impulses, their knee-jerk responses, and their first impressions. They don't waste much energy analyzing things, nor are they much swayed by logical considerations or the ideas and viewpoints of other people.

Whenever mind (Mercury) is the more emphasized of the two principles, the natives lay primary stress upon their cleverness, skillfulness, and perspicacity (rather than upon dogged self-will) to support their decisions. They are more light-hearted than the solar types, but also more light-weighted: they lack the stamina and staying power of feeling because they put primary emphasis on thinking.

The Astronomical Basis of Mercury's Synodic Cycle

Now there are two ways in which either intent or mind can be given greater emphasis, and these are symbolized by the two dimensions of Mercury's synodic cycle. These two dimensions are: 1) Mercury's relative distance from the sun; and 2) Mercury's position east or west of the sun.

Because Mercury's orbit around the sun lies within the earth's orbit, from our earth-centered point of view, over a period of several months Mercury appears to oscillate back and forth around the sun. Sometimes it appears to move towards the sun; sometimes it appears to move away from the sun; but it never gets too far from it. Sometimes Mercury is visible in the east just before sunrise; sometimes it can be seen in the west just after sunset; but most of the time it is too close to the sun to be visible at all.

When Mercury is near the sun, the solar principle has *dominance* over the Mercurial principle. Solar natives are all force, fortitude, stick-to-their-guns bullheadedness: they make knee-jerk decisions, and that's that forevermore. On the other hand, when Mercury is relatively far from the sun, the Mercurial principle dominates the solar principle; these natives are thoughtful and analytical about their decisions, but are also hesitant and vacillating.

The other dimension of Mercury's synodic cycle – the planet's position east or west of the sun – is symbolically a matter of one principle taking *precedence* over the other; it's a matter of approach or basic style, rather than stance or basic position. When Mercury is *oriental* (from Inferior Conjunction to Superior Conjunction) it is a morning star, rising before the sun in the east; and when it is *occidental* (from Superior Conjunction to Inferior Conjunction) it is an evening star, setting after the sun in the west. When Mercury is oriental the attitude is characterized as being eager (Geminian), and when it is occidental the attitude is characterized as being certain (Virgoan). The terms "Promethean" and "Epimethean" – which are indeed quite apt – have been used by some authors instead of "eager" and "certain". The conjunctions partake in nature of the preceding hemicycle: thus Superior Conjunction is eager and Inferior Conjunction is certain.

To avoid confusion, the terms "ahead" and "behind" will be used to mean ahead and behind in the zodiac; and the terms "leads" and "trails" will be used to mean oriental and occidental. That is to say, Mercury leads the sun when it rises before the sun, at which time it is behind the sun in the zodiac; and it trails the sun when it rises after the sun, at which time it is ahead of the sun in the zodiac (this is because zodiacal, or yearly, motion is opposite to diurnal, or daily, motion). Observe too that when Mercury is at Greatest Western Elongation it is oriental, and when it is at Greatest Eastern Elongation it is occidental.

The natives whose minds are basically eager (Mercury oriental) are unrestrained, experimentative, and guided by their own impulses. They feel no need to refer their decisions to any authority except their own inclinations of the moment; nor do they suppress their spontaneity in the name of voluntary submission to social sanction. Rather, they look at life in terms of convenience and expedience. They have an attitude of ready anticipation towards life, and they are animated by a well-spring of optimism and faith in the future.

The natives whose minds are basically certain (Mercury occidental) are restrained and cautious, and are oriented towards goals and purposes. They base their decisions upon a guiding philosophy of social responsibility, in which each member must contribute his or her share, and they are scrupulous in observing their part of the bargain. Where the eager natives enjoy, the certain natives construct; where the eager natives act, the certain natives comport themselves.

They have a basic attitude of wariness towards life, and they are animated by a strong faith in principle and duty.

The synodic cycle of Mercury, in its entirety, consists of six marking points (two conjunctions, two elongations, and two stations) which delimit six intervening phases (see Figure 1).

Mercury's synodic cycle begins and ends with the Superior Conjunction, abbreviated SC (the *astronomical* cycle begins and ends with SC; the *astrological*, or symbolical, cycle begins and ends with Inferior Conjunction, abbreviated IC).

At SC, Mercury is on a direct line with the earth and sun, on the far side of the sun from the earth, and moving at its maximum direct speed in the zodiac (see Figure 2). It then appears to move ahead of the sun in the zodiac, decreasing in speed, until it is moving at the same speed as the sun at its Greatest Eastern Elongation (GEE). As shown in Figure 2, the elongations are the points at which the lines of sight from the earth to Mercury are tangent to Mercury's orbit, so that the angle A between the sun and Mercury as observed from the earth is at a maximum. This maximum elongation can vary, since if the tangent point happens to fall near Mercury's aphelion, then the radius r is maximized, so A is a maximum maximum (around 28 degrees); and if the tangent point happens to fall near Mercury's perihelion, then the radius r is minimized, so A is a minimum maximum (around 18 degrees). Insofar as interpretation is concerned, the actual distance of an elongation does not seem to be significant; i.e., the maximum elongations do not exhibit elongation characteristics to a greater degree than do the minimum elongations. Position in time near an elongation seems to be more important than the actual separation involved (however, see the note at the end of the section on Elongation).

THE MARKING POINTS AND PHASES OF MERCURY'S ORBIT

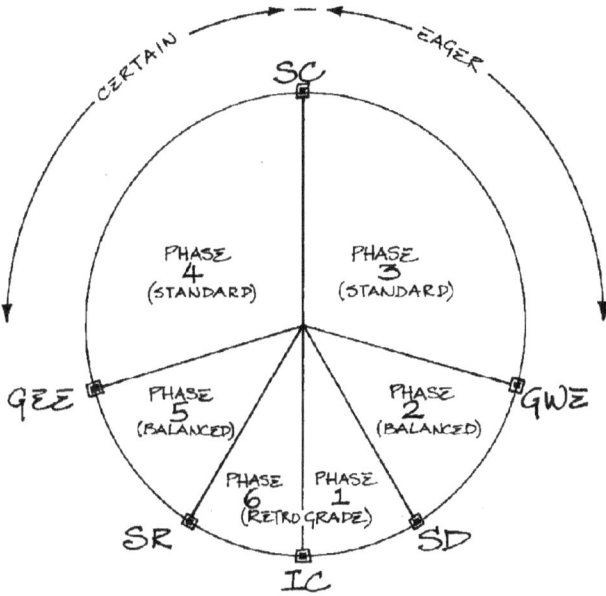

▣ IC	INFERIOR CONJUNCTION
SD	STATIONARY DIRECT
GWE	GREATEST WESTERN ELONGATION
SC	SUPERIOR CONJUNCTION
GEE	GREATEST EASTERN ELONGATION
SR	STATIONARY RETROGRADE

Figure 1

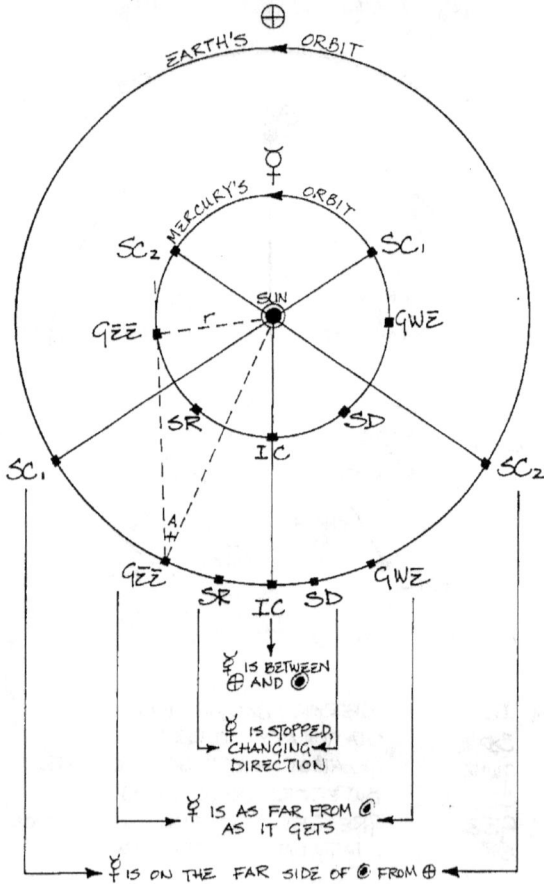

Figure 2

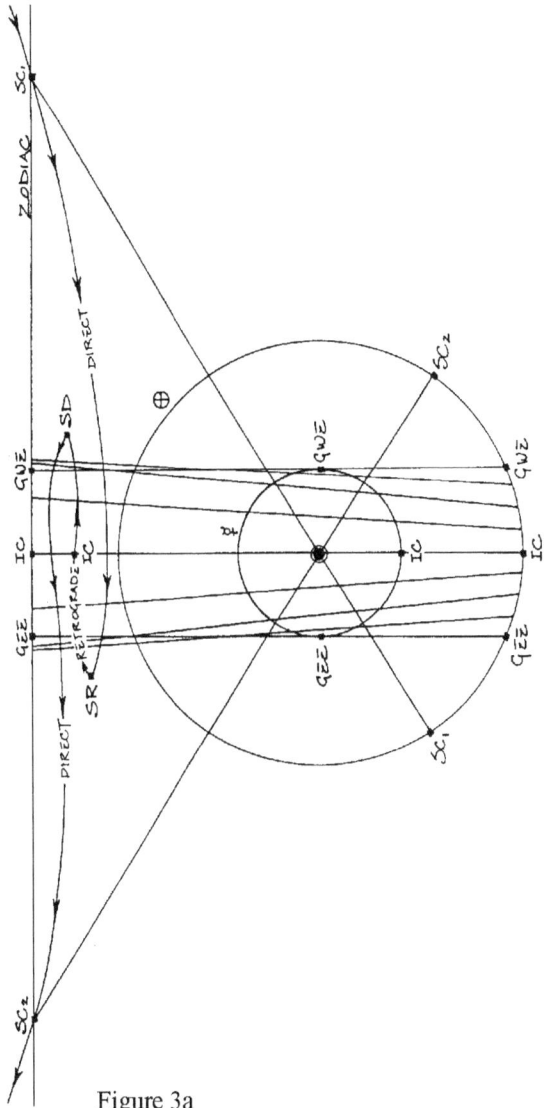

ILLUSTRATION OF RETROGRADATION

Figure 3a

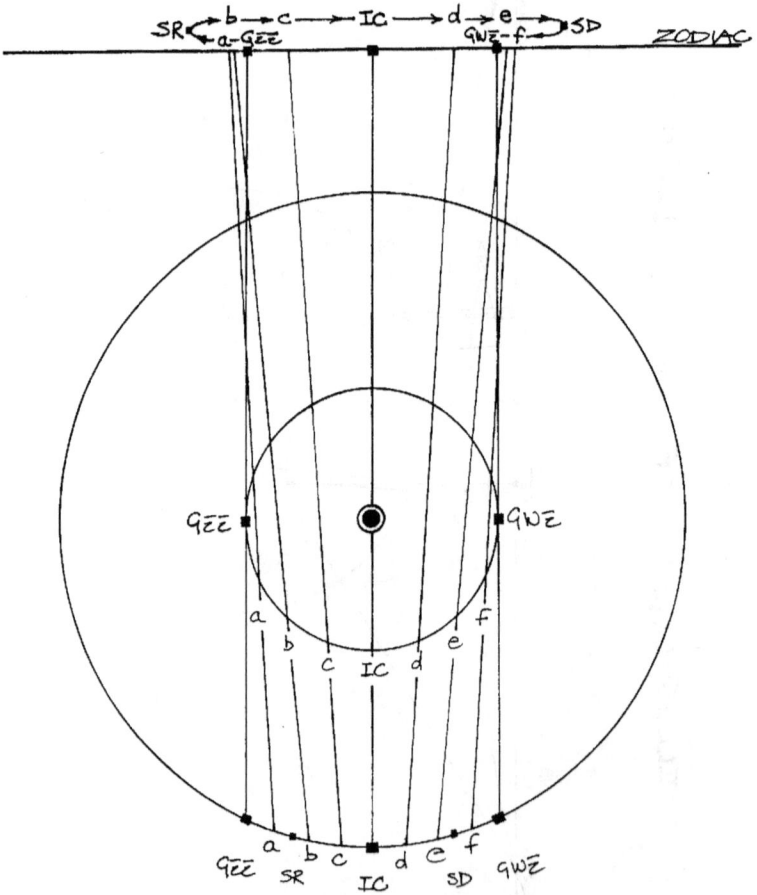

Figure 3b

After GEE Mercury's speed appears to fall below that of the sun, and the sun begins to overtake Mercury, whose speed decreases until it appears to stop (Stationary Retrograde, or SR) and then begin moving backwards in the zodiac. Figures 3a and 3b illustrate the phenomenon of retrogradation. After GEE Mercury's zodiacal longitude increases, but somewhere between positions a and b the earth "overtakes" Mercury, like a faster car overtaking a slower one, and Mercury appears to begin moving backwards.

Mercury and the sun move towards one another, the sun moving forward and Mercury moving retrograde, until they meet at Inferior Conjunction (IC), at which point Mercury is on a direct line between the earth and the sun, moving at its top retrograde speed. Normally Mercury does not actually cross the sun's disk, but rather passes "above" or "beneath" the sun. An actual transit of the body of the sun is known as *cazimi* in astronomy, but in astrology the term is used to mean merely an Inferior Conjunction exact to within a quarter of a degree, the apparent radius of the sun.

Mercury then falls behind the sun in zodiacal longitude, decreasing in retrograde speed, until it appears to stop and begin moving forward again (Stationary Direct, or SD). Mercury's direct motion increases in speed until it equals that of the sun at its Greatest Western Elongation (GWE). It then begins to overtake the sun until they meet again at Superior Conjunction. The entire cycle takes roughly 116 days (but is subject to considerable variation), and breaks down typically as follows:

Phase 4:	SC to GEE	=	35 days
Phase 5:	GEE to SR	=	10 days
Phase 6:	SR to IC	=	13 days
Phase 1:	IC to SD	=	13 days
Phase 2:	SD to GWE	=	10 days
Phase 3:	GWE to SC	=	35 days

However, the actual number of days in a phase of a given cycle is subject to some variation. The tables in Appendix 3 give the exact times when Mercury reached the marking points of its synodic cycle for the period from 1900 to 2050 A.D., together with simple instructions (no calculations or previous astrological knowledge required) for determining the position in Mercury's synodic cycle into which you, and the people you know, were born.

Quite arbitrarily, since some sort of orbs of inexactitude are needed for the marking points (rarely is anyone born at that exact minute), we will assume that a conjunction in zodiacal longitude has five degree orbs, so that an Inferior Conjunction is in effect for roughly two days, and a Superior Conjunction is in effect for roughly five days, both before and after the exact time of the conjunction. The elongations will be taken to have the same orbs as the SC, and the stations will be taken to have the same orbs as the IC. Hence the following table results:

Marking Point	Allowable Orb of Inexactitude
IC, SD, SR	± 2 days
SC, GWE, GEE	± 5 days

There are some cycles in which this allotment of orbs squeezes the balanced phases out of existence. In such cases it's better to use one's own judgment rather than to rely upon what is at at best a loose rule of thumb.

Generally speaking, it is best if Mercury is neither too near nor too far from the sun. At either extreme of the cycle (conjunctions and elongations) intent tends to get tangled up in its thought forms. Thought forms can come to dominate and overpower intent. They are created by intent, and are a part of intent, but they can also force intent to do their bidding, just as we individuals can force God to do our bidding. As we shall see later on, thought forms are actually living beings with wills of their own, in the same sense and to the same degree that we are living beings with wills of our own (although thought forms are much simpler than we are, just as we are much simpler than God is).

It is said that Mercury is a malefic planet because it symbolizes the thought forms which we choose to represent us in this lifetime; and it is only when we stop giving our thought forms the upper hand that we can truly make Mercury, the principle of mind, our proper servant. To reassert control over our thought forms – which basically involves decreasing their importance – is to realize that they are only the tools of experience, and not the experience itself. Mind is not reality; mind is but a tiny black speck moving hither and thither across the blazing brilliance of reality.

The sun symbolizes the life force, and when Mercury is conjunct the sun it becomes enervated, drained, and incapable of proper function. When Mercury is near the sun the mind is overwhelmed, so these natives tend to find their thoughts and impressions uncontrollable, unaccountable. These natives' inner communications function poorly; they are strangers to themselves. Although they allow all the power of intent to flow into their thought forms, they become thoroughly caught up in them and become their unwitting slaves.

By contrast, the elongation natives are quite capable of distinguishing between intent and thought forms, but they accomplish this by blocking energy output from intent to its thought forms – by being overly detached and trifling. They have too much inner communication: they squeeze the juice out of life by over-rationalizing it.

Mind seems to function at its best when Mercury is neither too near nor too far from the sun – i.e., in Phases 2 and 5. Indeed, these are the phases in which the planet Mercury attains its greatest brilliancy in the sky. In these phases a good balance is struck between intent and its thought forms: neither principle dominates the other. It is at this point that the clearest communication – cooperation and good faith – becomes possible.

The Conjunctions

If you were born with Mercury conjunct the sun (within two days of IC or five days of SC) there is very little separation between your intent and your thought forms. You tend to operate on instant, gut-level impressions and responses rather than on reflection and thinking things through. You rely more on intuition and cunning rather than on logic: you have an unerring sense of where your own advantage and other people's weaknesses lie. You possess powerful concentration and focus: once you have made up your mind about something you are indomitable. You have the greatest personal force of any of the Mercury types because you stand by your decisions and opinions come hell or high water; and standing by one's decisions is indeed the key to all personal power and success in life.

The problem with Mercury conjunction is that the decisions you stand by are usually not your own, and therefore are not necessarily in your best interests. Mercury symbolizes the child within each of us who can never get very far away from its parent, symbolized by the sun. With your natal Mercury conjunct the sun, you cling tenaciously to those thought forms which you created as a child; even in adulthood you hew very closely to the thought forms your parents inculcated into you. You were a "good" and obedient child; and later on became a "good" and obedient citizen. Mercury conjunction natives are the backbone of society.

Actually, what we are saying here about Mercury conjunction natives is true of everyone to one degree or another; the other types are variations on the theme of the basic conjunction type. The conjunction represents the extreme case, and thus epitomizes the entire cycle. No one ever escapes parental conditioning; however, greater separation between Mercury and the sun permits greater freedom of choice.

The sun symbolizes God as well as the parent because to a child the parent *is* God – the creator, the all-in-all, the source of everything. As a Mercury conjunction native you act and react exactly as your parents taught you to do when you were little; perhaps not with regard to superficial concerns, but certainly in the important things in life: intimate relationships; major commitments and responsibilities; and the scary stuff hiding under the bed (i.e. situations which you cannot control).

You don't examine or question your motives or reasons but rather charge ahead in the sure and certain knowledge that God – your parent – is on your side. Thus your decisions have great power and force of will behind them but evince little objectivity, discernment, or depth of understanding. You tend to be closed-minded, with blinders (emotional walls) which only permit you to see what you want to see, and you are critical and disapproving of anyone who doesn't measure up to your own prejudices.

Probably one or the other of your parents was a harsh, dominating, and repressed individual who gave you very little in the way of true love – acceptance of who you were (note that approval for a job "well-done" – meaning done the way the parent wanted it – is *not* true love or acceptance). And you feel constrained to uphold this role in turn for your parents – to approve of them unquestioningly, and to expect unquestioning approval from others in turn. The only thing you are consciously aware of is that you loved your parents; you can't see objectively how they programmed you and how much anger you feel towards them beneath the surface. Your parents never permitted you to express feelings of anger at them openly, hence you never learned how to handle anger within yourself. Instead, you pretend that you're not angry – that everything is copacetic; you don't have any emotional problems, and the people who do have such problems are just being self-indulgent. Mercury conjunct sun implies denial.

Just as your parents did to you, you don't permit other people – at least the ones you have power over: children, spouse, employees – the space to have feelings of their own: i.e., to disagree with you. A true love relationship always admits of disagreement; however, you tend to take any disagreement as an attack on you personally. When subjected to blame or criticism, you hiss and snap like a cornered animal. It's not that you feel you are in the right per se (although being right always seems to be the issue); rather, you assume that you must constantly defend yourself against the presumed judgment of being found wrong, and thus miss the point that (usually, anyway) nobody is judging you or attacking you.

You cannot conceive of disagreement in good faith. Your constant assumption in any relationship is bad faith – that someone has to be the winner, and someone the loser – and you'll be damned if that's going to be you. You assume that if the other person disagrees with you, then ipso facto they must be acting in bad faith. This is because the bad faith model of relating to others – scoring little victory points instead of listening to the other person's feelings – was the only model you had as a child. Your parents stamped you out; so all you know is stamping other people out (before they can stamp you out).

This is why your intimate relationships so often turn into power struggles; and you can never see your own role in creating this reality for yourself. All you can see is that the other person refuses to cooperate – therefore, they must be acting in bad faith. You can't see the anger you throw at them covertly, unconsciously; or that your negative feeling towards them actually presses down on them like a physical pressure and makes them erupt at you. And the angrier they get just proves all the more how wrong they must be: if they are so immature and indulgent as to be unable to control their emotions, then of what value is their point of view? They must just be angry people looking for an excuse to be unhappy, and blaming it on you.

The fact is that you don't really control your feelings; rather, you repress them. True self-control is not based on fear, but rather on detachment. Controlling one's feelings entails consciously acknowledging their existence within oneself, and then consciously processing (selecting or rejecting) them. What you tend to do instead is to block unwanted thoughts and feelings before they even become conscious; you have an instinctive fear governor – instilled by your parents – which immediately changes the subject (censors your thinking) whenever undesirable feelings come close to surfacing. Like children and primitives, you believe in magical thinking – that is, you believe that your thoughts have power, that thinking an evil thought will make that thought come true, such as being angry at Mommy will kill Mommy. Therefore you repress all thoughts you consider evil as soon as they raise their ugly heads – even before your mind can consciously formulate them as complete thoughts.

In truth your beliefs here are essentially correct – that "evil" consequences do originate in thinking. However, repressing evil thoughts without first processing them consciously is as bad as being obsessively preoccupied with them – it's just a different form of clinging to them, which is what eventually makes them come true. We can only truly release "evil" thoughts by first letting them fully enter consciousness – admit to ourselves that we *do* have these thoughts and impulses – and then reject them; or possibly even accept them if conscious reflection shows that they're not so evil after all. For example, maybe we do have valid reason to be angry at our parents; and maybe only by feeling that anger consciously will we ever be in a position to truly forgive them and release that anger.

Mercury conjunction natives don't know how to relate intimately with other people because they don't know how to relate intimately with themselves. Because you had no model of true acceptance when you were growing up, you feel as though other people are besieging you, and you are terrified of being unmasked by them, of being confronted with your shame. Hence you adopt a mask of shamelessness, closing your ears and closing your heart.

Shame and glory are what we call ego – they are how all of us are trained as children. They are not thought forms per se, but rather casts of mind, attitudes, ways of looking at things (ways of organizing thought forms). Nor are they the same thing as our true intent; but we are taught to defend them just the same. We can say that the Mercury cycle as a whole symbolizes how different types of people handle their shame: shame hides things (conjunctions); turns aside from what it doesn't want to face (elongations); or closes up into itself (stations). All shame is shame at one's feelings; or rather, shame at having repressed true feelings, at being a phony, at having allowed oneself to become separated from our true intent. Shame is the force of clinging – when there is no clinging, there is no shame. Observe that glory (pride) and shame are the same thing. Pride is a mask for shame – we are only proud of the things we are ashamed of; we are only proud for having sold ourselves out somehow in our quest for glory (approval).

As a Mercury conjunction native you express your shame as a supercilious contempt for others, whom you thus make live out your own shame openly even as you contemn it. You project an idealized, exalted image of yourself, and then work like hell to live up to it. The image is of a good and honorable person; but in your own heart, you don't quite believe it. On a subconscious level doubt gnaws at the image: perhaps underneath it all you are really a killer, a pervert, an uncontrolled savage! You don't dare take a chance on letting your feelings out of their cage without a whip and a chair.

The reason you clamp down so hard on yourself – and, by extension, on other people – is because you feel as though you are sitting on top of a powder keg which will blow up if you ever relax your grip for an instant. What you fail to understand is that it is the clamping down (repressing) which creates that pressure you feel inside that you're terrified of losing control over, and that only by relaxing your grip will the pressure ease up.

The truth of the matter is that in spite of your misgivings you *are* a good and honorable person. But lacking faith in the purity of your own primary impulses, you cling desperately to your thought forms as a drowning man clings to flotsam. You will not abandon your images no matter how threadbare they may become; no matter how loudly life may scream in your face that the images are false, you feel compelled to defend them to the bitter end.

You are haunted by the ghosts of feelings which were never dealt with directly in the moment of their occurrence, and so never dissipated their power over your consciousness. Because you deny your feelings, you cannot separate yourself from them, nor see that there is some enduring intent which exists apart from your thought form concepts of yourself. You possess an iron will, which enforces a severe inner discipline.

Often there is one thing – some one specific situation or possibility (the recurrence of a situation from childhood, such as abandonment, rejection, or powerlessness) which you deeply fear but towards which you are inexorably drawn as if mesmerized. That is, you feel a compelling need to continually, or at intervals, reenact your childhood traumas. This dynamic masks a fear of death which has never been directly acknowledged.

Both conjunctions are essentially ending points rather than beginning points, even though it is true to say that the cycle as a whole begins at IC. This is because the beginning of mind – its point of departure – is death. Death and mind are the same thing, as we shall see later on. The conjunctions are the points at which eagerness (SC) or certainty (IC) die, so there's a more acute awareness of death here – hence a greater clinging and fear – than elsewhere in the cycle. You never open up your defenses for a minute, never let yourself go, nor permit yourself a heartfelt response; rather, you only permit yourself to feel what you think you should feel under the circumstances, in conformity with your thought form conceptions of acceptable feelings for such situations.

The challenge of any conjunction is to learn to separate the two planetary principles involved and operate them independently. In the case of a conjunction with the sun this is especially difficult because the principle of intent is so insistent in its expression that it thoroughly overpowers and distorts any channel made available to it – it burns up anything in its way. Another way of saying this is, that intent will out: it will have its own way. Our true feelings will force us, through pain and suffering, to acknowledge their existence whenever we try to deny them. In the case of sun conjunct Mercury, which symbolizes intent overpowering mind, the result is tremendous fortitude on your part, but dedicated to the service of false self-images. To separate a planet from the sun means to separate the self from the parent; to overcome your fear of and anger at your parents and to address your own inner needs rather than to mechanically uphold those of your parents.

In spite of your apparent lack of self-awareness, you nonetheless achieve a certain depth and delicacy of feeling because of the mythic terms in which you cast your life. You are obsessed with the problem of evil; you daily reenact in your own life the fall of Satan and the struggle of good versus evil. It seems to you as if Satan and his minions are everywhere you look (which happens to be true, but which is also the reason why you're afraid to look into yourself). Your noble – if grossly naïve and self-serving – idealism seeks to encompass all of the pathos of the human condition, and as such reflects a close tie to the Spirit. Conjunctions operate on a level of feeling – you are very intuitive and in close touch with your heart center. In fact, the reason you are so closed-up is precisely because your heart is so big, and therefore extremely sensitive to pain and hurt.

Your lesson is to become more attentive to your own preconceived mental patterns and prejudices. Instead of assuming, for example, that attack is the only possible form of communication and coercion is the only means of agreement, you have to drop this assumption – which entails seeing it in the first place – to make other forms of communication and cooperation possible.

The antidote to fear is courage; the antidote to misunderstanding is trust. Mercury conjunction natives have what it takes to be truly successful and happy in life: decisiveness, conviction, self-control, and determination. With a modicum of thoughtfulness and understanding (which are obtained by listening to the people you are intimate with) you can take your true place as a role model of forbearance, self-discipline, and righteousness.

Inferior Conjunction

When Mercury is at Inferior Conjunction, it is moving from occidental to oriental, so the mentality tends to clutch at a certainty which is no longer quite so certain. Without question, the Mercury IC native is the most complex, multifaceted, and deepest of the Mercury types – the hardest to understand or predict – combining the highest degree of self-awareness with the greatest capacity for self-deception.

As a Mercury IC native, you are always quick to take the offensive, but in the most defensive manner possible. IC women are often extremely alluring – not in a crassly coquettish or flirtatious way, but with a primal sexual openness and intimacy – a naïve vulnerability which disarms men and invites them to submission. IC men often project an image of honorableness, reasonableness, punctiliousness, disinterestedness, and high-minded seriousness of purpose, which invites the trust and confidence of others. To your casual acquaintances, you IC natives project an image of purity and nobility – you seem to be paragons of childlike innocence, in need of protection from the cold, cruel world. Beneath these superficial appearances (your first line of defense), however, lies a shrewd, intuitive grasp of human motivation, and a drive for power and control over others: a belief that life is tough, so you've got to be tough; life is harsh, so you've got to be harsh. You IC natives keep a stiff upper lip, and never permit yourselves to feel (much less show outwardly) any sign of weakness or indecision. While IC is no more passive-aggressive than SC, you are more obviously passive-aggressive: you bare your teeth, whereas SC grits its teeth behind a Cheshire cat smile. Or, you may marry someone who rages at you (expresses openly the anger which you, yourself are repressing); whereas SC always strives to ameliorate and spread oil on troubled waters.

Beneath the surface you possess an overpowering, intimidating personality which bristles at contradiction. You must do things in your own way, in your own time, and you will not be crossed. Although you pride yourself upon your emotional stoicism and you fondly believe that no one knows what you are really feeling inside, the fact is that you radiate intense emotional vibrations which are extremely intimidating to those who must deal with you intimately (your second line of defense to keep people at bay). You are forever trying to secure a complete control or grasp over life, which nonetheless never seems quite susceptible to your analysis or management. There are just too many things happening that your parents never told you about.

You see others as being uncooperative, but in fact you are intolerant, uncompromising, and unwilling to make allowances. You cannot bear to admit that you have been in error or at fault. Although often riven with self-doubt, you will never show it, nor any other sign of weakness; yet you take any rejection very much to heart. You are puzzled by life, by trying to uphold rules that don't seem to work. Inside every Mercury IC native there is a frightened little child who is crying and crying, but who is too afraid of being hurt to reach out to be comforted.

Inferior Conjunction is the beginning and end of Mercury's synodic cycle: it symbolizes the most primitive and unconditioned impulse of mind, whereas Superior Conjunction symbolizes a conditioned, temporizing impulse of mind. The characteristic which distinguishes the IC from the SC (and which makes IC so much more frustrating to communicate with than SC) is that the IC's are exceedingly acute – they see everything with chilling clarity and insight – and then they close their eyes to it. Superior Conjunction isn't like this at all – SC is clumsy and klutzy and evasive; SC plays the clown, refuses to get serious. But IC is all brass tacks and intensity. These natives understand that life is a serious business; but this knowledge, instead of girding them for battle, usually has the opposite effect of making them throw up walls upon walls, to shield themselves from what they fear is the truth.

IC is the Mercury type which registers the greatest pathos and *Angst*. They have the flimsiest psychic defenses, the highest degree of emotional receptivity and sensitivity to psychic pain – and hence the highest capacity for self-delusion in order to escape from that pain. It can be truthfully said of the SC natives that they don't know what they're doing; but the IC natives always know what they're doing, and yet are so paralyzed with fear that they cannot bring themselves to face themselves squarely. Their keen awareness of their own vulnerability produces a terror in IC natives which forces them to deny what is right before their eyes, to strike before they can be struck at, to close up before they can be hurt. Only when Mercury is cazimi – exactly conjunct the sun, when birth occurred within two hours of the exact time of the IC – is this terror absent; in these (extremely rare) natives there is a calm, detached clarity.

Precisely because IC is the point of greatest naïveté – sharpest sense or intuition of what is right and true – there is also here the greatest potential for a thoroughly objective and intellectualized self-understanding of any Mercury type (the balanced phases are not intellectual by any means – they're too simple; and while the elongations may have intellectual pretensions, they don't go very deeply into themselves). There is an unremitting intellectual groping going on at the IC as nowhere else; thus the highest potentials of the entire cycle are inherent right here at the beginning: sober and precise observation, analysis, and interpretation; single-minded ferreting out of truth, articulated with fearless spiritual authority. Indeed, every now and again you IC natives come out with a bit of lucid, penetrating, and cogent analysis – unerring insight which cuts right to the heart of matters, and quite startles the people who have been battering their heads against your adamant willfulness.

However, most of the time you rarely reach these heights, but rather, clam-like, you gingerly extend a foot forward a bit and then quickly close back up into your hard shell. Yet your deep-felt need to understand what is going on within and around you endows you with an integrity often absent in the complacent and self-satisfied SC native.

Superior Conjunction

When Mercury is at Superior Conjunction it is moving from oriental to occidental, so the mentality tends to grab after an eagerness that is no longer quite so eager. Unlike the hard-boiled IC native, you cultivate an image of tenderness: you seem to be soft, sweet, outgoing, and friendly – a huggable, loveable teddy bear. SC men project an "aw shucks" awkwardness and self-effacing bashfulness; SC women project warmth, playfulness, and sensitivity, and are easily moved to tears. However, this apparent harmlessness and tractability are basically just your first line of defense to disarm potential adversaries; beneath the surface you can be as hard-headed and emotionally repressed as the IC type – a smug, overbearing, know-it-all.

Where Mercury IC is a lone wolf, Mercury SC is a social creature; you are always evaluating yourself in terms of how you imagine other people are evaluating you. In spite of your underlying contrariness and inflexibility, your apparent softness elicits tenderness and sympathy from others. People like you because you try to be harmless and mildly indulgent towards them, which inclines them to be similarly indulgent towards you. You seem to be so sweet and innocent that people bend over backwards to give you the benefit of the doubt. Easily mortified or disappointed, you close up like a mimosa at the slightest hostile touch. You have an air of helplessness – "please don't hurt me!" However, your self-coddling, self-stroking, self-congratulating, self-delight quickly loses its charm for those who must deal with you intimately. You readily revert to the role of victim who is being abused by circumstances, but in fact it is your own insensitivity to everyone except yourself which is your own worst enemy: you never have a moment's doubt but that you are absolutely in the right (it is just such underlying self-doubt which animates the rumination of the IC native).

Your basic approach to life is to close your eyes, cross your fingers, and hope for the best. You are naively optimistic and overly sanguine. You bet your entire stack on your image of the moment. You throw yourself headlong into situations and relationships (on some well-meant impulse) with little forethought or regard for the consequences, and as a result you frequently find yourself out of your depth, mired in complexities which you hadn't anticipated, and from which you are powerless to extricate yourself. You prefer a roller-coaster existence, with little regard for conscious steering. Through all the triumphs and defeats you try to project a front of suave imperturbability and disinterested objectivity, which however is belied by your strong need to be constantly proving yourself, justifying yourself, testing yourself, exceeding what you perceive to be the expectations of others. You sustain yourself with a boundless supply of hope, and a tremendous faith that the good guys will win in the end.

The Elongations

When Mercury is at either one of its elongation points (GWE or GEE) it is furthest from the sun, so there is considerable separation between mind and intent. Unlike the Mercury conjunction native, who operates principally on a level of feeling, the Mercury elongation type operates principally on a level of mind. You elongation natives have mind developed to a high degree of refinement, embellishment, and decadence. Instead of relying upon gut-level instinct, you must puzzle everything through, and convince yourself (and other people) through logic and reasoned argument. Where the conjunctions sweat and bleed to defend their thought forms, the elongation is wholly a creature of practicality and expedience – a hummingbird who flits about sipping a little of life here and a little of life there – but who also feels rather distant or estranged from the Spirit.

Now the conjunction may be considered to be an underuse of mind – that is, a refusal to take intelligent responsibility for the choices of everyday existence. Conjunction natives tend to sleepwalk through life, focusing all their attention on those areas in which they have some degree of superiority or control, and ignoring everything else. By contrast, the elongation may be considered an overuse of mind – a refusal to act on the pure promptings of the heart without first thoroughly rationalizing them. Where the conjunction types are stuck in their thought forms – utterly committed to them to the death – the elongation types can shift thought forms around with great agility.

You are a butterfly, discarding old thought forms readily, without any sense that you are thereby discarding a part of yourself. Hence you can pick and choose behavior patterns, likes and dislikes, to a greater degree than the Mercury conjunction types (who fear change). For one thing, you have a more realistic picture of your relationship with your parents, and a more objective view of them as people, than the conjunction types do. On the other hand, you have more self-doubt than the conjunction types, because your mind is further removed from the ultimate source of self-assurance.

Where the Mercury conjunctions rarely share their thoughts and feelings (indeed, they have a horror of sharing their thoughts and feelings, and thereby making themselves vulnerable; they may even have a secret fear that others can read their minds in spite of all their precautions, which indeed they can); you elongation natives, by contrast, tend to think out loud. You are generally quite frank and open about what's on your mind, although cagey GEE is considerably more circumspect and diplomatic than the chatty GWE.

The conjunction types clearly sense that all power in life comes from standing by one's already-made decisions; their problem is that the decisions they stand by are not their own, but those made for them by their parents and society. The elongation native, on the other hand, stands by no decisions at all; hence you have less power over your life than any other Mercury type, no matter how clever and incisive you may be. The question that the conjunction natives never ask themselves – which you elongation natives never stop asking yourselves – is: "Suppose I'm wrong?"

You are able to see everyone else's point of view, as well as the pros and cons of your own viewpoint; but this facility necessarily weakens your decisiveness (your willingness to make a commitment or take a firm stand). Where conjunction natives rely on immediate, knee-jerk responses; or immediate dismissal of ideas to oblivion (once they've decided something, their minds are made up forever); you elongation natives rely on continual self-analysis, sifting and refining your thinking, over and over and over. The conjunction operates on blind faith; the elongation on lack of faith.

Both conjunctions and elongations strive for glory, but the conjunctions cut off the other side of the coin – the shame – until it piles up and up to a crisis. You elongations, on the other hand, can see the shame as well as the glory. You analyze a lot of your shame as you go along; don't repress as much pain and hurt in the moment; and therefore are less surprised in the end. It is your conscious awareness of your own shame which weakens your conviction and feeds your self-doubt (your awareness of the falseness of your own images). The Mercury conjunction types don't have this problem because they repress their shame completely and rarely permit themselves a moment's conscious doubt – hence their forcefulness and unshakeable conviction of rectitude.

You are aware of all your thought forms, therefore you know quite clearly that everything you do, say, and think is phony; whereas conjunctions have their thought forms pasted down pat with no loose edges. Typically, elongation natives will readily accept the theory of thought forms because it is a good description of what they already know; whereas the typical conjunction natives will utterly reject the theory of thought forms: they are so close to their thought forms that they have no comprehension of what a thought form could be – it doesn't describe anything that they have experienced for themselves.

Although lacking in the constancy and staying power of the conjunction, you maintain a lighter spirit. Because true humor depends upon being able to see two sides of a question at the same time, you elongations have a better sense of humor than the conjunctions, who can laugh *at* other people, but not *with* them. You also tend to be far more open sexually than the conjunctions – not because you are any "sexier" per se (which is a matter of personal planets posited in certain signs, such as Scorpio and Capricorn) – but rather because you are less repressed; more relaxed within yourself and at home with your impulses; less inhibited by parental and societal fiat (what the neighbors might think). You are also more tolerant of variant behavior – both sexual and nonsexual – in other people, unlike the conjunctions, who cannot bear to see anyone else acting out openly that which they themselves are taking great pains to repress.

You are constantly watching yourself perform, and you are fascinated by what you see. You are alert and adroit, and have an ironic or droll point of view. Unlike the conjunctions who feel compelled to defend their positions at any cost, you just shrug your shoulders and walk away. You are a master of the sidestep; you lack a sense of real moral commitment to anything beyond your momentary designs. You are a bit too superficial – you believe that you have everything all figured out, so that you're one up on everyone else in the game of life. Where the self-confidence of the conjunction types is bravado (underneath it all they don't for a minute really believe in their own swaggering rectitude), the self-confidence of the elongation type is overweening (you believe in it a bit too much).

In a threatening situation you pause a moment for reflection, to try to watch what's happening and to figure things out. Thus you tend to be more coolheaded in a crisis than the conjunction native, who abhors a vacuum and always has to rush in blindly with some response or other. You have a gift for picking up the feelings of other people or the undercurrents of a situation, and for addressing and articulating them lucidly; thus you are usually quite apropos. You are a good communicator because of your basic openness and candor.

But in spite of your apparent mental clarity and straightforwardness, you maintain a vaguely patronizing attitude. You are mercurial and flippant; you take nothing to heart; and thus you are no easier to communicate with on a heart level than the repressed conjunction types. When someone is in pain, you would like to feel with the sufferer; but you are emotionally barren. You cannot put together a response deeper than well-meaning platitudes no matter how hard you try; and so you end up faking it (and know you're faking it).

You dally with life; to you it's only a movie on a screen. You are glib, always ready with an excuse for yourself. You're too busy watching yourself, preening yourself, gauging your effectiveness, to give wholeheartedly of yourself to your experience, or to exercise decisive control over your destiny. Where the conjunction types yield nothing, the elongation types defend nothing; but as a result your words and deeds lack the authority of conviction. Your life, therefore, tends to be a patchy, disorganized travelogue bereft of the seriousness of purpose which endows existence with meaning. You often feel stranded in your own rationalizations; out of synchronization with your world; left behind by a drift of events or feelings which you never fully understood or appreciated. You never have a secure sense of belonging, but feel like a stranger or interloper in the world. Indeed, you pride yourself on being a sojourner; but you are aware enough to feel the chill of your own coolness. What the elongation needs is a good dose of humility and a little less self-delight. You are good at listening to people, but must learn to hear them as well. There is a call here for a bit less cleverness and a bit more wisdom.

<Note that the minimum (17° 52' separation) and maximum (27° 50' separation) values of Mercury's elongations form a curious pattern:

	Minimum Elongation:			Maximum Elongation:		
	Date	Sun	Merc	Date	Sun	Merc
GWE	Sep 27	LI 4	VI 16	Apr 5	AR 15	PI 17
GEE	Feb 18	AQ 28	PI 16	Aug 12	LE 20	VI 18

In other words, when Mercury is at minimum elongation, the sun is weak by sign (either in its fall at GWE or in its detriment at GEE); when Mercury is at maximum elongation, the sun is strong by sign (either in its exaltation at GWE or in the sign it rules at GEE). This symbolism suggests that the sun's strength (as well as Mercury's) is augmented by greater separation between the two bodies, and reduced by propinquity.

However, Mercury is stronger by sign at minimum GWE and maximum GEE, and it is weaker by sign at maximum GWE and minimum GEE. It shall be left as an exercise for the reader to interpret what this symbolizes.>

Greatest Western Elongation

When Mercury is at its Greatest Western Elongation, your mentality is as eager as it can be: you are peppy and perky, ardent and impulsive, quick to seize any opportunity to prove your skills and show your stuff. You thrive on challenge and the chance to come to grips with life in its nitty-gritty aspects. You are uninhibited, sprightly and spunky, and have great personal flair. Candid and outfront, you have nothing to hide, and you take great delight in letting it all hang out. Whatever life role you choose, you play it to the hilt with unabashed theatricality, fanfare, and applause for another fine performance. You are sharp in your judgments and incisive in your outlook; nonetheless you have little patience for those who do not agree with you or support you. You are a consummate actor, with a brazen self-superiority or above-it-allness which can irritate people; your close associates often find your chintzy arrogance or blasé insouciance a bit overdone. You don't seem to know when it's time to turn it off; when you're overindulging yourself; basking in the glow of your own mirror; and it can take a sharp shock to bring you to. Although you conceive of yourself as a loner, you feel rather lost without your audience. Yet you have unlimited enthusiasm and faith in yourself, which in its proper moment inspires everyone around you.

Greatest Eastern Elongation

When Mercury is at its Greatest Eastern Elongation, your mentality is as certain as it can be. You have a quiet yet almost regal aplomb, and a strong sense of gravity or dominating presence. You have high principles which govern your actions, but you are sufficiently detached from your prejudices that you feel no need to impose them on others (at least not overtly). You are under no special incumbency to prove anything to yourself, therefore you can afford a tolerant, broad-minded, and democratic attitude towards others. You are cordial, subdued, decorous, and highly solicitous for other people. You tend to see yourself as the impartial facilitator or arbiter in any group of which you are a part. You are a consummate politician, artfully keeping yourself aloof from partisan strife, and steering clear of compromising entanglements which might limit your scope of action. You are observant and shrewd; you will not overtly cross anyone if you can help it, nor give needless offense. You maintain a studied neutrality or reserve in the face of confusion or complexity, hence you usually manage to land on top in any shakeup. On the other hand, your intimates find you cold and non-committal – too caught up in your game of chess to make a response from the heart.

The Stations

When Mercury is at either of its stations (SD or SR), there is sufficient separation of mind from intent; and there is also a powerful decisiveness. However, here mind and intent are in such perfect balance that there is no motion or growth in any meaningful direction. You stand like a boulder in a stream, unmoved and unaffected as life swirls by around you. The shock of unforeseen events against the customary patterns of thought and behavior of the conjunction and elongation natives serves to change (or at least disrupt momentarily) those thought forms in those natives. But as a Mercury stationary native you are mentally at equilibrium within yourself to begin with, hence you are quite impervious to the environmental and relationship pressures which make for learning and growth.

Where the conjunction recoils from confusion or uncertainty, and the elongation schemes to turn it to account, the stations simply turn it off. Your understanding of what is going on around you and of your position in the middle of it is acute as far as it goes; but you refer your reactions to a stereotype of unconcern and indifference. Where the Superior Conjunction affects imperturbability, the stationary native really *is* imperturbable – maddeningly so. You basically just want to be left alone.

Mercury conjunction natives believe they are "right" because God (their parent) is on their side: they think that they are faithfully carrying out instructions received from on high. Mercury elongation natives, on the other hand, believe they are "right" because they've figured out all the angles and possibilities – they've doped it all out for themselves. But you Mercury stationary natives believe you are "right", period. There's no reason for it – you need no excuses or justifications. In theory, you stationary natives have the highest potential of all – the firm conviction (lack of doubt) of the conjunction types, combined with the detached impersonality of the elongations. The problem is that you are completely self-obsessed, nonreactive, unresponsive to the needs of others. Your private space is all-important.

One might suppose that in the stations there would be a proper balance of energies, a true play, between the individual intent and its thought forms; and indeed there is a greater spirit of play at the stations than elsewhere. Stationary Direct is a fancy-free type; and even hatchet-faced Stationary Retrograde exalts in its rebelliousness and contumacy. But although there is a more playful spirit here than in the super self-serious conjunctions or the flighty, nervous elongations, there is also a greater clinging. The stations cling even more than the conjunctions do, because the stations are the doorways to the balanced phases, and thus represent the clinging before the release. All clinging is the magnetic tug of seeking glory and avoiding shame; and the stationary native clings to self-centeredness in a way which would make even the conjunctions and elongations blush; i.e., you enact shamelessness openly for the rest of the cycle. This is because you know better, but you do it anyway.

Mercury conjunctions comprehend no one's feelings but their own, and not even those most of the time. Mercury elongations comprehend feelings intellectually, but cannot release their intellection long enough to really feel with others. As a Mercury stationary native, you feel; you know; but you pretend otherwise. You pretend you don't understand by zealously guarding your own space and distance. Like the other two types, you still don't trust in the Spirit. In one way or another, all three types use thought forms where what they should be using is feelings. They defend concepts and beliefs when they should be asking questions and seeking answers.

As a Mercury stationary native you groove your existence in either the solar mode (SR) of sullen withdrawal into self, or in the mercurial mode (SD) of passing over experience lightly. In either case there is a delight in perversity and contrariety. You are pigheaded and inflexible, unyielding in the face of any surprise that life could possibly spring on you. You are uncompromisingly independent and free-spirited. You make your own rules and expect the world to bend itself to them, and you are delighted to find that it quite often does so. You have a compelling personality which either commands (SR) or seduces (SD) the acquiescence of others. You live in your own world, deciding for yourself where your responsibilities and obligations will lie. While you are punctilious in the discharge of what you consider your duty to be, you can be mulishly begrudging of your energies beyond this point, no matter what the situation may be demanding.

Your lesson is to learn to go out of your way, to make a bit more of an effort than you really think is necessary, to shake off your stodgy complacency. Since you lack the nagging self-doubts which plague the conjunction and elongation types beneath their surface savoir-faire, you must make this decision from within. Life will present opportunities but never motivation; and you Mercury stationary natives are usually quite comfortable with exactly how you are.

Stationary Direct

When Mercury is at its direct station, you are cheerful, expansive, and maintain at least a superficial semblance of reasonableness and tractability. You seem to agree with everyone you meet, and broach no objections to their thinking or plans; but then you go your own way and follow your own inclinations without so much as a fare-thee-well. You have an air of fastidiousness or snootiness, like someone who just can't be bothered. You hold yourself above contention, and generally resist appeals to your reason through a studied indefiniteness or impracticality; and yet you know damn well what's going on, and everyone knows you know it. Where the Stationary Retrograde native keeps the world at bay with a snarl, the Stationary Direct type blots the world out with the confetti of vagueness. You are pleasant but flighty – you will not let yourself be pinned down or committed. You smile and nod and hold to your own course, making as few waves as possible. Thus although you are as obstinate and determined as the SR native, you tend to engender far less opposition while being equally exasperating to the people who must deal with you. It is difficult to be angry at a person who is so easy-going, with such an attitude of live and let live.

Stationary Retrograde

The Stationary Retrograde native raises stubbornness to a high art. You are dogged and stern, unyielding to the point of unreason. You hunker down, grit your teeth, and dig in your heels in the face of any sort of outside demand place upon you; and indeed you greet every issue in life with such grim determination that one would suppose you to believe obstinacy to be a virtue in itself. An astute observer can catch the precise moment of your choler rising, when you involuntarily set your shoulders, clamp your jaw, and narrow your eye. You ask for no succor and you want none; you have firm lines which are not to be crossed, and a dignity which is not to be compromised or impugned. It's all just a big show you put on to force the other guy to back down and leave you alone, but it is extremely convincing and efficacious. Although you have a rather dour and forbidding demeanor, you are also extremely self-disciplined and thorough. You will not abandon an idea until you have exhausted all of it possibilities, and your tenacity will admit no counsel of despair. Your complete self-dedication to everything you do lends a nobility to your character, and compels the respect of others.

The Retrograde Phases

Statistically speaking, there are relatively few natives born into the Mercury cycle right at its marking points (or within orbs of same); the majority of nativities fall somewhere in the middle of the cycle, in one or another of Mercury's phases.

Insofar as interpretation is concerned, there is no hard cusp effect between phases; rather, the meanings of succeeding marking points and phases shade into one another. The marking point types (already described) may be regarded as the more sharply defined extremes of the intervening phases (to be described presently). Because the phases are arranged in pairs around the IC / SC axis, we will consider them in pairs, rather than in the serial order in which they occur in the cycle. This presentation illuminates certain important connections between corresponding phases in the cycle, but unfortunately it also obscures the progressive nature of the cycle itself (moving from Phase 1 to Phase 6), and also the progressive nature of each constituent hemicycle (Phase 1 to Phase 3, and Phase 6 to Phase 4).

The three pairs of phases are termed the retrograde phases (1 and 6); the standard phases (3 and 4); and the balanced phases (2 and 5).

In Phases 1 and 6, Mercury is retrograde and not too far from the sun. Here your attitude is concerned with your personal dignity and sense of the fitness of things. There is a greater interest in these phases in the issues which are raised by a given situation, rather than in the situation itself – that is, it is the principle of the thing which matters most to you – and this gives you a highly idiosyncratic slant on life. Your reactions are not what one would expect; not how most people would react. You are completely unpredictable. For example, you can be philosophical in a situation where most people would feel disappointed; or crestfallen at things most people would take in stride. You can be animated by a compelling sense of urgency in a situation where most people are patient and forbearing; but then be placid and collected when everyone else is tearing their hair out.

In the course of the average day, any number of whims and fancies dart into the mind of the average person; but only rarely will he or she act on one, since to do so entails getting sidetracked from the larger issues of life. However, to the Mercury retrograde native, there are no larger issues; or rather, the larger issue is the freedom to be able to act on whim. You have no sense of discrimination whatsoever between the important and the unimportant – you frequently ignore the one for the sake of the other. You tend to make issues out of things which no one else considers significant, and you steamroll over the logic and sensibilities of anyone in your path. You have to be the originator, not the follower. You tend to discount any disagreement with your own prejudices as a lack of intelligence, since it is incredible to you that any assumptions other than your own could possibly have any validity from their own side. Thus you have a pronounced psychological blind spot. There is little soul-searching in these phases (except right at the IC), hence there is a greater robustness here than in the balanced phases. You have a gift for focusing your attention entirely on the matter or project of the moment, to the exclusion of any other consideration or competing demand, which gives you a genius for handily accomplishing things which other people would deem impossible.

You are completely hipped on your own ideas. You possess a winning candor and a knack for enlisting the support – willing or unwilling – of others in the implementation of your own personal vision, because you act out of a deep faith in the power of the Spirit to sustain you. You have a naïve yet unshakeable trust in your own impulses, in the certainty of your inmost feelings, which gives you a reserve of inner strength and fortitude. In an emergency, you are a rock. But this also makes you rather solipsistic and isolates you in your own world. What makes communication so difficult for the Mercury retrograde type is that while your behavior and thinking are wholly erratic, you are nonetheless convinced that only a blockhead could fail to follow your impeccable logic or to agree with your apodictic conclusions. Where most people check things out or discuss them first, you Mercury retrogrades do things first, and discuss them (if at all) afterwards. The fait accompli is your main medium of persuasion.

You are difficult to reach on any level but your own, or on any terms but your own. There is a definite willfulness beneath your whimsy – as you cater to your own whims, you expect everyone around you to cater to you also. There is not much awareness here of the separation between intent and its thought forms: you are completely wedded to your own peculiar set of mind. You rely overmuch on your own intuition and thus fail to draw lessons from your history (mistakes). Your main lesson is to temper your unbridled intuition with a modicum of respect for the sensibilities and convenience of other people.

Phase 1: IC to SD

In Phase 1 Mercury begins to lead the sun, so a rational eagerness makes its first appearance. Like the Phase 6 type, you have an exaggerated sense of personal dignity, but it is very important to you that you be understood and appreciated. Albeit a bit fussy and finicky, you burst with friendly interest and the desire to help and advise. You are a tireless worker, and a natural-born organizer. You love to teach and preach, and you are always up on your soapbox; thus you make a good instructor or salesperson. Unlike the furtive Phase 6 native, you confront people directly. You pride yourself on your analytical faculties; you have a critical, legalistic mind which is fond of argument and which delights in spotting loopholes and errors in the thinking of others. You are querulous and love to bicker, as if for sport. You reduce all communication to contention, which you can then dominate by maintaining your own position at all costs and forcing concessions from other people by wearing them down to a frazzle. You take your own thinking so much for granted that you make no allowances for differing interpretations, and are impatient and bluff or indelicate in your handling of people. Thus you provoke dire confrontations unwittingly, with no awareness that your own obduracy might be a contributing factor, and no understanding of the fact that other people resent being brushed rudely aside. If they're in the wrong, they're in the wrong; right? That's their problem.

You are puzzled by rebuff, but usually lack the objectivity to surmount it because you honestly believe that you have only the best of intentions, and are acting in the best interests of all concerned. Although you have a penchant for quibbling, you also have a keen sense of fair play and take pains to be aboveboard and honorable. When you're not sidetracked on minor issues you have a gift for cutting through rigmarole and getting down to the real business at hand.

Phase 6:   SR to IC

The Phase 6 native has the certain cast of mind, so you act out of a sense of compliance with socially-approved norms and expectations. But Phase 6 is the loosest of the certain phases, the most individualistic and quixotic. Although friendly and outgoing in a social situation, you are basically a loner, a traveler of no fixed abode, and you live by the law of your own heart. You hide behind a mask of pleasant respectability, but you have a decided taste for the outré; hence you may number rank weirdos among your good friends, or engage in occult pursuits which would astonish your casual associates. You are truly an original. Albeit articulate and sardonic, you are not easily understood because you don't want to be understood – this is your privacy, your inalienable right. Where the Phase 1 natives are constantly poised to attack and expect the world to rearrange itself around them, you are poised to strategically retreat. You are shrewd rather than feisty and pugnacious; you parry rather than thrust, but like the Phase 1 type, your underlying assumption is conflict rather than communication. You feel no need for explanations, neither your own nor those of other people. You have a fortress mentality, and are ready to pull your wagons into a circle, psychologically speaking, at a moment's notice. This is not a defensiveness – you are too convinced of your own rectitude to be defensive – as it is a demand for consideration and respect. Although you are indomitable in your own convictions, you are surprisingly tolerant of and open to those of other people, and you are motivated by a great intellectual curiosity.

The Standard Phases

Phases 3 and 4 together account for almost two thirds of all nativities, thus they can be considered to symbolize the standard or normal types of mental functioning. There is a bit of torpor in these phases – an absence of the individual creativity and self-motivating and sustaining enthusiasm found in the retrograde and balanced phases. The standard phase natives are outer- rather than inner-directed in the sense that their everyday behavior is conditioned largely by the standards of shame and glory of their cultural milieu. By contrast, the everyday behavior of the retrograde or balanced phase natives is more the product of their own intuition or their inner necessities of the moment.

As a standard phase native you tend to view the world in terms of personal opportunity – for enjoyment (Phase 3) or for advancement (Phase 4). Your self-images are couched in terms of your social position; therefore, you are critically dependent upon feedback from your social environment for an assessment of your current status – you lack the inner surety of the retrograde or balanced phase native. On the other hand, you are less caught up in questions of meaning and interpretation. You don't see life itself as the issue (the problem; the opportunity); rather, you see life as a series of disconnected problems and opportunities. Thus you can afford a breezy, matter-of-fact attitude in your everyday dealings, which carries you smoothly over the shoals of life with a minimum of thought on your part.

Phase 3:   GWE to SC

In this phase Mercury leads the sun, so the mentality is of the eager type. You are spontaneous, uninhibited, and will do or say whatever is on your mind at a given moment, so that your remarks and actions are usually quite pithy. You seek your psychological equipoise in your individuality and your own self-expression. There is not much that escapes your notice; you are quick to pick up and capitalize upon whatever feelings are in the air. You tend to be broadminded and open to new ideas. Unlike the Phase 4 native, you are not bound by convention: you see life more as an art than a science – an endless play of possibilities. Your customary state of mind is enthusiasm for this or that current affair or interest. This is the Will to Party: you basically like to just hang out and have a good time.

On the other hand, you don't have much stick-to-itiveness, and your life often seems to be lacking in purpose or direction beyond momentary gratification. In between enthusiasms you easily fall into a mental rut, or become bored when you don't have a constant stream of stimuli from outside to engage your attention. There is often an underlying sense of nonfulfillment: a recurrent feeling that you're not getting anywhere or accomplishing anything of permanent value.

You have little consciousness that many of life's difficulties could be obviated or ameliorated with a bit of intelligent forethought on your part. You tend to be too caught up in what you want right this minute to have much perspective on your history (except for your fondly remembered triumphs) or your future (except as the projection of your current schemes). You believe that yesterday is gone and tomorrow will take care of itself. On the other hand, you have a keen sense of life as fun – a point often missed by the somber Phase 4 type.

Phase 4:   SC to GEE

In this phase Mercury trails the sun, so the mentality is of the certain type: you have to be sure of yourself before you act. You seek your psychological equipoise in your acceptance by your social group: in worldly success, in fulfilling expectations, in having an impressive resumè. You are well-organized; you consider carefully, plan ahead, and cautiously jockey for position in life. You avoid real risk-taking because you must feel yourself to be in a defensible position at all times. You can be a bit stuffy and opinionated, and overly sensitive to offense or affront.

You have well-defined ideals or standards of conduct to which you refer all your actions, and a disciplined submission to these standards. However, you can always justify the self-serving aspects of your empire-building – the skill with which you turn any situation to personal advantage – because ultimately "the rules" are elastic enough to be altered or reinterpreted at will to suit your convenience: you take "the rules" to mean whatever you need them to mean at the moment.

Because you must always feel that you are heading in some definite (and approved) direction, towards some definite (and praiseworthy) goal, you are extremely ambitious – sometimes cold-bloodedly so. Except near the conjunction, you can clearly see into your own ulterior motives, and therefore you tend to be distrustful of the motives of others. You greet the world with an attitude of suspicion, and as a result are rather inhibited. There is a definite need here for a general lightening up, and for a realization that your ex cathedra judgments have no sanction outside of yourself.

Generally speaking, neither the eager nor certain attitude is correct. The certain types try to hedge against the future, to prepare for all possible contingencies, which is impossible: "Life is what happens while you're making other plans." While it is impossible to plan our lives, it *is* possible to visualize goals for the future and to reach them by undaunted effort – by making the correct choice at every fork in the road; but it is impossible to anticipate these forks before we come to them. This is the eager attitude – to just let things happen and keep our fingers crossed and hope for the best.

The correct point of view is to visualize future goals with certainty, but then to let go and abandon ourselves to our fate with eagerness. And this requires a keen sense of balance.

The Balanced Phases

Phases 2 and 5 are the phases in which there is a proper separation between mind and intent – in which the interaction between the two principles is symbiotic rather than combative. Only in the balanced phases is there true trust in the Spirit, and therefore no need for pretense. Balanced phase natives don't create thought forms and then blindly follow them forevermore (as conjunctions do), nor do they strew their path with weak thought forms which lack force and conviction (as elongations do). The balanced phase natives have their intuitive channels wide open, so they are attuned to their own true feelings – the impulses of their own hearts – rather than to social and cultural canons of acceptance and approval. These are the only Mercury phases which have no great stake in being "right" – in particularly caring what other people think of them.

What these natives balance is shame and glory; they take greater care in obeying the dictums of their own hearts rather than in currying and preening their self-images (thought forms). Only in the balanced phases is the striving for glory not the mainspring of all action; these natives are past clinging to glory, for they have faced their shame.

As a balanced phase native you are humble, plainspoken, and unprepossessing. Usually you feel yourself to be a misfit, at least in youth. There is often some sense of psychological disadvantage or handicap which you must overcome early on, and the effort required equips you to use your experience as a teacher. What you learn is how to separate yourself from your thought forms, so that your ego is not alternately exalted and crushed by the vicissitudes of life. But unlike the coolly detached elongation types, you come to cherish life in itself; to treat it (and the people around you) with delicacy and restraint. You try to find a proper balance or sense of acceptance within yourself – a level of being on which you can live comfortably with yourself; feel good about yourself; strike an easy, relaxed pace in life; be willing to compromise and live in peace with other people (rather than project your own inner turmoil onto them). You are perhaps the best communicator of all, even though no one understands you, because you put everything on a basis of good common sense – i.e., good faith. The hallmark of the balanced phase native is your utter reasonableness. You are candid, open, and straightforward. You communicate in the language of gentleness, and touch other people on a feeling (rather than thought form) level.

Nonetheless, the balanced phase native can be the most stubborn type of all: you will never act against your principles, whereas all the other types can be made to back down (except perhaps the Mercury retrogrades – who knows what they'll do?). Just as you respect the space of other people, you know your own limits as well. You trust the Spirit because you trust yourself – you are sufficiently detached from yourself to be satisfied of the essential goodness of your own primary impulses – and you are in turn willing to trust other people, and life in general.

You give more of yourself to your experience than natives of the other phases; you assess your own motivations in terms of the impact your actions might have on other people and the world around you. You have been chastened by life; you no longer have the vigor to be constantly pushing yourself forward (it takes natives of the other phases a good deal more pommeling to arrive at this point of exhaustion). Thus you may appear to lack decisiveness and worldly ambition. You may project an image something like a sad sack or waif. To natives of the more aggressive phases you seem wishy-washy: an ineffectual oddball whom the world is passing by. There is an ineffable sadness about the balanced phase native, but also a heartfelt sincerity.

These are the most reflective phases; the ones which most thoroughly digest and internalize their experience; the least susceptible to being fooled by superficial appearances. The highest degree of intelligence is manifested in Phases 2 and 5.

Phase 2:   SD to GWE

In Phase 2 Mercury leads the sun and begins to pull away from it: mind becomes the vanguard of intent. Phase 2 is as spontaneous, adventurous, and open to new experience as Phase 3, but without the flightiness and egoistic capriciousness. Where Phase 3 natives tend to be pushy or effusive, and to keep their relationships as convenient and superficially pleasant as possible, you make a real effort to reach out to understand other people and their feelings, and to give them their due. You possess an uncompromising earnestness. You have learned to accept yourself, with all your limitations and shortcomings; thus you reject nothing, but accept the experiences and viewpoints of other people as being valid from their own side and hence worthy of respect. You possess the greatest breadth of understanding of human nature and motivation of any of the phases in your simple faith in the power of the human spirit.

You are real – unaffected and outfront – at times self-effacing and deferential to a fault. You are more interested in doing a job well than in receiving any particular credit for it, and you are encouraging to others to achievement on their own account. You have an unremitting urge to make some sort of sense out of life; to put things into perspective; and to create something of value out of your experience. The impulsive enthusiasm of Phase 3 becomes true conscientiousness in Phase 2.

Phase 5:   GEE to SR

In Phase 5 Mercury trails the sun: mind becomes the servant of intent. You have all the caution of the Phase 4 type, but without the unfeeling ambition and drive. Where the Phase 4 native has a strong moral sense but tends to be rather flexible in applying it, the Phase 5 native's morality is an unshakeable conviction of the heart – which makes you as stubborn as a wet boot.

You have an unremitting urge to *be* someone – not in the self-aggrandizing manner of Phase 4, but in the knowledge that you have a unique contribution to make: a unique task in life that only you can fulfill. This becomes your staff and banner, and gives you a deep sense of obligation to do your best and give your all. You have an innate sense of the indispensable value of the individual in the cosmic scheme of things, which provides you with the greatest depth of understanding of human nature and motivation of any of the phases. You are dependable, the sort of person upon whom other people instinctively rely and to whom they usually assign their meanest tasks. The intellectualized ideals of Phase 4 become true conscience in Phase 5.

Phases 2 and 5 are the equilibrium phases; as a native of any phase matures, he or she more and more comes to resemble a balanced phase native. It might be supposed that this fortune of birth confers a great advantage upon the balanced phase native – and in a sense, it does. But one might also put it that life forces upon the Phase 2 or 5 native at an early age a point of view of resigned acceptance (lack of importance) which natives of the other phases have more power and determination to resist.

Chapter II: Waking Mind

"We are speaking not of people who still have to prove their social usefulness, but of those who can no longer see any sense in being socially useful and who have come upon the deeper and more dangerous question of the meaning of their own individual lives.   To be a particle in the mass has meaning and charm only for the man who has not yet reached that stage, but none for the man who is sick to death of being a particle.   The importance of what life means to the individual may be denied by those who are socially below the general level of adaptation, and is invariably denied by the educator whose ambition it is to breed mass-men.   But those who belong to neither category will sooner or later come up against this painful question."

> – Carl Jung, *The Practice of Psychotherapy*

Society Teaches Us to Deny our Senses

The basic axiom of magic can be stated as: "It's all in the mind." What this means is that there is not some one, objective reality going on out there which we are perceiving with our senses, but rather something of the nature of a psychedelic light-show which we are able to stabilize and organize with our senses. According to this view, our senses are not input devices, but rather output devices; they don't perceive reality, they create it (project it outwards), using whatever programs society has installed in their thought form computer.   From the magical point of view what we call reality – or waking mind – is but a highly specialized form of dreaming, which we as a human society have learned to define and uphold together, and to pass along in turn to our children.

The world of a newborn is largely a world of feelings; there are sights and sounds and smells (sensory thought forms), but the only thing that really matters to a newborn is how things feel. For example, a newborn doesn't see a person in front of him – all he sees are moving shapes; but he can *feel* the presence of a person. Similarly, all of the places in an infant's immediate environment – all the spots around his crib where his eyes may light – have unique feelings associated with them. When the infant's eyes happen to rest at a given spot, he does not so much see the spot as feel the feelings associated with that spot. Every time his eyes happen upon that particular spot he always has the same feeling. Although he cannot control his eyes or use volition to seek out and find a particular spot, every time his eyes chance to fall upon a spot he has seen before he can recognize it by the feeling it gives him. To the infant, the feeling that a particular spot gives him is primary; only later does he come to realize that every time he feels that particular feeling the same scene is registering to his vision. The scene he is seeing with his eyes becomes a kind of shorthand notation – a thought form – of the original feeling associated with that scene.

Similarly, the newborn hears all sounds indiscriminately, like a tape recorder. But to the infant, each of these sounds has a feeling: there are happy sounds, sad sounds, fearsome sounds, etc. The infant's world has a certain mood at each passing moment which is reflected in the sounds it makes. The infant is attuned primarily to the mood of the world rather than to the actual sounds per se, which serve more as a shorthand for the feelings. After a while he comes to recognize that certain sounds are associated with certain feelings, for example that his mother's voice is associated with the feeling he has of his mother. The sound of his mother's voice, as well as the sight of his mother's face, are thought forms which come to be associated with the feeling of his mother. In time, as the infant goes along, the thought forms he has created of the world around him will gradually come to replace the feelings he feels for the world around him.

This occurs because all of the adults in the infant's environment (especially, but not exclusively, his mother) are calling the infant's attention away from his feelings and placing primary importance on his thought forms. They give consensual validation to the thought forms, but not to the feelings.

What transpires between a mother and her baby is so extraordinarily intimate that most adults have lost all conscious memory of what that kind of intimacy is like. It is wholly telepathic: the baby can feel exactly what the mother is feeling even if the mother is not consciously aware herself of what she's feeling. If the mother feels angry, for example, even if she is repressing her anger, the infant will feel *anger*, as if the feeling of anger was his own. Where most of the rest of his environment tends to be rather tranquil and easy-going, the feelings the infant receives from the adults around him are powerful, attention-grabbing, and very hard to ignore.

The intense feelings which his mother and other adults impose upon the infant force him to create a shield of inattention (avoidance of direct feeling) to fend them off. This shield of inattention is called *importance*.

Thought form defenses – strategies of inattention – screen out other people's feelings and thus bolster the infant's integrity as an individual (his self-importance, or sense of having feelings of his own), but they also make it impossible for him to feel what other people and the world around him are feeling.

While the mother can pick up some of this telepathic exchange, the extent to which she operates on a basis of thought forms rather than feelings is the extent to which the infant will also substitute thought forms for primary feelings. From the infant's point of view, his mother is right up there with him on some of the things he feels: she addresses his feelings of hunger, need for tenderness, etc.; but she is *not* there with him on other things he feels. For example, she does not share the feeling of that beautiful, captivating yellow spot with him – she has that wavelength blocked up. To her it's just a blotch of old yellow paint that fell on the crib once when the ceiling was being painted; she can't see what the infant sees in it or feels about it.

The mother can somehow see things without feeling them. For the infant to put his attention on his feelings about what he sees leads to isolation from his mother, since she does not feel those feelings with him. She looks at the yellow spot but can't feel the feeling of it; perhaps what she feels at that moment is anger instead. So the infant, who can't distinguish his mother's feelings from his own, has his own feelings of beauty for the yellow spot obliterated by the angry feelings now coming from that spot.

The point is that the emotional static coming from the adults in the infant's surroundings, by its sheer insistence, bends the infant's perceptions around until he can no longer feel what he is seeing or hearing. He can no longer trust his original feelings about the things in his world because they are too changeable – the thought form notation "dead yellow spot with no feeling to it", which is being validated by the mother (as she tries to scrape it off), has more apparent stability than the "dancing, dazzling, joyous yellow spot" had. The thought form notation is a more useful tool in the adult world than the original feeling was, even though that original feeling was *joy*. The infant's world is, for the most part, a very pleasant place where the infant can just relax and feel good, for no particular reason at all; and the world, for the most part, feels good back at him. By contrast, the adults' world is a clattering, intranquil place, but it's nonetheless very compelling.

For one thing, it's focused. The baby isn't stupid, he quickly comes to realize that the adults around him are far more capable than he is, and he senses that this capacity has to do with their ability to focus their attention.

The infant cannot focus his attention, choose what he will pay attention to, as an adult can. In the infant's world, no particular sight or sound is more important than any other sight or sound. Some sights and sounds feel good; others feel bad. An infant hasn't enough control or focus to choose one over the other, to seek out only good sights and sounds and to avoid or shut out the bad ones; he has to take whatever is presenting itself to him in the moment, whether it is pleasant or horrendous. The idea that "good" sensations are more important, or to be preferred, to "bad" sensations is not within the infant's compass since he can't do anything about it anyway.

The adult assists the infant in making a selection of where he will place his attention instead of just taking everything in passively and indiscriminately. This involves cataloguing everything in the universe according to a scheme of relative importance. One and only one particular thought form (a sight, sound, thought) will be considered to be of utmost importance at any given moment, and all the rest of the sensory and emotional input which bombards the faculties in the selfsame moment will be considered of lesser importance, or ignored altogether. Importance is a screen of inattention, a criterion for selecting just one of the innumerable possibilities of where attention will be placed at any given moment in order to bring just one piece of the nebulous picture into high focus. The feeling that something is important is sufficient of and by itself to bring that thing into focus and to disjoin it from its surroundings. It's magic: to feel something is important is to be able to separate it from its background and hold it in place.

This definition of importance is just one way of looking at it. We could as easily have defined importance to be a type of glue, which glues our attention to certain characteristic conceptual thought forms. Indeed, when we feel importance in our bodies, it feels like glue – a heavy, viscous substance which exerts uncomfortable pressure, particularly in the regions of the heart and solar plexus: that "wad of dough in the tummy" feeling when we are frightened or angry. But defining importance as a screen or blind which enables us to focus attention is more useful in understanding its function in the psyche.

Adults take it for granted that we only see a single image with our two eyes; however, we had to learn how to do this. A newborn sees two images, and it takes some time for him to learn how to ignore (screen out) this fact so as to blend the two images into one. It is in fact quite a strain to maintain one's eyes focused on a single image, but adults have become so used to the effort involved that we don't realize how unnatural and uncomfortable it is (this is why gazing exercises involve relaxing the eyes – and the gaze – by lightly crossing the eyes, to create a double image. See the "Photograph Gazing" chapter of *Magical Living* for detailed information).

It should be pointed out that this or that thing in the infant's world can stand out even without importance; e.g., the yellow spot can become the center of attention for a while in the infant's awareness as long as he continues to feel it. However, the infant cannot purposefully maintain his attention on the spot unless it has somehow become important to him. When all he is doing is feeling the spot with his eyes, purposelessly, for no other reason than that it is enjoyable, the spot does not stand apart from its background.

Importance is basically what is born at birth and dies at death, although it is also true to say that an infant is born with an instinctive sense of importance attached to the thought form of crying. When an infant feels something is important he cries (and soon learns that this thought form will call mother even when direct telepathy fails). That something is important can never be a true feeling. That is, we don't experience importance as a primary feeling in the same way in which we feel fear, hunger, joy, pain, etc. Rather, the feeling of importance – that something is important – is basically a learned behavior which takes the crying instinct as its point of departure. We don't need other people to teach us how to be afraid, or hungry, or joyous, or in pain; but we do need other people to teach us what's important – what is desirable and what should be avoided.

To be able to think – that is, to be able to cut off original (or true) feelings and substitute importance in their place – requires a tremendous amount of effort. Since feeling and thinking cannot take place at the same time it is necessary to deny the one in order to be able to do the other. The here and now is apprehended with the feelings, not the mind; to think is to feel that there is something more important to pay attention to than what is happening here and now. Since relaxation can only exist in the here and now, importance can be considered the negation of relaxation.

As long as the yellow spot holds the infant's feelings he can keep his attention on the spot effortlessly. However, for the infant to keep his attention focused on a particular spot by volition is a strain. Those of us who have ever been really drunk know how difficult it is to focus our attention in that state; now imagine the plight of an infant trying to do the same thing, but without even the memory of focused awareness to steer by.

It must be appreciated that the infant's world is a world of boundless infinitude; he has no sense of being limited or helpless. It is the adults in his environment who impose upon him their own distrust of focuslessness and the feeling of wholeness which is the infant's birthright, and instead substitute their own feelings of importance. Importance is a nagging, irritating, unsettling feeling, which will not leave one alone or in peace. One cannot be at peace as long as there is something important (pending). In short, to feel that something is important – which is part and parcel of being able to focus on it, to think about it, to separate it out from its background – is a thoroughly exhausting position to maintain for any amount of time. It requires the complete suppression of one's true feelings of joy and peace to feel that something is important. The ability to think – the process of converting the world from a feeling of unity to fractured categories of importance held together by a driving sense of urgency – is usually completed by about age three, and is maintained at the cost of intense pain and suffering for the rest of the life.

In comparison with an infant whose senses are keen, alert, and alive, adults are like zombies whose senses are so dull that we seem to move about in a drugged stupor. Adults don't see much of what goes on in the world around us. We are immersed in our thoughts; we're in a hurry. A pretty leaf lying on the sidewalk doesn't have much importance in our scale of values. Moreover, we turn aside from any sight which might tend to make us *feel*. When we look at other people, for example, we can only see the most superficial details of their physical appearance; we can't let ourselves feel with them (feel what they are feeling).

Nor do adults customarily hear anything of the world except for the dull drone of talk or the constant repetition of the same music. We only hear what we want to hear – we've lost the infant's sense that the world is serenading us all the time. To an infant, the world is always new and vivid: every pleasant taste is orgasmic; every fresh smell is orgasmic; every soft sound is orgasmic; every gentle touch is orgasmic.

Perhaps our greatest sensory distortion of all is reflected in the way we adults touch the world around us, perhaps because of all the senses, touch is the closest to feeling. The chief reason we wear clothes in warm weather, when it would be more comfortable to go naked, is to dull our sense of touch. Wearing clothes does mask our vulnerability (provides us with a screen behind which we can hide from other people), but its main function is to cut off our feeling of the world – the dance of the breeze across our skin, the warmth of sunlight, the thrill of raindrops. We bundle ourselves up against the cold to dull our awareness of the chill of death, to soothe ourselves into a stupor, while children play joyously outside in their shirtsleeves. It's not that children don't feel the cold or are too stupid to put on a coat – it's that the cold is their friend. We adults have made it our enemy.

We prefer comfort to touching. In particular, our use of shoes (except when our feet really do need protection) is an egregious waste of precious healing energy which the earth would otherwise give us through our feet. We cut ourselves off from all direct contact with the earth, our mother, and then we wonder why we feel like lost children in an alien environment.

We also disconnect ourselves from the things in our world: we grab things, bandy them about, and throw them down. We don't have a feeling of relationship with the things about us the way an infant does. Feeling connected means, that instead of treating things as insensible objects, treating them as if they were as capable of feeling as we are. A sailor knows that his ship loves him; a child knows her dolls are alive; and most of us have at one time or another felt emotionally intimate with our automobiles. These feelings are no mistake – this is true mingling with the objects in our environment, relating to the world on a basis of true feelings, as an infant or magician does, rather than on a basis of thought forms (learned concepts, such as that a car is just a "car", and any feelings we are picking up from it are just our imagination). This is where each of us must begin again to learn to love, because if we can't love inanimate things, which have no malign intent, there's no hope of our ever learning to love something as bewilderingly complex as a human being.

This means paying attention to what we're doing when we are touching or handling things; being grateful to our tools for the help they give us; lifting things gently and placing them where we want them; dealing with them with the same delicacy and respect with which we ourselves would prefer to be treated. We toss things about carelessly or leave things in a mess, and then wonder why we feel that life is tossing us about like an insensible object, and why our life is a mess. We can't make that connection in our minds, of where those feelings are coming from.

Our adult concept of ownership – our belief that we possess objects – is one of the main ways we cut ourselves off from them. Indeed it is more true to say that they possess us – they have us in thrall to our fear of losing them; and they know it; and we know they know it. We become ashamed to face the objects in our environment, and we close our hearts to them by proclaiming that we "own" these "insensible" objects, therefore we are better (more important) than they are. We feel ashamed because we know we have betrayed ourselves, betrayed our own true feelings, in exchange for some pathetic sense of glory.

The feeling of importance, which is the principle that undergirds focus and thus is the basic building block of adult (waking) consciousness, has two manifestations: shame and glory. These chase each other around in an endless circle, and generate the energy necessary to drive importance. That is, they keep the attention occupied in an endless loop. When attention is caught in an endless feedback loop – a self-reflection in an endless series of mirrors – it takes on a frantic urgency which we feel as importance. We feel it is important to seek glory and to hide shame.

We are taught to feel the validation of our conceptual thought forms by other people as glory; and to feel the beckoning of our own true feelings as shame. We are taught to seek the one and to hide the other: to deny our senses and feelings, and to substitute instead a false distinction which other people will applaud. It is an endless loop because glory cannot be arrived at without shame: to seek glory is to seek a lie, and lies bring about feelings of shame because we know in our hearts that we are not what we claim to be – more important than anything else.

Now while it is true that most human societies have historically recognized the need for a sense of importance in order to focus individual and group attention, not all societies implemented importance by setting up a shame / glory cycle. Indeed, there have been human societies on earth which consisted of enlightened beings who set up and defended schemata of importance categories, but more as art for art's sake rather than something to shed blood, sweat, and tears over. These societies played life more as a game than we do; the individual was motivated because he or she believed things were important (as in our society), but importance was based on the best allocation of energy resources in the now moment, the most skillful employment of whatever opportunities were at hand, rather than the reduction of all the joy in life to a striving for glory and hiding shame. They buttressed importance with competence and self-love.

Be that as it may, our society took the glory road, in which importance is equated with personal glory (approval by the social group) and hiding shame (stifling one's own true feelings). In our society, the driving force which runs the spinning wheel of shame and glory and thereby buttresses importance is not competence, but irresponsibility; not self-love, but self-hatred. Self-hatred is the glue which binds our society together, and which enables us all to deny our own senses for the common weal. Its basic component is the assumption that what we do when we're awake is more important (more "real") than what we do when we're asleep.

A human being does not naturally sleep all through the night and stay awake all day long. Our hunter ancestors, like infants, slept off and on when they felt like it, and divided their sleeping and waking hours indiscriminately between day and night. Although our vision is keener during the day, our feelings are keener at night, in the dark. An infant isn't afraid of the dark; on the contrary, to him it is reminiscent of the peaceful, enjoyable, warm state he knew in the womb. He finds the daylit world jangly and nerve-wracking. Only later, when his mother has become the most important thing to him – far more important than his own feelings – does the dark become a forbidding place, since he can no longer see his mother (since he can no longer feel her). Adults are the ones who are afraid of the dark, though they repress this fear and laugh at the children who act it out openly for them. They are afraid of the dark because they are afraid of feeling their own feelings; and because they are afraid of feeling their own feelings, they hate themselves.

It is far more natural for a person to sleep on and off during the day, and to be awake on and off at night. A person vents a great deal of anger, fear, impatience, etc. by being able to sleep it off. In cultures where they take a siesta during the day, the pace of life is generally more relaxed than in countries where people relentlessly drive themselves all day long every day.

Sleep is the ultimate conservation of health – the feeling of inner balance and stability. Instead of fighting sleep with drugs, caffeine, or busyness; instead of holding the daylit world to be supremely important and the world of sleep wasted time; we should allow our bodies to dictate when and where we should sleep. In dreamless sleep we make the deepest contact with our love for ourselves; by cutting ourselves off from sleep, we cut ourselves off from self-healing and self-love. The main cause of our self-hatred, the chief reason we are all so neurotic and out of kilter with our world, is because we've been awake too long.

Society Teaches Us to Deny our Sexuality

When we say that the action of mind is to repress direct feeling and substitute thinking (conceptual thought forms) in its place, what we are defining is adult mind, everyday mind, or waking mind. In actuality mind exists on various levels, and it is still mind acting on a higher – or more fundamental – level which creates feelings in the first place.

What we call feelings, emotions, desires – including the entire range of feelings such as hunger, thirst, grief, joy, anger, ecstasy, fear, longing – are at root, sexual. The basic energy of the universe is undifferentiated sexual energy. It is in dreamless sleep that we attach a notation of differentiated feeling to the original sexual impulse; and it is in dream consciousness – our infant's mind – that we attach a (sensory) thought form to that differentiated feeling. However, at root, all desire and all feeling are sexual; and all emotion is merely the vocabulary of dreamless sleep, just as sensory thought forms are the vocabulary of dream mind and conceptual thought forms are the vocabulary of waking mind.

Note that sexual energy is not a hot, breathless, agitated rush to climactic orgasm. True sexual energy is the feeling we have when we are out in nature, all by ourselves, naked and completely relaxed. It is definitely a sexual feeling, but it is neither heterosexual nor homosexual, nor does it point towards climactic orgasm. "Heterosexuality", "homosexuality", and "climactic orgasm" are thought form vectors which society imposes upon our sexual energy to channel it in some direction, to turn what is essentially a state of peacefulness and wholeness into a state of striving. In other words, what sexual feeling we don't repress altogether (experience as shame or glory), we are forced to experience as pursuit of some external object or goal rather than as being relaxed and at peace within ourselves.

True sexual energy is a cool, tranquil, placid state of great pleasure and union. It is the usual state of mind of a fetus in the womb, as well as of a newborn. There is little sense of separatedness in it; no urgency, no importance. It is our original mood, our true feeling about the world. Climactic orgasm is the product of focus. To be able to have climactic orgasms we must strip all joy and pleasure from our moment-to-moment existence every day, and concentrate it down to a few seconds of intense sensation. If you refrain from having climactic orgasms for a couple of months, then you begin to notice that all your senses (particularly touch) have a pleasurable, sub-orgasmic piquancy that they lack when you are having climactic orgasms regularly.

The reason why children are happier than adults (unless they've been abused by them) is that they have not yet imposed that climactic orgasm straitjacket on their feeling of essential aliveness and wholeness. They don't have that agitation pushing them forward (if they are men) or holding them back (if they are women). They aren't caught in that web of predator / prey which snares most adults. In short, children don't put importance on their sexual feelings: they just *feel* them. That is what happens at adolescence – for example, all the social expectations put on a man that he isn't a man until he has conquered a woman. Although sexual desire is quite normal, and is especially heightened at adolescence, the "vectorization" of sexual desire – the importance of sexual release – is a socialized phenomenon. Society has us inflame ourselves sexually and then clamp down hard on ourselves (thus producing weird, distorted sexual desires – rather like clamping down on a balloon).

Society finds it necessary to vigilantly control and direct the sexual feelings of its individual members, since it is by redirecting these energies that it can impose order and social focus, getting everyone moving in more or less the same direction and at the same speed. Society believes that it must straitjacket our natural sexual feelings because the action of waking mind – the creation of conceptual thought forms – is effete by itself; waking mind by itself can do nothing except focus attention. It can conceive of great things, but it hasn't the power to actually move things around. Only higher mind, i.e., dreamless sleep – what we call intent or true feelings – can actually make things happen: create a reality. However, true feelings by themselves have no direction, no focus, no preference, although they do have an equilibrium state of just feeling good; and hence they have no reason to do anything unless waking mind is giving them orders. So society goes in and begins issuing the orders to seek glory and avoid shame. Both shame and glory are perverted sexual impulses.

The fact is that most of the feelings we have for one another are sexual feelings, both heterosexual and homosexual, and society forbids us to recognize them consciously much less to express them openly. For example, in our society we must keep our bodies scrupulously clean and scent ourselves, to cut off all feeling coming from our olfactory sense. In fact, the odor of our bodies is as much a sexual attractant for us as it is for any other animal species, so society has us cut that sense off cold, and so distort it that we are offended by our own smells, and would never dare to smell each other as dogs do. The reason we feel so turned off by the smell of some people who haven't bathed is precisely because we're so sexually turned on by them – and we must deny ourselves the feeling that goes with that smell. Our odor at any given time carries a lot of information about what we are feeling inside; our smells are as distinctive as our faces, but even more primal, i.e., sexual. So society has us fumigate over that sense.

The way society keeps us all in line is through our sense of shame. Yet our sense of shame isn't sexual at all – it's societal. We are ashamed of how we have let ourselves be used; of how we've turned ourselves into unfeeling robots in the drive to glory. Glory and shame go hand in hand. Precisely the extent to which we have been striving for glory is the extent to which we bear shame. We are not ashamed of our sexuality: on the contrary, what we are ashamed of is having repressed our sexuality – at society's behest – in the name of glory. But society has us convinced that it is our own natural sexual feelings we're ashamed of, rather than of having repressed those feelings; and thus it leads us into the loop of shame and glory.

Glory is the sense that we are better than everyone else. In our society, the root of glory is the idea that *we* don't have weird sexual desires, therefore we are worthwhile beings. *Our* rude sexual impulses are under control; therefore we deserve glory, for having achieved this feat of self-mastery. But this is all a sham: everybody's still "doing it", or wishing they could "do it"; they're just pretending they're not.

The main technique by which society inculcates hiding shame and seeking glory is toilet training. In our society toilet training is instilled with a sense of shame – indeed, the most important result of toilet training is that individuals learn to feel ashamed of themselves before their parents and to hide (repress) their shame. What children are learning is not so much how to control their sphincters as how to feel ashamed of themselves. Toilet training necessarily depends upon anger and fear because it involves clenching up. After children learn to clench up their bodies, clenching up their feelings is the next logical step. Feces symbolize our feelings: learning to hold our feces inside is a symbol for learning to hold our feelings inside so that we don't make ourselves smelly (vulnerable) to others.

What happens at this point – how children handle their fear and anger at their parents for imposing toilet training on them – depends upon the children and the parents. If our mother made a battle out of our toilet training, then we tend to become rebellious and make our feces (anger) in our panties to force her – and later in life other people – to wipe our bottoms (bear our shame) for us. In short, a lot of our personality traits are a direct product of our experience with toilet training, which is as severe an exercise in concentration as any advanced mind training technique – not only is it the root of our shame, it is also the basis of our constant inner dialogue, the incessant thinking which occupies our attention most of the time we are awake – except that it is imposed on us when we're two years old. Indeed, this is basically what is symbolized by Mercury's synodic cycle – different ways that different types respond to toilet training.

RESPONSES TO TOILET TRAINING
A GALLERY OF MERCURY TYPES

Jawohl, Frau Obersturmführerin! Your wish is my command!

THE CONJUNCTION

What on earth is she trying to put over on me here? Oh well, might as well humor the old bat since she seems so intent on it.

THE ELONGATION

Oh dear, poo-poo. How terribly distressing. Someday we'll have to do something about that.

STATIONARY DIRECT

Oh yeah? Well shove it up yours too!!

STATIONARY RETROGRADE

In a general kind of way, conjunction natives are toilet trained at an earlier age than are elongation natives. Mercury conjunctions are usually toilet trained the same way as puppies – their mothers rub their noses in it – not literally, perhaps, but with the same indelicacy and force. Their mothers wash their genitals similarly: roughly, rudely, contemptuously. This is why these natives find it difficult to be soft and vulnerable to others – their first model of an intimate relationship was usually rough and disrespectful of their feelings, and they thus learn to be disgusted by their own feelings and intolerant of the feelings of others. Mercury conjunctions become the "good" children who shut their mouths, hold their feelings inside, and do as they're told. By contrast, elongation natives are usually toilet trained rather late since they tend to be fascinated by and proud of their feces, so it's more difficult for them to take toilet training seriously. Their mothers made a game out of the whole thing rather than a shameful, onerous imperative; so there is less incentive to give up toilet training on both sides. Elongations are naturally looser and more relaxed than conjunctions, and not as awed by their parents. Because they are never "properly" toilet trained, elongations never learn how to hold their feelings inside; even into adulthood they tend to hold their feces (feelings) up for public display and admiration, and at their worst spew them over other people.

When we have our minds hooked up to the concepts inculcated by our society of sexual normalcy, we are simply acceding to our slavery by the system for its own purposes. The question we must each decide for ourselves is whether these are *our* purposes. By maintaining postures of sexual normalcy we gain social acceptance, but we lose all sexual spontaneity and freedom to be able to communicate with other people intimately. We must always maintain a façade of sexual disinterestedness or else we are stigmatized socially.

Only by throwing off our guilt at our own nakedness – our vulnerability and desires – can we really feel at home in our own feelings: completely vulnerable and relaxed in the presence of other people, just the way we felt as infants, without the need for constant vigilance over our feelings; constant pretense, faking it, stifling all sexual attraction.

The fact of the matter is that we all have hidden agendas in all our interactions with one another, and the overwhelming majority of these are sexual at root. There are sexual electrons going back and forth, and not just between the sexes. Two men or two women are also involved in a little sexual dance or mating ritual every time they meet. The competition we so often feel with members of the same sex is 100% sexual. All the little games of one-upsmanship, power over others, feeling ourselves to be better than others, etc., are sexually based. If we were actually having the sex we are repressing into competition, we would be a whole lot happier, but we'd be so busy making love that we wouldn't get anything else done.

For example, women often think that the competition they feel with other women is a competition for men, for the attention and approval of men; but this just isn't so. Two women who feel competitive with each other are in fact sexually attracted to one another, but are not permitting themselves to feel the attraction directly; instead, they twist it into competition. Two women who find themselves fighting over the same man should realize that they are sexually attracted to one another, that the man has nothing to do with it, and just make love to each other, since that's what they're truly feeling.

Similarly, the back-slapping, beer-drinking camaraderie of men is frankly homosexual. They are flirting with one another, strutting like peacocks for each other, because they're physically turned on by each other. Of course, very few of these macho men are consciously aware of what's going on: they wouldn't think of their behavior as sexual at all, let alone homosexual. They consider themselves to be real men, contemptuous of women and homosexuals; yet that's precisely what they are.

There's nothing subconscious about these agendas we have going with one another, except we have ourselves trained to pretend they aren't occurring. It's only by banishing the thought forms which are in control of censoring a particular emotional reaction that we can stop for a moment and see what is actually going on "beneath the surface".

Most of our interactions with other people consist of thought forms; but every now and then there is a little flash of direct feeling – an emotion thrown from one person to another – which is a naked instant, like a flash of lightning, in which everyone can clearly see and feel where everyone else stands. The emotion involved can be love, hate, lust, anger, humor, etc. Whatever emotion is thrown is invariably an expression of sexual attraction. When two or more people can feel the same thing – no matter what the nominal feeling is – they are basically having an orgasm together.

However, these little flashes of direct feeling and knowing occur very fast, and our conscious minds (because of our social training) tend to skip right over them, to immediately deny that they occurred, to ignore them by the mutual consent of all concerned, except in rigidly defined situations. But there is nothing actually hidden about these agendas, except for the thought forms of being flustered and averting eyes which immediately cover up what just happened a moment ago.

Most of us, at one time or another in our lives, have experienced powerful flashes of mutual sexual attraction with certain individuals; but the fact is that we would have flashes like that all the time with practically everybody if we didn't have thought forms in place ready to jump in and censor such feelings the instant they raise their heads.

Homophobes, for example, are in a particularly desperate position: they are homosexuals who feel overpowering desires which they can scarcely control, and hence can't bear to see anyone else acting out openly the feelings which they are struggling so mightily to repress.

The fact of the matter is that homosexuality is quite normal. This is not to say that it is moral, but merely that it is normal. Practically everyone at one time or another experiences strong sexual attractions to certain individuals of the same sex; but society has trained us to repress these feelings even before they become conscious.

There can never be such a thing as abstract rules or standards of morality, because the self-same act which is true feelings in one context may just be thought forms in another (this is where many conventional religions lose the thread). There is no one correct answer to the question of what one is "supposed" to feel or "supposed" to do in a given situation. All there are, are different choices, different lessons, ultimately none of which matter in the least. There is no such thing as "right" or "wrong" – all there are, are true feelings or thought forms.

It might at first appear that homosexuality is unnatural because it is non-functional in the evolutionary scheme of things (although the same argument could be brought against e.g. golf). This is correct at the present time, but only in the recent past, since the invention of meiosis. Our original sexuality – that is to say, the sexuality which arose with the invention of mitosis and which is still our basic sexual memory – is homosexual. All one-celled beings are females, and they are also homosexual in orientation. Just as our everyday (waking) consciousness is rooted in dreaming, so too is our heterosexual drive rooted in homosexuality. Even at the present time women are basically homosexual and men heterosexual in orientation (of course this is a sweeping generalization: there is lots of individual variation).

To openly avow our homosexual feelings, or any true sexual desires, in our society today is to face some very heavy shame and self-hatred raps which society reserves for such deviance. And yet the only way to deal with this and get back to our true feelings is to consciously acknowledge these impulses within ourselves; to be willing to relate sexually with everyone we feel sexual with. This doesn't necessarily mean having sexual relations with everyone we know (though for some people it could mean that) – but rather just acknowledging openly those sexual agendas that are happening; just acknowledging that that other person turns us on. That's all that is required: we don't necessarily have to act on all our impulses – all we have to do is acknowledge them consciously: "Yes, this is part of me, I acknowledge that" – and then let the impulses go.

The reason for sexual openness and making ourselves vulnerable to other people (letting them see our true feelings) is to make a direct attack on our sense of shame – our shame that we can't allow ourselves to feel with other people. We are ashamed to be using those people out there just as a mirror for our own concepts, our reflection to see how we look, how we're doing, like checking our hair in a mirror.

Other people aren't mirrors – they're living, feeling flesh and blood just like us. They don't need our plastic, synthetic smiles and inquiries about the weather; they need our love. But how can we share love with them unless we let ourselves feel with them? And of course that means letting ourselves feel sexual with them, since sexual repression lies at the root of all emotional repression.

The evil use of people is not desiring them sexually, but rather pretending that they aren't flesh and blood, that they don't deserve our best feelings, that all they are there for is our own greater glory. To get rid of the glory we must attack the shame.

We must recognize it and see how utterly ashamed of ourselves we are for having allowed ourselves to become such phonies and liars. If we can feel the shame, we can get rid of the need for glory.

Society Teaches Us to be Irresponsible

The reason why we are so easily misled and tricked by society (and by ourselves) is because mind – although it fancies itself to be so important – is in fact sterile. Feeling is always the primary impulse behind any perception – the response to what is actually going on right here and right now. The content of sensory thought forms is basically feeling. Conceptual thought forms are counterfeits of true feelings – little notations which do have feelings to them (called "importance coverings") which can be quite compelling and convincing, but which nonetheless are phony versions of what we truly feel about what is going on. And conceptual thought forms are readily manipulated by society.

For example, apathy is a phony version of disinterested-ness; infatuation is a phony version of love; pride is a phony version of impeccability; approval is a phony version of appreciation; knowledge is a phony version of wisdom; self-pity is a phony version of anguish.

It must be pointed out that our true feelings are, in fact, reality. Reality is nothing more nor less than our true feelings right this moment. That's all reality is, and that's all we are: a feeling at a particular moment. However, we have the option of denying that feeling, of pasting a thought form reason for not feeling that feeling directly over the primary feeling itself. We can use our minds to frustrate our desires, and the chief strategy of inattention we use to do this is irresponsibility.

Fundamentally, irresponsibility entails reacting with some stock thought form reaction instead of responding to what is actually happening. Responsibility is nothing more than connectedness. Responsibility is feeling connected, and irresponsibility is feeling disconnected. When we know that there is a connection there – that it's not all self-glorification – then we are taking responsibility for ourselves and for the world. Any time we are repelled by something someone does, or find something about them unacceptable, we can be sure that we are lying to ourselves, cutting ourselves off from (repressing) that part of our own selves which they are exhibiting openly; and we hate ourselves for being so irresponsible (disconnected) – although we usually lie to ourselves and convince ourselves that it's them we hate; and then we hate ourselves all the more for telling that lie.

Irresponsibility begins when an infant is subjected to the adults' bombardment of helplessness and self-pity. An infant doesn't feel self-pity (which arises with irresponsibility just as shame arises with glory. In fact, all shame is just a manifestation of irresponsibility, and all glory is just a manifestation of self-pity). An infant only feels connected. He feels connected whether he likes the feeling or not. If there's a pin sticking into him, he hasn't got the mental wherewithal and defenses to convince himself that there's *not* a pin sticking into him, or to blame someone else for his pain and try to stick a pin into them. An infant just lies there and howls, but he takes full responsibility for his pain because he hasn't any choice but to feel it; he doesn't see any way out of it.

Self-pity is a mood which informs the thought forms of irresponsibility. Any time we feel self-pity, we can be sure we are acting irresponsibly. Our thought forms of irresponsibility make us believe that we don't know what we really want, and that we don't understand what is happening to us. This is a falsehood – we *do* know what we want, and we all know exactly what is happening every minute: this is our intent. But we pretend otherwise so that we'll feel justified in pitying ourselves. We even have thought forms to plump up our glory in our self-pity, which make us believe it's romantic or sensitive not to know what we want; to be wistful, sighing, longing for we know not what; to feel blown hither and thither at the mercy of forces beyond our control.

The term *unbending intent* means taking complete responsibility. Once the decision is made to do something, one must be willing to go to whatever lengths are necessary to make it happen. To be a magician means to be thoroughly undaunted and unfazed – to go to any extreme required to realize one's desire. This is what holds the average person back: not only social constraints about conventional morality and "dealing with the devil", but also the general lethargy and mediocrity which society encourages. Only magicians are willing and ready to go to the utmost extreme necessary to realize their desires, thus only magicians are really taking responsibility for their world, and only magicians are in a position to control it.

The pinnacle of our irresponsibility is the creation of our customary moods. We are taught to believe that our feelings originate within ourselves, but this is untrue. Most feelings come from without – from the tonality (astrology) of the moment, from the physical place where we are located, from spirit forces surrounding us, as well as from other people. We put up our customary moods in order to maintain a semblance of stability and equilibrium, to screen out what is actually going on around us, impinging on us, by focusing our attention on ourselves. In fact, we have no "self"; there is NO SELF. What seems to us to be our "self" is a stock set of moods we use such as annoyance / irritation, seriousness, giddiness, cuteness, dullness, busyness, piousness, sweetness, toughness, etc. which we put up as a front most of the time so that we don't have to feel connected to what is really happening. We have our ready reactions of irritation, self-seriousness, levity, etc. at hand so that no matter what happens, we don't have to take any responsibility for our response; we are above it all – cool, unaffected, in control. They are phony masks we've chosen to portray ourselves to other people.

Our customary moods are forgotten thought forms, inculcated into us by our parents before we could think or speak. Thus our customary moods are either direct copies of our parents' moods, or else complementary copies of our parents' moods – e.g. our parents' oppressor moods can create in us both oppressor moods and victim moods. And, of course, we have different moods or masks for different people. The purpose of these moods is to make us feel *bad*.

Making ourselves feel bad is a form of self-pinching, of convincing ourselves that we're real. As long as we hate ourselves, then there must be some "we" there, and some "ourselves". We base our sense of personal continuity upon self-hatred; it becomes the glue that ties everything together for us by making us feel bad. By feeling that good old familiar bad feeling, we know we're us (and not somebody else). Of course, we could do the same thing with self-love, with feeling good about who we are and what we're doing; but that can only be done by taking responsibility for ourselves.

In other words, if at any given moment we feel bad, that means that at that moment we have abdicated all responsibility for ourselves and for the situation. In choosing to feel bad instead of good – and it is always a free choice – we are choosing to be irresponsible, helpless, self-pitying. In choosing to feel good, no matter what happens, we are taking complete responsibility for ourselves and the situation. There is nothing whatsoever that life asks of us beyond feeling good. That is all that is required of us, ever.

Society Teaches Us to be Phony and to Hate Ourselves

Self-hatred stems from denying senses and inputs which a human would normally accept. In our society we are not permitted to accept ourselves as we are, but must change most of our natural tendencies in order to make it – be accepted – by society.

We are taught that we must come across with one central face or mood; otherwise we are considered insane. We are taught to express our opinions rather than our feelings; we are taught to be dishonest with ourselves. The question, "How do you feel about this?" rarely means "How do you *really* feel about this?" but rather "What have we taught you to think about this?" Most of our conversation is like having to defend a thesis before an inquisitional audience.

Thinking for oneself is considered subversive, and our society takes elaborate precautions to make it quite unnecessary for people to think for themselves. Other societies have done it through more brutal, less subtle tactics; but it is always done through fear – fear of what people might think or what they might say; fear of ostracism at best, or of violence and brutality at worst. This is why we develop our thinking faculties to such a small extent.

We learn not to trust our own thinking; in fact we feel it's dangerous to do so, when there are so many "experts" around to tell us what to think – doctors, lawyers, academics, therapists, etc. Advertisers and the media tell us what to believe and desire. We can't do *anything* for ourselves. True thinking is the acceptance of our own abundant inner knowledge, our intent; but to deny our connection to other people and the world around us, we are taught instead to adopt a false thinking based on a scheme of importance categories.

Importance categories means comparisons: only by making comparisons – making us believe that we are above some people and beneath others – can society keep us from feeling with them. Society asks of us that we deny ourselves love so that in the subsequent search for that something we know is missing in our lives, we will try to substitute glory. Since only a fool would choose glory over love if given a fair choice, society doesn't give us a fair choice. It doesn't give us any choice at all.

Look around: who are the ones who are really being loving (besides the children and the saints)? Just the lunatics and simpletons. Not all of them, by any means (many lunatics occupy a position of vulnerability as part of a self-hatred agenda); but there are also many simple and crazy people walking around with their hearts wide open. They aren't people who *can't* fit into society; they're people who don't *want* to fit in. At some point they took a good, hard look at the adults' world and decided they wanted nothing to do with it. All mentally ill people are making themselves extremely vulnerable by rejecting society's demands on them that they act "sane". Successful lunatics staunchly resist all attempts to teach them comparison.

Comparison is the basis of all feudal society, of which our society is a prime example. We are taught to hold the poor and wretched at a disdainful arm's length, and to slobber and fawn over the rich and successful. Comparison is a thought form matrix or generator which stamps out a thought form for every human being we know (even for plants and animals). Since this is the sort of information which will likely surface when you start doing the active imagination exercises in Chapter IV, we'll describe it and other common glory thought forms which arise in active imagination from a theoretical viewpoint here.

Comparison works as follows: we are taught to cut off our true feelings for the people we meet, and to substitute instead thought forms of those people. The thought forms include what they look like, and also all our little judgments and opinions of them – what we approve or disapprove of about them, what we want or fear of them, etc. What we call our personalities are just random collections of thought forms we have picked up in our travels – memory banks of all our prejudices, likes and dislikes, what qualities we consider admirable (mirroring our glory) or despicable (mirroring our shame), what sort of person turns us on, what sort turns us off, etc. So for every person we meet, our comparison generator searches through this library of ready thought forms, and matches up what's there with this creature who stands before us.

When first someone comes into view (i.e., if on some level we have to connect with another human, even if only on a level of glancing at the driver of the next car stopped at a red light, without apparently acknowledging the other's presence); whenever we first become aware of the approach of another human, even if we (and he) have no intention of making any conscious sign of recognition, the comparison thought form generator comes into play to decide which thought form to put out there to face the guy with. For a pretty woman, we pull out one stock response; for a cop, quite another; for a drunk or a bum, yet another. Whatever kind of people we meet, we have a stock of ready thought forms to greet them with, and the comparison generator picks out one which will immediately establish who is more important.

When we genuinely like or are repelled by someone, that is our true feelings. It is only on a concept level, by a process of comparison, that we can relate to other people on a basis of superiority. We feel we are better than plants and animals (sometimes we use the words "better" and "better off" interchangeably). For every person we know we create a thought form which compares us to them and thereby denies our true feelings for them: "We are better than (Tom, Dick, or Harry) because of (rationalization)." The function of comparison is to find a rationalization to justify why we are better (more important) than everyone we know (or if we are living out shame rather than glory with a person, why he or she is more important than us).

Another thought form generator is expectation. For each person we know, we have a little list of what we want from them. Every time we meet someone, we size them up and try to decide what sort of validation we want or could possibly get from them. For example, from our parents we can expect such-and-such; from the beggar we give a dime to, something else; from little children, something altogether different. We try to stay completely away from people we don't want validation from, such as drunks, people who turn us on too much sexually, people who are in great suffering and pain, etc. People whom we do not want to compare ourselves to we don't see as sources of possible goodies. Expectations of others and fear of others are the same thing. Expectations of others implies a concomitant fear of those expectations not being fulfilled.

Another thought form generator is pure glory. The glory generator is a database or sort which examines everything which happens in our lives and decides how it can be used to contribute to our greater glory. The face we turn to others when we are putting our best face forward is the pure glory generator. It uses other thought forms, whichever is most apropos, to exculpate us of all guilt or responsibility for our failures and errors, and to push ourselves up higher so that everyone will see how marvelous we are. The glory generator has at its disposal an array of ready thought forms which we learned at various points in our lives (largely from our parents), and which it can grab out of the bag as a ready response to any situation. Having to show off or look good, for example, is a thought form most of us picked up from our parents when they encouraged us to show off, repeat that cute phrase or action over and over, do their bidding in front of other people. This type of thought form tries to show us off to best advantage in whatever pose we think will most impress a particular audience.

Another common glory form is the dress rehearsal form, which anticipates scenes and conversations with other people and runs fantasies in which we always win or get our way, and everyone is suitably impressed with us. This type of form is always plotting and planning a future, and in that future there is always glory for us. Indeed, that's the only place glory really exists: glory can only exist in some future we never arrive at, for glory is the counterfeit of the love we are denying ourselves in the here and now.

Another common glory form is the false watcher, which is our self-consciousness or need to keep referring everything back to ourselves. This type of form takes anything that is going on and glamorizes it, and imagines other people applauding us for it. The false watcher thought form is in fact society's way of papering over death. We do have a true watcher watching us, and that watcher is our death. The false watcher is society's way of eradicating death from people's awareness, to make people act as if they weren't going to die, to make people forget about death as much as possible. Only by making people forget about death can they be led into believing that there could be anything more important than the fact that they could die in the next instant. And part of banishing awareness of death is substituting a glory thought form of watching ("watching oneself in glory; watching oneself with approval / approbation") for the true watcher thought form, which is death.

Another important glory thought form is talking. Next to having orgasms, talking is the most draining, wrenching, exhausting activity we engage in. Now, talking can express true feelings, when true feelings are being expressed by it; when that happens everyone is more attuned to listening than to thinking about what they are going to say next. But thought form talking is all lies: people don't tell each other the truth about what they're thinking or doing; they just babble inanities to each other in order to keep from sharing true information about what is really going on. For example, we all tend to assume that our individual perceptions of the world are more or less alike; and this lie has been reinforced by all the homogenization of inputs among all people world-wide that modern technology has made possible. But it is not true; our individual perceptions of the world are decidedly *not* alike; but society won't let us get together and compare notes and possibly discover that truth for ourselves. The only talk permitted is thought form talk, not talk about our true feelings.

We force our politicians and leaders to act like phonies to publicly enact our own phoniness for us; and in some cases (e.g. Nixon) we also force them to live out our shame and fear of being unmasked. The amount of glory we strive for is precisely equal to the amount of shame we hide; and the people before whom we are unmasked are the very ones whose approval / approbation we sought. Glory from other people is only necessary as long as we don't feel a true sense of worth within ourselves.

Society teaches us to be dissatisfied with the people around us, instead of just accepting them for themselves and what they offer us freely. Society gives us our model of what can reasonably be expected from e.g. a parent, spouse, or child; and oddly enough, one of these expectations is an elusive thing called "love". Society teaches us to hate ourselves, to deny ourselves any semblance of love, to turn ourselves off to the people around us, to despise the people around us; and then it has the temerity to teach us to expect love from them! In fact, it isn't real love that society teaches us to expect from other people, but rather approval. Approval involves burying all true feelings of love because it is always contingent and subject to withdrawal on a moment's notice. This is what much of a parent / child relationship is based on: the parent withholds love in favor of approval. To hold approval or disapproval over someone is to put oneself in a controlling or dominating position over them. Our need to control or dominate other people is the projection of a need to control or dominate our own anger. If we can somehow contain the anger of someone else, we can successfully contain our own. This is the basis of much of the black magic that underlies everyday relationships: forcing other people who are under our control to feel our repressed anger (to bear our self-hatred) for us.

In teaching us to fear disapproval, society successfully divides us by making us fear each other, since we all wield approval / disapproval over one another. We're all deathly afraid of being unmasked, hurt, betrayed. We're afraid to approach other people with our normal desires directly for fear of rejection. So we have to hide our desires of other people with some sort of phony self-effacing or scheming and manipulation; and when we can't stand the shame anymore we let ourselves get caught and unmasked, to relieve the tension which all that phoniness builds up.

In our society, only simpletons and lunatics don't fear other people; otherwise, our constant assumption with one another would be trust. To submit ourselves to other people for approval is highly unskillful – it means giving them a handle to jerk us around with (in the event they choose to reject us). A lot of our "good faith" is just asking other people to stomp on us – our "good faith" is a phony copy of good feelings, an agreement we have to make precisely because we don't trust the other person.

True feelings can't be rejected; they just *are*. True feelings address what is really happening, so there's no way they can be rejected. If we feel hurt, it's because we ourselves have made the decision to feel hurt. If we gave true love and joy, then what difference does it make if the other person was open to it or not? True joy comes from giving love; if true love was given, its inevitable corollary is true joy.

How, Then, Can We Know Our True Feelings?

Our true feelings – our intent – are not merely a response to what is happening; our true feelings *are* what is happening. Although we believe that we are separate from what is happening to us; and that how we feel about it all is yet something else again; in fact there is no difference in our original (dreamless sleep) mind between ourselves, the world around us, and our feelings about ourselves and the world around us. These distinctions arise on the level of dreaming (infant's) mind, and they reach their highest degree of sharpness on the level of waking (adult's) mind; and while they can at times be useful distinctions to make, we must be aware that they are false distinctions. To believe that they are true distinctions is the cause of all suffering.

The problem is not that we create thought form copies of original feelings – this is just the natural action of mind. The problem comes up when we consider those notations to be more important than the feelings they replace. To believe that we are unhappy because of something that's happening "outside" ourselves; or that we would be happy if this or that would happen; is to get tangled up in the shorthand record of what's going on, and thereby miss out on what's *really* going on. If we believe that the superficial appearance is the important thing, then we'll never get down to what is really creating that superficial appearance. Most New Agers adhere automatically to the credo, "You create your own reality" – without fully appreciating what this truly means: that we have at our fingertips illimitable freedom if we are willing to accept complete responsibility.

Importance is our sense of being trapped by life. Whatever is important to us – whatever areas of life we have chosen to be important to us in this lifetime – is what makes us feel trapped and helpless. For example, if we believe that money is important, then we'll always feel trapped by money – either trapped by our belief that we lack money, or trapped by our fear of losing it. No matter how much money we have or don't have, we are trapped by our obsessive concern over money. Clearly, money doesn't have anything to do with our "money problems"; money is just a thought form we use to symbolize the decision to be worried and jealous and unhappy.

If we're not getting what we want, then the fact is that our true feelings don't really want it, no matter what our thought forms might be telling us. If we have ourselves convinced that we want love, or success, or riches; but we can't seem to make it happen in the world "out there", then we can be sure that our true feelings are that we don't really want it because we don't believe we really deserve it. If we could see ourselves objectively as other people do then we would in fact be able to see precisely how we are tripping ourselves up – pushing away the very thing we claim that we really want. But as it is we have our true feelings stifled and listen only to our thought forms, so we can never understand why we can't get life to give us what we want. All we know is that we can't get what we want (happiness) no matter how hard we try; it never occurs to us that all the trying is just pushing what we want further and further away.

The reason for this is that our true feelings *are* reality, whereas our concepts are just a copy of reality; and to make things happen in reality we must work with our true feelings, not our thought forms. Thought forms don't have any power behind them – e.g. we can't manipulate other people with thought forms, only with true feelings. If we first decide (on a thought form level) what it is we want from people, and then start making moves (on a thought form level) to get it, we'll only trip ourselves up.

We are taught to believe that love comes from without, from other people; however, true love comes from within. Love is not something we get; love is something we give – or better said, something that flows through us. We can't sit back and expect other people to hand us love just because they're our parents, spouse, or children. True, this can happen on occasion, just as it has happened on occasion that we've found money lying on the street and picked it up and it was ours. But to expect money to come to us in that way is absurd; and to expect other people to give us love just because we've stuck them in a supporting role is also absurd.

Love must be unconditional – it can't have the string attached that love will be given in return, because love offered with conditions isn't true love. Love doesn't discriminate between who is the parent and who is the child, or who is the spouse and who is the stranger. All of these roles are transitory – the child in one life is the spouse or stranger in the next.

Pretty much everyone in the world has the attitude of, "Okay, you give me love first and then I'll respond." That's why there's so little love in the world – no one wants to be first, because they mistakenly believe that to love is to open oneself to hurt. But true love cannot result in hurt feelings; on the contrary, hurt is proof that there were strings attached all along. True love doesn't depend on a feeling of gratitude or arousal or whatever. True love is offered freely with no thought of recompense. And if other people reject it, or purposely try to hurt us – that's their problem, not ours. We can give them love anyway – unconditional love. We have no one to blame but ourselves for the lack of love in our lives.

We bury what we're actually doing with people under a mountain of thought forms. Our waking minds are not smart enough to figure out why we are interacting with people, what lessons we are actually trying to learn from them. Our thought forms of manipulation only tell us that we want to get money from a person, or have sex with that person, or get some other kind of validation from that person. So we go ahead and act on those thought forms, completely ignorant of the actual agenda we've got set up with that person, and of course we blow it, even if we do succeed in getting what our thought forms told us we wanted.

Manipulating other people on a feeling level means (or should mean) dealing with them with detachment and distance; respecting their space, and not permitting them to encroach upon ours; going to them with what we desire of them openly and candidly; happily receiving whatever they choose to give us; and in no way demanding anything from them beyond this. It means letting ourselves mingle with them on a feeling level, rather than directing the flow of things based on some thought form rationale of what we think we want from them. It means quietly and peacefully letting people interact with us, with no expectations of them.

How do we know who is worthy of our love? Loving other people doesn't necessarily mean having to stand for their guff. For example, if a person comes to us and asks for something, how can we know whether he is trying to sniggle us for something or rip us off; or whether he is truly deserving and we should be generous and give it to him? Thought forms determine all these outcomes in advance, depending upon who the guy is, what he means to us, what we can expect to get from him in return. A thought form might have us be stingy and say "no", no matter what the merits of the case might be; or a thought form might have us be bleeding hearts who get ripped off by all kinds of people, no matter what the merits. In either case, on a thought form level, we wouldn't be addressing this guy in front of us at all, as to whether he needs it or not. Maybe he doesn't need it at all – maybe he's full of baloney. The point is, that dealing with a person on a level of true feelings means taking responsibility for the fact that he's right there in front of us; we have a relationship going on with him whether we like it or not, whether we want one or not. If he's right there in front of us we must have called him to come, so we must take responsibility for that and deal with him and whatever he wants of us. And we can only do that by staying open to him and feeling what he's feeling (seeing things from his point of view, whether we agree with it or not), rather than judging him, protecting ourselves from him, rehearsing what we will say to him, etc. True feelings about a person can't surface when they're being crowded out by thoughts of gain or control.

Thought forms can never get us what we really want. All they can do is fool us into believing that we're doing everything possible to get what we want. They make us anxious and pushy; when we overreach ourselves and get caught they create the shame of embarrassment; when we do seem to get what we were pushing for, we get a charge of glory tinged with shame, which spoils the true joy we would have felt had the thing come to us on the merits, rather than by our wiles.

Thought forms of desire (rather than true desires) create their own raison d'etre; they keep us on a treadmill of dissatisfaction to keep themselves going. For example, our thought forms of wanting love from the opposite sex are designed to keep us miserable because we don't have the love of the opposite sex. It's the function of this type of thought form to make us want love – not to fulfill that want. The thought form itself doesn't want that love fulfilled, because the moment that love is fulfilled the thought form created to want that love ceases to exist (becomes unimportant to us, which is the same thing as death to a conceptual thought form). The thought form can operate only as long as love is wanted; so in addition to keeping us glued to a wistful longing for that love, the thought form will sneakily attempt to defeat any attempts to actually get that love, all the while fooling us into believing we are doing everything possible to get the love. That's why we find ourselves seeking love only from people who will reject us and not from the people who would gladly give it to us (them we reject ourselves). That way we can pretend we are doing all we can to get love without there being any danger of actually getting it, and thereby keep the thought form of wanting love going on forever.

That's why all our little thought form moves, our little ploys and calculations, so often go awry: they are intrinsically designed to be self-defeating. Trying to impress other people, for example, usually turns them off; trying to protect ourselves from hurt opens up the possibility of other people breaching our protections. In fact, the real hurt we're protecting ourselves from doesn't exist: all hurt is egoism – hurt can only arise from disappointment, and disappointment can only arise from expectation: we create the hurt in the very instant of trying to protect against it. If you snatch a toy away from an infant, he doesn't protest, or even feel ripped off. But try the same thing with a one-year-old! By then the kid has developed a sense of hurt, and a defense against that hurt (since the two arise together).

There's nothing wrong with wanting things from other people, or desiring things in the world "out there", so long as we don't feel it's important whether we get them or not. If we feel that it is important to us that this other person does something; if we are anxious about something someone does or doesn't do; then we have substituted a thought form of importance for the original feeling (feeling good within ourselves no matter what that person does or doesn't do). This doesn't mean that we can't prefer that the other person do this or that – we certainly prefer that he or she love us rather than hate us – it merely means that we feel no special sense of stake or urgency in whether the person does it or not. To give up our sense of importance means to truly not care a fig one way or the other about the outcome of anything; but this doesn't mean we necessarily have to like everything that happens to us (we still keep our thought forms of like and dislike; we just detach the coverings of importance from those thought forms). This means we don't try to weasel out of things we don't like, nor sneak around like children who know they're being naughty to get the things we do like.

Nor does it mean we sit on our hands and vegetate, or go limp and expect the universe to come through with no effort on our part. "Letting things happen rather than making things happen" doesn't mean we go into a stupor and just "let it all rest in the hands of the Lord." That is another thought form of irresponsibility – "Let God do it if He so desires." We have to cooperate creatively with the Spirit: not go passive, but not push push push either. This means acting when it's time to act, when prompted by the Spirit, and refraining from action prior to that time. It means holding back and waiting patiently until the moment has enough power behind it to carry our desires forward.

When we act on our true feelings, we set up a definite intent to accomplish what we desire, but we don't actually do anything to make it happen (beyond systematically visualizing it happening). We make no overt moves, but let the universe bring it to us in its own good time, when we have completed the inner work necessary to pave the way. If we are making conscious moves to accomplish something, we can be sure we are operating on a thought form level, and we might as well relax since thought forms can bring us nothing but shame. If instead we wait patiently, when the time is ripe, when we least expect it, the Spirit will suddenly pop what we want up right before our eyes; and then (and only then) we make a big swoop and grab it.

That swoop can never be the move of a thought form. For one thing, a thought form would never have the utter self-assurance, audacity, and personal power behind it that the swoop of a true feeling has. When we reach out and grab something with a true feeling, there is no doubt or hesitation or anything of the sort behind it.

When we operate on true feelings, we concentrate all our desires on what we want; we visualize it happening with complete confidence that its realization is a certainty – and therefore, since it is a certainty, there is no sense of urgency about it. We know it will happen when it's supposed to. Or not, as the case may be (in which case we know it wasn't in our best interests; it wasn't our heart's desire).

When we operate with thought forms we feel a strong sense of urgency, of an opportunity to be grasped or lost, of time slipping away. It's not the calm certainty of true feelings, but uncertain vacillation and disquiet. Squandering our energy on thought forms keeps us on a treadmill of frustration all the time. Not acting on our thought forms – just wishing for something with all our hearts but taking no overt action to make it happen – builds up the power required to make it really happen. Denying the importance by not acting on it produces a great pressure which eventually forces the Spirit itself to open the floodgates. Wishing for something with the certainty that we will get it is all that's required to make it happen (whether or not it starts out as true feelings, wishing for it with certainty is enough to make it true feelings).

To be able to operate with our true feelings, we first have to know what our true feelings are. In a general way, anything we want that will bring us glory or avoid shame is not a true feeling. Operating with our true feelings means opening ourselves up to what we *really* want – not what other people and our society have put us up to, or misled us into thinking that we want.

For example, it is perfectly natural for us to want success in life – that's our true feelings. But our thought forms detour us away from our true feelings of desiring success as a measure of a job well done, the contribution we have made; as something deserved because of the effort put forth, as an outward token of completed inner work. The thought forms which seek success want it for reasons of status, validation in the eyes of other people and society – glory pure and simple. Obviously this type of success-seeking is not only phony, but it hangs us up in all the wrong things (seeking the token rather than the work). True feelings drive us to find happiness within ourselves, rather than to seek society's version of what we should be happy with. True feelings are always trying to make us feel good; they're always trying to steer us in the direction of true joy. Therefore, our true feelings always try to make us feel shame about striving for false joy.

What is the difference between self-assurance and self-importance; between faith and fooling ourselves; between true hope and inflated hopes; between true joy and false joy? The former are true feelings (light fibers) and the latter are thought forms. In the former we relax into our true feelings, and in the latter we squelch our true feelings. That's the difference – with true feelings, we just relax. With true feelings, we release our own designs and let go of our hold (control). True release from our problems can only come after we give up grasping after a release. The grasping after a release is what keeps release at bay. Only when we truly reach the end of the rope and have to let go and drop into the abyss can we feel true release. Spiritual growth is basically just a matter of exhaustion.

What we all need is grace – a direct lift from the Spirit to get us over the hump. Average people don't know what grace is: they think it's winning the lottery, or finding true love which drops down from heaven with no effort on their part. This is false: grace has to be prepared for. When magicians take complete responsibility for themselves and their situation, then grace will come to them automatically. And this can only happen when they eradicate their self-pity and realize that they're all alone, facing an abyss with no supports or protection. No deity is going to intercede for them or save them; and certainly society isn't going to. They're going to have to take complete responsibility for saving themselves. Then and only then will the way be cleared for the Spirit to fill them.

Self-pity is a retreat when life gets too intense or threatening: it takes some of the sting out of life. Without self-pity life seems overwhelming and uncontrollable (which it is). Self-pity is the presumption that we are important enough for God to care about. By contrast, feeling our true feelings means feeling the raw, unpredictable aspects of life: standing naked and completely vulnerable to life, prepared to take whatever life dishes out.

If something we were counting on didn't come through for us and we feel disappointed, that means that our true feelings didn't want it to come through, because we don't feel we really deserved it. We feel we didn't deserve it because it wasn't true joy, it was just for glory rather than something we had taken complete responsibility for. It wasn't our best; because, if it had been our best, we wouldn't have felt disappointed. What we're disappointed in is ourselves. If it is something we truly deserve and know that we truly deserve, then by the fundamental laws of the universe, we will eventually get it; there's no need for a lot of thought form machinations, and there's no need for a cushion of disappointment.

Our disappointment works in a loop with our inflated hopes to keep us on a roller coaster of expectation / disappointment all the time. Inflated hopes are not the same thing as true hope, but rather a thought form copy of it which inevitably leads to disappointment. True hope is a fierce yearning based on certainty, whereas inflated hopes are a thought form employed to paper over the thought form of doubt. Inflated hopes are hopes for things we don't really feel we deserve; when they come crashing down into disappointment, we feel hurt; but since they weren't our true desires we can stand the pain. What we are afraid of is the hurt of not realizing our true desires. We set up inflated hopes to replace true hope in our thinking and then watch them crash and feel disappointed, but we never have to put our true desires on the line. To have our true desires crash would be tantamount to rejection by the universe itself. So to avoid that possibility (which of course is impossible), we substitute false, inflated hopes which can be validated in the world of society for our true hope. When these false hopes crash we may have been rejected by society, but at least our true hope is safe and sound in the crypt we've built for it. We delay the gratification of our true desires indefinitely so as not to put them on the line. It is doubt in the sustaining power of the universe, doubt in the Spirit, which is doubt in our own true feelings.

In general, the way to recognize a true feeling is that there is no doubt about it, no question about it, it rings clear and true. Usually most of us have some moments like that here and there, particularly when powerful emotions are upon us, but few of us live like that from day to day – manifesting that clarity, self-certainty, and decisiveness with every act. Most of the time we run on thought forms.

When we first begin the painful process of detaching the importance coverings from our thought forms (reordering our priorities and discovering the awful truth about ourselves, and how we have been conditioned by our parents and society) it is difficult to discriminate between true feelings and thought forms in the moment they arise. The first step is to get a grip on what just happened the moment before: whatever actually happened was a true feeling – what we really wanted (asked to happen) in our hearts; whereas if there is a sense of disappointment to it, a feeling of regret, then it was a thought form. If we can recognize in retrospect which was which, we've made a good start on recognizing them in the here and now. Where in the past did we blow it? Every place where we are aware that we blew it, every place we feel ashamed of, is a place where we denied our true feelings.

Doing something which makes us feel bad in the end is never acting on our true feelings; only doing things which make us feel good is acting on our true feelings. Obviously we all have the capacity to act contrary to our true feelings – to choose to feel a thought form cover of importance rather than a true feeling. We can eat chocolate compulsively to remind ourselves of the love we're not getting and call that happiness; but that isn't a true feeling. We're not enjoying that chocolate – we're hating it, and we're hating ourselves for eating it.

True joy is joy we feel for no particular reason; it's the joy we feel when it's a beautiful day and we have nothing in particular on our minds except that it's great to be alive. That is true joy, and anything desired beyond that is an illusion, a thought form.

False joy is always joy because of … . When we're feeling false joy, we are joyous for some reason: because something we wanted to happen happened, or because we're expecting something we want to happen to happen. It feels similar to true joy, but it is not at peace as true joy is: there's a little chugging engine behind it, a sense of urgency and importance. False joy is a veneer over a true feeling of shame – shame that we are seeking false joy rather than true joy.

Ultimately the only way to discriminate between thought forms and true feelings is by the way they each feel. If we feel vague feelings of doubt, shame, smugness, expectation, fear of disappointment, etc. – anything other than feeling good about ourselves – then it was thought forms. But if we feel calm, in control of ourselves (never mind the situation), not urgently pushing pushing pushing to get our way, nor cringing helplessly, nor soothing ourselves with self-righteousness or self-pity and making excuses for ourselves, then we are acting on our true feelings. If there is complete confidence and peace in our hearts beyond any shadow of a doubt, then we are feeling our true feelings.

Chapter III: Dream Mind

"Our thinking consists of tautological transformation;
it is incapable of comprehending a reality."

– Hans Hahn, *Infinity*

The Theory of Light Fibers

In this chapter we will discuss waking mind and dream mind as if they were two different faculties; but in fact waking mind is but a more highly developed and specialized facet of dream mind.

It is the function of waking (adult's) mind to substitute conceptual thought forms for original feelings; to replace the direct perception of feelings with thoughts, so as to impose a semblance of order and focus on what would otherwise be the chaotic experience of random emotional impulses such as we encounter in dreams. We still create (sensory) thought forms in dreams – otherwise we couldn't remember them – but it's a much fuzzier enterprise than it is in waking consciousness. This is because the *feeling* of a sensory thought form is paramount – the thought form part is just a symbol for the feeling.

Dreams which consist of sensory thought forms – that is to say, dreams which can be remembered by waking mind – are just a tiny fraction of all the dreams we have. Most of the activities, life decisions, interactions with other people, etc., which go on in the dream state happen in dreamless sleep – a level on which thought forms don't exist. In other words, although we still create thought forms (things still happen to us) when we are dreaming, this is not the true functioning of dream mind.

It is the function of dream mind to create differentiated emotions out of the undifferentiated sexual energy which is the basic stuff from which everything in the universe is made. At the bottom of everything which exists there is pure sexual energy which – when seen unto itself with no trappings or coverings – appears to consist of fibers of living, pulsating, white light which permeate everything, and sparkle and glow. (For excellent drawings of humans interacting on a light fiber level, see Barbara Brennan's book *Light Emerging*). That is all there is to anything, until dreamless sleep separates this sexual energy into separate emotions, which appear as different hues of light – the entire spectrum of feelings known to human beings: love, hate, fear, joy, fatigue, satiation, everything. All emotions are merely undifferentiated light fibers of sexual energy to which dreamless sleep has assigned different hues. Then, on a level of dreaming, these light fibers are attached to sensory thought forms – "objective" sensory events.

In this book we will use the terms light fibers and feelings or true feelings interchangeably, though in fact feelings are merely colorations of light fibers – jotted notations made by dreamless sleep to keep track or keep a record of undifferentiated sexual energy. So while it is true to say that whenever we are feeling a feeling we are in direct (non-thought form) connection to a light fiber, we would be in even more direct connection to that fiber if we could get beneath the emotion and experience the sexual energy which underlies it.

So dreamless sleep attaches a notation of emotion to pure sexual energy, dream mind then attaches a physical / spatial context to that emotion, and waking mind attaches a conceptual or temporal context to that sensory thought form. Every thought is an image picture; and because thinking is linear, it imposes a semblance of linear order on time.

Feeling is spatial; that is, what we call space is merely the sense of having feelings and what we call time is the sense of having thoughts – hence everyone's need for their own personal space or right to their own feelings, and their own time to make up their minds. Physical, three-dimensional space is a symbol for feelings, just as time is a symbol for thoughts; hence space still exists in the dream state, but time doesn't (certainly not in the same sense in which it exists in the waking state). Our sense of personal continuity in the dream state is not based upon a linear, sequential, unfolding of events, as it is in the waking state, but rather is based upon an awareness of self as experiencer (i.e., one's death). That vibrant, alive quality that dreams have is actually awareness of death. In dreams we are aware of death every second, willy-nilly, because there's nothing solid in dreams to cling to: there's no way of toning down the intensity of what we are experiencing. We're face-to-face with death every second. That's why we feel more alive in dreams than we do in wakefulness – because we are seeing with the eyes of death; we are one with death when we are dreaming, which is why we can't die in dreams – we're already dead. In wakefulness we make a separation between ourselves and our deaths – an absurd pretense, but a useful one for certain purposes – and that's why wakefulness is duller, less vivid, less joyous than dreaming.

The point is that what we call time is an illusion: the universe is not continuous, but rather explodes into being and dissolves into nothingness with every passing instant of "time". To us, space and time are real, and light fibers and thought forms are symbols for space and time, but in fact, exactly the reverse is true. Space and time are just an adult mind version of Santa Claus and the Easter Bunny; indeed, Santa Claus and the Easter Bunny are considerably more real in the cosmic scheme of things than what we call "space" and "time".

In fact, everything's all going on at once in an eternal now moment (which is the way the Spirit sees things). The future exerts as much pull on the present as the past exerts drag – i.e. the present is shaped as much by the future as it is by the past. Newton exerted as much influence on Kepler and Copernicus as they did on him. And our forebears who invented agriculture had computers and spacecraft in the backs of their minds. All this was foreseen – it's no accident.

One way of looking at it is that the Spirit creates the light fibers in the first place, and we – who are bundles or agglomerations of light fibers – take some of that light fiber energy and make thought forms out of it. Just as it's the Spirit's *lila* (play or sport) to create the universe, so too is it our individual spirit's play to create thought forms. That's just what we do, like baloney slicers slice baloney: there's no particular *reason* for it.

Light fibers may be considered to be the intersection of the universe with the individual. They don't belong to the individual in the same way in which his or her thought forms do, but rather may be considered the force of the Universal Spirit moving through the individual spirit, giving it the breath of life. All we are is "knots" in the fabric of universal light fibers – points where light fibers "cross". These knots of light fibers have the power to create thought forms (all beings in the world, whether animal, vegetable, or mineral, not to mention spirits, have this power, as does the earth herself. The earth's light fibers, called ley lines, cross at certain spots on the earth, and these are power spots. Spirits often take up abode at such spots).

In everyday life three things are always going on at once: something is being decided, something is being felt, and something is being experienced (as an "objective" event). The real McCoy – the actual decision-making level – is dreamless sleep. We cannot consciously remember what transpires there because there are no thought forms on this level – just light fibers. On occasion we do remember a decision made in dreamless sleep, and that is what we experience as a prophetic dream, or sometimes as dream wars with other people. The part of everyday life which most closely resembles dreamless sleep is orgasm – that is to say, orgasm is an intrusion of dreamless sleep into waking consciousness. However, physical, climactic orgasm is a pale, pale reflection of dreamless sleep.

Above the level of dreamless sleep there is dreaming, which basically involves feelings. Although there are sensory thought forms in dreaming, they are beside the point – what is important is how things *feel*. The thought forms are just symbols for the feelings. What is really happening is happening on a light fiber level (something is being felt), and this feeling event is symbolized on a thought form level by some physical event. We believe we are reacting to the physical event by feeling an emotion, but in fact it is the emotion which is calling up the physical event.

Everyone has a level of magic on which they are manipulating other people and being manipulated by them: interacting with people by directly mingling light fibers with them. This is called desire, the action of Venus; however, it is directed by mind (Mercury). For example, if we start to feel something which we're not supposed to feel, such as being sexually turned on by someone we're not supposed to be turned on by, then something in our minds puts its foot down and squelches that feeling. The feeling that was starting to emerge was a desire line (action of Venus), and the squelch was carried out by a thought form (action of Mercury).

Similarly, when we are overcome by emotion such as grief, anger, hilarity, fear, or whatever, so that our very thinking process is numbed, that is a desire line emerging so forcefully that it brushes aside all thought forms in its path (Venus overcoming Mercury). Whenever we feel a desire, we emit a line of light from our navels which reaches out to the object of our desire and tries to reel it in like a fish. People who go window shopping, for example, throw desire lines out this way and that at everything they see. The only reason we don't get everything we want immediately is because our thought forms interfere, the principal obstacle being doubt – doubt that we could actually bend the universe to our will – but also unworthiness, self-pity, and fear are common thought forms which prevent the realization of our desires (ploys by which our Mercurys obstruct our Venuses).

The difference between Mercury conjunction and elongation is (going back to our example of being sexually turned on by someone *verboten*): both Mercury conjunction and elongation natives will immediately repress the unwanted sexual desire. However, the Mercury elongations are quite aware that they're doing this as they do it, whereas the Mercury conjunctions repress desire so fast that they're not even aware that they're repressing it. If you asked them, "Were you sexually turned on just then?" they'd deny it, and be telling the truth. They could even pass a polygraph test.

They have no conscious memory whatever of what just transpired. They use apathy to hide from themselves the mechanism by which their thought forms override their desires, and they therefore believe they are free of unwanted desires since they can't see themselves repressing them. However, this sort of discipline is not true discipline since it is animated by fear, not joy. It tends to rigidity and dullness rather than acuity (true perception).

The point is that Mercury (mind) makes the choices of what it wants, and Venus (desire) carries out the necessary instructions on a level of feeling. If mind happens to be in a confused state, it will issue contradictory or self-defeating orders to desire. Mind can become confused whenever it puts attention on schemes of importance categories rather than on what is actually being felt at any given moment (intent).

Although all we really are is feelings, we are taught to distrust feelings and instead believe that we are the sum total of our thought forms, arranged into a hierarchy of importance categories. Our thought forms fit into a well-ordered scheme in which each form is more or less important than any other. For example, our bodies are thought forms, and every part also is a thought form; we would more willingly part with our feet than our hands (presumably), and with our hands rather than our heads.

In most of our (magicians and lunatics excepted) importance schemes, the most important thought form of them all – the last fig leaf to which we cling when all else is stripped from us – is *separatedness*. Separatedness is the granddaddy of all thought forms, both sensory and conceptual. It is the basic assumption which supports the activities of mind. It is more of a matrix than a thought form per se; it is the shaper of all thought forms. As long as we are operating on a level of mind (waking or dreaming), we are necessarily separated from what's really going on (light fibers); or another way of saying this is, when things are perceived via mind, they appear to be happening outside of us or separated from us. Only when we are directly feeling something – perceiving it without a sense of separation – are we at one with it. That's when we are directly connected to our light fibers.

Just as our bodies are merely thought forms, so too is all of the world around us. We come closest to getting beyond these superficial appearances when we are *feeling* the world around us – feeling the breeze blow on our faces or whistle in our ears. If we could just follow that feeling we could enter into the breeze directly and become one with it, and blow with it across the earth. There isn't any us and there isn't any breeze – there's just light fibers.

All art is a thought form symbol (painting, poem, piece of music) which puts everyone who experiences it in touch with one another and the artist on a level of feeling. That's all the everyday world is also: a thought form symbol which connects up the people who experience it. To get at the true symbolism (feeling) we would have to get rid of the importance, the petty likes and dislikes, the mine-and-yours thought form gloss which waking consciousness puts over the symbols.

Consider a comedian. If the comedian is a good magician-comedian, he'll hook up to a light fiber which dreamless sleep has given the emotional coloration of "funny", and he'll hook up the members of his audience to it as well, so everyone agrees that the comedian was funny – they crack up laughing. The particular skit which the comedian did is unimportant. All of us have seen some hilarious bits in which the comedian did a complete deadpan in an off-the-wall situation. The humor arises from the fact that there is a funny light fiber attached to a thoroughly banal and unfunny thought form. It isn't the comedian's words or ideas that are funny, it's his timing, or ability to hook up to a funny light fiber and take his audience with him. It's his spirit which is light and funny, not the particular thought form through which he manifests it for display. That's why the audience goes out of the theater repeating the "hilarious" bits to each other and cracking up each time, whereas when they repeat the same bits to someone who hasn't seen the comedian in person, they can't see the humor at all.

Actually, we are all comedians putting on one big comedy act called waking consciousness, though not all the light fibers we hook up to are funny, by any means. We can get agreement on the thought form level because we've agreed to agree on that level; but we don't all get the same agreement on a feeling level because we have our feelings blocked by importance.

Separatedness is the same thing as death – that is, separatedness and death are just two different labels for the same phenomenon, and instead of saying that "separatedness is the basic matrix of mind" we could just as well have said that "death is the basic matrix of mind". When we feel that we are watching ourselves – that there is some part of us that is watching our every move – that part is our death thought form. It is constantly looking over our shoulder; it's the sense we have that something out there is watching us (The Spirit is watching us too, not to mention lots of other beings, both angelic and demonic; but our root self-consciousness, the sense that we feel within ourselves that something is watching us, is our death thought form. Observe that this is not the conceptual "watcher" thought form, which we use to watch ourselves with glory; that watcher is a phony copy of the true watcher – death – which is utterly cold and dispassionate).

Another way of saying this is: the sense we have that we are perceiving – that there is some perceiver there perceiving – is our death thought form. Without that sense of a detached perceiver there, we wouldn't be able to focus on anything: everything that we see, hear, touch, etc. at every moment would bombard our senses with equal impact. We would be overwhelmed with information; indeed, we would have no sense that "we" exist at all (just as an infant doesn't) – we would be pure perception. To use mind – to be able to focus on one thing at a time by separating it out from its background – is to create a perceiver which is perceiving; and that's what we call death. The separatedness thought form creates the death thought form to act as a witness (actually they're just two ways of looking at the same thing – one impersonal and one personal).

Light fibers are deathless, but thought forms – issuing from chance intersections of light fibers – do die. Thus, if we identify ourselves completely with our thought forms, we will believe that we die when our bodies die – since the body is merely a thought form – or perhaps believe in an afterlife which is some glorified version of waking consciousness, to paper over our fear of death. However, since we can operate quite well without our physical bodies (e.g. in dreaming and astral projection), this is clearly a false point of view.

We still have our body and death thought forms in the dream state (we most certainly have a body there, and we still have an aversion to death); moreover all five of our "physical" senses are fully operative in the dream state. But our dream bodies aren't physical – they don't need food, can't feel pain, and don't die. When we are fearful of death in a dream, we are fearful of something which can't happen. If we're about to die, we just wake up (in some other reality).

The body and death thought forms are in fact just physical symbols for the more abstract thought form combination of doubt, forgetting, and isolation – the three characteristics of separatedness. Doubt is the limitation of physicality; e.g., we doubt that we could fly in our physical bodies, although the only thing preventing it is our doubt thought form. This thought form is largely responsible for making waking consciousness so slow.

The forgetting thought form is largely responsible for picking out a particular path of personal history and future through the thicket of possibilities. Forgetting is responsible for making waking consciousness so obsessively focused and narrow in scope.

The isolation thought form provides the energy to support waking consciousness – to keep everyone awake and striving, striving, striving. On a thought form level people strive to isolate themselves by glorifying themselves above their fellows on the one hand, and by hiding their shame away from them on the other. On a light fiber level people strive to break out of this false prison of isolation and seek true love. It is this seeking true love through the obscure mists of shame which society puts on the individual which animates all the individual's experiments with society's glory and shame: society capitalizes on this energy by teaching people to deny themselves love, and then redirecting their frantic efforts to get back to it again.

Body and death are the creation of all three of these thought forms: people are isolated in their bodies and their deaths; doubt makes death inevitable; and forgetting is death's particular pastime.

Arising together with our body thought form we have our world thought form. The world thought form is the one which everyone has been imposing on us since the moment we were born – it is the creation of everyone around us (or better said: our response to everyone around us). Without a world thought form we wouldn't be able to handle the world – we'd be in the same position as a newborn, unable to satisfy any desire in the world.

The problem with the world thought form is that it's easy for society to get in there and twist us around with that form – force us to jump through all sorts of hoops to get what we want. The only two alternatives for avoiding this are 1) lunacy, or 2) separating the world thought form from its covering of importance. This means taking complete responsibility for the world – being diligent, scrupulous, and thorough – but putting no light fiber energy into it whatsoever. This is what most people do with their church services, the pledge of allegiance, and the national anthem: they rigorously go through all the motions, but they don't actually give a damn. And that's what we must learn to do with everything in this world: go through all the motions, fulfill everyone's expectations, but be entirely indifferent as to the outcome.

We do need a world thought form because we do need that mirror; not to check to see how well we're doing or how fine we look, but rather to feel what is going on inside ourselves. We can only see our own feelings objectively, understand them, get them under mental control, by somehow getting them outside ourselves where we can examine them dispassionately. That's what the world is for – to enable us to see and understand what is happening inside ourselves.

We must stop making war upon the world and blaming it for all of our problems. There should be a symbiotic relationship between mind and feeling, rather than a tyranny of one over the other. The calm, cool, sober judgments of mind should act in concert with the raw, naked power of feeling. So we do need a world thought form if we expect to impose any sort of order upon the world, because the world is essentially chaotic, not ordered. Order and mind arise together – they are the same thing.

Consider the universe to consist of a zillion pick-up sticks heaved into the air so they come crashing down in a jumble; but at some certain place five of the sticks, by sheer coincidence, happen to fall in such a fashion as to form a perfect star. What we do (what mind does) is to focus all our attention on those five sticks (ignoring everything else), and then to marvel at how ordered the universe is, and how intelligent we are to have perceived that order! In actual fact, the supposed order of the universe, and the putative perceiver of that order, arise together and fall together, and only abide for an instant.

Personal History and Future

When humans were still hunters, they did not draw as sharp a distinction between being awake and being asleep as we do today, since they slept in snatches when they felt like it instead of in long stretches during the night. Similarly, they didn't draw as sharp a distinction between past and future as we do now because they didn't need to – they were more centered in the now moment, hence they experienced their past and future in a more immediate fashion than we do today. They didn't define themselves as much in terms of personal history and future aspirations.

We say, "I am no longer who I was back then" – separating who we are now from who we were at an earlier age. We say, "Someday I will be or do such-and-such" – separating who we are now from who we will become. But our hunter ancestors didn't have that much of a sense of separation – things that happened to them a long time ago, or that would happen to them some future day (what we would call prescience), were more a part of who they conceived themselves to be now than they are for us. They were in closer touch with their intent – the feeling of their past and future; they didn't have as many thought forms interposing a linear order upon their consciousness, imposing some ponderous past and inexorable future upon their present.

As we have striven to make clear in these pages, all that really exists in the universe is light fibers, or feelings. The function of mind is to organize light fibers by pinning them to certain thought forms. Some of these forms mind calls "desires" and points them towards a future; and some of these forms it calls "memories" and points them towards a past. But this is not a true distinction because mind is necessarily linear. What's really going on is that every single desire and memory that we have ever had creates unto itself (is a record of) an entire *probable reality*. Every light fiber (every feeling) is an entire universe. Everything we desire creates an entire world in which that desire is realized – i.e., every desire creates its own future. We don't desire something for the future, or in the future; but rather the future only exists as there is a light fiber of desire reaching out to it and creating it. And our minds choose which possible future to go with, out of all the available futures.

Similarly with memories. Every memory is a thought form record of an entire universe (a decision we have made). We mistakenly believe that we have had a linear personal history – a series of events which led up to where we are right now – and from here we will have a linear future. And there is one "us" who has had this personal history and who is going to have this personal future.

In fact, there are an infinite number of "us's" who had an infinite number of personal histories in back of us; and there are an infinite number of "us's" who will have an infinite number of possible futures. The action of mind is to select a path going backward and forward: it selects one particular set of memories going back, and one particular set of desires going forward, out of the culture and *Zeitgeist* (thought forms) it finds at hand.

All of the thought form material that's left over – all of the "could have beens" and "might have beens" and "should have beens" – are the probable realities for a given lifetime (and are in fact accessible via a technique similar to past life regressions; this is described in the companion volume *The Great Wheel*). Probable realities are parallel lifetimes, which branch off from this one at each point where a decision, large or small, is made. That is why we must stand by our decisions; otherwise we are draining the energy we need in this lifetime to realize our true desires off into other probable realities. Probable realities are no more nor less real than this lifetime. There are always probable realities in which we get (or got) what we want (or wanted). Mind picks which probable reality to go with from the smorgasbord of possibilities.

Fundamentally what mind is grabbing onto are light fibers (feelings); it swings from light fiber to light fiber like Tarzan swinging through the jungle. Mind makes a little notation of each feeling; mind records it in a thought form, and in so doing it separates it out from everything else. Mind makes just one jotted notation of that fiber; it could just as easily have picked any number of other notations – and indeed in other probable realities it did so – but in this probable reality it happened to pick that notation. Seen from above it seems to be wholly arbitrary since there are any number of ways that a particular fiber could be associated with an event: any number of other events could have as easily happened to symbolize that feeling. The event that actually occurred (or is desired) is irrelevant; the event is merely conjured up as a way of remembering that memory (the feeling of that memory).

Now this is not a very good way of doing it. It would be better to get back to feeling that feeling again as is done in recapitulation, as will be explained in *The Great Wheel*, if what we want to do is really remember that memory. The point is that what we call our personal histories and futures are completely arbitrary, just picked out of a hat. And mind, by creating thought forms, is doing the picking. Events never happen anywhere except in our imagination. The feeling happened, but the event is merely a thought form record of the feeling. If the feeling was, say, of catastrophic fear, then the event could equally well have been being raped or tortured, falling down a well, or being told we have an incurable disease. We ourselves select which event will go with that feeling, in accordance with what we have been taught, what we expect, the general social situation, etc.

Babies come into this world with lots of loose light fibers, which they one by one peg down in memories and other thought forms. A memory (like a desire) is a way of grabbing onto a feeling and pickling it in brine. Master magicians still have feelings just like an average person does – they feel fear, love, dislike, lust, anger, thirst, cold, discomfort, etc. They don't exist in an eternal state of tranquility and bliss. If the feeling of the time is depression, they feel depressed; if the feeling of the time is anger, they feel angry; if the feeling of the time is intense outpouring of love, they feel that. They don't wish they were feeling something other than the feeling of the time, or pretend to themselves that they're feeling something other than the feeling of the time. They just feel feelings, and then let them go. They don't grab them and pin them down in memories or other thought forms. They don't fear fear, love love, dislike dislike, lust after lust, get angry at anger, etc. They don't make a big deal about how they feel; they don't feel any need to create a dramatic production to preserve their precious feelings for all eternity, to show how sensitive they are. They don't need to exalt their memories – their personal history is completely fluid. In fact, they can have different memories of the same event (in lucid dreaming or gazing they go back to the event and let themselves feel the importance coverings surrounding the event. By feeling them they can change that "past" and make something else "have happened". Thus they can have two memories of the same event, or rather two different events occupying the same space in time. Or yet another way of putting it is, they erase the barrier which separates those probable realities).

Magicians stay fluid by grasping each moment anew. They ride the moment instead of being dragged through it by thought forms. Most of us have most of our light fibers tied to the people around us, the things in our environment, our memories of the past and desires for the future, etc. Magicians have all their light fibers free to seize the moment, to act fully in the moment, not tied up in personal history and future expectations. The only reason a thing has happened is because we believe it has happened.

For example, consider a person diagnosed as having some fatal disease (e.g. AIDS). The person chooses a moment in which a doctor says to him, "You have AIDS; you're going to die", and he makes that thought form of fear into an overwhelming belief when he could as easily – after the initial fear – just laugh it off and refuse in his heart to believe it. But instead, he makes the thought form into an overwhelming belief by assigning tremendous importance to it, and he then carries that belief through the rest of that probable reality.

Of course, at the moment the doctor said, "You have AIDS", another probable reality branched off in which the doctor said, "You don't have AIDS". These two probable realities interact on each other: in the AIDS branch, there is a wistful longing for the non-AIDS branch; and in the non-AIDS branch, a constant fear of the AIDS branch. The wistfulness of the AIDS branch may send messages to the non-AIDS branch like: "Enjoy your health! Appreciate what you have!" And the non-AIDS branch may send messages to the AIDS branch saying, "Cheer up! Life has its bright side too!"

If at any moment the AIDS patient realized that the AIDS is just a belief he could change – only a reality that he is creating by believing it every moment – then at that instant it would collapse and the person would be cured. But this becomes harder and harder to do as the person becomes "sicker and sicker"; i.e. believes more and more in his sickness, thus making it into an overwhelming reality (of course, this is a greatly oversimplified example; what is really going on out there in the universe is far more complex and infinitely ramified than anything mind could ever conceive of).

Everyone, at every moment, is creating their own reality. They call upon other people to play roles for them in the creation of their reality, as others call upon them in turn to assist in the creation of their own realities. That is to say, contrary to popular belief, we are not partaking of the same reality; rather, everyone is walking around with their full attention glued to their own TV sets, watching their own show (their own reality). These realities interpenetrate and make use of some of the same materials, but they are *not* the same.

When mind attaches a thought form to a light fiber it is selecting one possible event notation out of an infinite number of possibilities available to it, all of which are equally real. Mind selects just one of these and calls that one its "personal history" or "desires for the future"; the others it forgets and relegates to other lifetimes or probable realities. Without mind to make such a selection we'd experience all our lives at once – or rather, we'd experience the world as pure feeling, as we do in dreams. We'd hop around from one life to another without the sense of continuity or linear march of causality which we experience in wakefulness. It is precisely dissatisfaction with this sort of butterfly instability of dream consciousness which motivated humankind to perfect waking consciousness in the first place.

Expectation (eagerness/disappointment) buttresses Doubt and stabilizes Desire.

Familiarity (hope / fear) buttresses Forgetting and stabilizes Memory.

Importance (shame / glory) buttresses Isolation and stabilizes Mind.

Forgetting is the thought form which makes the world of concepts possible. Concepts are a linear, one-dimensional version of reality. In order to maintain our concepts we must simplify everything; reduce everything to black and white, either / or, yes or no; impose a duality on a system of organization (better said: disorganization) so complex that it boggles the mind. The only way mind can manage or handle the blizzard of information coming at it is by forgetting most of it and concentrating on a tiny fraction of the original system.

Without a forgetting thought form we could easily remember every meal we've ever eaten, and every breath we've ever taken. But that would be equivalent to flooding our conscious mind with so much information that it would no longer be able to function (to conceptualize).

As noted previously, the entire universe is bursting into being and vanishing again into nothingness every instant. Familiarity is the screen which disguises this moment-to-moment disruption by forgetting it. In other words, familiarity is a focus on the monads of existence which ignores (forgets) their interstices. Familiarity is the gloss or impression that there is something in the universe which abides; it covers the holes in the fabric of reality by slowing the rate of consciousness down, so the holes whiz by too quickly to be seen – in precise analogy to a motion picture.

For the most part, there is very little of the principle of memory present in what most people consider memory. Most conscious memory is thought forms, not true memory. It's like the difference between a snapshot of a person at a moment of great emotion, and being the person at that moment. The snapshot is a record of the moment, of the emotion, just as most conscious memory is a record of emotion; but it isn't the emotion itself. Only in recapitulation, where the feeling of the memory is more vivid than the thought forms, is true memory functioning.

Conscious memory is necessarily distorted. We all know how vivid our experience is when we are in the throes of orgasm, or about to crash in a car, or have just been told that a loved one has died. Well, every moment of our lives is that vivid, or would be if we let it be. We tone it all down, filter out the raw feeling present in every moment, since waking mind cannot function in an environment of raw feeling.

The chief function of mind is forgetting; that is to say, forgetting is the main bulwark of our inattention, of which importance is a highly refined and stylized embellishment. In order to think, we must forget what we are feeling. Mind has to forget that there is a grotesque monster there about to devour us, so that it can turn all its attention to counting how many angels can dance on the head of a pin. In order to do all the routine tasks of everyday life we have to ignore the fact that we are literally living in the midst of total chaos and insanity, and experiencing complete annihilation with every passing instant. It's the equivalent of trying to balance a checkbook while having an orgasm or facing a firing squad. That's why waking consciousness is so depleting: it is truly an incredible strain to ignore the powerful feelings which we are feeling so that all our attention can be focused on some triviality.

Importance can be considered to be a specialized form of forgetting, precisely as mind is a specialized form of memory. Forgetting, like importance, enables us to focus by ignoring (screening out) available information. We tend to make a distinction between conscious thought forms (those we are aware of and can manipulate) and unconscious thought forms (those we're not aware of, such as the thought forms which regulate our metabolism, digestion, blood circulation, etc.; also memories of our infancy and early childhood); but in fact there's no essential difference between the two types of thought forms. Thought forms are thought forms, and the only difference between the conscious and unconscious ones is forgetting.

Each thought form (and the corresponding self-existent "I" who witnesses it) comes into being for a flash – for one instant only – and then dissolves into nothingness unless it is attached to a light fiber. Each thought form observer / observed duality ("I") which springs into being for an instant has a gloss of importance. This gloss of importance makes the individual self-existent observer feel important – at least for the instant that he or she exists. At each passing instant the observer must remember or regrasp importance (focus) out of undifferentiated nothingness. One could say that attaching thought forms to light fibers means making the thought forms familiar, since only thought forms anchored to light fibers can be remembered. The list of all remembered thought forms constitutes a lifetime – but there are zillions (albeit a finite number) of ways that those same thought forms could be assembled, and each of those zillions of ways is a probable reality for that lifetime. There is no central, abiding "I". This lifetime is a single line of memory – or better said, there are zillions of "you"s sharing this probable reality. The reason why you can only remember one of them is because of forgetting. Forgetting performs for different lines or sequences of thought forms what importance does for individual thought forms: forgetting keeps different lines of thought forms (different probable realities and past and future lives) separated.

Forgetting was invented together with meiosis. A one-celled being is immortal and eternal, and instantly aware of any changes occurring in any of its ramifications (antecedents and descendants). It exists in an eternal NOW moment. Moreover, it is also aware of all the anatomical processes going on inside itself. In other words, pure dream consciousness (the consciousness of one-celled beings) is relatively undifferentiated, and it encompasses a great deal more information than does waking consciousness (the consciousness of us multi-celled beings). There's just too much information available to one-celled beings for them to be able to do much focusing. For example, a one-celled being would not be able to differentiate as clearly as we can between "hunger" and "satiation", since it experiences both of them at once in distinct ramifications of its total being. But we experience "hunger" and "satiation" at different "times" – i.e., we can focus upon either "hunger" or "satiation" separately.

The first thing our forgetting thought form has us forget is that our realities are our own creation – that we set the whole thing up quite consciously, and then forget that we've done so. We quite literally forget that we've asked for a given experience by cutting ourselves off from those light fibers; the fact is, however, that everything that happens to us we have asked for (intended). And light fibers are still operative – working to get to the original feelings – even after we've forgotten the thought forms that go with them (the asking for it). The forgotten thought forms still remain attached to the light fibers, but are no longer in control of them. Rather, the thought forms are manipulated by the light fibers in a jerky fashion, like spastic puppets; whereas remembered thought forms, albeit also puppets, are rigid and efficacious. These are the ones which hang around at the fringes of conscious mind; the forgotten ones don't – they are outside the ken of conscious mind, which can no longer control them or call upon them as it can remembered thought forms.

The only difference between thought forms under the control of conscious mind and thought forms out of control of conscious mind is the forgetting thought form. Forgetting is a thought form manipulated by our death thought form, in the manner of the chess game in the *Seventh Seal*. Forgetting something is a form of death; when we forget something, a part of us dies – it is as if death has taken another counter in the game. People who have forgotten their true feelings, their joy, have already largely surrendered themselves to their death. Our death thought form, working through our forgetting thought form, cuts our conscious mind's connection to a given memory.

To live with all of our memories is to lose our sense of linear time. Only by ridding ourselves of our forgetting thought form (by recapitulating all of our memories) can we forestall our deaths completely, since then we are in possession of all the memories (feelings) of all our past and probable lives, as well as this one. At that point we're not really centered in any given one of them anymore. The point is that the basis of mind, of reason, is death; you can't have one without the other.

All of the great inventions of meiosis – sex, duality, individual self-existence, and death – are products of forgetting. If we could recapitulate our entire lives, and remember all our past and future lives; i.e. if we could consciously access all of the thought forms which comprise the totality of our being (as one-celled beings do), then we would hover over the sum total of who we are in all of our ramifications – we would be instantly aware of everything that was happening in all of our lives and realities; but we would concomitantly have rather limited scope of action (decision) in any given one of them. A one-celled being is very aware – totally aware – but also incapable of much more than instinctual action. One-celled beings learn and evolve, but their capacity for making decisions is just not in the same league as us multicellulars.

Here's the answer to the mystery: what we consider to be "ourselves" is just a given thought form at a given moment. Time doesn't exist – at least not as a line. It's more like a plane, an infinite now moment, in which everything is happening all at once; but each individual thought form involved thinks that it is a real, separate being with individual self-existence and a personal history and future. Each of the infinite thought forms which makes up "us" – all the things we have ever experienced or will experience; all of the monads – since they are discrete – of every instant of awareness in all our probable realities from this life and all our past and future lives – thinks that it is the real "us". Each one thinks it's the top dog (most important). And from any given thought form we can move to an infinite number of possible futures or remember an infinite number of possible pasts. And once that decision is made – the decision to move from the standpoint of any given thought form now moment to any other given thought form future moment or remembered past moment – mind will stamp upon that decision the notation: *Makes Sense!* (is "real").

Admittedly, some probable futures or pasts are more likely than others; it's more likely that your next thought form will be moving a bit further along reading this sentence rather than suddenly appearing on a Caribbean beach sipping a piña colada. That's the sort of thing that happens in dream consciousness – the jump from thought form to thought form tends to be a lot more random than in waking consciousness.

But it's nonetheless a random process, shaped by tendencies from human and individual memory, whose only claim to fame is that it makes sense – there's no doubt about it!

Mind is what makes sense out of this selection. This is easier to see in dream consciousness where even the most outrageous and improbable (from the point of view of wakefulness) thought forms can pop up and yet make perfect sense at the time we are dreaming them. Similarly, our waking consciousness (experience of everyday life) also only makes sense because we have decided to let it make sense. Our behavior in everyday life appears to be ridiculous to people of other cultures, as does theirs to us. The canons of what makes sense vary from culture to culture, as they do from dreaming to waking. The point is that all mind is, is a gloss over raw awareness – the feeling that whatever is happening (being perceived) makes sense. That is all that mind does: it doesn't organize or assemble anything. All it does is separate itself from what is being perceived (which are actually not two different things) and then say, "That makes sense! That is a good idea! That is a good decision!" Thus mind is just a gloss which assigns importance to things, just as memory is a gloss which assigns familiarity to things. Just as all mind does is to say, "That makes sense!" all memory does is to say "I recognize this!" This is why we say that importance is just a specialization of familiarity, and mind is just a specialization of memory, which broke off at the time of meiosis.

Things make sense in dreams which don't make sense in waking because there is less mind (importance) there – the thought forms tend to be sensory rather than conceptual – so it doesn't matter as much whether the sequence of thought forms follows strict rules. There are a lot more choices on the menu in dreaming, but they're not as controllable. When we're half asleep, or drunk or drugged, or in a state of shock, things seem more distant; unreal; don't make as much sense; nor do we care whether they do or not. When nothing makes any sense, we're totally incapable of acting (making decisions). Some lunatics are in this position, as are newborns. While bacteria and protozoa also act and make decisions, for them it's much more of a knee-jerk chemistry than it is like playing contract bridge or programming computers.

When we say that mind and death are the same thing, we must realize that death is not a sudden moment in time, as most of us believe, but rather a slow process that begins when we start pinning our light fibers down to thought forms of importance; that is to say, it is a slow process of forgetting. People who have just died find themselves in a state not unlike waking consciousness when they're falling-down drunk. It's just that their death thought forms have become more important to them than their body thought forms. The "moment of death" is just a thought form notation for this particular decision, which they could just as easily make or have made at any other moment in their lives.

Our thought forms don't really vanish when we die (or banish them); rather, they merely crack loose from their importance coverings. If we banish a thought form we are saying to it, "You are no longer important." When we die, most of the things we thought were so all-fired important now become less important than death. So we loosen the thought forms from their importance coverings, but we don't separate them completely. They become like a ring of scar tissue around the light fiber they were attached to, which then dips into the immediate thought form material available to it in another lifetime or reality to reconstruct the situation or a similar one. Thought forms never really cease to exist – they get buried in the dusty archives of the akashic records – but our connection to them becomes more remote and tenuous.

The sum total of all the dead, scaly material clinging to our light fibers blocked by importance is what we call our lifetimes. They are like a collection of scenes or tableaux strung together by mind into a lattice of threaded beads. All of the beads (or life events) which directly connect to a given bead are probable realities. From that bead, mind can take any number of directions to another bead. The black threads connecting the beads are death – we literally die from moment-to-moment. We always have to pass through death (forgetting) to move to the next bead (scene); and if we take a turn which leads to a long run of black thread till the next bead, that's "real" death and the next bead is birth in another lifetime.

Another way of saying this is, we have ourselves separated into a bunch of little pieces, each of which feels isolated and disconnected from (more important than) the rest. However, within each little piece we have tremendous focus and stick-to-itiveness ("fear of death") – a willingness to keep up the struggle to stay awake and separated no matter how much of a bummer it is.

All we mean, when we refer to "ourselves", is a bunch of thought forms, which are actually in great flux. There is no, central, abiding "us" there in the sense in which we are accustomed to thinking. We are all multiple personalities, and the only difference between people with multiple personality disorder (such as Eve, Sybil, or Truddi) and the rest of us is that people with out-and-out MPD are unable to lie to themselves as effectively as the rest of us: as a defense against the pain of severe childhood trauma they are unable to maintain the fiction of a central "I": they parcel out their pain to different "I's" to make it more bearable.

The "you" who is reading this sentence is actually a very different being than the "you" who read the previous sentence, and this is not meant in a trivial sense (that a few cells have split in the interim) – it is meant in the deepest sense possible. The belief that you are the same person from moment to moment is an illusion, a lie. To maintain this illusion you must snatch yourself back from death every instant, be on the qui vive every second. It is precisely this clenching up against death which creates and sustains waking consciousness (gives us the focus and control we lack in dreaming).

What makes waking mind seem linear is that instead of seeing the lattice, with all its interconnections, from above (as a one-celled being does with its ramifications), we have narrowed our focus down so all we can see is one bead at a time, and one thread leading away from that bead. The "you" who is reading these words right now in this lifetime think you're just sitting there reading a book – you have no idea how this is reverberating on all your other probable realities and lifetimes. What is going on inside you right now is not just going on inside you in this lifetime.

Which probable reality we find ourselves in at any given moment is largely a function of what conscious choices we are making for ourselves, or else what thought forms we are letting live our lives for us. Consider, for example, a light fiber of joy. Suppose our waking mind has attached to that light fiber a thought form of "getting a raise". Since most of us have thought forms working at cross purposes, there are various probable realities in which that basic "getting a raise" thought form could be physically realized. If we truly feel in our hearts that we deserve the raise because we've done a good job and we want our world to reflect our joy in accomplishment, then we'll take a probable reality branch in which we receive the raise and are joyous about it. However, if in our hearts we know we don't deserve the raise but are only desiring it for our own glory, then we can either take a probable reality branch in which we get the raise and feel false joy about it, or else we don't get the raise and feel disappointed about it. In the latter two cases our true feelings (our intent – the original light fiber of joy) is trying to steer us to true joy by making us feel shame (false joy or disappointment). Just because we block the natural action of the light fiber with our thought forms doesn't mean that the light fiber isn't still operative and calling all the shots; all it means is that we experience the joyous impulse as shame rather than joy.

In the above example, all three probable realities are equally real. Which one we choose for this lifetime (this personal history) is a function of which choice of the three we decide to make for this lifetime: one choice we make by going along with our true feelings, and the other two we make by going along with our glory thought forms, at the moment when the universe pops that possibility (of getting a raise) up before our eyes.

But in another lifetime, to that very same light fiber of joy to which in this set of probable realities we attached the thought form of "getting a raise", we could have attached any number of other thought forms depending upon the circumstances of that life. For example, in other lives that same joy fiber could mean "successfully hunting that mammoth" or "becoming emperor of Rome" or "receiving many alms"; and in each of those lives we can choose different probable realities based on whether we got what we wanted or not.

But whether or not we get what we want is irrelevant; it's a blind to what is really going on. People who get more or less everything they want are no happier than people who don't. In a general kind of way this has to do with Venus: people who have Venus conjunction sun tend to play the victim / loser, and people who have Venus at elongation tend to play the oppressor / winner. But it's all just thought forms, and all it leads to is shame.

A child's anger at a deceased parent for having abandoned him; a woman's feeling of guilt for having been raped; a parent's self-recrimination for an unavoidable accident suffered by her child; are all valid feelings because those probable realities were indeed chosen in preference to happier ones. For example, the parent whose child died in an accident, who spends weeks thereafter ruminating on "If I hadn't done this ... " and "If I'd only done that ..." is actually reviewing all her decisions (branching points into other probable realities) which led up to this reality. Some psychologists believe that it is infantile for a child to blame himself when his parents divorce; yet the child is absolutely correct: he chose that probable reality. This is what is meant by "taking responsibility for our already-made decisions" or "taking responsibility for the situation in which we find ourselves"; because that is what we have chosen for ourselves: that is our intent – the place we have to start from. In Viktor Frankl's book *Man's Search for Meaning* he describes the various opportunities he had to leave the concentration camp or to obtain advantages which, had he accepted any one of

them, would have led to his death. And the chain of events –
the miracle – which led to his ultimate survival was the
decision he made at each branch point to consider the needs of
his patients above his own needs.

In order to achieve anything in life we have to balance two
things: 1) Desiring the thing desperately, with all our hearts;
and 2) Not caring in the least whether we get it or not. Fierce
desire is not a thought form, but an intent, a command to the
Spirit. But concern over whether we get it or not is a thought
form (a symbol for the true desire). Concern over whether we
realize our desires is what causes all the emotional wear and
tear which wastes the energy needed to actually realize them.
Just as the importance we attach to our memories makes up
our customary moods, so too does the importance we attach to
our desires make up our customary concerns. Customary
moods and customary concerns are matrices which tend to
crank out thought forms of a given type (e.g. depressed, giddy,
rapacious, passive, lecherous, etc. etc.). So actually
importance is not ruled by Mercury; rather, it is assigned by
the moon and Venus. Mercury is actually sort of a traffic cop
that keeps bundles of light fibers (memories and desires)
organized and moving along in orderly fashion. Mercury is
the ego, or sense of a self-existent "I". It consists of our
thinking – our constant internal dialogue – which gives us our
sense of stability and continuity.

Why are things important to us? Either because they are
familiar to us (or unfamiliar to us, as the case may be, in
which case we assign importance to the process of
familiarizing them – having that one "covered" by our thought
forms); or else because we expect something from them.
These are our reasons why. We tend to mold new thought
forms according to our reasons why – i.e., new thought forms
tend to have the same moods and concerns (reasons why) as
our old thought forms. The reasons why is the Mercury part –
the thought form gloss over a memory or desire (a reason why
that memory or desire is important). Since time doesn't really
exist, it isn't true to say that the mood or concern predates or
causes the reason why it exists; but it is true to say that the

mood or concern is primary, and the reason why – the thought form gloss which justifies this mood or concern – is secondary or of lesser significance.

Following the spiritual path means losing importance – and in particular this is done by detaching importance from things which previously occasioned moods or concerns. That is, to be free of moods and concerns – to feel that nothing is important – is enlightenment.

What tends to fool us is the fact that some people do seem to get more or less everything they desire on a thought form level. Some people just make that choice (to be lucky) for a particular lifetime. This is the "Richard Cory syndrome" – the illusion that getting what we think we want has anything whatsoever to do with our happiness. It does have to do with our happiness as long as we know what we really want in our hearts, but not if what we think we want is phony stuff like gadgets and designer clothes and other people envying us, instead of loving and being loved. The practice of magic – at least white magic – is not so much a way of getting what we really want as it is a way of knowing what we really want.

Thought forms (which is to say, mind) cannot accomplish anything; all they can do is fool us into believing we are accomplishing something. Let us say that in all three probable realities in which we wanted a raise we made more or less the same thought form moves to make it happen: butter up the boss, spruce up our appearance, ostentatiously work overtime, etc. In two probable realities we got what we wanted and in one we didn't, but all the little ploys had nothing to do with it in any of those realities. In the reality in which we got the raise because we knew we truly deserved it, all the little ploys were unnecessary. Indeed, in probable realities in which we are going for true joy we rarely use thought form ploys at all, because we sense we don't need to: we're doing a good job, and that's what matters. In the probable reality in which we got the raise even though we knew we didn't deserve it, and in the one in which we didn't get the raise because we preferred to wallow in self-pity, the only purpose our little thought form ploys served was to increase our sense of shame for refusing true joy.

In lucid dreaming (a technique which will be described in the companion volume on Venus) it is possible to see a lot more of these interconnections than can be seen in waking consciousness. There we can hover over waking consciousness just as recently deceased people do; until they narrow everything down to their death thought form and thus leave this sphere. When all a person has left is his or her death thought form, they are born into another body in this universe or some other.

In actual fact, we are nothing more than our death. Our death is the complete written record of our life. It is all contained in our death. Our death can be likened to a microdot which contains our entire life in one little point. It is us, or everything we know as "ourselves".

We are like the little point which moves on an Etch-a-Sketch board or computer drawing program, blazing out a path through life (making a squiggle on a previously blank screen) and leaving a trail behind it. The entirety of our being is like that blank screen, and the squiggly path is this particular lifetime. It has a beginning and an end, and is delimited. That delimitation is death.

In other words, just as our sense of space is our sense of having feelings, and our sense of time is our sense of having thoughts, so too is our death our sense that there is some contained entity which is having those feelings and thoughts. Death is our sense of containment, of boundedness, of singularity, of discreteness. It is a species of glue which binds random light fibers and thought forms together into an integrated, cohesive whole.

The death thought form creates the body thought form to symbolize this sense of discreteness, solidity, stability, boundedness. What we consider our unity – our individuality, our continuity, our "us-ness" – is actually our death. When we cling to our sanity, our sense of being centered in a stable environment where things are more or less predictable, what we are clinging to is our death. Wakefulness could not exist without it.

The main difference between how we perceive in dreams and how we perceive when we're awake is that being awake is deathier – there's more death to it, more to lose, more to cling to; whereas in dreams there's not as much "us" there – not as much sense of a detached perceiver perceiving. Things just are.

Newborns have very little sense of being focused in a body. They don't know it's a body, or their body; they just have feelings. They learn to associate those feelings with their body thought form later on, as they discover their body. Infants don't even feel feelings as their feelings; they just feel. The sense that what they feel is their feelings is in fact their death, which they create, fill out, and grow into along with their body. When they die, they shed their body thought form in the same way in which they first created it – by releasing the feelings they had associated with it. They don't feel those feelings as bodily sensations after they die, just as they didn't when they were first born. But usually people lose their body thought forms a lot faster than they assumed them, so they don't realize that it's just the inverse process of what they did as infants.

The adults help the baby construct his body thought form because they already agree on what the baby looks like, and then they impose that thought form on him. He has a hand in it too, of course, but newborns are still so fluid that what they look like changes from moment to moment and from day to day. They haven't learned to hold themselves in a rigid pose, as adults have.

Another way of looking at death is to consider it to be an entity. The same source which emits light fiber emanations (The Spirit) also emits death. Death is just a "negative" light fiber. Each light fiber, albeit deathless, carries a death underside. Death is just another way of looking at a light fiber – at its dark aspect rather than its glowing aspect.

Death is the blank screen upon which all of our lives are painted. Those lives don't exist; they're just momentary plays of light and shadow. However, to us they seem utterly fascinating and absorbing. To get to who we really are we would have to pull all of that obsession (light fiber energy pinned down by importance) out of all of those lives. As we do this (via recapitulation), we find less and less of what we now consider to be "ourselves". We find the barriers which separate us from other people and the world around us becoming less and less distinct. It becomes harder for us to feel where we end and the next guy begins.

The "us's" of all our past and probable lives are really no more us than that guy standing over there; and he is as much us as anything else. But he branches off from the totality of who we are at a more remote point than our past and probable lives do. Just as our past and probable selves are no less us than the us of our present lifetime (but are more remote from it), so too is everyone and everything else in the universe as much us as we are, but they are even more remote from our present self than our past and probable selves are.

Opening our hearts to other people goes a long way towards reestablishing these connections, overcoming the boundaries that separate us from others. All of these boundaries are death. That's all death is – boundedness. When we are facing our death we are consciously acknowledging our boundedness, limitedness (not helplessness). That is what is meant by "directly confronting our death." It's a matter of being humble and respectful. Our death is not the same thing as our intent; however, only when we are directly confronting our death (poignantly aware of our death, rather than passing over it, brushing past it, ignoring it, pretending it doesn't exist, treating it with disrespect) are we in direct touch with our intent.

This is why when we channel the spirits of deceased people they are usually mellower than they were in life, because they are no longer bounded by their fear of death but instead are facing death directly, and they can thus feel their connectedness to e.g. other people which they didn't permit themselves to feel in embodied life. Thus the first step in opening our hearts to others is to banish our "fear of death" thought form.

Fear of death isn't necessary unless we live our whole lives on thought forms (mindlessly). If we are going to live our lives like automatons, then of course we need some sort of automatic reaction like fear of death to keep us from crossing the street when the light is red. Magicians, on the other hand, would feel death lurking there, and wouldn't even go near the intersection. But average people move about in a stupor of thought forms, so they need a fear of death thought form to keep them out of the more obvious difficulties at least. For all that, fear of death doesn't work nearly as well as being alert does.

Observe that in reality there is no such distinction as importance – but if we were to say that one is more important than the other, certainly our death is more important than (primary to) our life. Our life is just a symbolic reflection of our death; it's not the main issue at all. To think that our life is more important than our death is not only gross stupidity, but plays right into death's hands.

Death is neither malevolent or benevolent – it just is, like the force of gravity. Gravity can both hurt us and help us, depending upon how we use it (or let ourselves be used by it). So too with death. Death actually calls all the shots and we have to dance to its tune, really; but we can do that either elegantly or spasmodically. Master magicians waltz with death; caress it fondly; and then seduce it.

Importance is the means by which we consolidate death, or grab onto it (though what we believe we're doing is pushing it away). Importance is the illusion that we are controlling our death, when actually the reverse is the case. It's like hanging on for dear life to a runaway stallion and all the while trying to pretend that everything's just fine and dandy. The runaway stallion we cling to is death, and the pretense that we are in any way, shape, or form in charge of the situation is importance. It's what keeps us from enjoying the scenery as we gallop along.

Without our fear of death thought form we would be more aware of our past and probable lives (at least the feeling of them, if not the actual thought forms) as well as of the feelings of other people. We'd be able to feel them as our own feelings. And thus we'd lose much of our sense of individuality. That's how lunatics and magicians live: they still have individual lives, things happen to them, but there's less of a difference between something happening to them or to someone else. Something which happens to them is no more important than something which happens to someone else. Their feelings are no more important to them than someone else's feelings.

Death is the basic delimiter – the mechanism which separates light fibers into individual light fibers, and thought forms into individual thought forms. Our individual awareness is the product of our death – without our individual death we would have no individual awareness.

Our death is just a way we keep score, keep count, keep track of things: it's how we separate this moment from that one, and this lifetime from that lifetime, and me from you. Without death the whole thing would just be one big stew. Death is what props us up – if it were not for death we would not have any sense of there being an us there at all. After all, what are "we" anyway? The sum total of all our experiences (memories) and expectations (desires). Right? What else is there? Nothing, right?

We, of ourselves, are absolutely nothing. Zero. All we are is something that is going to die. That's the only reason we have life at all, is to die. We are something that death conjured up, as an afterthought, to give itself a raison d'etre. And then, once it created us, we took off like a lumbering Frankenstein monster, and it tagged along to watch what we did.

All death is doing is watching us. It doesn't approve or disapprove of what it sees; it isn't conscience or shame; it just watches dispassionately. And what we are is death watching itself. It has nothing to do with us whatever. We are just a reflection in death's mirror – a symbol for death. We have no primary awareness: just as the moon only reflects light, we only reflect (are a symbol of) death's awareness of itself. We only exist as death is watching itself through the metaphor of our lives.

And that's why we say that death is mind: because that sense that we have that we are being watched is our death watching us. Without our death there watching us, we are nothing – nothing but a little point on a random walk through an infinite jungle in which nothing makes any sense whatsoever – there is no rhyme nor reason to anything (no mind).

Mind (order) can only exist when there is something there watching the path that this random blip on the screen is taking. And that's what we call death. Just as each individual thought form has a life of its own, so too does the collection as a whole, which we call "ourselves". What binds all those thought forms together into an organized whole is our death. Many of those very same thought forms are bound together in quite different forms of organization (by other deaths) and these are the probable realities related to this same lifetime.

On the next level up come all of our past and future lives, which taken together with this lifetime and its probable realities form a "Super-Us" entity which we have called our dream mind. Just as on a waking level we separate ourselves from (forget) all our other waking selves in other lifetimes and probable realities, so too on a dream level do we separate ourselves from other people, and other beings generally.

The next level up is dreamless sleep, in which all there is, is unity (no thought forms). It is only by remembering the feeling of this level, which everyone experiences every night, in our everyday waking consciousness that we can hope to truly unite with other people. To unite with other people in waking consciousness, to truly feel with them, means to overcome all sense of importance with them. This feeling of non-importance is not something we have to conjure up from scratch: we know this feeling better than we know our own selves; it is as deep as we go – we have only to remember it. It's right there in front of our eyes all the time, staring us right in the face, but we're too busy being distracted by this or that important thing to stop and *see* it.

A Brief History of Consciousness
(with Future Prospects)

To an infant, being awake is similar to what dreaming is like to an adult – inexplicable, but somehow or other you manage to muddle through. Dreams are what everyday life would be like if we didn't have importance riding herd over it. The things which happen in dreams are more symbolic of pure feeling – there's not this constant sense of who we are, and what we're after, and how we can make a buck out of it, and everything else society has taught us, pulling all the strings. If we stopped using importance so much – as magicians and lunatics do – then the everyday world would be more like dreaming: it would be even weirder than it is.

In fact, the everyday world is just as chaotic and out of control as the dream world, but we pretend that it isn't. We pretend that this is all reasonable and rational and ordered. That's what everybody validates for everyone else: we concentrate all our attention on seeking this validation from other people, all of us scratching each other's backs.

The difference between dream mind and waking mind is that in dream mind we are not constantly referring things to other people for validation. Accomplished dreamers get as much (more!) self-validation from their dreams as most of us waking folk get from the rewards and back-patting – or excoriation and rejection, as the case may be – of other people. In dreams we go by how we *feel*; not by what the neighbors might say. In dreams we are not seeking the validation of others, but are validating ourselves.

The specialized emotions (anger, lust, fear, joy, etc.) are the equivalent in the dream realm of thought forms in the waking realm. Light fibers are just light fibers – it's dreamless sleep which separates them into distinct "emotion forms" such as anger, lust, fear, etc., and then passes them up to dream mind, which attaches sensory thought form events to them; or up to waking mind, which attaches conceptual thought forms (memories or desires) to them and identifies these with a past or future in a continuous personal history. Dreamless sleep itself is difficult to talk about except to say that just as waking consciousness is the tiniest cork adrift on the sea of dreaming, so too is dream consciousness the merest bubble of froth on the sea which lies beneath it.

Most of us have all our awareness tied up in the world of waking consciousness (we can't even remember our dreams – that's how little importance we give dreaming). Waking consciousness is where we are the most alert, eager, and animated; we have little awareness tied up in the world of dreams, hence we tend to find the dream state chaotic and unmanageable – we are uncomprehending observers there. Things happen to us in dreams and we react to them and try to deal with them, but for the most part we remain passive, shuffled around by events, instead of being active participants.

By contrast, many of the people whom society considers primitive or savage, simple or crazy, spaced–out or irresponsible generally, are people who just happen to have little of their awareness tied up in the waking world. They find the waking world chaotic and incomprehensible. Most of their attention, interest, enthusiasm, sense of fit place, ambition (if you want to call it that) are centered in their dreams. Their dreams have zest and spice, and give them the freedom and scope and sense of purpose that the rest of us find in the waking world.

Although we still create thought forms in dreams, the medium of the dream state is a lot faster than is the medium of the waking state. It's like the difference between walking through air and walking through water – things are faster in air, slow-motion and sluggish in water. Similarly, the very stuff of waking consciousness is more viscous than the stuff of dream consciousness – conceptual thought forms are heavier and slower-moving than sensory thought forms. It takes a long time for things to happen in waking consciousness – things go on and on for years without changing very much; there's a lot of repetition of the same old crap over and over and over. Whereas in dream consciousness things change fast:

a slight pang of fear and WHAM! – there's a monster there. One has to be very alert and nimble to change with it.

It requires a great deal more skill to be a good dreamer than it does to be a success in the waking world where, after all, the only thing required is to be a good robot. Thus society's greatest artists are actually to be found among its most "useless" members. If it weren't for the lunatics and simpletons (and a handful of magicians) among us who are holding the two worlds together for us, all of us would be truly lost – completely caught up in self-hatred and self-destruction. Note, however, that some so-called irresponsible people are actually quite centered in the waking world, and their lunacy or irresponsibility is merely a pose or protection. E.g. most alcoholics fall into this category – they are not true dreamers.

The reason why the dream state is so mutable is that there is little sense of separatedness in it. It is importance which stabilizes attention; the attention we have in dreams has little importance to it, so we can't control what we will pay attention to (what will happen next). Whether we are dream artists or dum-dums on the dream plane, what we experience there is far more immediate, vivid, gripping, and intense than in the ordered waking world. It all happens so fast that we can't separate ourselves from it as we can and do in waking life. We don't get weekends off and two weeks paid vacation in the world of dreams, and there's no TV to watch – no way to make it stop happening or pretend it's not happening. We must either be on the qui vive every instant (as true dreamers are), or else stand there in a stupor (as most of the rest of us do); but we are inevitably so caught up in it, so much a part of it, that although we are experiencing our feelings in symbolic form in dreams, there is little sense of separation there. Mind exists, but it's not developed.

Mind cannot develop until there is a clearly defined sense of separatedness, which gives mind a pause, a moment's rest or leisure, in which it can reflect on itself. It's that moment's rest or lull which gives birth to a sense of time and linear continuity.

Waking mind is actually a complete illusion – like the insouciance of a drunkard staggering across a battlefield where bullets whiz by all around him but who is somehow protected from it all by his blissful indifference. *That* is waking mind. It is so totally a fiction (the sense that we are separate from everything around us) that it can only be maintained by the constant validation of other people. Only by all of us reassuring one another constantly that we are separate individuals (thought forms) can we jointly uphold the fragile structure of waking consciousness.

What happens in *lucid dreaming* is that all of a sudden we become aware that we are dreaming: we wake up within a dream and consciously realize that we are asleep. At that moment we activate our separatedness thought form in the dream state; we become self-conscious in the dream state; we separate ourselves from it and watch ourselves acting – just as we do in waking consciousness. Once we've activated the separatedness thought form within a dream, we can then call upon any and all of the thought forms which arise as a consequence of separatedness. That is to say, we can bring reason in to run dream consciousness. Lucid dreaming is our task as human beings – our joint intent; the reason why we're here.

The theory of evolution is somewhat correct in its assertion that all life on earth evolved from one-celled beings. But actually physical evolution is just a notation, a symbol for what is really going on, and that is the development of consciousness.

We can infer an evolution prior to mitosis; according to the materialistic view it goes: gas cloud – star – planet cooled – land and water separated – atmosphere developed – i.e. all the requisites of what materialists term "life" came about and then "life" happened. But from the magical point of view – even accepting the materialistic model – consciousness was present all along and guided this evolution. It didn't spring into existence at mitosis – it just took a radically different form. It began to employ thought forms, which had not existed heretofore – at least not in this corner of the universe.

The materialists are correct in asserting that evolution does occur through random processes; however selection is a matter of the Spirit. Although there is a guiding intelligence directing evolution, this guiding mind has to patiently wait upon the fortuitous conjunction of random events (like the five pick-up sticks falling into the shape of a star) in order to further its intent. Indeed, this is precisely the manner in which magicians must patiently wait upon the Spirit in order to further their own intent.

At a certain point in history, which we shall call the invention of mitosis, there appeared one primordial cell, which was and is and will be forevermore the great-great-great-great-grandmammy of us all. And this cell began to reproduce by dividing.

Note that there is no a priori way of determining which way evolution (time) is running. We consider that we are a higher form of life than one-celled beings, so we suppose we came after one-celled beings in the evolutionary scheme. But viewed objectively, all one-celled beings are immortal, selfless, and exist in a state of nirvana – precisely the goals which we are supposedly striving to emulate in our spiritual practice (en passant, when a one-celled being divides, it has an orgasm which makes our orgasms seem tepid by comparison). So who is to say which is the "higher" form of life?

As mentioned previously, the consciousness of a one-celled being comprises the sum total of all of its ramifications (antecedents and descendants). Although individual ramifications may have individual experiences which are sensory thought forms – e.g., this one may desiccate and die; that one may find a rich food source and prosper; the other one may imperfectly divide and mutate; nonetheless the consciousness of a one-celled being is unified: it experiences all these individual happenings simultaneously, in an eternal now, rather than sequentially. Cf. human survivors of near-death experiences, who often report having seen all of the events of their entire lives flash by them, one scene at a time, in no time at all: that's how a one-celled being perceives its lives. To a one-celled being there is no sense of precedence (time) – the child is truly the father of the man. To a one-celled being it is impossible to determine whether time runs forwards or backwards – whether a single ramification divided (the way we see it) or whether two ramifications united. And one-celled beings are immortal: although individual ramifications may cease to exist, the being as a whole lives forever. Indeed, all multi-cellular beings on this earth are descended from the same single primordial cell, which is why we are all one: we are not separate entities at all but just ramifications of that primordial first living cell. We're like different fingers on the same hand, but we are united in dreamless sleep.

Dream consciousness, the consciousness of one-celled beings, consists primarily of feelings (thought forms are secondary). One-celled beings, like human beings, are capable of feeling hunger, thirst, joy, love, satiation, etc., as well as a host of other feelings which humans can't access. These feelings – the stuff of dream consciousness – are made of orgasm. I.e. one-celled beings exist in a mood (or frame of mind, if you want to call it that) which very closely resembles what we call orgasm, which is why they can't get very much accomplished. They have very little sense of self-existence because their normal experience of being in the world is so intense.

What we call individual self-existence – as well as sex and death – came about at the same point in history, and thus can be considered to be different aspects of the same phenomenon. All one-celled beings may be considered to be females, and their sexuality (whether considered as division – as we see it; or union – as they see it) is homosexual. At a certain point, which we shall call the invention of meiosis, one particular cell mutated when it divided and formed a male, which began to swim around and inject its DNA into its sisters. In a sense, the male sex is like a disease to the female sex, which then became incapable of reproducing without it. Half the infected offspring carry the disease of females, which is being male.

Nonetheless, the consciousness of meiosis (waking consciousness) was actually a great improvement over the consciousness of mitosis (dream consciousness) because of the greater degree of order and stability it afforded. The consciousness of individual ramifications – now called past and future lives, and probable realities – was enhanced at the expense of a sense of wholeness and unity. Individual ramifications came to have a greater consciousness of self – a watcher, a detached observer, a mind, an individual death. The distinction between sleeping and waking also arose with meiosis – indeed, all duality arose with meiosis, as did time.

When did the Mona Lisa come into existence? When Leonardo painted it? It can be argued that all those atoms and molecules in the paint and canvas always existed, long before Leonardo came along. So too did time exist before meiosis, but only when multi-celled life came along was time arranged in a pattern of importance. Time did not exist before meiosis because one-celled life doesn't have the wherewithal to experience time, just as time is less there in the dream state than in the waking state.

The following chart summarizes the differences between single- and multi- cellular consciousness:

SINGLE-CELLED LIFE	MULTI-CELLED LIFE
Dream consciousness (sensory thought forms) Awareness in space but not time Little sense of individual self	Waking consciousness (conceptual thought forms) Awareness in space and time Strong sense of individual self

IS IMMORTAL	DIES
Individual cells die, but a one-celled being lives in the awareness of all its antecedents and descendants. No division made between conscious and unconscious – everything is NOW.	Total consciousness divided into many different past and future lives which do not consciously remember one another. Memory compartmentalized.

SINGLE SEX	MALE & FEMALE SEXES
Single-celled life is all female and is narcissistic (homosexual) in orientation. Thus homosexuality is the root sexual impulse, and heterosexuality was grafted on later, at meiosis.	Heterosexuality arose with the invention of the male sex. Thus females (generally) are still basically homosexual, where males (generally) are basically heterosexual.

Unlike single-celled beings, we multi-celled beings limit our awareness to a single ramification of the totality of ourselves: we forget our past lives, future lives, and all the probable realities that branch off from our present life (ramification). We still pass information between individual ramifications of our selves, as one-celled beings do, but we do this subconsciously, in dreamless sleep (we are united in consciousness with all our past and future lives in dreamless sleep). In waking awareness, however, we forget or ignore this information, just as play- or movie-goers ignore the fact that what they are experiencing isn't really happening. The advantage of this division into separate pieces is that there is much greater focus within each piece – our consciousness is far more intricate and elaborate than that of a one-celled being.

Another way of saying this is that our waking consciousness is created by toning down or filtering out the intensity of feeling; just as the feeling consciousness of one-celled beings is created by toning down or filtering out the intensity of primal orgasm. Orgasm (white light fibers) is the basic raw material out of which everything is made.

The next major step after meiosis – from our human standpoint, at least – was the invention of agriculture some 12,000 years ago. Up until that time human beings, like other animals, operated fundamentally on feeling and instinct. If we were to encounter today a human from as recently as 20,000 years ago, we would consider it to be an animal: there's no level on which we modern humans would regard it as being what we consider to be human. The transformation in consciousness from animals to thinkers was accomplished by repressing feeling. The natural state of consciousness of animals and infant humans, as well as lunatics, is feeling – they are incapable of all but the most rudimentary thought processes (note that memory – and hence learning – is not yet thinking). Thinking can only take place when feeling is held in abeyance (repressed). Thinking and feeling cannot take place at the same time – feeling takes place in the now moment (thus sensory thought forms are basically just feelings); whereas thinking, although it takes place in the now moment, is primarily concerned with past or future (the content of conceptual thought forms consists of events that have happened or will happen). The device which is used to repress feeling and make thinking possible – as we have mentioned before – is importance; i.e. in order to think, something must be considered to be more important to pay attention to than what is going on (being felt) in the now moment. Importance is clenching up – it is the denial of relaxation and peacefulness. The humans who invented agriculture implemented importance with two basic techniques: 1) Control of the body's urge to defecate; and 2) Control of the body's somnolence.

What happened at about the time that agriculture was invented was that humans adapted the basic "constant vigilance for a predator" thought form, which is common to many animals, to the abstract and symbolic act of toilet training. Heretofore humans, like most animals, would defecate where they list. They could hold their excrement in for short periods of time, as cats and pigs do, so as not to foul their nests; but they were unable to hold it in for anywhere near the length of time that we modern humans can do. Indeed, this is basically the only difference between us and our pre-agricultural ancestors; all civilization takes off from toilet training, and so does most of our suffering. We modern humans walk around all day long with a major piece of our attention focused upon our sphincters, but we get so accustomed to maintaining this unnatural pose of constant vigilance and fear of soiling ourselves that we take it completely for granted, and don't realize how much energy we have tied up in it, much less see that it is the reason we are so uptight and unhappy all the time.

Now it is true that babies can usually talk before they are toilet trained; moreover, it's obvious that some babies (at least) are quite aware of what e.g. money is even before they are able to talk. Thus it is obvious that humans are able to think before they are toilet trained; however, this thinking is discursive and unfocused. It only becomes truly constructive when it is sustained and focused, which requires that it be undergirded by importance – the constant, moment-to-moment denial of relaxation – which only occurs after toilet training. Thus toilet training is the cornerstone of our inner dialogue: our inner dialogue is a constant repetition of the thought form "I exist!", "I exist!" ("Glory!", "Glory!") – hence it is the basis for our sense of continuity and individual self-existence. If we stop our inner dialogue (through mental training, or shock) then obviously our sense of continuity and individual self-existence ceases also.

Toilet training is a masterful invention – control of the sphincter necessitates control of the mind (constant vigilance). It is the matrix of what will later become sexual and emotional repression: holding in our feces becomes a symbol for holding in our anger at our parents for having foisted toilet training on us – we fear our anger at our parents and repress it at the same time we repress our desire to defecate. This repression of anger is our entry point into participation in modern society.

The second great pillar upon which modern human civilization is based – which also involves repressing anger and frustration – is sleep deprivation. Our hunter ancestors were basically doing what we would call dreaming as their normal mode of being. There wasn't such a sharp distinction between being awake and being asleep. Then people slept in snatches, as infants do, and they alternated hunting off and on with dozing. Most of their hunting was done in a state of mind that we would call sleepwalking (a trance state). Sometimes people who are very ill or dying get into that state, where they are half asleep and half awake and not differentiating between what is dreams and what is awake. But hunters, unlike the sick person, were very alert and active in that state.

Ancient humans were more magical than we are. They permitted dream material to freely intrude into their awareness, whereas we moderns have mechanisms in place to immediately repress any such intrusion into our reality. Separation of time into 16 hours of wakefulness and 8 hours of dreaming – forcing our bodies to stay awake for such a long stretch of time – is as stern a discipline as toilet training, and helps block the intrusion of dream material (magical events) into wakefulness. Ancient humans mixed the two together in their awareness – waking life was as ineffable as dreaming, and everything was a source of wonder and mystery. We moderns have learned to tone down our sensory impressions, to take everything around us for granted by not paying attention to anything except our own incessant mental chatter. This makes our lives utterly boring and meaningless, but nonetheless provides us with our ability to focus our attention, to be methodical, concentrated and deliberate.

Although waking consciousness originated with meiosis, the invention of agriculture was its apotheosis: order, regularity, sleep 8 hours at night and work 16 hours during the day. Humankind had outgrown dream consciousness; it had found dream consciousness too unstable, too ephemeral, and therefore too limiting for its free expression. Therefore it literally constructed, piece by piece, thought form by thought form, over the surface of dream consciousness, the floating edifice of waking consciousness. Humankind began to think and reason.

The first and most basic separation was the sharpening of the duality of being asleep versus being awake (which duality originally arose with meiosis). Pretty much all serious attention was put on wakefulness at the expense of dreaming. This was necessary to stabilize waking consciousness. When dream stuff intrudes into waking consciousness we get moments of discontinuity, and this just won't do. It's bad technique. We can't have differential calculus then. We have to say that discontinuity is unreal, and that people who experience discontinuity are crazy, or tired and overworked and in need of rest. We have to pretend that discontinuity doesn't exist in order to stabilize wakefulness: any sudden start or shock or fright is a rift in our sense of continuity – or better said, a mad grab for our sense of continuity to mask such a rift. We have to get everyone to validate this pretense – to pretend that they're not experiencing discontinuity. It's a valiant effort, but it takes a heavy toll. Inevitably we crack; we lose our grip; and at that moment we are forced to (horror of horrors) feel feelings! This happens when we experience crises in life – the feelings we have been repressing to sustain waking consciousness just pour out, and mind invents some little notation or other ("My spouse died!", "I have AIDS!", "I'm bankrupt!", or whatever) as the reason we are feeling those feelings. But in fact the feelings are primary; the thought form is conjured up after the fact to give us an excuse to *feel*.

The reason why society finds it necessary to so stringently regulate all interpersonal contacts, to make them as unfeeling and loveless as possible, to turn even the joy of childbirth or the resignation of death into sterile medical procedures, is because if everyone all of a sudden woke up out of waking consciousness and realized that we are not all separated, that everything is all connected, then the fragile structure of waking consciousness which humankind has struggled and sacrificed for millennia to painstakingly erect would collapse.

Lucid dreaming is the capstone of why the human race started all this business back at the invention of agriculture. It was in a position similar to that of a baby who first notices that he has a hand there that he can spasmodically control, and which he wants to develop into a useful tool instead of a curiosity moving hither and thither, only vaguely subject to conscious manipulation.

So too humans found that their dream consciousness, to which they were as ably adapted as a fish to its watery environment, nonetheless was capable of greater development and definition. They wanted to give it a shot, just for the hell of it. That's the nature of the human spirit – curiosity. That's why humans developed thinking and lions (for example) didn't. Lions aren't very curious; lions are lazy, they're not into so much of a struggle ethic as humans are; also they are better adapted to their environment and so have less of a need to be clever. Although all animals can think and learn (create thought forms and empower them with light fibers), none of them has developed the faculty of mind to anything like the extent humans have done. That is merely humans' particular intent in this particular reality, just as vultures eat carrion and fireflies blink. There are other versions of this same reality in which animals other than humans developed consciousness to its ultimate perfection (such as the land of the Houyhnhnms, which is in no way less real than this world we live in). Humans did this as part of what might be termed a bargain or business deal, between what might be termed the human God, and what might be termed the gods of the other animals, on what might be termed earth, in what might be termed millennia ago in this so-called time-space reality. However, the whole thing is just one mad, crazy dream.

What was actually invented at the time agriculture came about, was the lie. On the dream plane, in the realm of feelings, it is impossible to dissemble. We humans were taught how to lie by demon advisors, whom we called in to teach us what they knew (humans had always been in close touch with the spirit realm; but only in the last few thousand years before the invention of agriculture did they come under the direct influence of demons). In other words, the invention of agriculture was the point at which the human race forged a blood alliance with the race of demons, who raised us up from animaldom and helped us become something more like them. Agriculture wasn't so much a matter of humans domesticating and farming plants and animals for their own use as it was the demons domesticating and farming humans for their own use: to suck our energy – the froth of our despair, frustration, and anger. This point is perhaps the main difference in belief between Christians and magicians (besides the viewpoint of God as caring versus the viewpoint of God as completely indifferent): Christians believe that humans were formed in the image of God, whereas magicians believe that humans – at least modern, thinking humans – were formed in the image of Satan. What both belief systems have in common is a fall from a state of primeval grace.

Philosophers of language tend to be fond of extolling the glories of human language as our "triumph" over the animal kingdom. In point of fact, language is but a vestigial remnant of humans' primordial telepathic ability, which we moderns have been taught to repress along with our other senses. However, we modern humans still rely upon our latent telepathic powers when language fails us. For example:

1) Mothers know exactly what their babies want; some mothers even let their milk down a few minutes before their babies wake up.

2) Lovers know the exact instant that the decision is made to go to bed together for the first time.

3) In foreign countries, we usually know exactly what they're saying to us, even if we don't know a word of their language.

4) We often know when we're being observed from afar (lift our eyes from reverie to the exact spot from which

someone is watching us); this awareness is a remnant from our hunting days.

5) We often recognize someone we know from way far away, long before we can make out their features, posture, or gait.

6) And, of course, prophetic dreams, precognition, intuitive hunches – the types of so-called ESP that practically all of us have experienced at one time or another but cannot consciously control, but which our forebears relied upon in place of thinking and language. To them it wasn't "E"SP – it was a normal part of SP.

These sorts of telepathic communications are not a matter of body language or subliminal cues (as the materialists would have it); rather, they are examples of true telepathy, which was a part of humankind's original equipment.

The most important concomitant of the invention of agriculture was the invention of the lie. As long as people could communicate telepathically, lies were not within the realm of possibility, since everyone knew exactly what everyone else was feeling every minute. Similarly, even we modern humans are not as easily fooled when we're dreaming as when we're awake: in dreams we can sense exactly who or what is evil or to be avoided, in spite of superficial appearances.

When mindlessness replaced mindfulness, thinking replaced feeling, and the inner dialogue replaced paying attention to the now moment, on a social level verbal communication replaced telepathy. And the gist of verbal communication is the lie: all thinking is a lie, in the sense that it is the denial of feeling, of not paying attention to the now moment. IT'S ALL A LIE. That's the gist of waking consciousness. All rationalism comes down to science; and all science comes down to mathematics; and all mathematics comes down to logic; and all logic comes down to a proposition known as The Law of the Excluded Middle, which states, in effect, that "either a statement is true, or else it is false." And that statement is false. The ability to lie – to ourselves, and other people – is what "elevates" us above the rest of the animal kingdom, and enables us to work hand-in-hand with demons.

Demon consciousness is far more elaborate, refined, and aesthetic (you might say) than human consciousness. In fact, demons are as far above humans, consciousness-wise, as humans are above animals; and their opinion of us is about like our opinion of animals. On the other hand, they are even nastier and more uptight than humans are (further separated from the Spirit). Actually, they're pretty slimy and sleazy. The point is that it's the demons who taught us how to lie, and the lie is what makes modern society, which is a pack of lies, possible. When good faith and mutual respect are gone, lawyers and contracts and lists of duties and obligations are necessary.

Humans, guided by their demon mentors, intuitively perceived that a greater degree of mind would result from a greater sense of separatedness. And so, over millennia, by painful trial and error, they tried different experiments in separatedness. Agriculture was the big move, and then it got into greater degrees of division of labor and social complexity. Humankind went on a rambling, meandering walk for several thousand years. And it discovered that any separatedness which depends upon denial of true feelings will only lead to self-hatred and self-destruction.

And now, at this time, humankind has pretty much reached the limits of waking consciousness, having cut itself off from its very roots in dream consciousness. It will now enter into lucid dreaming. Dream consciousness is too erratic and mutable; waking consciousness is too ordered and routinized. Only in lucid dreaming do we have a healthy balance of mind and feeling working together (instead of one dominating the other). Lucid dreaming is the true union of reason and direct feeling – it is our true estate and destiny (For an excellent nuts-and-bolts approach to the practice of lucid dreaming, see *Exploring the World of Lucid Dreaming* by Stephen LaBerge and Howard Rheingold). It is the reason why humankind, at the time of the invention of agriculture, explored and refined waking consciousness. At that time waking consciousness was to humankind what lucid dreaming is to us today: a new frontier to explore and develop.

Lucid dreaming allows us to take a pause for reflection on the dream plane – to make it stop happening for a moment to critically evaluate and redirect the experience, instead of being wholly caught up in it, forced to be constantly shifting and adjusting ourselves to it, as our hunter forebears had to do. Hunters had to more or less go with the flow, and they were better or worse hunters as they were able to be flexible and quick to see and grasp opportunities and avoid pitfalls as they arose. They were nimble, but not very capable of planning, organizing, or thinking things through. If there was an easier way to do something, they probably wouldn't have been able to figure it out (not enough separatedness).

The great triumph of waking consciousness is the high degree of corroboration or validation by consensus available in it; this is the very gist of waking consciousness. We can't do it in dream consciousness (except now and again, like ships that pass in the night). When we are asleep we are having as many (nay – more!) interactions with the people around us as when we are with them in waking consciousness. The only difference is that it's fuzzier – we cannot bring it all into focus together. This is why waking consciousness was invented – to be able to get that kind of consensual validation which is not possible in dreams (the fact that it's all a lie is not the point – the point is that we can do it at all). This is the reason for the development of consciousness in the first place, as a means of joining together – gluing all the pieces back together.

The important thing to remember about consensual validation is that it is completely an illusion, a pretense, a lie. We are not; repeat NOT seeing the same thing (partaking of the same reality) when we look at something. There is NO objective, external reality out there. Society just has us convinced that we are all seeing the same thing because it has all our attention pinned down to the things we can agree on.

If we suddenly found ourselves plopped down in another person's body, with all that person's perceptions, we'd think we'd landed on Mars. We all know what it's like having to work for or with an extremely dominating and overbearing person whom we can't tell off (e.g. a parent, teacher, or boss). We have to bend ourselves completely out of whack to deal with such a person's weird adaptation to the world. But actually everyone's world view and perceptions are that alien to our own, except that we don't usually notice it since society has us paper over it, unless for some reason (e.g. that we're their children, or married to them) they're shoving it down our throats.

Society has us all make an agreement that instead of feeling together through the unblocked light fibers between us, which would be true agreement, we instead block the fibers between us with importance and pretend to agree on a thought form level. In other words, the supposed agreement that we're all seeing the same thing when we look at something is a pretense – we are only pretending to see the same thing. Children are trained to see what the adults around them are seeing, i.e., to agree with the adults around them on what their eyes are telling them. But magicians (or lunatics) looking at the same scene won't necessarily see the same thing at all, because they don't have the same expectations of what is being seen.

For example, a magician or lunatic looking at a banana tree sees a happy, waving creature who is just bursting with joy and doing a little dance in the breeze. But that is not what an average person sees who is looking at that same banana tree. Since nobody wants to come out and say that the emperor is stark naked for fear of being thought a lunatic, everybody pretends to agree that "Yes, this is a tree" or "Yes, that is a rock", etc. "Tree" or "rock" are just thought forms that we all agree on, in precisely the same way that we all agree on the English language. We all speak English; similarly, we all see a rock there. But not everyone speaks English, and not everyone is going to see a rock there in the same sense in which we do.

The function of separatedness is to make things stop happening for a moment, and in that hiatus people can get together and say, "That is a rock", and have everyone else agree on it. All these agreements between people are *not* cordial affairs. They're made (at least in our society) with threats of force and violence. A baby reaches to touch his penis and the hand is pushed away; if he continues, the hand is slapped. If we see a rock as something other than a "rock" and have the temerity to voice our opinion, we're locked up in a loony bin. So fundamentally we all agree that a rock is a "rock" because we're terrified of it being something else.

So we say (to ourselves and to others), "Okay, that's a rock – a dead, inert piece of nonliving matter, whose only importance is to give me something I can be more important than." We cut off our light fibers which go to that rock, and the light fibers which go to everyone else in the world through that rock, and we all say "That's just a piece of inert matter." We can all agree on that because we all have our light fibers blocked up by that same thought form.

Now a rock wasn't a "rock" until someone came along and attached that thought form to it for everyone else. Somebody had to invent that "rock" in the first place. For example, it is correct to say that the Renaissance artists invented perspective. Before that time people's visual perception of the world was like a jumble on a flat field (as medieval paintings – and primitive people's paintings to this day – attest). It wasn't that medieval artists weren't competent painters – on the contrary, they were faithfully reproducing the world as they saw it – they were dreaming in their everyday lives more than we do today. They didn't see depth in the same sense in which we do. We owe our depth perception to the Renaissance artists who invented that thought form for everyone else.

Similarly, we create our body thought form and secure agreement from everyone else as to what it looks like. We all do that for each other; we create the waking world together. But it isn't the same for all of us, as we suppose it to be (e.g. we look very different to the people who are madly in love with us than we do to the people who can't stand the sight of us).

Our problem is that the world doesn't look the same to us on a thought form level, and yet we're all trying to force each other to see it our way. For example, if there's an object in front of us, we first of all agree on whether or not it has any value, or importance. If it does, then we agree on who owns it. We all agree to see that object as an object with certain attributes. Once we can all agree that a rock is nothing more than non-living, inert matter – if we can get agreement to that fantastically egregious distortion of reality – then getting agreement on the details (size, color, shape, etc.) isn't that hard. It's just a matter of calling one wavelength of light "red" and another one "blue", etc. We all call that one "blue"; but how do we know that we're all seeing the same thing when we call something "blue"?

The fact of the matter is that we *aren't* seeing the same thing. We're all seeing vaguely the same thing, as we also do in normal dreaming; but some people are more intuitive or spaced-out and experience that thing on more of a feeling level than others. We all know that colors, for example, can evoke certain emotions; for some intuitive (and crazy) people, the emotion is actually far more pronounced than the visual sensation of the color (which is but a thought form notation of the feeling, which most people get hung up on).

What is so frustrating about waking consciousness is that we can get other people to validate some of our importance categories for us, but not all. Worlds in which everybody validates everyone else's thought forms are called heaven worlds, and worlds in which nobody will validate anything for anybody else on any level are called hell worlds (there's pretty much total isolation in such places). Here on earth we're about in the middle: we can get people to agree that a rock is a "rock", but we can't always get them to agree that we are wonderful and loveable and terrific. The rock doesn't bang into their own importance agendas like the intangible stuff does. It's the itchiness of being unable to get total validation that runs our society: the sense of nonfulfillment, the drive to connect on a thought form level (where such connection cannot take place), is what keeps society humming.

Part of the agreement we all make is that not only will we agree on what is happening (on a thought form level at least), but we will also agree on what has happened and will happen. We all get together and agree on probable pasts and futures. The very purpose of waking consciousness, we might say, was to obtain as high a degree of consensual validation among humans as possible: everybody agreeing on what they were seeing and experiencing as a means of joining together.

But what happened was that the consensual validation became the important thing, and the joining together was forgotten. Everybody agreed that it was important to get everyone else to agree with what they were seeing and experiencing, but they fell to fighting among themselves to try to force one another to agree. The minimum compromise of what most people could agree on is what we call "society".

So people forgot why they had developed consensual validation, and threw themselves wholly into consensual validation until they got pretty much everybody in the whole world connected up to the same network of wires and radio waves. Importance was important in the development of consensual validation, for how else could society get itself together except as an agreement? What was wrong was making validation from other people the most important thing – even more important than joining with them.

Importance is the feeling of having a blocked light fiber. People blocked up the light fibers between them, which gave them a sense of urgency to try to unblock those fibers, and then they redirected that sense of urgency into forcing each other to agree with them. They began to use the fibers to suck each other rather than to give and take (love).

Importance is not itself a thought form, but rather a thought form covering. It is a feeling – or rather, the denial of a feeling. It is a casing, like a sausage casing, into which a light fiber can be stuffed, and it is controlled by the thought form which created it. In a manner of speaking, importance coverings are our thought forms' thought forms. Just as the Spirit does for us, we give our thought forms a certain amount of independence. Actually, about all we can do is to create them and destroy them; other than that, they roll their own. And we are subject to their control, just as the Spirit is subject to our control. If we don't like the way some of our thought forms jerk us around, how do you suppose the Spirit feels about us some of the time?

Not only are we subject to our thought forms, but we are also subject to our thought forms' thought forms – the light fiber energy which we gave our thought forms originally, which they have in turn bestowed upon their importance coverings. Thought forms don't persist from lifetime to lifetime, but these importance coverings do. They try to recreate banished thought forms, and to reconstruct similar thought forms in different lifetimes.

When we go into past life regressions the first thing we can attach to are the importance coverings, not the thought forms, of a particular life. We reconstruct the thought forms which were attached to the light fibers later (i.e., we first feel the feelings, and only later do we understand "why"– what situation produced those feelings).

The reason why we substitute thought forms (at least conceptual thought forms) for light fibers in the first place is because it seems important enough to remember them for future reference. Their importance coverings make some thought forms more important in our estimation than others, and make waking consciousness more important to us than dream consciousness.

Nothing is more important than anything else in a dream. True, we can have dreams in which we are striving for something that is important to us, or trying to avoid something which thereby becomes important to us. But this is merely dreaming about importance; importance doesn't undergird the entire dream state as it does waking consciousness. Waking consciousness is a "Great Chain of Being" in which some things are more important than others. Just because we may strive to achieve something in a dream doesn't mean that it's important to us to achieve it – it just means that we're striving to achieve it. Maybe the next moment we'll be off somewhere else and have lost all interest in what we were so mightily striving for a minute ago. If something we are striving for is important to us (more important to achieve it than not achieve it), then we're not dreaming – we're awake. The feeling of importance still exists in the dream state to the extent that we still feel that there is an "us" there; however our "usness" is more sporadic than in wakefulness; we're not constantly checking back on it to make sure we're still there, like we do when we're awake. In fact, that's the definition of going to sleep – laying down our self-importance, our sense of personal control and continuity, our phoniness, when the strain of maintaining this position becomes overwhelming. We get tired and go to sleep. This is an act of great trust and love, which is why we enjoy going to sleep so much: it's about the only act which most of us perform in our daily lives which is in line with our true feelings.

The importance which is still present in dreaming – more familiarity than importance qua importance – is minimal. For example, we still have a human body in dreams, not an animal body or an amorphous "self". That's because of importance: it is still important in dreams to have a human body, so we keep it. If we lost all importance there would be no sense of an "I" there at all – no dichotomy between perceiver and perceived, no thought forms. That is what dreamless sleep is like – it's all ONE – no distinctions are made between anything. Nonetheless decision-making still takes place in dreamless sleep, even though, from the standpoint of waking consciousness, there's no one to decide anything and nothing to be decided.

The half of humanity which is awake (on the other side of the globe) keeps the general thought form structure intact for the people who are asleep; and then they hand it over to the awake ones and go to sleep themselves. Similarly, the "useless" people who are more alive on the dream plane than the waking plane are holding all of humanity to its roots in dream consciousness; the rest of humanity couldn't go to sleep if there were not some humans who were holding that doorway open. There are hell worlds in which everyone is awake all the time – indeed, that's the definition of a hell world. There's no one around to show the others how to reenter the dream state. This is all done with light fibers; the

Chinese don't have to phone the Americans to tell them its time to wake up, nor do people have to go to a primitive tribe or lunatic asylum to be able to go to sleep. All humans are connected on a light fiber level, and they pass this information back and forth on that level.

Another way of looking at it is: among our infinite selves in other lifetimes and probable realities, there are some magicians, lunatics, etc. who are keeping the totality of our being rooted in the dream state, no matter how seemingly entrapped in waking consciousness the rest of our selves are.

What happens in lucid dreaming is that we preserve the thought forms of waking consciousness, but without their coverings of importance; that is to say, lucid dreaming is waking consciousness sans importance – it's what waking consciousness could be (and will be) like when we get rid of our importance. To do lucid dreaming consistently we have to loosen the thought form coverings in the waking state: i.e., come to a general conviction in our daily lives that nothing is all that important. The exercises in the next chapter are designed to help lose importance.

The point is that the thought forms of waking consciousness can be activated in the dream state once they have been cut loose from their importance coverings. To go to sleep without the thought forms of waking consciousness (separatedness) is to discard 12,000 years of human history. The hunters of old could just go to sleep and dream. What we can do that they couldn't do is bring separatedness to bear upon that state.

In lucid dreaming we are not actually centered in any given lifetime. It's like being on the main platform of a train station: from there we can take any number of tracks and go on any number of journeys, but we do keep our ticket for a return train on the track by which we arrived at the station. As long as we keep our return ticket intact we can always return to the track (lifetime) from which we started. After we die, we are also in lucid dreaming, but without a return ticket. We also find ourselves in that train station every night, in our dreams, but we usually don't stray too far from the track we came in on: the thought forms of our present lifetime, which make up most of the material of normal dreaming. Also, we're not usually there lucidly.

What pulls us back to this lifetime (has us keep waking up in this one) are light fibers which we have attached to this lifetime and its thought forms. That's what pulls everyone back out of dreamless sleep. Actually dreamless sleep is the real thing – this lifetime is like a kite tethered to dreamless sleep by a light fiber.

Death takes a different form in lucid dreaming than it does in waking consciousness. In lucid dreaming we are facing our death every moment, whereas in waking consciousness we are ignoring our death most of the time – screening it out with thought forms, "fear of death" and its derivatives (that we use to cover our fear of death) being the basic ones. Separatedness can still exist in lucid dreaming because the state of lucid dreaming is undergirded by the awareness of death, just as the state of waking consciousness is undergirded by importance.

What importance is, then, is the denial of death. Importance seeks to use the light side of a fiber by denying its dark side. It's a trifle absurd, but it works – importance can actually hold death at bay (up to a point). Of course, we can also keep death at bay by being completely aware of it on the one hand, and not caring a fig about it on the other. But the way most of us do it is by pretending it doesn't exist on the one hand, but actually living our lives in terror and dread of it.

It is the importance coverings which pass information between lifetimes. If we leave an unresolved issue (a blocked light fiber) in one lifetime, the covering that something important needs to be done will pass over into another lifetime. The precise memory of why we feel that e.g. something important needs to be worked out with such-and-such a person may be lost: our thought form images of a given person come loose when we die. But the light fibers to which they were attached – the feelings that there is blocked energy in the light fibers connected to that person – remain. All we know is that there is something important to be done with that person (and if we're operating on a level of thought forms rather than light fibers, we don't stand much chance of figuring out what that is: what lesson we are seeking to learn with that person). If we manage to unblock those fibers in a given lifetime – to get the love energy flowing with that person – then the notation of importance vanishes. If we don't unblock the fibers in this lifetime, then the covering of importance grows.

What makes things important is the denial of love: denying love creates a sense of urgency to get back to it again. However our thought forms, for their own survival, make us believe that what we are feeling is their importance to us – they derail our search for love to a defense of them.

The difference between a good (innocuous) thought form, such as we could also have in lucid dreaming, and a bad thought form (one that should be banished) is that a bad thought form has a covering of importance, and a good thought form doesn't. Consider, for example, the thought form "8 + 5 = 13". In order to memorize this thought form in the first place, it had to be important to learn it. We received glory from our teacher and parents and schoolmates when we learned it, and anyone who was slow to learn it was made to feel shame. Glory and shame are the carrot and stick which in our society animate importance (the ability to focus our attention on memorizing things like "8 + 5 = 13" when our true feelings would prefer to be gazing out the schoolroom window).

However, now that we are adults, "8 + 5 = 13" is no longer important to us. Since most adults know that 8 + 5 = 13, knowledge of this fact doesn't bring much glory – it can't be made a basis of comparison or snobbery. We can still remember "8 + 5 = 13" whenever it becomes momentarily important to do so, but its importance disappears immediately thereafter.

In short, a bad thought form is one which we use to enhance our glory or hide our shame. The great majority of our thought forms do not have coverings of importance, and hence do not fit into our scheme of importance categories.

But a lot of them do have such coverings: practically all of the light fibers which join us to other people are blocked by importance – a sense that we are more important than them, or that they are more important than us – unless they are people with whom we feel complete love and openness, with no reservations whatsoever. Observe that in the dream state we interact with other people directly and react to them directly. We don't plot little schemes involving them, nor analyze what we expect to get from them, nor protect ourselves from them by ignoring them, etc. There just isn't that kind of time in the dream state: time out to stop feeling something directly and think about it instead. This is why we say that dream consciousness is more of a state of love (wholeness and unity) than is waking consciousness. "Love" doesn't mean rib-tickling giddiness every minute; love just means openness to whatever's there – pain, joy, happiness, suffering; whatever is happening. Loving someone doesn't mean slobbering all over them – it just means (detachedly) wishing them the best.

Our hunter ancestors didn't feel that they were more important than the game they hunted, for whom they had the greatest respect. They didn't feel a sense of triumph over the animals they killed, like most modern-day hunters do; nor did they indulge in pitying them. They just could directly feel what the animals were feeling – indeed, this is how they hunted them: by tuning into the animals' feelings and tracking them telepathically. Because they didn't feel they were in any sense better than the animals they hunted, they didn't feel affronted when other animals or humans hunted them in turn: although they certainly strove to avoid it, they didn't have a sense of personal stake – of shame or glory – in the outcome. They sensed that in the totality of who they were, there would be lifetimes and realities in which their flesh would sustain the very beings which they were hunting in this lifetime. Hunting, then, was an act of love – an understanding by which hunter and hunted exchanged loving energy through different lifetimes, each one alternately sacrificing their waking consciousness to assist the other in sustaining theirs.

Ancient hunters hunted telepathically by attuning themselves to the wavelength of their prey, and actually feeling their preys' feelings. They could project their awareness forward into their prey. All predatory animals have this faculty, which is a precursor to astral projection. I.e. astral projection, like telepathy, was a natural part of pre-agricultural humankind's original equipment, which we modern humans have repressed. Good hunters could thus anticipate the actions of their prey; but if the prey was a good magician, it could always outwit hunters who weren't.

The relationship between hunters and prey was a love relationship in the truest sense of the word. Most definitely it was a contest, and a contest to the death; but it resulted in a great sharpening and honing of skills for both humans and prey. Humans and animals thus worked together to build waking consciousness. There was great love and respect there, even though we were killing and eating each other. It wasn't paradise – there was always pain and suffering in it, as there are in dreams today – but there was no cruelty. It was an environment of love. The extent to which separatedness already existed was the extent to which there was still suffering; but it wasn't suffering due to an absence of love (blocked light fibers).

Then humankind, guided by its demon mentors, found it could increase separatedness (heighten focus) by blocking the flow of energy through light fibers, by substituting a feeling of importance for connectedness (love). The thought forms' coverings of importance are true impressions made in dream consciousness. Humans saw that they themselves couldn't effectively stop the intensity of dream consciousness long enough to separate themselves from it. They didn't have the strength to stay awake that long. So they built a little machine, a little robot, to do the job for them; and that robot was importance.

Humans don't create importance directly themselves – they have their thought forms do it for them. Humans are still too closely tied to the dream state to be able to operate wholly on a concept level: they let their feelings interfere with their thinking as much as they let their thinking interfere with their feelings. However, their thought forms, being pure concept (no need to sleep), *can* stand up to dream consciousness. How thought forms create the coverings of importance and make them sufficiently durable to be able to withstand the rigors of dream consciousness is beyond human comprehension. About all that can be said on the subject is that they're just able to do this, in the same way that we humans are able to create thought forms in the first place.

Because we surrender our sense of importance when we go to sleep, importance is minimized in the dream state. But actually, the distinction between being awake and being asleep isn't as clear as we usually imagine: when we run past life regressions; or even watch TV – any time we are so absorbed in any activity that we lose all sense of self perceiving self and are operating on pure "flow"; we are actually closer to being in a dream state than in a waking state. The less we are consciously controlling what is happening, but rather just letting it happen by itself, the closer we are to dreaming. The act of "going to sleep" is just a thought form we use to convince ourselves that we're not dreaming half the time anyway. We use the acts of "going to sleep" or "waking up" to separate out the two modes – to make a distinction where in fact little distinction exists. It's like two people who have been living together for years finally getting married – it's a symbolic thing, there's not much objective difference between the two states. It's as if we made up some sort of distinction like "write with your right hand on Tuesdays, Thursdays, and Saturdays" and "write with your left hand on Mondays, Wednesdays, and Fridays". If we got everyone to do this and make it an automatic habit, then after a few centuries the human race would have invented another distinction in consciousness (indeed, this is in fact what different cultures do). People would find that life on Tuesdays, Thursdays, and Saturdays was very different from life on Mondays, Wednesdays, and Fridays. But it's all an artificial distinction. The dichotomy of "going to sleep" and "waking up" wasn't invented by humans, but humans perfected it – just as birds invented flying and humans perfected it.

But although importance is minimal in dreams, separatedness *can* exist in the dream state. If we can strip the covering of importance away from separatedness, then we've got lucid dreaming.

Humankind cannot get to lucid dreaming from a position in wakefulness because it forever barred return by that path when it conjured up self-importance. We can examine the dream state via gazing from a position in wakefulness, but we cannot fully enter into it (unless we're very accomplished dreamers). To enter into lucid dreaming from a position which starts from being awake is called astral projection. Talented dreamers have a facility for astral projection, and this can be the quickest way for them to go (See LaBerge and Rheingold, *op. cit.*, or Robert Monroe's *Journeys Out of the Body,* for information on how to do this). But it would take most people too long to learn astral projection; it's easier for them to come at it through lucid dreaming. This is a better path for people who think too much, since it minimizes thinking. We have to start from being asleep, and then beckon our separatedness thought form to come to us without its covering of importance. If the covering of importance comes too, then we wake up. That's why so many of us find it difficult to maintain ourselves in a state of lucid dreaming without waking up: one must be calm in a lucid dream, otherwise one tends to beckon importance.

The covering of importance was definitely necessary to enable humankind to sustain waking consciousness long enough to stabilize separatedness – it made separatedness durable. It enabled humankind as a whole to develop reason, mathematics, physics – all of waking knowledge. It was a tremendous feat which far exceeded its founders' wildest hopes, but it had a tremendous cost: all of those blocked light fibers caused feelings of great pain and torment.

Now suffering certainly exists on the dream plane, but since light fibers are not blocked there, there is little sense of personal suffering. Suffering there is as bearable as anything else; it has its own rewards, etc. Anyway, there's no way to avoid it, so we just accept it without making a big deal about it. Suffering doesn't take on the tremendously personal aspects that it has in waking consciousness, where we're always suffering because of this, that, or the other thing; and we're such crucified martyrs who suffer so unjustly and wallow in misery and despair; and we have such a personal stake – sense of urgency and importance – in the outcome; as if the outcome was anything other than an arbitrary notation.

What happens in waking life is that we have the option of blocking light fibers – in this case, a light fiber to which dream mind has attached the emotion "suffering". Instead of accepting our suffering, taking responsibility for it, *feeling* it, we can block the energy from that fiber and instead feel some form of importance – self-pity, apathy, whatever – to occupy our attention and block the direct feeling of pain. Then waking mind puts some tag on it like, "I'm suffering because of so-and-so" or "I'm suffering because I dread the future" or (in the case of deniars) "I'm not suffering at all." In any event, that blocked light fiber will endure in its blocked state until something comes along and unblocks it (we are willing to feel our pain directly). This is why thought forms' coverings can outlast the thought forms themselves. If we don't unblock a fiber in this lifetime, we'll have to unblock it somewhere else down the line. That agenda, which carries with it a sense of importance (it feels important to get that fiber unblocked), becomes our true feelings – the choices we make; the lessons we seek to learn – in this, that, or the other lifetime. If we refuse our true feelings; refuse to accept responsibility for the choices we have made for ourselves in a given lifetime; refuse to unblock the light fibers which we chose to unblock in that lifetime; then we keep compounding the blockages from lifetime to lifetime.

Knowing our true feelings means not wishing for something else besides what we have already decided for this lifetime. This is because we have made a decision, and we have to stand by it – otherwise, we have no power. We can only get power by sticking to our already-made decisions;

otherwise we really are just blown hither and thither. Our already-made decisions for this lifetime – our intent – are our roots: they're the only place we can stand. They are what this life symbolizes to us. If the basic feeling we have chosen to feel in this lifetime is struggle, then to shrug it off, to pretend it's not happening, to try to get out of it somehow, to make up thought forms to keep ourselves out of the struggle – is to deny our true feelings. All it is, is a symbol anyway. If we're not getting what we think we want from life, then obviously we're out of touch with what we're really demanding.

Choosing to be born into this life is like choosing to jump out of an airplane; once that choice is made, we have to take responsibility for it. We have to accept responsibility for whatever situation we find ourselves in – whether we like it or not, whether it is fair or not, whether the other fellow is pulling his share of the load or not. Even if he is pulling 0% of the load, that just means that we will have to pull 100%. That is the only way to really change anything. As long as we are indulging in self-pity or blaming the other guy for our unhappiness, we're just running around in circles and perpetuating the problem. Only by accepting 100% of the responsibility are we in a position to break out of the dead-end circles of self-pity and unblock the light fibers which are pinned down by it.

The way to unblock a light fiber is to remove the feeling of importance which covers it. The most fundamental and important fiber to unblock is the one which considers being awake more important than dreaming. When humankind – or any individual – comes to the conviction that what they do when they're awake is no more important than what they do when they're dreaming, then the development of this present phase of consciousness, since the invention of agriculture, is basically into the home stretch.

This conviction is speeded along by losing importance: by unblocking, one by one, all the other blocked light fibers; that is to say, reaching the conviction that this or that "terribly important" thing – particularly the things we are afraid of or angry at – just isn't that important. This loosens separatedness from its matrix of importance coverings on the waking side. This is the purpose of recapitulation of our memories – to get back to the feeling of a memory by recollecting the event tag which waking mind affixed to it, and then to snip off the importance covering from that light fiber by allowing the feeling of the memory to be felt directly.

How does one lose importance? The same way one obtained it. Thought forms are cut off from light fibers the same way they were attached in the first place: through repetition. We first banish the thought form (make a firm decision to destroy it) and then we continually reject those thoughts as they arise as the importance coverings attempt to reconstruct the thought form. Eventually, by refusing those thoughts, we sever them altogether from the light fibers to which they were attached – we lose that importance.

This is exactly what repressed people (people in denial) do: reject certain thoughts as they arise; but repressed people are not consciously – voluntarily – rejecting those thoughts. Rather, they have a fear governor – derived from their parents – which rejects those thoughts for them, before they become fully conscious. In other words, they don't use intent (conscious decision) to control importance, they use importance to control intent (and to create more importance). When repressed people reject a thought, they aren't pushing that thought away, but rather are actually attaching more importance to it – clamping down harder on it, grasping it harder. Magicians, by consciously rejecting thoughts, eventually dissipate the importance they have attached to them; repressed people, by clamping down harder each time, increase the importance they have attached to them. Thus their repressed thoughts acquire more and more power all the time – require more and more energy to keep them repressed – until finally the people break and what they most feared comes true.

This is a burning issue in our time. Societies which lose their mental discipline – particularly their sexual discipline – become decadent. The partisans of so-called "traditional values" are quite cognizant of this fact, and would like to stem the tide of dissoluteness and dissolution by returning to the sexual and social repression – the Puritanism – which obtained earlier in our history, or which obtained in such repressed societies as Nazi Germany or Communist Russia. However, this is probably not a viable solution: the dogs are loose – there's no going back to that period of lies and phoniness and misery.

The question which confronts us magicians is whether it is possible to combine sexual openness with sexual discipline – i.e., whether it is possible to openly acknowledge the sexual agendas which are taking place beneath the surface of everyday life without necessarily acting them out; to be able to consciously acknowledge that one is sexually turned on by e.g. one's own parent, child, sibling, best friend's spouse, etc. etc. – rather than repressing these impulses, as a Puritan does – without the impulsion to act on them. These feelings stem from other lifetimes and realities – they are normal impulses, in the sense that everyone feels such feelings; how can we label them "evil" or "unacceptable" without lying to ourselves?

The Puritan is afraid that if he permits himself to be consciously turned on by e.g. his daughter, then he will be unable to control that impulse (not act on it). The Puritan is not disciplined in the least; he is merely fearful. True discipline involves making a conscious decision – a choice which presupposes acknowledgement that all choices are valid: that nothing is "unthinkable"; that within ourselves there exist a myriad of conflicting impulses, and that it is not wrong or immoral to consciously acknowledge that these impulses exist, even if it may be unskillful to actually act on them.

Libertines are the slaves of their impulses, and Puritans are the slaves of their fear of their impulses. But surely there is a middle path here; surely it is at least possible that people will make the right choice – the disciplined, considerate, loving choice – of their own free will, if they are given the opportunity to do so. In a Puritan society they are never given that choice: the social stigma against sexual perversion is too strong. This doesn't stop anybody – they still "do it" in back alleys and under the cover of darkness – it just makes for general hypocrisy and augmented self-hatred. Besides, it's repression that creates perversion in the first place.

Obviously our society is presently (turn of the millennium) going through a period of overexpansion – having only very recently overthrown a Puritanical mindset, it is swinging way to the other extreme of sexual hedonism. Hopefully this is just a phase: it is natural that the sexual feelings – and also the anger at society which manifests as the glorification of senseless violence in the popular media – so long repressed will overexpand when they're finally released. Hopefully things will swing back towards voluntary – not imposed – sexual discipline of their own, because people have to understand that personal power, effectiveness, and success can only come from discipline. Sexual and emotional license are dissipative rather than constructive: they are as bad as repression. Nonetheless it is healthy that society, and each individual, pass through such a stage on the way to true (arising from within) discipline.

When humans first decided to try to get things into tighter focus, they cut themselves off from the animals they were hunting. They began to consider it important to kill their prey, to celebrate their kill, to glorify themselves in victory, to separate themselves from their prey, to block the light fibers which had carried the love they exchanged with their prey heretofore, in the Age of Innocence, when humans and animals could still "talk".

This led to a decadent age of hunting – the last few thousand years of hunting were a pretty sorry mess (although there are pockets of true hunters left here and there in the world to this day). There was a "Biggest Son-of-a-Bitch in the Valley" kind of mentality going on – a lot of brutality of humans against humans as well as against animals. This is when humans' alliance with demons began: the Late Upper Paleolithic.

So the true feelings of humankind at that point collectively decided that this was a dead end. There was a lot more focus in hunting this way – one could devise all sorts of ingenious and sleazy methods for ensnaring game and one's fellow humans – but there was so much self-hatred in it that it wasn't worth the meager gains. So humankind stepped back and reconsidered its position. That's when it invented agriculture, as a somewhat more peaceful and pleasant endeavor than murder and pillage (though throwbacks to the brutal stage of human development certainly still exist in the world today. We're all still like that, actually, just beneath the surface).

With agriculture, humankind cooperated with nature instead of brutally raping it, but still remained separated from it. Humankind was delighted with this new invention. There was still a good deal of self-hatred wrapped up in it, but at least it was more relaxed and relaxing than the last stages of hunting had been – closer to true feelings because it felt better. Humankind sensed it was on the right track.

With agriculture came the idea of a sense of future which was at least as important as the present. One could, and indeed had to, make plans for the future (something the hunter had little need to do). The new consciousness also demanded a stronger sense of rootedness in the past to establish possessoriness and develop technology, as well as a greater concern for the future. And for the first time there came such ideas as excess of production, vending (as opposed to bartering, which had existed in hunting times), markets, specialization and division of labor, etc. At this point we're up to the historical record. Thus, the perfecting of waking consciousness required the invention of agriculture in order to: 1) separate being awake from being asleep; 2) separate the past and future from the present, and 3) physically (economically) sustain the new social organization which resulted. Note that agriculture was the byproduct of the new change in consciousness, rather than the cause of it.

At the present time in humankind's development, after all these millennia of strengthening it, the separatedness thought form – or rather, the light fibers to which it is attached – is strong and bright enough to stand on its own, without all the claptrap and paraphernalia of doubt, isolation, forgetting, shame and glory. Recall that a thought form has to be repeated over and over to give it the strength to endure – to put intent behind it – hence the repetitiveness of prayers and incantations, not to mention advertising. Once something has been sufficiently intended via repetition, you can take the importance covering off, and it will stand alone (like "8 + 5 = 13"). So after all this repetition, separatedness can be moved lock, stock, and barrel over into dream consciousness, since it is now strong enough to tackle dream consciousness directly, without the gloss of importance it needed in wakefulness. In dream consciousness there is little doubt, isolation, or forgetting; yet in lucid dreaming separatedness works just as well as it does in waking consciousness.

How, then, can separatedness be carried over from waking to dream consciousness? The answer is by 1) cultivating lucid dreaming, so as to give separatedness a new base; and 2) by losing importance in the waking realm. This is done by shifting the hours spent awake and asleep each day back to something reasonably resembling what they were in the days when we were hunters, even if all this means is a catnap during lunch break and a stroll around the neighborhood in the middle of the night; and also through various mental training techniques such as listening to sounds, gazing, etc. which serve to shift around that which we consider important. Assiduous cultivation of lucid dreaming on the one hand, and of losing importance on the other, can then move separatedness to its permanent base in dream consciousness. It will take humankind as a whole some time yet to get to this point.

Note that no major upheaval in present society would necessarily be required to make this shift, unless humankind stupidly proves to be incapable of responding short of a total crisis. There are probable realities which go either way, which we as individuals can choose or decline to participate in, by believing what we choose to believe. All that's required to save humanity is for most people (not necessarily all) to lighten up just a little bit. We don't need everyone to don sackcloth and ashes and take to caves and become enlightened; nor do we need everyone to fall in line and believe as we do. All we need is for most people to become just a tad less greedy, selfish, suspicious, intolerant, closed-hearted. Just for most people to lighten up a teensy bit – that's all we need to tell our demon pals to go scat, and for the human race to enter into lucid dreaming together.

In the state of lucid dreaming everyone instantly knows the truth, so pretense is impossible. By contrast, most of what transpires in waking consciousness is a pack of lies: people are talking about one thing, but what is really going on under the surface is something altogether different. It isn't like that in lucid dreaming – what we see is what we get. There's no room for phoniness because those importance coverings don't exist in lucid dreaming – that agreement is more important than truth.

As in waking consciousness, two people who are lucidly dreaming together can also see the same thing happening; this is the genius of separatedness. We are not actually separate beings at all; rather, we are different aspects of the same being (primordial first cell) which are pretending to see the same scene from different points of view. It's all one: "you" and "I" are not two separate beings, but rather two different aspects of the same super-awareness – like two eyes in the same head. We only pretend to be two different beings. This pretense underlies both dream and waking consciousness, but is more pronounced in waking. In lucid dreaming all our light fibers are connected and working, and yet we can still maintain the pretense that "You and I are separated, yet we are still seeing the same thing happening." The difference is that in lucid dreaming we know it's a pretense, a notation, a symbol, a short-hand record of what's really going on between us on a light-fiber level. We just have that particular model available to us as well; but the model isn't the important thing – in lucid dreaming we know that the important thing isn't whatever appears to be happening on the surface, so we don't get bogged down in bickering about it. Only in lucid dreaming can we get both thought form agreement and feeling agreement. We are both united, and yet separated. It's a perfect balance. It's actually a form of juggling, and until we get practice at it the normal tendency is to go one way or the other (to wake up, or to drift off into normal dreaming).

The reason why even in lucid dreaming two people can look at the same thing and agree on what they're seeing on a thought form level as well as a feeling level (i.e. can agree on an object's color, shape, size, etc.) is as follows: all of our individual realities, our ideas about what is blue, or round, or 3 inches long, etc. are not the same. We aren't giving those concepts the same meaning, but are only pretending to. It's like the difference between Einsteinian versus Newtonian mechanics – as long as we are only looking at this one little piece over here, Newtonian mechanics works pretty well. So we agree to put all our attention on that one little piece. We now agree on a Newtonian universe, though people before Newton's time certainly didn't, nor do "primitive" peoples to this day. The universe wasn't / isn't mechanistic for these people, but rather *alive*. Perhaps our children or our children's children will have an intuitive feel for the Einsteinian model – will incorporate that thought form into their everyday awareness of the world. The point is that we have so curbed our own senses, so limited the scope of information which we permit ourselves to process mentally (which we did to narrow our focus down to waking consciousness) that we can indeed get agreement on such insignificant details as color, shape, size, etc. We have so collectively distorted our own senses that we have been able to agree to agree that that rock is blue and round and 3 inches long. In order to be able to even think in such terms as "blue", "round", or "3 inches long", we have to block up a bunch of light fibers. It's like looking at a child dying in a grief-stricken mother's arms and only being able to think, "She's wearing a blue dress with round collar, and the kid's hand is 3 inches long." That's all waking consciousness is: a bunch of people standing around discussing stupid, irrelevant details and completely closing their hearts to what is happening right in front of them.

However, it was necessary that humankind pass through a phase like this in order to get the "blue" and "round" and "3 inches" kind of details worked out. Waking consciousness is a mean, cruel place, but it served its purpose. Thanks to our collective experience of waking consciousness, we are now able to bring this superficial agreement back into the dream state, but without all the hatred and agitation. In lucid dreaming we are still able to maintain the pretense that that rock is blue and round and 3 inches long, but we have all our light fibers which go to it and through it working as well. But we also have the option of using the "blue" and "round" notations as well, if we so desire. There's no contradiction here: waking consciousness doesn't have to be at odds with dream consciousness. There doesn't have to be a war going on. It's just that we are so imbued with the assumptions of waking consciousness that naturally we cannot conceive of life going on more or less as it does in normal everyday life, but with everyone being truly joyous instead of bringing one another down.

Waking consciousness has been irretrievably screwed up by all the selfishness and tit-for-tat nonsense which humankind has laid over it. It's like a battlefield strewn with stinking corpses. It should be left behind altogether since there's nothing left on that battlefield worth salvaging – all that's there is shame and glory.

But the discipline, the warrior spirit, and the calm reason which were learned on that battlefield should not be lost. They will merely be applied back in the original world of dreams. In dreams there is no richer or poorer; there is no need to strive for glory, and there is no need to hide shame. Everything there is more symbolic – directly known and understood. There are fights to the finish there, and overwhelming fears; but also we are lighter and less encumbered by doubt, and therefore capable of great feats of courage and will. And it has the added advantage that we don't die.

We never die in dreams, we just wake up. That is humankind's true estate – we don't die. Death is just a thought form conjured up to support waking consciousness. Waking consciousness represents a heroic effort by humankind to do what King Canute couldn't, and hold back the tide of dream consciousness. Staying awake is a horrendous strain, extremely taxing for the race as a whole as well as for each individual human being. Death is the only respite. Only by offering some such retirement plan – the knowledge that you do get a rest at some point – could society seduce its members into the heroic effort of denying their true feelings in order to stay awake.

Lucid dreaming is not something essentially different from waking consciousness, only we get to it from a position of being asleep. When we start out from a position of being awake, we call it "everyday life". What do you suppose the horseless carriage is? Or the radio, TV, airplane, space rocket, computer? They are all wild, crazy dreams. A hundred years ago that's exactly what we would have considered them. And that's all they are – dreams. Humankind just incorporated that dream material into waking consciousness. That is the sort of thing waking consciousness is good for: to originate dream material of that sort. That kind of business requires slow, patient development; and the dream plane is too unstable and mutable to do that kind of stuff on. The dream plane is too here and now – it doesn't allow for the detachment that a sense of past (history) and future (planning) can give. We need a greater sense of separation to be able to do things that slowly. That's why it is so difficult to do things like dial a phone number or read a sentence in a normal dream – these activities require a greater degree of separatedness than normal dreaming affords, to be able to bring that kind of minute detail into focus.

That's the genius of waking consciousness: everything is so clearly focused and delimited (even if we all become extremely myopic and uptight in the process). We lose scope and agility, but in return we get focus and a methodical way of getting at things.

So now humankind must move separatedness away from the petty bickering and striving for glory which has heretofore characterized its development. The shame and glory bit was a sidetrack, but it worked; humankind developed a strong sense of separatedness from the experience. Now it must learn to take that sense of separatedness and let it flow, let it be fluid, instead of heavy and stagnant as it has become in waking consciousness. Humankind cannot get to lucid dreaming from a position of being awake because it sealed that exit when it began to put its primary attention on waking consciousness. As mentioned before, waking consciousness *is* lucid dreaming, but we can't see that because we must keep up the pretense that what we're doing is real and important. Therefore we can't see that it's all just a dream.

So the only way left for humankind to get to lucid dreaming as its everyday consciousness is from a position that starts from being asleep (this will be the subject of the companion volume on Venus). But it was necessary to mention this point because the only way to get at an understanding of what mind is, is to understand how it functions in different environments – in dream consciousness, waking consciousness, and lucid dreaming. Mind is most highly developed in waking and lucid dreaming, but only in lucid dreaming is it truly at it freest and most artistic, since it is not pinned down to the heaviness of importance.

Chapter IV: Active Imagination

"O wad some Pow'r the giftie gie us
To see oursels as others see us!
It wad frae mony a blunder free us,
And foolish notion."

– Robert Burns, *To a Louse*

Examples of Active Imagination

In the preceding chapters we have discussed the action of mind – the creation and perpetuation of thought forms – from various points of view. Now we will examine the question of how thought forms may be manipulated to our advantage, instead of allowing ourselves to be manipulated by them, using a technique devised by Carl Jung called active imagination. A serious practitioner is advised to read one of the specialized works on the subject (e.g. *Inner Work* by Robert Johnson), but the basic technique is explained in the following pages.

As mentioned previously, about the only things we humans can do with our thought forms are create them and destroy them; apart from that, they have volitions of their own. This is because thought forms are living beings, who are no less real than we, their creators. However, thought forms are much simpler entities than humans. They don't have the rich emotional tonality of humans; in fact, they are limited to one emotion each: the emotion of the light fiber to which they are attached, or some distortion of same. They are not stupid, by any means, and in fact can be extremely perceptive and pithy within the narrow scope of their own prejudices and points of view. Precisely because they are so simple – being pure concept – they can see things much more clearly than we humans can. Thought forms don't have much depth or dimension, but they do have the same passion for life which characterizes all living beings. In other words, thought forms can be considered to be conditioned patterns of behavior or reaction, positions which are being defended, which have a logic, a rationale, and a will to live all their own.

The personalities of individual thought forms – their feelings – mirror different facets of our own personalities (by definition). If we tend to be sassy and flippant, our thought forms will also tend to be sassy and flippant. If we tend to be gloomy and morbid, our thought forms will be gloomy and morbid too. Most of what we mean by, or can point to, or consider "ourselves" is just a random collection of thought forms.

Observe that thought forms serve needs in our psyche; that's why we created them in the first place – to respond to some need. The problem is that our needs change as we go along in life, but our thought forms don't. They are capable of modifying themselves to adapt to the vicissitudes of changing circumstances, but they won't modify their basic purpose, and their basic purpose is to keep themselves alive (important to us). The reason why we find it so difficult to truly change ourselves is because our importance has to be durable – otherwise we'd go insane. Only crazy people can't focus their attention on the world – they mix up dreaming with being awake. To keep the two worlds separated we need a strong sense of importance. Another way of saying this is: focus (importance) and awareness work inversely; therefore, to increase awareness we have to lower importance. The goal of active imagination is to get to a place where we can turn focus / importance off and on at will, rather than having to maintain the switch in the on position all the time we are awake, which necessarily curtails our awareness – awareness of colors; sensory impressions; the feelings, "hidden" sexual agendas and motives of other people, etc.

Active imagination entails isolating or bracketing thought forms as a first step to modifying or eliminating them – that is, becoming consciously aware of them and thus able to separate them out from the background of mental chatter. To isolate a thought form is to no longer take it for granted, which is the first step in stripping the importance covering from it.

A good preliminary exercise for isolating thought forms is called knifing. This entails rephrasing your beliefs in as many ways as possible, negating each clause in turn. For example,

"I hate my mother because she never appreciates me."

"I love my mother even though she never appreciates me."

"I hate my mother even when she appreciates me."

"I love my mother because she always appreciates me."

Etc. etc.

The idea is to actually feel (connect with) the feeling represented by each of those thought forms. Here's another example:

"If I stand up to him, he'll be angry and attack me."

"If I stand up to him, he won't be angry or attack me."

"If I don't stand up to him, he'll be angry and attack me."

"If I don't stand up to him, he won't be angry or attack me." Etc. etc.

The point of allowing yourself to feel all the different viewpoints is to give yourself an option, instead of having to jump into and defend one particular viewpoint as a reflex action. This makes a space for yourself, gives you a choice, and enables you to dethrone your thought forms' importance by setting up contradictions. The point is to see that you could (in theory, at least) just as easily defend the exact opposite position if you chose to.

There are lots of ways of channeling thought forms directly. Normal thinking can be considered to be a form of channeling thought forms, but it tends to be mindless: in normal thinking our thought forms are doing all the talking, and we're just sitting there dumbly. To interact with our thought forms we need a more *active imagination* than normal thinking affords. Jung's method utilizes artwork, modeling, dance and other creative activities to interact with our unconscious thought forms. But perhaps the easiest way for the beginner to communicate with his or her own thought forms is by automatic writing.

Now, automatic writing is as simple and straightforward as its name implies; there is no trick to it whatsoever. If they had taught it to you in seventh grade (as perhaps they should have) you'd have been doing it all this time and not giving it a second thought. Rest assured that anybody who really wants to do it can do it. There's nothing to it, although it does seem to work best when you have a strong need for information about problems you are facing, rather than when you're just idly curious.

Choose a time when you are relaxed, alert, calm, and will not be interrupted. If you are an astrologer, you can use a lunar planetary hour; but this is merely a help, not a necessity. Either lie or sit down, as you prefer, with a pen and notebook in hand (though it can also be done on a typewriter or word processor). Writing down both your questions and the replies as they come, "ask" if there is any thought form who wishes to address you. If you don't feel an impulse to write, then coax the thought form to appear: "Please come and talk to me. I am really trying to be open right now, I have this problem that I'd really like some information on, and I want to hear what you, my thought forms, have to tell me." Etc. Use your own words and sentiments, mean (feel) what you are saying, but don't stop writing until you start feeling an answer coming.

Needless to say, this exercise won't work unless you do it in good faith, i.e., have an open mind and heart about it, and truly want it to work. If you are harboring some idea such as, "This is the bunk!" or if you are afraid of hearing what your thought forms might tell you (which usually involves facing up to a lot of shame), then obviously you're not going to be able to do automatic writing.

Usually in automatic writing a few words or phrases spring into your mind at a time, a little faster than you can write them down, so that you often don't quite grasp the gist of what it is you're writing until you go back and reread it. Sometimes you get whole blocks or paragraphs at a time. You may also feel the feeling you felt when you created the thought form (get a feeling of its personality). You might see memory pictures pop up before your mind's eye, or get flashes of dream-like scenes as you write. Note all of that stuff down, because it's all relevant. It may not make sense at the moment, but it will eventually if you keep a written record of it.

If nothing comes to mind in response to your entreaties; or if all that comes to mind is gibberish, it means that you are blocking – your conscious mind is too fearful to yield control of your writing thought forms to your subconscious mind. Your conscious mind might say, "This isn't working; I'm not doing this right; there must be some trick to this!" in its effort to subvert the process. Don't fall for this ploy! Keep trying, keep on writing, even if all it is, is gibberish. Whatever is written down is valid, so believe in it and trust in it no matter how much nonsense it appears to be. Sometimes rereading "gibberish" a day or week later reveals that it wasn't as nonsensical as you believed at the time. In other words, don't judge yourself: you get enough of that from other people – you don't have to do it to yourself.

Only trust can open you enough to write automatically; otherwise you tangle yourself up with doubt. Doubt is the enemy of all magic, and it can completely tear down automatic writing at the outset. Faith is the key to success here as elsewhere, and a strong curiosity is a valuable asset also. Bear in mind, too, that the fact that you are even willing to try to do active imagination shows that you've got thought forms in there who are just busting to communicate with you. It often helps, if you find yourself blocking, to switch to your non-dominant hand. Just keep on writing, don't stop, and at a given moment your conscious mind will relax its grip and you'll start writing automatically. Then, just write down what the thought form has to say, asking any questions you like along the way.

Ask the thought form what its name is, and what function it serves in your psyche. Ask about its history; for every thought form came into existence at a certain moment in time, created by you in order to handle a certain situation, and to automatically handle all similar situations (decisions) in the future.

Thought forms are often in possession of memories and other information which your conscious mind has forgotten, or else doesn't want to face. Thought forms are invaluable sources of information on what past lives you ought to run, which probable reality branches you should trace, and what memories you should recapitulate. They can even interpret your dreams for you. They can give you unbelievably accurate and insightful information about all your relationships and circumstances in life. You can invite particular thought forms to address you (those who possess the particular information you are after); or you can just invite one to come in who has some pressing comment to make regarding your current situation in life.

Remember that the thought forms you created as a child are still children, so it's frequently difficult to understand what they're trying to communicate to you. Needless to say, they have the most important information of all, so pay utmost attention to them and write down everything they say. Later you can ask another thought form to come in who can interpret the first thought form's message in a way you'll understand.

Indeed, the main limitation on active imagination as a technique is that it can't be used to get at thought forms which were installed in us when we were preverbal (before we learned to think and talk). These are what we called forgotten thought forms. They aren't forgotten at all, but rather can't be recalled to mind because they can't be framed as concepts: they can only be felt or apprehended symbolically as quasi-dream images. The only way to manipulate them is through recapitulation, a technique which is described in the companion volume *The Great Wheel*. However, even though they can't be addressed or banished directly, it is still possible to strip away their importance coverings using creative visualization and nature spirits.

In doing active imagination you have to be open to whatever it is your thought forms want to tell you. This doesn't mean you have to agree with them, since they do have their own quirks and prejudices which are not necessarily in your best interests; you can even grow fond of some of the little buggers, even if they don't deserve it.

Here's an example of one of my own active imagination sessions:

BM: Is anyone available to talk to me?

Schlemiel: Yes, here I am as always.

BM: Who are you?

Schlemiel: I'm your Schlemiel.

BM: Well, sir, what do you have to say for yourself?

Schlemiel: Not much. I don't have much to say. I'm just trying to keep my head down and avoid controversy. I came into being to deal with your parents. They were / are extremely overbearing when they want to be, and the easiest way to handle them when they're in that mood (and when you don't feel like fighting) is to just do the shuffle your feet and "yassuh" number.

BM: Nancy can't stand you.

Schlemiel: Wrong, pal. That's false. Nancy married you because you are a wimp. You know that – you've often said it. She would never have married a strong man whom she couldn't dominate. She married you precisely because she knew you'd let her walk all over you.

BM: Well, she doesn't like you any more. She wants you out.

Schlemiel: What about you?

BM: I don't care. Somehow I believe that my wimpiness is connected to my heart. I may be a wimp, but I don't get a charge out of running all over people.

Schlemiel: That's my line, pal. You've just adopted my point of view. Actually it's possible to keep people from running all over you without your running all over them.

BM: How?

Schlemiel: I dunno. That ain't my department. I'm just a schlemiel.

BM: You sure are. You're the one who's afraid of people?

Schlemiel: Deathly. And why shouldn't I be?

BM: You mean if I banished you I wouldn't be afraid of people any more?

Schlemiel: Not as much, and not in the same way. I'm the one who used to apologize all the time. I don't do that any more because you put a stop to it. Similarly, I suppose I could be modified to stop cringing and cowering in front of people.

BM: Are you responsible for my failures?

Schlemiel: No, that was your demon, may his soul rest in peace. But I helped him. I was the thought form that expected failure, just as I expect people to dislike me and to abuse me.

BM: Precisely what function do you serve in my psyche? You don't protect me.

Schlemiel: No, I don't. I'm just here for convenience, I suppose. It's convenient to have a handy reaction you can pull out of the bag when you're up against a tyrant and you don't feel in the mood to fight.

BM: I'm thinking of banishing you.

Schlemiel: Naturally, I expected it. You're not telling me anything I wasn't expecting all along. That's what everyone does to me. But your heart isn't in it, is it?

BM: No, it isn't. You aren't hurting other people, like Jealousy and Hatred are. I sort of feel comfortable being a schlemiel.

Schlemiel: Naturally. That's why I'm going to be harder to get rid of than they were – your heart isn't in it.

BM: But are you holding me back from success?

Schlemiel: Yes, I am. All of us thought forms are.

BM: How many of you guys are there?

Schlemiel: Lots. Strictly speaking, every thought you've ever had is a thought form, but in practice there are only about ten of us that are holding you back. I'm one of the main ones because I make you timid.

This is a rather typical example of how I do active imagination; but since everyone does it somewhat differently, you shouldn't suppose it will necessarily be like this for you. My active imagination tends to be rather prosaic; for some people it's really outlandish – three dimensional, technicolor, and wired for sound. Some people do it more by drawing pictures or making music or dancing than by writing. Everybody does it differently: there's no right or wrong way of doing it.

When first starting out to do active imagination it is a good idea to just invite thought forms to communicate with you, rather than to command them. This is because (unless you are very self-attuned and have been doing active imagination all along without knowing it) you probably have a number of thought forms who have important information for you that they have been trying to communicate for some time. Now that you are offering them this chance, let them have their say before you rush in there with your own preconceived ideas of what you want to know. But once the initial tumult has died down, it is a good idea to seek out and communicate with several of your most important thought forms.

Probably the most important thought form to talk to is your death; in fact, the death thought form should be sought out and talked to on a regular basis. However, unless you've got a pretty good stomach, you shouldn't talk to your death thought form until you've had a lot of experience with active imagination, because the death thought form is pretty hard to take. It knows EVERYTHING about you, is completely unsympathetic, and is just smacking its chops in anticipation of the feast. Once you get to know it, though, you'll find it's the very best friend you've got.

Another very important thought form you should talk to is your body. Just as everyone's body is different, so too does everyone's body thought form have different advice to give. Some people are intrinsically libertine, and others are intrinsically ascetic; some people should follow a high-protein, meat-based diet, whereas others should be vegetarians. The specific information which each of our body thought forms has to share with us is quite different and individually tailored – there is no one correct diet or universal standard of sexual conduct, for example.

Not only is the body a thought form, but all of its parts are thought forms also, and it is quite possible to call upon them for information about health matters. Here is an example of active imagination done by a woman who was experiencing bleeding in the second month of her pregnancy:

Woman: My body, can you help me get in touch with the thought form who controls my uterus?

Body: Yes. You will be having bleeding all through your first trimester, but it does not mean that there is anything wrong with your baby at all, or for that matter that you have placenta previa. It is your body's way of expressing unhappiness. I know it seems very weird to you and that you've never heard of anything like it before, but you are not the first woman to have this complaint. In fact, if you would like to talk to your uterus, I suggest you do so right now. You might be surprised.

Woman: Uterus, would you please talk to me?

Uterus: Yes, I will be happy to. You can hardly believe the incredible work that I am being called on to do. I know you take it all for granted – like the most normal thing in the world to do. Doesn't every woman have a baby? But it still doesn't change the fact that I am being forced to do a lot of extra work with which you, frankly, are not helping me. For example, I could use more herbal teas. I know you don't like them, but I do. Make an alfalfa-raspberry mixture every day and drink three cups.

Also, eat meat or drink that iron tonic for these first three months. I just need more physical help in what I'm doing. You should be eating the chard that is wasting in the garden. Right now make the children eat what you want, not what they want. Drink more water. Put brewer's yeast in your yogurt. And rest. I just need it, that's all, and you've got to accept it. Rest at least two hours during the day. If you feel ashamed of this (which you do), too bad; I don't, and I'm the one who is doing all the work. Otherwise I get overtired; I just do. Maybe other women don't need two hours of rest, but you do. For your gestation you need oodles and oodles of meditation and dream experiences. Do you think that the Virgin Mary ran around all day long? No, she contemplated the stars and the moon – just as you should do.

So if you're too stupid to know what you should be doing, I'm not; and I talk with blood whenever you get out of line and think that this thing of gestating a child is done on some sort of automatic pilot while you go merrily off to play. I need your conscious support and awareness. You help me and I'll help you.

Along with the body thought form, two other thought forms which all multi-celled creatures have in common and which should definitely be consulted early on in the practice are the anima and animus – the female and male sides of our personalities (These terms are used here in a somewhat different sense than Jung used them). Because most of us are so sexually repressed (have most of our light fibers of sexual energy blocked up), the only way we can find out what our true sexual feelings are is by going to our animas. The anima, or female side, is the more important of the two thought forms: the male side is subordinate to, or an outgrowth of, the female side; therefore the anima should be consulted first. All sexual turn-on is due to the anima, and the anima is basically homosexual rather than heterosexual (this is true in a general sort of way for both men and women; but again, everyone is different). Heterosexual attraction is due to the animus (male side) in both men and women. There's no point in belaboring the description here; just ask your own anima and animus any questions you like yourself, and they'll tell you. The point is that they can give you invaluable advice concerning your sex life, which (if you have the courage to follow it, since it can be quite shocking) will make you a great deal happier and self-accepting (unblock a lot of light fibers).

You should also speak to whatever thought forms are making you unhappy; they'll come forward and speak their piece. Know that doing active imagination is like lifting the lid on Pandora's box – inviting a direct confrontation with all your shame and irresponsibility – so be prepared! But know too that there's always a little hope at the bottom of the box.

Here's one final example of my own active imagination:

BM: May I speak to my anger thought form?

Anger: (gruff) Here I am. What the hell do you want?

BM: What do you have to say for yourself?

Anger: I don't have one goddamn thing to say for myself. So buzz off.

BM: You have nothing to say before I banish you?

Anger: Not to you I don't. I hate your guts.

BM: So it's true what they say about all anger being self-anger?

Anger: What the hell did you think, stupid!

BM: Where did you come from?

Anger: Where the hell do you think? From your parents, of course. Now if you've had your fun, go away and leave me alone. I said, Beat It!

BM: May I banish you?

Anger: Who the hell cares. Just go away!

Banishing Thought Forms

When you come across thought forms in active imagination which are working against your own true feelings, it's a good idea to banish them. There are some people who just can't bear to put the pistol to their thought forms' heads, and for these people it is possible to talk it out with their thought forms and come to an understanding (complete modification of the thought forms' purpose). But I find it easier just to destroy them. I, personally, had to banish upwards of 200 thought forms before I began to feel a sense of personal control over my life; but of course, some people will have to banish more or fewer thought forms, depending on how neurotic they are to begin with. It's not hard to do – after the active imagination (communicating through automatic writing) is done, you can knock off a dozen or more thought forms in a leisurely afternoon.

When you're talking to a thought form in active imagination, just ask it frankly, "Would I be better off if I banished you?", and it will tell you the truth. Thought forms are compelled to tell you the truth in all factual matters – though they also have their own personal opinions. They must tell you the truth because they stand in roughly the same relation to you as you stand to God – i.e. ultimately they're just marionettes dangling from your light fibers, even though a lot of the time you let them pull the strings.

The thought form might say something like, "Yes, you would be happier if you banished me, but then you would be more vulnerable and unprotected." or something of the sort.

They don't want to be banished. But they aren't living your life, they aren't responsible for what happens to you, and they don't really give a damn; any more than you care about God and what would make God happy. So if you're letting your thought forms call all the shots, then you're subjecting your life to forces that will bang you around a lot. Thought forms aren't accomplishing anything for you – they're just chattering in the background, making you think this and that and the other; but they don't have much to do with what's really happening at all.

The astute reader has perhaps asked the question, "If thought forms are so easy to banish, why not just banish my death thought form?" In fact this can be done, but it's not quite as simple as banishing an everyday, garden-variety thought form. Certain thought forms are much stronger or more pervasive (important) than others – are attached to more brilliant light fibers; and while these forms can be banished, they tend to return immediately unless their importance coverings have been completely stripped away. In the case of the death thought form, this means recapitulating, one by one, all of your memories; that is to say, cutting the forgetting thought form from all of the light fibers to which you've attached it, thus forcing death to give you back all your marbles, as it were.

Many of us have at one time or another banished our death thought forms unwittingly; any time we have narrowly escaped death just by an act of will, we have temporarily banished our death thought forms. Rest assured that other probable realities branched off at those moments in which we went with our death thought forms rather than our true feelings.

Therefore, even though we can't banish these powerful thought forms – death, separatedness, forgetting, doubt, etc. – permanently, it is possible to banish them, or at least weaken them by banishment, temporarily, but long enough to sneak some magic by them. For example, it is often useful to banish the forgetting thought form immediately before going into a particularly knotty recapitulation; or to banish separatedness immediately before doing some inundation technique (or making love, for that matter). The thought forms return immediately, but repeated, continuous banishment does permanently weaken them. For example, you could also banish the death thought form permanently by doing a continuous banishment ritual against it all day long every day, in the manner of the Pilgrim's continuous prayer; but there are actually easier ways of doing it than this. Even a complete recapitulation – as daunting as it may sound – is easier than that; and there are always shortcuts.

It's also a good idea to banish the doubt thought form before any activity about which you feel dubious. Your doubt thought form can also tell you (in active imagination) precisely where you are putting your doubts – setting yourself up for disappointment and hurt – and in that sense it can be used to predict the future (although the future really can't be predicted: everything's too fluid; the decisions are being made moment-by-moment. All your doubt thought form – or any other oracle – can tell you is the wind speed and direction at any given moment, but not where the leaf is going to land). You can banish the doubt thought form any time you need a surge of confidence, e.g. before an exam, or before walking into the boss's office to ask for a raise. Continuous banishment of the doubt thought form would build up your overall self-confidence, but as noted before, there are easier ways to do this, such as the resort to nature spirits.

Now before banishing a thought form it is necessary to hear it out completely, and ask if you may banish it. Of course, it will try to talk you out of it. But you can't just banish a thought form without a fair hearing, because your thought forms are a part of you, and you must have respect for yourself. You can't just snuff out an important part of yourself like *that* – you have to give it its due, see in yourself why you brought that thought form into being, and then decide if you want to keep it. You can't treat other people as mere objects of convenience, dismissing them, and their feelings, when it is no longer convenient for you to respect them. Similarly, you can't treat yourself with disrespect; you have to know why you are banishing a thought form – what you want to change in yourself, and why.

You can use any banishing ritual you like to banish a thought form. I, personally, use a Greek folk dance (Vari Khasapiko) to dance my thought forms off; but you can use any old ritual you like, or just make one up. The point is that the ritual or dance should be done with true repugnance for the thought form and a complete determination to stamp it out.

Fast on the day when you plan to rid yourself of thought forms. You can do as many forms as you want on the same day, but you must have the same conviction and determination to get rid of each one in turn. That takes some time with each form, to work yourself into a state of mind to banish it. Talk to each form before you get rid of it. Thank it for its help; ask it if it has any last words. Be respectful, but merciless. Then do your ritual or dance. Afterwards, you can use automatic writing to check to see if you succeeded: if you call upon the thought form and it doesn't answer, that means it's gone.

You may not feel any immediate difference after banishing a thought form, although for some people it is very traumatic (Mercury conjunction natives, in particular, often find banishing thought forms a wrenching experience since they can't easily separate themselves from them – they are afraid they might be killing a part of themselves thereby. It's hard for these natives to even work themselves into a state of mind to banish thought forms, since they tend to agree with them 100%). Moreover, banishing certain thought forms which control perception – such as "fear of death" or "having to think constantly" – can be like taking a psychedelic drug in that thereafter the world takes on more of the vividness of dream consciousness.

In any event, within a day or so of banishing a thought form you'll feel more detachment in the area ruled by that thought form. Banishing a thought form gives you a space, a free moment, in which you can make a sober, reasoned decision about how you'll react to a given stimulus, instead of being compelled to react out of some stock set of neurotic reactions which may not be appropriate to the present situation.   You get a pause in there instead of a blind, thoughtless, headlong rush to react. You can watch yourself as you react; you become consciously aware of what you're doing as you do it.

When you banish a thought form, the compulsion to react in a given fashion vanishes, but the tendency to react in that fashion doesn't. This is because when the thought form is banished, the light fiber to which it was attached is left flopping around loose; and if you don't soon make a new thought form to fasten it to, the importance covering left on it will try to recreate the old thought form you just banished. You will feel this as the old habit or feeling of the thought form tugging at you. Don't give in to it: that would recreate it for sure. It's usually easy to refuse to surrender to the impulse – even for lifelong habits or addictions – since once the original thought form is destroyed only a little vigilance and common sense are needed to keep the old habit at bay. But you must fasten the loose light fibers to new, constructive thought forms. The techniques used to do this are creative visualization in conjunction with the resort to nature spirits.

Light Fiber Techniques:

Creative Visualization

When all is said and done, active imagination is just a manipulation of thought forms; and while this is a necessary preliminary to wipe the slate of waking mind clean, it doesn't lead to real, permanent change. It gives us insight and helps us to straighten ourselves out on a concept level, but it can't actually transform us – put us in direct contact with our true feelings.   It can only put us in contact with a conceptual picture of our true feelings. In the following sections we will discuss several elementary techniques for actually manipulating light fibers themselves – that is, for making things really happen in the world "out there". The first of these is creative visualization, which is used to change our basic beliefs – e.g. our beliefs that we are poor, or ill, or lonely, or unhappy.

Our basic beliefs are the armatures of thought forms which support our customary moods and concerns. One common basic belief, for example, is the notion that we're here on this earth to suffer. Those of us who share this basic belief have a cadre of thought forms at hand to twist everything that happens to us around to support this basic belief: e.g., since we're so good and wonderful and don't deserve this terrible fate that has befallen us, that just proves once more that we're here to suffer. Basic beliefs are not themselves thought forms, but rather clusters of thought forms learned from our parents, usually, which all try to evoke the same customary moods and concerns. You can banish all the thought forms which support a basic belief and still leave that basic belief unchanged, although doing this is the first step to changing it; creative visualization is the second. This is because banishing thought forms doesn't of itself destroy their importance coverings – although there's no way to get at the importance coverings until the thought forms themselves are cleared out of the way.

The way to change our basic beliefs is by truly wanting to change them, in our hearts – not our minds. We change beliefs in our hearts by simply deciding that isn't what we want for ourselves anymore; and then the beliefs will change. This is the purpose of creative visualization – to change beliefs. It's a matter of changing our mood from self-pity to eager expectancy; only after our own beliefs are changed can the universe be changed around.

The first basic belief that has to be dealt with is the belief that things "just happen" to us, rather than that we have in fact called them to us. It doesn't even make any difference whether this is true or not: only fools would go in there on the assumption that they have less than 100% control over what is happening to them, and thus can get by taking less than 100% of the responsibility for it.

Once we have intellectually convinced ourselves of the truth of this axiom, or at least adopted it as a working hypothesis, we can then get down to changing specific beliefs. Our thought forms can tell us which ones to work on. Not only that, but our thought forms can also tell us precisely how to phrase an affirmation, or what photos or images we should use in a treasure map, in order to change a given belief – e.g. a belief in our poverty, illness, or loneliness. That is to say, the thought forms we are about to banish can recommend the precise thought forms which should replace them.

Creative visualization is a form of self-hypnosis. In fact, all magic is a form of self-hypnosis. In fact, all waking consciousness is a form of self-hypnosis. You hypnotized yourself into thinking that you are poor, or sick, or lonely; and you can just as easily hypnotize yourself back out of it again (by comparing yourself to people who are poorer, sicker, or lonelier than you are, rather than by being jealous of people who are better off). If you believe that the world is a drag, rest assured that the world will become a drag; conversely, if you believe that the world is magical, the world will become more magical than you could have ever dreamed possible.

It is to be expected that you will be doubtful and hesitant at first; but if you have even a modicum of belief in the possibility that what you are doing is valid, that will be enough to make it happen. Of course, the more heartfelt your belief, the faster and more impressive the result will be. Creative visualization is essentially the same thing as prayer, and has the same result, except that you don't invoke a deity. If you are accustomed to praying to a deity, then by all means continue to do so, since this can be even more efficacious than straight creative visualization (of course this depends upon who the deity is and what you're praying for).

Since there are some excellent books on creative visualization readily available (e.g. Shakti Gawain's), we will only summarize two creative visualization methods here:

1) Affirmations can be spoken aloud, voiced mentally, written down, or chanted. These are positive, uplifting statements: for example, "Every day in every way I am getting better and better"; or "I got that raise I wanted because I truly deserved it!"; which are repeated over and over, with feeling.

2) Treasure maps are collages of photographs or drawings which illustrate us getting what we want from life. The visual

images can also be accompanied by written affirmations. The visual images are examined and the accompanying affirmations read with the aim of conjuring up the feeling of that image coming true in our lives.

In using both affirmations and treasure maps, the important point is to get to the feeling of the desire, and not just do it by rote. To make it heartfelt, you should be in a happy, delighted mood – lose yourself in reverie. Try to connect with a feeling of intense longing – a pang of sweet anguish – in your heart. Actually, once you have the intent firmly set up, you can dispense with the visualization (mental imaging) part altogether and just feel the feeling of your desire as a pang in your heart. This is a more economical way of doing it in terms of energy expended. The pang feeling is not unlike the feeling of fear, except you feel it in your heart instead of your solar plexus.

Creative visualization should be done for at least ten minutes or so upon awakening, and again at night before going to sleep. Try to do your visualization as you drop off to sleep. This is difficult at first because the attention needed to maintain an image in the forefront of the mind (importance) is the opposite of the attention needed to enter the dream state (relaxation). The trick is to drop off to sleep with the feeling of your desire uppermost in your mind rather than the thought forms, which is a lot harder to do, and indeed is the equivalent of astral projection – entering lucid dreaming from a position in wakefulness. However, if you keep plugging away at it you'll soon get the hang of it – the necessary balance.

You should also visualize your desires during the day – just like daydreaming, but in the present rather than the future tense, e.g., "I'm so happy *now* that such-and-such is happening in my life!" The secret of creative visualization is to convince yourself that what you are wishing for is already true, and you're just hanging around for a few minutes in the waiting room while the universe finds it and hands it to you. To visualize a desire as if it were already achieved means to imagine it happening in the here and now, as if it were taking place in front of you. You mustn't set up any contradictory agendas such as, "In the event that this creative visualization doesn't work for me then I'll do this other thing." You have to put all your eggs in one basket, in the probable reality in which your desires come true, rather than cover your posterior in the event of failure. The more energy you can bring to bear upon your desire, the faster you'll start seeing results. But be patient: Rome wasn't built in a day.

Creative visualization is essentially a frontal attack on the doubt thought form, which will fight back with every trick it knows. It is helpful, therefore, if you are serious about your creative visualizations, to banish the doubt thought form frequently – perhaps once a day, upon arising – to keep it on the defensive. Your doubt thought form is what tries to hang you up in "Will this happen or not happen? Maybe it won't happen, so I shouldn't let myself get too excited about it so I won't feel disappointed if it doesn't happen, etc. etc." Creative visualization is a way of cutting across all those endless circles of doubt, by taking primary joy in the act of visualization itself. It's like playing with an imaginary companion: a child who has an imaginary companion doesn't care if it's real or not – he or she just has fun with it in the now moment. And that's the attitude you must bring to creative visualization – take primary pleasure in imagining it happening right now, rather than worrying about whether or not it will actually come true in some future. What you are trying to connect with is a feeling of JOY – not attachment to some specific outcome.

The difference between creative visualization and normal daydreaming is that in creative visualization there is no doubt: as in dreaming, the experience is too vivid and intense for doubt. In normal daydreaming, on the other hand, people don't really want the fantasy to come true. They're afraid of taking responsibility for that probable reality, for having that much power and control over their own destiny. Ergo, they detach themselves from their desire by projecting it into a future which will never come, instead of knowing, beyond a shadow of a doubt, that the probable reality will come true – by living that reality in the now moment, which is what is done in creative visualization. Successful people are already using creative visualization unconsciously: they have no doubt about their intentions.

Creative visualization is a light fiber activity, whereas normal daydreaming is a thought form activity. In creative visualization you are trying to connect with a true feeling (a probable reality in which your desire is realized), whereas in normal daydreaming you are idly indulging in some glory scheme. There's no true feeling in most daydreams, just the false joy of undeserved glory. In creative visualization you are not desiring validation from other people; you are desiring and calling forth a sense of merit and reward from within yourself. In daydreaming you say, "Everyone applauds me because I am so wonderful" whereas in creative visualization you say, "Everyone likes me because I like myself".

Both creative visualization and normal daydreaming tend to bring about the conditions they visualize. The trouble is that daydreaming can only bring about conditions in the world of society, not true happiness, because what is being visualized is not true happiness but rather a thought form copy of it. Daydreaming is phony – it has only glory attached to it, not true desire or true hope. Both daydreaming and creative visualization are commands to the Spirit, but creative visualization is a command of fulfillment whereas daydreaming is a command of lack. This is because it is a thought form's command, not ours, and thought forms don't want our desires to be realized because then they cease to exist (become unimportant to us).

In normal daydreaming you are standing back and watching yourself, applauding yourself, patting yourself on the back. The "you" in the daydream is just a puppet; the real you is watching this puppet perform. But in creative visualization, the real you is smack dab in the middle of the action, taking primary enjoyment from being in the scene that unfolds around you, rather than standing back and gloating over it.

In normal daydreams other people only serve as mute witnesses to how wonderful you are or how right you are; they are mere puppets who are impressed by you, or turned on by you, or repentant at how shabbily they've treated you; whereas in creative visualization they're warm, alive, and unpredictable, and you take great pleasure in being in their company. In normal daydreaming you write a rigid script, and usually run the thing over and over again, perhaps making little revisions here and there to enhance your glory; whereas in creative visualization the idea is to get to a point where you are so lost in the joy of it that you are no longer controlling the course that it takes any more – the other people in the scene (if there are any) are making all the suggestions about what will happen next.

Whereas normal daydreaming is a means of escaping from the rigors of life, creative visualization entails knowing that you called your outer circumstances to you for some reason; and knowing that you can also change that reason if only you don't lose sight of (feeling for) the ultimate goal. It means reaching out to probable realities in which there is joy, no matter how improbable they may seem at the moment, rather than to ones which will only reinforce your self-pity and self-hatred. The legend of Pygmalion and Galatea is not a myth – it's a true story.

When you catch yourself indulging in normal daydreaming, switch it to creative visualization. The point is to stop thinking and to let yourself *feel*; to give yourself permission to feel as much joy as you would feel if your desire were to come true, without making that joy contingent upon whether the desire comes true or not. Then it really doesn't matter whether it comes true or not; and this clears the way for it to come true. Having set up an intent by intense, singlepointed desire, you must then drop the obsessive concern and become indifferent as to the outcome. The trick to magic lies in the ability to turn the importance switch on and off at will.

Magicians set up an intent by putting 100% of their attention on it. Whatever their desire is, they have themselves feel an intense longing in their hearts for the object of their desire moment-to-moment, all day long, every day. With every indrawn breath they draw the object of their desire to them, and with every expelled breath they blow away the obstacles in their path. They do not permit themselves to think about, or to desire, anything except the object of their intent. Average people, who don't have the mental control to be monitoring their thoughts and feelings all day long, can still obtain a similar effect by just intensely desiring something as powerfully as they can. Desires that have been longed for for many years have enough strength behind them, by virtue of their sheer repetition, to serve as intents (commands to the Spirit). If there's something which you've desired obsessively for a long, long time, then you have enough intent stored up there already and don't have to do anything more except to drop it.

Once the intent has been set up by obsessive concern, the only way to make it happen, to let the Spirit free to do your bidding, is to drop the concern completely. What locks the Spirit up – keeps it from helping us – is our inability to just let go and abandon ourselves to it, to just trust it to come through for us.

Magicians are able to just drop an obsessive concern because they have their true feelings so finely tuned that they can switch them off and on at will. They are not as wrapped up in their desires and feelings as are average people. They don't have such an ego stake (success / glory versus failure / shame) in the outcome of anything, so they can throw their attention completely behind a desire, and just as completely release it. Average people can't do this – they cling, and cling, and cling to their desires and memories and thought forms. They don't know how to let go. They don't have the discipline to be able to just drop something without looking back. So what average people have to do is to trick themselves: after setting up an intent through obsessive concern, they should then arbitrarily choose some other area of their lives to become obsessively concerned about, and shift all their intense, obsessive desire to this other area.

In actuality, the mental control necessary to maintain one's attention fixed on a specific feeling all day long, and then to stop thinking about it cold, is not as hard as it sounds. You can call upon spirit helpers, or even your death thought form, to assist you by constantly reminding you to return your wandering attention to the object of your desire; or to quit thinking about it, as the case may be.

But it really isn't necessary to do creative visualization all day long. Just do what you can, in good faith, on a level you feel comfortable with, and everything will work out okay. The important thing to remember is that hope is the fuel that propels desire lines forward. This means faith not in ultimate success, but in ultimate self-worth. In the end you have to abide by the dictates of power. You win a few; you lose a few; that's the way it goes.

One further application of creative visualization which is useful in untangling light fibers with other people (to be discussed at length in the next section) is to try to remember times when you've been angry or cruel to other people. It would be best to actually go to them personally and ask their forgiveness; but if this isn't possible you can go to them in your visualization and humbly ask that they forgive you. Then imagine them forgiving you. You should humbly visualize yourself asking and receiving forgiveness from anyone you've ever felt angry at or have hurt. This helps in freeing up your karma (unblocking light fibers) that holds you back from opening your heart.

Defeating Black Magicians

Generally speaking, everybody has light fibers joining them to everyone else in the universe, but in a given lifetime or probable reality only some of these connections are important (although to a magician or lunatic they are all equally important). In normal human relationships there is a give and take of energy (love) through these light fibers, which is what happens when people are making each other feel good. However, there are some people who use these fibers only to take, not to give. These energy vampires are the black magicians.

True black magicians are not doing anything different from what everyone in waking consciousness is doing, namely extending the boundaries of waking consciousness, and also contributing their own little piece to it. As mentioned before, the strain of staying awake is incredibly intense and energy depleting. True black magicians are people who have found a way of maintaining waking consciousness by stealing the energy of other people – by making other people bear the strain of keeping them awake (bearing their self-hatred for them). This is done by blocking up all their light fibers so that no energy can escape from them, they are entirely non-reactive themselves, but they can still suck energy from other people by goading them to react. Black magicians, like evil spirits, feed from emotions: as long as a person has any emotion towards them at all – whether it be fear (the usual one), or anger, or love, or hate, or disgust – the black magicians can suck energy through the light fiber of that emotion. But the black magicians themselves are like brick walls – completely non-reactive emotionally – when any energy is demanded of them; thus no one can suck any energy from them in return. True black magicians stifle all love, all generous impulses, and give themselves wholly over to their own importance. Everybody does this, of course, to some degree or another, but some people are naturally better at it (more psychopathic) than others, or have the counsel of evil spirits to assist them. True black magicians are at the cutting edge of waking consciousness; vampires, for example, actually do exist and can stay alive for centuries. What is basically involved is vampirizing oneself – all the energy which the vampire believes he is getting from others he is actually draining from himself in other lifetimes, in which the power equation between himself and his victims reverses. Being a vampire is really a spiral downward into hell; there is no joy in it whatsoever, but only an overpowering need to stay awake at any cost, which builds and builds on itself to a horrible crescendo.

En passant: the question arises whether vampires have physical bodies, like ourselves. The answer is that they have enough corporeality to make their effects felt in the physical (waking) world; but the fact is that none of us have physical bodies in the sense in which we have been taught to believe. When we are dreaming, our bodies in dreaming operate with all five of the usual senses; so on what basis can we say that our waking bodies are more corporeal than our dreaming bodies? We have no objective way of determining whether, at any given moment, we are awake or dreaming. This is what society does for us: it gives us an objective (albeit false) basis of consensual validation from which to operate. Other people's validation is what makes the waking world seem so real and solid, when in fact wakefulness is but a specialized form of dreaming. Our waking bodies have a continuity that our dream bodies lack; however, this continuity and solidity are learned behaviors – we are not born with them. All we're born with is an ability to suck and cry – everything else we learn as we go along. Similarly, magicians (whether black or white) learn to use and control their dream bodies just as a baby learns to use and control its waking body. A vampire's body is somewhere in between the two in terms of corporeality. It depends on who is looking at him – after all, some intuitive (and crazy) people are quite capable of seeing ghosts, and spirits generally; corporeality is as much a matter of who is doing the observing as it is what is being observed. We can say, though, that vampires stand at one extreme of the progression: disordered personality – psychopath – sadist / torturer –black magician – vampire. The difference is a matter of degree and skill, not of kind. And needless to say, the popular misconceptions about vampires – that they bite you on the neck and suck blood; that they can't stand the light of day; that garlic or silver bullets will keep them away; or that there is anything whatsoever romantic or enviable about them – are fallacious.

In the everyday world where (thank God!) the S.O.B.'s are not as competent as true black magicians, the same basic black magic is going on but in a more polite and genteel fashion. Magic – both black and white – can be considered to be the strategic manipulation of importance. In white magic importance is erased, whereas in black magic it is made an end in itself. What a black magician does, by force or seduction, is to make his desires more important to his victims than the victims' own feelings. He imposes his desires upon his victims, while giving the victims' feelings no credence (importance) whatsoever. And this can only be done with the victims' connivance; there are no innocent bystanders in life. As long as the victims pay attention to the black magician, they cede him importance. In giving another person our attention, what we are giving them is love, even if that attention is forced or strained. For example, a torturer forces his victim to give him attention, but that is still love even though it masquerades as fear.

From the magical point of view, what the average person considers everyday society is a tangle of lies and evasions; of people casting lines into one another to suck each other's energy, all the while pretending they aren't doing this; of people making human sacrifices to propitiate the voracious gods of Money and War, and pretending there are rational reasons for this; of people allowing themselves to be swayed by the blandishments of evil spirits, while pretending that such spirits don't exist. In short, from the magical point of view, our everyday society is a blood pact made between black magicians bent on mutual destruction and abetted by a host of demons, transpiring beneath a thin veneer of civilized niceties and tea party hypocrisy.

Our present-day society forces us to suppress our intent and glorify our thought forms. So people are left in a quandary: they can only find a sense of worth in obeying social sanctions; but, on the other hand, to do that means that they have to suppress their true feelings and embrace society's concepts. Not all human societies demand such a sacrifice of individual spirit – only cultures which serve angry gods demand such blood sacrifices of individual members to appease the group deity. Any culture which values power, which is a concept, over love, which is a feeling, is a culture which has debased its gods and itself. Power is a never-ending thirst: people become happy to repress their sexual drive, to go to war, to do anything to increase their society's power – and by extension, their own – even though this inevitably leads to their own destruction. That is the real problem with black magic – not that it is evil per se, but that it's unskillful. It *inevitably* leads to self-destruction.

Black magic is bad faith and selfishness – any intent to suck more energy through a light fiber than we are giving in return. Any time we address other people we send a light fiber their way. A good feeling comes across as a bright, strong fiber which we are offering them, which they can either accept or reject. A bad feeling, an angry feeling, a fearful feeling, etc. comes across as a weak, dark fiber. It's an invitation to grab us by our phoniness and suck us. We only send such fibers to people we want to reject us and suck our energy. By contrast, a bright, strong fiber is a mandate – a command. It can still be rejected, but cannot be used to suck us.

The everyday black magicians are the people we know who make us feel bad, or dirty, or used. If there is something other than joy and openness going on in a relationship, you can be sure that black magic is at work. Two people who are not being straight with each other – who are not acknowledging consciously and openly the feelings which are passing between them – create an atmosphere of tension and strain, but they become so accustomed to it that they cease to notice it. In a tense relationship practically everything that is said, no matter how supposedly innocent or nonchalant, carries a dart of anger and frustration with it; but the set of ready thought form responses is so quick to the fore that nobody is consciously at the controls any more on either side. A dart just calls up a dart, and the thing goes on like zombie ping-pong.

Now a black magician can be foiled by non-reactive victims, who entirely refuse to react to the black magician's goads (to cede the black magician any importance). Black magicians, like demons, just can't stand being ignored – or worse yet, laughed at. However, the light fibers which the black magician has in his victims are themselves irritating, like mosquito bites. It is difficult for the victims who have such lines in them not to react to the black magician's provocations, particularly if they have a history of encounters with that black magician, and have built up a body of thought forms of him which predispose the victims to respond in the fashion which the black magician desires. Besides, if there is black magic going on, you can be sure that the victims are parties to it also – black magic is invariably a tango for two.

To have other people's lines in us – to have them encroaching in our space – drains us of energy. To have our lines in other people, which we feel as a constant need to be on their case, may give us an immediate jolt of ego power, but in the long run it weakens us by making us dependent on the people we are sucking, and extremely vulnerable to them if they should ever decide to turn on us. When the power equation in the relationship changes, as it inevitably does sooner or later, our erstwhile victims can use those same lines we stuck in them to suck from us; moreover, we'll still have our thought forms which compulsively activate those lines for them – thus we become the victims of the very trap we ourselves created, forced to jerk ourselves around by a cord which we ourselves handed over to our victims. In any case, black magic is inept because it *invariably* runs out.

This power equation, the exchange of roles between victim and oppressor, is an inevitable law of nature, although it can be spread over several lifetimes. The power in a relationship at any given moment resides in the hands of that person who has the least stake (importance) in the continuation of the relationship; and by the normal ebb and flow of things this seesaws back and forth over time, even over lifetimes. These trans-lifetime thought forms (karma) are what we have called importance coverings, and they are actually encoded in our very molecules. They can be glimpsed in past life regressions, but can only be manipulated from a position that starts from lucid dreaming. However, active imagination can be used to get at the lines of black magic which were created in this lifetime, and which if not detached will become the karma next time.

The reason why most people find their close relationships more problematical than their casual acquaintanceships is precisely because they have light fibers in their friends and family that they don't have in strangers and casual acquaintances. When other people have their light fibers in you, they can always "stick one to you" through those fibers. This is why master magicians have no fibers in anyone (except for people whom – for whatever reason – they are trying to influence or manipulate); nor do they permit anyone to stick fibers in them. To truly open your heart to someone it is necessary to get rid of the lines that join you to them. Opening one's heart doesn't involve lines at all – lines aren't conduits of true love but rather of self-reflection. As long as there are lines between two people, then thought forms of expectation begin to accrete (while lines *can* be a conduit for love energy, when you open your heart you don't need specific conduits to certain people – you just feel compassion for everyone. And that's easier to do if you don't have specific lines in specific people).

Note that you don't pull out all of the lines which you have in other people and they have in you; you leave in the good lines, where there is a healthy flow of energy back and forth. You only pull out the parasitic lines, in which energy is only flowing one way. First you must find out where those lines are, and how many of them there are. Go into active imagination, and beckon a thought form of the person whose lines you wish to sever. Just ask, "I'd like to speak to a thought form of So-and-so."

Usually we have a number of different thought forms (stock responses) for everybody we know – e.g. the people themselves, what we want from them, what we fear of them, our love for them, our envy of them, etc. Normally in our everyday dealings with people, we don't interact with *them* at all; we address only our own thought forms of them. If we're not making direct eye contact, then for sure it's just thought forms; but even direct eye contact in a spirit other than openness ("flashing" on the person) is still thought forms. When we first meet people, we react to their appearance, social class, what we expect to get from them, whether we feel turned on or threatened by them, and so forth, rather than to *them*. We don't relate to our parents, spouse, boss, or children, so much as we react to our own images / expectations which we have created of "our parents", "our spouse", "our boss", or "our children".

Here's an example of one of my own person thought forms:

Lena: I'm Lena.

BM: Are you really Lena, or a part of me named Lena?

Lena: I'm a part of you named Lena, but I am what Lena gave you. I am your loving, tender side, who can accept anything without question and be joyous in it. It was me who reverberated so much at meeting the disciples of Father Divine.

BM: What do you want to tell me?

Lena: You owe it to me to be happy. That is what I want for you. You have often wondered what you could do to pay me back for all I did for you. It is simple: be joyous. Be happy. That's it; if you do that, I will feel amply rewarded. And you have a tremendous opportunity to do this. The kids are great, and Nancy's wonderful. You have everything you want; now just be happy. Do that for me. That's all I wanted for you ever since you were a baby. Be happy and your happiness will bless me and make me happy. Okay?

Here's another example of a person thought form, this time of a good-natured but unsavory mooch who lives in my neighborhood:

BM: May I speak to a thought form of the Old Man?

Old Man: Hi! I'm the Old Man!

BM: You sound young.

Old Man: I *am* young. That "old" stuff is just a blind. I'm young because I have lots of energy. I suck off of lots of powerful women. I suck off of my church. I suck off of you. I pamper myself.

BM: May I banish you?

Old Man: If you like. I have plenty of energy without yours.

BM: I think you're a pain in the ass.

Old Man: No doubt. I think you're a selfish, egotistical snob who is choking on his self-importance. You're such a self-righteous ass it makes me want to laugh! And so stupid! And so easy to diddle!

BM: Anything more to contribute?

Old Man: No, but if I really need something from you, I'll be back.

BM: May I speak to another form?

Fear of Old Man: I'm your fear of the Old Man. You can't help but fear someone who has a line in you. It's natural. But you're not that afraid of me. Though I had to chuckle at your reaction to Peter's statement that I was the Angel of Death. Not to mention your fear that I might be a bodhisattva because I'm the least likely person you know who might be one.

Our thought forms of the people we know are born when we first meet (or even hear about) them, and they grow and become more elaborate at each new contact. They are the sum total of all our images and expectations of people – the history of our experiences with them. Without such thought forms (i.e. after banishment) we start from scratch with those people. That is, after banishing our thought forms of people, we still have the same feelings about them and the same opinion of them, but not the same immediate reaction to them. We can see them with detachment, as beings in their own right, apart from whatever gratification or irritation they may have in store for us.

To sever lines, call upon your thought forms of the person whose lines you wish to work on in active imagination. Speak to each of these forms in turn, and ask them to tell you how many lines that person has in you, and where in your body they are located; and how many lines you have in that person, and their location. Also ask for a history of each line, because each line was put in at a certain moment in time, for a certain reason. For example, if the black magician desired your love, he probably put a line in your heart; if he desired your anger or fear, he probably put a line in your head; if he desired your lust, he probably put it in your genitals; and if all he wanted was to bleed you dry, he probably put it in your navel.

Also ask the thought forms where and when you stuck lines in the other person. Then choose a day to pull out all of these lines. It helps to abstain from orgasmic sex for a few days before pulling out lines, and you should eat minimally the day before the ritual. Fast on the day of the ritual. Then call upon all the thought forms related to the person, one at a time, and ask them if they have any final words. Then liquidate them with your banishing ritual or dance.

Then pull out the lines, one by one. To pull the other person's lines out of your body: take a firm stance, and imagine you are gripping with both hands a rope or cord stuck in the given part of your body (where the black magician put it). Try to actually feel it in your hands. You can look at a photograph of the person while you do this, or just visualize him or her standing there before you. Then, with a movement of great repugnance, determination, and finality, jerk the line out of your body and cast it to the ground. Do this in turn with each line that the thought forms told you about. You don't have to actually "see" the light fiber (though some sensitive people do) as long as you can "feel" it – i.e., imagine it is there.

Next, pull your lines out of the other person. Take a firm stance, and imagine you are gripping a line which goes out from your navel (or wherever) to the given part of the other person's body. Imagine the person is standing right there in front of you. Then with a sharp, determined jerk, pull the line out of the person and cast it to a tree.

If that person was really bringing you down, you should feel immediate relief and release after doing this exercise. Sometimes you don't even realize the extent to which they *were* bringing you down until you get their damn lines out of you. You should feel more youthful, since that's what black magicians vampirize – other people's youthfulness and joy. The next time you meet that person you'll be surprised by how different you feel about them and by how much clearer your understanding of the dynamics of the relationship is (you'll have much more detachment).

To cut the lines we have in others and they have in us is like breaking a hypnotic spell. For the first time we can see exactly what is going on, and in time to stop reacting to it automatically if we so choose. If another person says "Please pass the salt!" with a dart of anger behind it, we can clearly see the dart of anger before activating a dart of our own, and we can choose not to activate it if we so desire. We can just pass them the salt as if they'd asked for it nicely; we're not compelled to throw anger at them with the salt, as we would be if we still had lines in them and they had lines in us.

Once you have cut a black magician's lines out of you, you have to keep them out. The black magician will instantly know what you have done, and if he's worth his salt at all he'll try to stick more lines in you immediately, the next time he sees you. You may even have a dream about him in which he's trying to goad you into reacting to him (most of us transact much of our light fiber business when we're asleep). Just refuse the black magician's goad and you defeat him. If you have a dream war with someone, it means that you "won": the other person failed to stick a line in you, since such lines can only be put in in dreamless sleep; therefore, if you remember dreaming about such an encounter, it means you succeeded in moving the battleground from dreamless to dreaming sleep, where the other person's attacks are fruitless. After a while the black magician will give up trying to goad you. It's not hard to refuse the goad once you've gotten rid of your thought forms of him. If he does manage to stick more lines in you, just go through the entire procedure (active imagination and pulling out lines) again. Marriage partners sometimes have to pull their lines out of each other over and over again to untangle a real mess.

Besides pulling his or her lines out, the other way to deal with an unavoidable (parent, teacher, boss, spouse) black magician is to regard him or her as your petty tyrant. See Carlos Castaneda's *The Fire From Within* for details.

There are two major ways of using other people to diminish our importance: following an enlightened guru, or enduring a petty tyrant. In either case the idea is to submit to another person who will not validate our importance for us – who will not mirror glory back at us (plump up our self-pity), but rather who will force us to feel ashamed of ourselves. Since there are a good many more black magicians walking around out there than enlightened gurus; and since most of us already have one or more relationships going with people with whom we are locked in an unavoidable importance tussle; enduring a petty tyrant – dealing with him or her honestly but non-reactively; keeping them at arm's length without rancor or defensiveness; enduring their self-hatred without taking it personally – can be a royal road to losing importance.

Only a fellow human who is truly dedicated to causing us unhappiness can help us get rid of our importance to the last drop. Without a petty tyrant we reach a certain point in our spiritual practice in which we are sufficiently happy and content that we no longer care to make the effort to continue to lose importance. Only a petty tyrant can force us to keep on keeping on. And the only difference between a petty tyrant and any other black magician who is oppressing us is our attitude towards them. Any person who deliberately tries to make us unhappy is a black magician; if we realize that this person is actually helping us to see clearly where our importance lies and swallow it (since they won't validate it), then they become our ally and our very best friend.

Casting Out Demons

In addition to our fellow humans, there are other parasitic beings which can drain our energy, and these are called demons. There are basically two types of demons: demons of anger and demons of melancholy; though, for example, every kind of addictive drug, mental illness, or incurable disease, has its own special cadre of demons proper to it.

The person who lives only to be irritated and hassled all day long; the person who is irresistibly impelled towards dissoluteness and self-destruction; the person who lives only to be ill or depressed – these sorts of people for whom life offers no joy whatsoever but is only a travail – these are the people who are in an advanced stage of demon possession. By the time such people reach old age they are truly sad to behold: they don't have much soul (feelings) of their own left, except for pain; they are just hollow collections of thought forms being manipulated by demons. There's generally no cure for them, since these people are past listening to reason. There's no way you can persuade them that life is anything other than a depressing, irritating, meaningless hassle. Their demons have them convinced: they are so possessed that they feel that to give up their demons would be to give up their very beings. Their demons give them strength and rationalizations, such as their automatic dismissal of any suggestion that their own negative mindset could possibly have anything to do with their problems. Their demons make them mistrust and reject any manifestation of joy, and crave money, or success, or a comfortable routine instead.

Now demons are not thought forms. Thought forms originate within people, as the natural byproduct of their thinking. Demons, on the other hand, come from outside of people – they are summoned into hosts at their behest, usually at a time when the hosts are very weak and need a strong protection against attack or pain. If a host dies or exorcises a demon, it doesn't disintegrate (as thought forms do) but instead flies into another host who has called it for his or her protection.

Demons cannot properly be characterized as evil – there is no such thing as good or evil (except that us guys are good and those guys over there are evil). Demons are just doing their thing, they have to eat like everyone else, and it wasn't demons who set up the rule that all beings must eat – destroy other lives in order to sustain their own. That was the Spirit's idea: the Spirit is the author of life and death, and set things up so as to eat the rest of us. Is the Spirit evil, then?

When you call a demon into yourself, it shares your power as a true partner. You give it the power to create thought forms (to which you are subject), and to shoot out light fibers to draw circumstances to you (e.g. of rejection, hatred, pain) to which you are karmically bound. You surrender volition to the demon, and it takes over a lot of the controls. Unfortunately, you are the one who has to bear the consequences.

Demons *do* protect their hosts, at least initially: they give their hosts a hard edge, a steel plate cover over their hearts to hide their vulnerability and belie their pain. But eventually demons consume their hosts completely: strangling their hearts, sucking them dry of all energy and joy, and fooling them into defending their misery to the death.

Generally speaking, first world, wide-awake, stressed-out societies such as Japan, Germany, and the U.S. have a larger proportion of demon-possessed souls (on a guess, probably more than half) than do laid-back, sleepy and dreamy societies such as those in Latin America (probably less than half). Examples of societies not especially influenced by demons can be found among present-day hunting and gathering tribes. Also, Mercury balanced phase natives (as a rule) seem to have less truck with demons than do natives of the other phases.

Since so many people in our society are possessed by demons, it is a good idea to examine the possibility of whether you also might be possessed by a demon early on, while you still have some ability to reason on your own account left, and enough strength and joy to cast the demon out. Not everyone is possessed by a demon, by any means; but enough of us *are* to at least make it worthwhile to put the question.

To inquire as to whether you are possessed by a demon, just ask some of your more trustworthy and right-minded thought forms. If they indicate that you are indeed possessed by a demon (or demons), don't panic. It's not all that hard to exorcise a demon – all you need is the desire to exorcise it. The hard part is having that desire in the first place, because the demon will try to convince you that you still need it; it will make you fearful of giving up its protection, or angry or disbelieving at the very suggestion that you could be demon-possessed.

If your thought forms tell you that you are possessed by a demon, call upon that demon in active imagination, the same way you communicate with thought forms. Note that when you are speaking with your own thought forms, they are compelled to give you truthful answers. But demons, because they come from outside yourself, can tell you lies and try to trick you; so take whatever they tell you with a grain of salt. They are excellent salesmen. They are, however, compelled to answer you if you address them directly and command them to answer your questions – i.e. they can't hide from you or pretend they're not there unless you yourself want to lie to yourself.

I first stumbled across my own demon in active imagination – some of my thought forms made reference to it since they were created by it and fronted for it. So I called upon my demon to talk to me in active imagination, and we had a conversation. It told me that I had called it to come into me at birth to protect me from my mother; and later on it had helped me to deal with various tormentors: teachers, schoolmates, my wife, and others who I felt had built up their own self-importance by tearing down mine. My demon gave me a flinty, sneering arrogance, which buttressed my sense of self-worth in the face of these useless scum who oppressed me. The demon worked through my own thought forms of anger and self-pity.

To exorcise a demon, first call upon it and talk to it in active imagination. Ask it what it has to say for itself, and respect what it says, since you're the one who called on it in the first place. Thank it for the help it has given you in protecting yourself against life, but tell it that now you want to be joyous instead of protected, and that it must leave.

You can't fight against a demon – that only makes it stronger. You can't be fearful or angry when you cast out a demon; on the contrary, you must be joyous and abandoned. On the day when you decide to exorcise a demon, fast all day long. It's better if you have not engaged in orgasmic sex for at least several days, for strength. Try to cultivate an attitude of eager expectancy towards the exorcism, and on the chosen day engage in activities which are happy and fulfilling. If you are an astrologer, use a Mars planetary hour for the exorcism itself; but this is merely helpful rather than necessary. Joy is the main weapon you use to cast out a demon, so be happy.

Whatever filled you with joy as a child is what you should do on the day of the exorcism: if you were happiest at the beach, go to the beach; if you were happiest playing with dolls, play with dolls; if you were happiest being with your father, be with your father (or his photograph).

Then at the end of the day, do a joyous dance with the intention of shaking the demon out of your body by jumping about and shaking your whole body joyously. You should therefore do this in a place where no one will see or hear you, or else your fear of discovery might inhibit you. Sing and be wild and light; shake your whole body vigorously; and at a certain moment you will feel a shiver up your back, or a feeling like a weight slipping off, or a sensation like the release of claws that had been dug into your back, or something of the sort. If you're clairvoyant, you'll actually see the demon leaving (en passant: this technique of jumping up and down and shaking your body is also very effective in casting off angry and self-pitying moods, illnesses, and negative vibrations which other people try to lay on you).

This is the usual way to cast out a demon, but some people defecate them out. It's all the same. The point is that the exorcism has to be done with joyous abandon, happy in the knowledge that you are finally getting rid of this demon who has been stifling your heart, and now a new life will open up for you.

Once the demon has left you, leave the spot immediately. Try to avoid the spot where you cast off a demon for at least a year. It has no noxious effect for anyone else, however; demons only enter hosts by invitation, but for you to return to that spot would be an invitation. Note that it sometimes happens, when someone casts out demons, that the demons return that night to terrify the person (to try to get back inside of them). If this should happen to you, just hang in there: it's only one (interminable) night of hell, and after that they'll leave you in peace. Maybe spend that first night with someone you trust to hold your hand if need be.

You should feel physically lighter and younger after you cast out a demon. You can always check to see if your exorcism worked by going into active imagination and asking to speak to your demon once again; if it doesn't answer, that means it's gone.

Your friends will notice the difference in you; they'll say you're more relaxed now, a nicer person to be around. On the other hand, you're going to be more vulnerable also. Casting out a demon does not, ipso facto, make you happier – it only makes it possible for you to be happier. To be happier, after leaving the shadow of black magicians and demons, it is necessary to put yourself under the shadow of joyful and nourishing spirits.

Tree Spirits

Like everything else in life, the spiritual path has a trick to it that they never tell you about. They tell you how you *should* think and feel: "Accept all things evenly, as coming from God"; "Desire nothing, cling to nothing"; "Let the world be as ashes in your mouth." What they don't tell you is that this state is impossible to achieve in a real, meaningful way by one's self. We need a guru or an embodied spiritual agent acting upon us to truly transform ourselves. Not even Jesus or Gautama Buddha did it by themselves: they were receiving lots of guidance and support from the spirit side; the Buddha even used a tree spirit to get enlightened, the technique which will be described presently.

The reason for this is that we, by ourselves, can banish thought forms, but we can't keep them from returning unless we have considerable will power to begin with. Since most of us are pretty flabby, we need to borrow strength to be able to control our impulses. It takes self-confidence to have self-confidence; it takes discipline to have discipline; it takes faith to have faith, and hope to have hope. If we're starting out from zero, as most of us are, especially once we've removed the thought forms which offered us protection in the form of phony self-confidence, phony discipline, phony faith, and phony hope, then we have to have someone or something giving us energy to prop up the confidence, discipline, faith, and hope which we lack. If we have a human guru, then this is his or her main function as far as we are concerned. A guru doesn't really teach us anything so much as point a direction, and then support us like a crutch until we are able to walk in that direction by ourselves.

This is done through a "bending" of light fibers: the guru's light fibers act directly upon the disciple's fibers and bend them in the same direction as the guru's fibers. They force the disciple's fibers to conform to, or match, the guru's fibers. There's nothing out of the ordinary in this – this is precisely how parents bend their children's fibers as well. It's a magical process which can't be described in words, although it can be *seen*. The overt process connected to it – the parent fastening his or her own thought form to the child's light fiber (better said: the parent teaching the child a thought form congruent to the parent's to attach to the newly bent light fiber) – is what we call learning by imitation. But this is just the mind level of what's happening: the most superficial manifestation of a very complex process, much of it taking place when both parties are asleep.

For those of us who don't have gurus, it is necessary to go to nature spirits to borrow the energy we need to keep ourselves straight. The light fibers of nature spirits gently engage our own, and by their brilliance they dissolve the importance coverings left by banished thought forms. They align our fibers with theirs, and shake off the extraneous casings which imprison our fibers. The only difference between a human guru and a nature spirit is that the latter operates much more slowly and gently than the former; it can take months or years of going to the same nature spirit daily to obtain the same effect that a human guru can give with one swift blow.

In particular, the earth is a highly salubrious spirit, with great power not only to heal but also to absorb and dissipate negative energy and every sort of spiritual and emotional heaviness, as well as chronic illness. The usual procedure is to dig a trench perhaps two feet deep and somewhat longer than your body. Line the trench with sawdust or leaves so you will have a soft bed and pillow to lie on. Disrobe and wrap yourself in a sheet with only your face exposed. The sheet serves as a protection against e.g. ants. You can do without the sheet if you're the intrepid type. Then lie down in the trench and have someone cover you with a layer of earth up to your neck, with your head sticking out. Insect repellant can be used to keep bugs away. If you are very sick or are in desperate need of lightening up, you should remain buried for 12 hours (dawn to dusk) the first time you bury yourself, and for at least 6 – 8 hours on subsequent burials. Average people need only a 4 hour burial to tune themselves (there's not much point in doing it for less than 4 hours at a stretch). Although this may strike you as an odd thing to do, you might just find that being buried is one of the most enjoyable experiences you've ever had. The earth herself is your hostess, and she will do her best to comfort, nourish, and entertain you.

The sun is also a powerful spirit who can help you open your heart. Stand facing him (early morning is best) with your chest bare and your palms open to the sunlight. Feel his rays on your left breast warming up your heart. You should do this exercise for a few minutes every day. Semi-cloudy conditions also permit doing the exercise so long as there is some shadow.

Other useful nature spirits include water and rock spirits, which can cleanse and solidify us, respectively; and anyone who is only mildly psychic can find such spirits easily enough. They are often found in public parks, since these spirits often direct humans – who may quite unaware of what's going on on a conscious level – to create parks around them. But since tree spirits are readily available to almost everyone, we'll limit our further discussion to them.

People are using tree spirits all the time. Any time you have sat under a tree to read, or write, or relax, you have followed your true feelings to find a proper tree spirit, and then you've plugged your feelings into it. Your mind, your concepts, may be saying, "Oh, how lovely! Pretty day, blue sky – let's go sit under a tree." And you just sit there and don't know what is happening; but your body knows it. Your body goes there because it needs it; and it knows exactly where to go, what to do there, and when to leave.

Tree spirits are noble and generous beings, with a particular affinity for humans which is all the more remarkable considering the wholesale genocide we have practiced on them. It's not that trees mind being taken for wood; they understand the necessities of humans. But logging could be done with a trifle more respect for the lives being taken than is now being done. We should be respectful to our trees; and if we have to cut one down, we should tell it we're sorry and explain why we have to do it.

Society has trained us to feel that we must make other people accept our feelings and point of view in order for them to be valid. And this leads to difficulties, since we can't get validation from another person until we feel valid within ourselves; and we can't do that until we feel worthy of love; and we can't do that until we can validate and love others.

This is why trees are so important in the practice. The light fibers of trees spread out and envelope us without any thought form rationality of "I'm valid", "You're valid", etc. The tree just embraces us lovingly, with no judgments, and that makes our own fibers shine. It makes us know and believe in our true feelings from a light fiber (rather than a mind) point of view; little-by-little it puts us in a proper mood – makes us feel light and strong. Trees strengthen our essential being so we know what *our* desires are; not the desires of our parents, teachers, or society, but our own true desires, our intent, the reason we were born. Only trees can truly validate us because they don't deal on a mental level. Trees help to anchor us in our own true feelings – they give us steadiness and sobriety, so we are not so easily swayed by banished thought forms trying to reassert themselves.

In actual practice, it is most effective to resort to the same tree spirit or spirits every day – or better yet, every night, after you've already had a few hours sleep – for weeks or months at a time, rather than to go to different trees all the time (unless you have some specific need, such as a healing). This is because the effect of a tree spirit is incremental, and almost imperceptible at first. Only after you've resorted to the same tree daily for a long time will you begin to consciously feel what that tree is doing to you; although here and there you run into a tree who really socks it to you.

However, you can talk to a tree at any time, from your first visit, if you like; though there are trees that don't have much to say, and which frankly eschew small talk. However, no tree prefers this form of communication, and no tree will talk to you if you're acting stupidly. You "talk" with trees in your mind, like a two-way conversation going on in your thoughts. Perhaps the easiest way to begin a dialogue with a tree spirit is via automatic writing, the same way you communicate with your thought forms. But after a little practice it's easy enough to dispense with the necessity of writing.

When you first go to a tree that you've never met before, touch it very lightly. Say hello, introduce yourself, stroke the tree, and show it respect and affection. Ask what it can teach you or do for you, because every tree has its own special knowledge to share. Then thank the tree, kiss it goodbye, and leave. Stay at a tree until you feel it's time to go. Your first visits to a tree will probably be longer than subsequent visits, since once the tree knows you it doesn't take it long to tune your fibers.

It's best to sleep at a tree; next best is to doze, or just turn off your mind and listen to sounds, or meditate. But even sitting there thinking or reading has its beneficial effect; it's just that the tree can perform its work more easily if you have your mind turned off. You can bring a groundcloth, pillow, mosquito net, or whatever else you may need to make yourself comfortable. The tree is not going to be impressed that you are sitting in e.g. a lotus position, if that is not truly a comfortable position for you. The important thing is to just relax.

Observe that you must *not* kill bugs, because trees regard that as a violation of their hospitality – one of their guests killing another – so if bugs bother you, shoo them away gently, or use insect repellant or netting.

You have to touch trees very lightly, in all senses. You have to be respectful. If the tree directs you to climb it, you do so agilely and nimbly, not heavily and clumsily. You don't blather and wipe your self-importance over trees like you do with the people you meet; you keep your thought forms (excuses, doubts, etc.) to yourself, because trees don't relate to them.

It's a good idea to bring tree spirits little gifts now and then, such as flowers, pretty stones, or special foods you have prepared lovingly yourself (a token portion will suffice). You don't have to do this every time you visit a tree – you're not trying to bribe it, but just give it a little joyous gift now and then as you would to a dear friend. One wouldn't suppose that spirits would care about such things, but in fact they are delighted with little presents and the thoughtfulness behind them. They themselves will sometimes ask you to bring them a little something on your next visit.

Occasionally a tree spirit will give you a little gift in return: a piece of bark that breaks off in your hand by itself, or leaves or needles that fall on you as you sit or lie under the tree, or which stick to your clothes when you get up. Ask the tree, "Is this a little gift for me?"; and if the tree answers in the affirmative, thank it and regard its present as a true gift of power. Such power gifts should be placed in a small cloth bag and worn around the neck, or placed under your pillow at night, to keep the power of the tree spirit with you even when you are not physically with it. Whatever you do, don't break off a piece of bark on your own account: trees don't care for crassitude.

One thing you should ask the tree spirit is what its specialty is, since all tree spirits have particular virtues. Note that trees have their own proper awarenesses apart from any spirits which might be inhabiting (possessing) them – in the same way that your "soul" inhabits your body, which has an awareness of its own (for an interesting discussion about how an incoming human soul possesses the body of a fetus in the womb, see Dr. Michael Newton's *Journey of Souls*). In the case of spirits which possess trees, there are tree spirits who grant wishes, make you loving, build your self-confidence. There are trees who can help you lighten your spirit, and others who can put you in touch with repressed grief. There are trees who facilitate gazing, lucid dreaming, and seeing the future. There are trees who can help you put your life into perspective, inspire you artistically, and heal your body and spirit.

You might ask what would happen if you go to the wrong tree. The answer is that this can never happen; there is no wrong tree, and whatever tree you find yourself at is the right tree, no matter how you got there. Ideas like right / wrong – "Am I doing this right?" – such ideas only apply to the world of concepts. In the world of feelings, there is no right or wrong, only here and now. How do you feel? No one can answer that question but you; so take responsibility for what you're doing. The only way to learn how to trust your feelings is by trusting them.

Although trees don't operate on a concept level, they are capable of talking to you. But this is not the main way they communicate, and to turn your time with them into a dialogue would be to tangle yourself up in concepts again, and take time away from their true healing function. So once you've learned to talk to them, best let them initiate any conversations, unless you have some pressing question to ask.

Somewhere in your vicinity, in a nearby park or woods perhaps, there is one particular tree which is your own special tree, no matter who you are or whatever virtues are proper to that particular tree. There has to be such a tree near you, because you couldn't live in an area that was too far from a special tree of your own without soon going crazy.

It's worthwhile to search around a bit to locate your own special tree – and if you go looking for it, I guarantee you will find it, whether you can talk with trees or not. In all likelihood you know it already. Your special tree can tune all your fibers at once. Sleeping, dozing, or just sitting under your special tree relaxes you completely, removes all your cares, and soothes your inmost soul. You feel that you are at home, exactly where you belong. The warmth, joy, and complete acceptance which you feel at your special tree is enough to recharge your batteries for days.

If you do nothing else of the exercises and techniques given in this book, but only go to the trees (for a few minutes at least) every day or night, then you'll find after a couple of months that you are just plain happier all the time, without any obvious reason for it.

Summary

When originally invented together with mitosis, thought forms were only perceptions: observer / observed pairs, disassociated pairs of perceiver / perceived. Sensory impressions are the simplest, most primitive type of thought form.

With the invention of meiosis came focus – sequencing random collections of thought forms into strings of past and future. This is what we call "I" – ego or self-awareness. It is merely the arrangement of sensory thought forms into a sequence. Remembered thought forms are attached to light fibers of memory, and "yet to happen" thought forms are attached to light fibers of desire. In one-celled beings there aren't even lines (sequences of past and future); rather, all sensory impressions are happening at once.

Temporal consciousness, sequencing thought forms, is accomplished by forgetting, which in turn gives birth to importance (focus). In our momentary awareness we only experience one sensory impression at a time: focus implies one-at-a-time (there is such a thing as "two-at-a-time" awareness – what Castaneda terms "silent knowledge" – but in this type of consciousness time ceases to have much meaning; nor does space). Actually, we are not precisely focusing on just one thing at a time; rather, momentary consciousness is like a pyramid of forgetfulness with attention decreasing from the apex.

Sensory thought forms are perceived primarily with our feelings; conceptual thought forms are derived from sensory thought forms by not focusing on the sensory input, but rather elsewhere (on something remembered or desired). That is to say:

Sensory thought forms are perceptions of our feelings obtained by forgetting most of the information bombarding awareness at the selfsame moment and focusing on just one thing at a time.

Conceptual thought forms are created by forgetting the sensory thought form of the moment and substituting something remembered or desired in its stead.

It is the process by which those sequences of thought forms are strung together which society seeks to control. Actually, the process is quite random, although familiarity and doubt exert strong forces on what possible pasts and futures are most probable. If you jump out of an airplane, there is a probable future in which you just float up to a cloud; and another in which you land gently and safely in a soft tree; but the most probable future is "Splat!"

Conceptual thought forms are what make up mindless activity (paying attention to something other than the now moment) and sensory thought forms are what make up mindful activity (paying attention to one sensory input in the now moment).

Importance is a light fiber attached to a thought form. Importance is a focus of attention, which is shaped by memory and desire: we tend to consider important – or focus attention – on those thoughts which reflect our moods or are of greatest concern. When we attach light fibers (of memory or desire) to sensory thought forms, that's fine: that's called learning or creating. However, when we attach light fibers to conceptual thought forms, that's neurosis: it entails remembering or desiring something that doesn't exist. Conceptual thought forms never happen anywhere except in our minds. When all, or almost all, of our waking attention is pinned down in conceptual (as opposed to sensory) thought forms, then the internal dialogue is complete. Society is triumphant and we are its abject slaves.

We are awake only to the extent that we are thinking. If we are merely processing sensory thought forms – if we are either dreaming or acting mindfully in waking consciousness – then we are not actually awake. Acting mindfully and dreaming are rather the same thing; acting mindlessly (on importance) is essentially something else. That is to say, contrary to popular belief – our socially-conditioned definition of reality – the hard-and-fast distinction is not between dreaming and being awake, but rather between mindfulness and mindlessness: paying attention to the now moment versus paying attention to a past that never was or future that never will be. The difference between being awake or being asleep is an artificial distinction, like the special clothes popes and kings wear so people will know how important they are. In similar fashion, we make a big deal out of the difference between being awake or asleep just to show how important our waking selves are.

Waking consciousness per se isn't evil. It's only when importance becomes the main issue – i.e., when sensory thought forms are sporadic and conceptual thought forms are the norm – that we've got neurosis.

The "self" which is being focused upon or isolated doesn't actually exist. It's merely a vortex, or clenching up. For example, in a river, here and there, for whatever reason, vortices form. The vortices are just disturbances (non-uniformities) in the water of the river. And that's all individual sentient beings are: disturbances in the stuff of consciousness (light fibers). Where light fibers happen to "cross" or "agglomerate" or "agglutinate" they start issuing thought forms. But these agglomerations of light fibers have no more substance or self-existence than vortices in a river. And just as vortices in a river arise and eventually disperse, so too do individual sentient beings arise and disperse. They are not eternal. What keeps them going is importance.

Importance and familiarity are needed to focus attention. Normally sentient beings focus attention through a "self" (through an importance / familiarity gloss). Newborns, perforce, perceive with very little importance / familiarity (sense of self), hence their experience of the world is chaotic and uncontrollable. But once focus has been learned, it is possible to dispense with the gloss of importance / familiarity (screens of inattention) and perceive without using a "self" to focus attention. The difference between an infant's and a master magician's perception is that the former is chaotic and uncontrollable, and the latter – albeit equally chaotic – is more usable. The master magician is able to adapt to what he or she perceives, whereas an infant is completely at sea.

To truly perceive reality it is necessary to do so with no "self" there, which entails getting rid of importance. But we don't get rid of all importance (sense of self) otherwise there wouldn't be anything left – neither perceiver nor perceived. To drop all familiarity and importance is to drop all focus and selfhood – to dissolve back into chaos, to cease being a vortex. Since this is where everything is heading anyway, as the Second Law of Thermodynamics assures us, some enlightened sages decide to do just this. How much importance and familiarity to keep is an individual matter: the optimum amounts depend upon each individual's purpose and purposes. We must keep just enough importance to focus, and get rid of all the extraneous importance.

The eradication of importance can be reduced to three basic steps:

Banishing the "Fear of Death" thought form

Using creative visualization, and

Resorting to tree spirits.

1)   Banishing the "Fear of Death" thought form severs importance loose from the "Body" thought form, in which it is principally lodged. Beneath the thought forms of anger, fear, jealousy, annoyance, etc. behind which it hides, importance can be felt in the body as a heavy, doughy pressure in the trunk, especially around the heart and solar plexus. This pressure in the body is always seeking release (pushing outwards). It calls up thought forms such as anger, fear, jealousy, etc. to which it can attach darts of released energy. These light fibers thrown out by importance – that is to say, our customary moods and concerns – are like a fuel which it expends to keep itself going. That's why we die – we eventually use up all of our fuel (light fiber energy).

Another way of looking at it is that light fibers (i.e. feelings – desires and memories) are like morsels of meat which we toss to the tiger (death) which is stalking us, to keep it placated for the moment. But eventually we run out of meat, and the tiger gets us. There are two ways to beat the tiger: black magic, which entails stealing meat (energy) from other people to feed the tiger; and white magic, which entails turning on the tiger, standing up to it, and forcing it to back down and disgorge all the meat we've given it – that is to say, forcing death to give us back all our light fibers. We do this by recapitulating all of our memories and pulling back every desire (feeling of anger, fear, jealousy, etc.) that we've ever had. Note that feelings of love and joy don't have to be pulled back, nor do those memories have to be recapitulated, because we still own those fibers. Death doesn't get light fibers of joy and love, only fibers attached to thought forms of importance.

By banishing the "Fear of Death" thought form we begin the process of standing up to the tiger. This does not of and by itself eradicate importance, but it's a first step (intent). However, after banishing the "Fear of Death" thought form we do find ourselves in a state of greater alertness, and begin to notice little things that we'd heretofore overlooked, such as the fact that it is importance which calls up thought forms, and not vice versa, as we believed previously. That is to say, we can see that we don't react to a thought form event, but rather the emotion calls up that thought form as an avenue of release; and that what is being released is not the ostensible emotion of the thought form (anger, fear, jealousy, whatever) but rather a heavy, unpleasant sensation which issues from the neighborhood of our navels. These darts of energy are what demons and black magicians elicit and live from.

Once the "Fear of Death" thought form (and its attendant forms, such as e.g. "The Desire for Heaven") have been cleared out of the way, importance can be attacked directly. This is inevitably a difficult and painful enterprise because importance is so durable.

2) To oppose the powerful sense of importance based on society's scheme of shame and glory, we must conjure up another and stronger importance scheme to oppose it – i.e., to make something more important than shame and glory. To this end creative visualization is employed to replace negative, self-pitying thought forms, which bolster importance, with joyous, hopeful ones, which starve importance. This practice develops thought and mood control – the rejection of thought forms of glory and emission of darts of importance (feelings of anger, fear, jealousy, etc.) as they arise, and the replacement of them with thoughts of well-being and hope. Creative

visualization is pursued until the new standard of importance overpowers the old one. At this point it can be clearly seen that whatever was being visualized (health, wealth, love, whatever) has nothing to do with the case, but was only a thought form symbol of no importance whatsoever except as a standard around which attention could be rallied to oppose the importance of shame and glory.

3) Where creative visualization supplies us with thought forms to oppose the thought forms of importance, nature spirits supply us with the actual strength needed for the effort. We borrow the energy of nature spirits to set up a counter pressure outside of ourselves to resist the pressure of importance inside of us – to help us contain or hold in darts of negative energy which importance is constantly trying to emit. When we reach a point where we are in balance – where there is no sense of compulsion and no sense of restraint, but rather an inner peace and stability – then importance has been eradicated.

Glossary

In this glossary the materialistic philosophical or psychological equivalent of the magical term is given in italics in parentheses, e.g. Intent (*affect*).

Active Imagination – a technique devised by Carl Jung for consciously interacting with our thought forms

Conceptual thought form (*meme, schema control unit, agent*): a thought – a conditioned pattern of behavior or reaction (learned from parents and society); a position which is being defended, which has a logic, a rationale, and a will to live all its own

Conjunction – two planets (such as sun and Mercury) occupying the same position in celestial longitude

Dream consciousness (*REM sleep*) consists primarily of sensory thought forms

Dreamless sleep (*Non-REM sleep*) consists primarily of feelings (light fibers). It is the deepest level of sleep, on which we are reunited with our spiritual selves (Daimon)

Elongation – a point in an inferior planet's (such as Mercury's) orbit in which it appears to be as far from the sun as it will get (in a given cycle). A native born when Mercury is elongation sun

Familiarity – recognition: the feeling that what is happening now resembles something that happened previously

Hypnagogic imagery or hallucination: the jumble of dream images which flood the mind as one is dropping off to sleep

Importance – the feeling of urgency, of being driven, of something being more important than paying attention to the now moment

Importance coverings – Conceptual thought forms' thought forms, which stabilize them (give them the illusion of persisting in time). They are the "index" of rank in the bureaucratic hierarchy of conceptual thought forms (which well-order conceptual T.F.'s)

Intent (*affect*) – feeling, the stuff of dreamless sleep, just as sensory thought forms are the stuff of dream consciousness and conceptual thought forms are the stuff of waking consciousness. Our intent is our true feelings; our inner certainty; our innate sense of what is right and true, of who we are and what we must do

Light Fibers – feelings, intent (which to psychic vision appear as fibers of living, aware light)

Lucid Dreaming – dreaming in which we are consciously aware of the fact that we are dreaming

Magic – a coherent set of practices (basically lucid dreaming and recapitulation of present-life memories) for blending waking and dream consciousness (erasing the boundary of forgetting). Magic involves the conscious manipulation of the force which most people term "luck", by means of the deliberate cultivation of the faculty which most people term "intuition".

Marking Point – one of Mercury's conjunctions, elongations, or stations

Meiosis – the process by which a cell prepares for sexual reproduction; loosely, multi-cellular life

Mitosis – the process by which a cell divides; loosely, single-celled life

Native – the subject whose horoscope is being analyzed

Probable reality – a "parallel reality" which branches off from this lifetime whenever we make a decision

Recapitulation – a technique (similar to past life regressions) for reliving memories from this lifetime (described in the author's companion volume *The Great Wheel*).

Sensory thought form (*qualia*) – sensory or extrasensory perception of the now moment: sight, sound, smell, taste, or feeling (either physical and nonphysical). Sensory thought forms have a high proportion of feeling to them, such as the sight of a beautiful woman; the smell of roses; the roar of the ocean; the feel of slime

Society – the set of conceptual thought forms proper to a given milieu at a given time

The Spirit – the magician's God – it is the source of light fibers (i.e. everything that exists is a manifestation of it).

Unlike the Judeo-Christian-Islamic God, it is utterly indifferent, so there is no point in worshipping it or praying to it. Nonetheless it is subject to our command (intent) by means of unyielding determination and infinite patience

Station – a point in a planet's orbit where it appears to stop its zodiacal motion and begin moving again in the opposite direction; a native born when Mercury is stationary

Synodic cycle – a planet's orbit around the sun as seen from the earth (as opposed to sidereal cycle – a planet's orbit around the sun as seen from a fixed point above it)

Thought form (*mentation*) – moment-to-moment awareness; observer/observed duality; the content of each moment's awareness is a thought form (sensory when we are being mindful and conceptual when we are acting mindlessly).

True feelings – intent; what we are really feeling in our inmost hearts

Waking consciousness – consists primarily of conceptual thought forms

Zodiac – the sun's apparent yearly path through the fixed stars, which is used to measure astrological position

Appendix 1: The Progressed Mercury Cycle

The system of secondary progressions is an astrological technique for predicting important epochs of change in the life, based upon the equivalence: one day equals one year – that is to say, one day of astronomical time can be equated to one year of actual life span. If, for example, Mercury reached its Greatest Eastern Elongation twenty days after you were born, we would say that progressed Mercury reached GEE at age twenty years. Progressing Mercury to the marking points of its synodic cycle usually yields several predictions (in the average case) of times in your life when you have to perform radical surgery on your self-images. A birth time which is off by an hour only throws these calculations off by two weeks, so somewhat inexact birth times are no bar to applying the technique.

Instructions for Progressing Mercury to its Marking Points:

1) To the clock time of birth, add the number of hours of the standard time zone of the birthplace (Atlantic Standard or Eastern Daylight Time = 4; Eastern Standard or Central Daylight Time = 5; Central Standard or Mountain Daylight Time = 6; Mountain Standard or Pacific Daylight Time = 7; Pacific Standard Time = 8; etc.). This yields the Universal Time (UT) of birth. If the sum is greater than 24 hours, subtract 24 hours and advance the birth date to the next day.

Example: Birth on December 31, 1950, at 8:15 pm (20:15 hours) in Chicago.

On this date Chicago was on Central Standard Time (zone 6), hence the UT = 20:15 + 6 = 26:15. Subtracting 24 hours and advancing the day by one yields a UT of 2:15 am on January 1, 1951.

2) For the birth date take out the day number from the appended Table of Day Numbers. Express the UT in hours and decimal fractions (instead of hours and minutes), and

divide by 24 to obtain the day fraction. The day number plus the day fraction equals the birthday number.

3) In the Tables of Mercury's Synodic Cycle in Appendix 3, scan down the column for the birth year, and note all the marking points, with their dates and UT's, which occur in the several months after birth.

4) For each marking point: take the day number from the appended table; convert the UT's to hours and decimal fractions (instead of hours and minutes), and divide by 24 to obtain the day fraction. The day number plus the day fraction equals the progressed number for each marking point.

5) From the progressed numbers of the marking points, subtract the birthday number. These differences are the number of years and decimal fractions from birth until the progressions operate. Multiply the decimal fractions by 365 and add to the years to obtain years and days of age until progressed Mercury precisely reaches its marking points. If the progressed numbers are less than the birthday number (i.e. if the progressed dates fall in the year following the birth year), then add 365 to them before subtracting the birthday number.

Example: Birth at 2:15 am UT on 1 January 1951

Day number of 1 January = 1. UT expressed as hours and decimal fractions = 2.25. Day fraction = 2.25 / 24 = .094. Birthday number = 1 + .094 = 1.09 (there's no point in carrying these calculations out to more than two decimal places because the timing isn't that precise anyway).

From the tables in Appendix 4, the following marking points occur in the three months after birth:

IC - 1/ 1/51 @ 20:33 UT
Progressed number = 1 + 20.55 / 24 = 1.86 and
1.86 – 1.09 = .77
77 * 365 = age 281 days = October 1951

SD - 1/12/51 @ 15:29 UT
Progressed number = 12 + 15.48 / 24 = 12.65 and
12.65 – 1.09 = 11.56

11 + .56 * 365 = age 11 years, 204 days = July –
August 1962

GWE - 1/24/51 @ 3:20 UT
Progressed number = 24 + 3.33 / 24 = 24.14 and
24.14 – 1.09 = 23.05
23 + .05 * 365 = age 23 years, 18 days = January
1974

SC - 3/11/51 @ 10:07 UT
Progressed number = 70 + 10.12 / 24 = 70.42 and
70.42 – 1.09 = 69.33
69 + .33 * 365 = age 69 years, 120 days = April –
May 2020

Although the calculations work out to precise dates, the predictions are pointing to epochs in time spread out over several months at least. As with other major progressions, the associated events usually begin within a month or so after the calculated dates, and the effects last for some 4 to 6 months thereafter, although there is often a permanent reorientation of perspective or shift of gears in the psyche.

At all of progressed Mercury's marking points you are forced by circumstances to take more responsibility for the direction of your life, rather than permit yourself to just drift along, subject to the vagaries of outward circumstances. There emerges a more conscious awareness on your part of your own conditioned patterns of behavior and taken-for-granted assumptions; this comes about because some such pattern is highlighted or disrupted by an "outside" event. At these points in your life you have to establish new patterns of belief and behavior based upon new sets of presuppositions.

Table of Day Numbers

Jan	Feb	Mar	Apr	May	Jun	Jul	Aug	Sep	Oct	Nov	Dec
1	32	60	91	121	152	182	213	244	274	305	335
2	33	61	92	122	153	183	214	245	275	306	336
3	34	62	93	123	154	184	215	246	276	307	337
4	35	63	94	124	155	185	216	247	277	308	338
5	36	64	95	125	156	186	217	248	278	309	339
6	37	65	96	126	157	187	218	249	279	310	340
7	38	66	97	127	158	188	219	250	280	311	341
8	39	67	98	128	159	189	220	251	281	312	342
9	40	68	99	129	160	190	221	252	282	313	343
10	41	69	100	130	161	191	222	253	283	314	344
11	42	70	101	131	162	192	223	254	284	315	345
12	43	71	102	132	163	193	224	255	285	316	346
13	44	72	103	133	164	194	225	256	286	317	347
14	45	73	104	134	165	195	226	257	287	318	348
15	46	74	105	135	166	196	227	258	288	319	349
16	47	75	106	136	167	197	228	259	289	320	350
17	48	76	107	137	168	198	229	260	290	321	351
18	49	77	108	138	169	199	230	261	291	322	352
19	50	78	109	139	170	200	231	262	292	323	353
20	51	79	110	140	171	201	232	263	293	324	354
21	52	80	111	141	172	202	233	264	294	325	355
22	53	81	112	142	173	203	234	265	295	326	356
23	54	82	113	143	174	204	235	266	296	327	357
24	55	83	114	144	175	205	236	267	297	328	358
25	56	84	115	145	176	206	237	268	298	329	359
26	57	85	116	146	177	207	238	269	299	330	360
27	58	86	117	147	178	208	239	270	300	331	361
28	59	87	118	148	179	209	240	271	301	332	362
29	*	88	119	149	180	210	241	272	302	333	363
30		89	120	150	181	211	242	273	303	334	364
31		90		151		212	243		304		365

* in leap years add 1 after February 28th.

Progressed Conjunctions

At Mercury's progressed conjunctions you are forced to stand up for yourself and take active control in a confusing or chaotic situation. The two conjunctions (IC and SC) have similar meanings; however at SC you usually get to elect which way you'll go to overcome the difficulties, whereas at IC the decision is usually imposed on you from without and you have to accept it (adjust to it) as best you can. Another way of looking at it is: at SC you must take responsibility for yourself and make the world mirror it; whereas at IC you must take responsibility for the situation and mirror it within yourself. Hence SC tends to be benefic and IC malefic; but much depends upon the tenor of concurrent transits, progressions, and directions.

Progressed IC: You are plunked down in an unfamiliar (and a bit threatening) situation. There is a sense of being held down or trapped by circumstances, as if the world were closing in on you. Your own feelings don't seem to count for much. You are thrown on your own resources and forced to rely upon your own capabilities and pluck. You learn a lot about what you are capable of handling, and also about what your limits are. You have to stand firm and stick to your guns. And you find an island in the storm – a sense of calm within yourself which enables you to come to terms with your own feelings – i.e., to find freedom within yourself, no matter what is going on around you. You find you are able to make some space for yourself under even the most trying conditions.

Examples of Progressed Mercury Inferior Conjunction:
Jack London – April 1907: He had announced a year previously that he would sail around the world, and he borrowed money to build and launch a vessel on the strength of the articles and stories about the voyage which he promised to write. But delay followed delay, the boat ended up costing five times his original estimate, and it kept breaking down as fast as it could be repaired. Finally in April 1907 the cruise of the *Snark* got underway with a broken engine, a leaky hull,

spoiled provisions, and a crew of amateurs. Since the supposed navigator didn't know how to navigate, they were soon lost at sea. In the midst of this horrendous debacle London sat down and began writing *Martin Eden* (his finest novel). Eventually, by luck, they made it to Hawaii, where London fired the crew and got the boat shipshape to continue the voyage.

Ernest Hemingway – May 1928: The preceding winter and spring he had suffered a series of painful illnesses and serious accidents, which left him exhausted and depressed, and completely unable to write. He was homesick for America and wanted his pregnant wife to give birth in America, so he now moved to Key West. He quickly fell in love with the place, and threw himself into writing *A Farewell to Arms*.

Charles DeGaulle – June 1943: At the Casablanca conference five months previously he had been forced to take a back seat to Roosevelt and Churchill; and he was also being seriously challenged for leadership of the Free French. Now he defeated his main rival for power and united the different French resistance movements under his own leadership. He also moved his headquarters from London to the recently liberated Algiers – a symbolic act of defiance against his English and American allies. By the summer of 1943 DeGaulle was universally recognized as the undisputed master of the provisional government of France.

Progressed SC: You have been in a confusing and disorienting situation in which strong and conflicting currents of emotion have been buffeting you about; everything seems up in the air. Undaunted by the confusion, you make a firm decision to take control of things instead of drifting along helplessly. You must take the initiative yourself, but you are very lucky now, and the ideal resolution may seem to drop into your lap as if from heaven. You may find a new home, job, milieu, or base from which you can operate independently. At first you may have doubts about your ability to measure up; but you find you are able to tap into previously latent reserves of power within yourself – a calm faith in the sustaining power of the universe – that enables you to step forward and impose your own order on the chaos. You find yourself gazing upon new, enlarged horizons, with a greater self-confidence and sense of purpose.

Examples of Progressed Mercury Superior Conjunction:

Conrad Hilton – April 1912: "I was twenty-three years old. I had been working for eleven years. So far I had earned a partnership in a store in the town in which I was born. But it was my father's store. A.H. Hilton & Son. A.H. Hilton & Shadow? a small voice within me was questioning. Wasn't it time I formulated a dream of my own?" With the impending admission of New Mexico into the union in January 1912, Hilton ran for and won a seat in the new state legislature (over the vehement opposition of his father) and in April moved to Santa Fe, where he eagerly and idealistically threw himself into his legislative duties and the social life of the capital.

Jean Harlowe – August 1927: She had eloped with her boyfriend (at age 16) the previous March in order to escape from boarding school, and upon her return she was immediately expelled from the school and sequestered by her outraged parents. Cut off from her erstwhile husband; the subject of scandal in her home town, she went through a period of depression, losing weight and starting to smoke. Then in August her parents moved to Los Angeles, which delighted her, and where she soon began to get bit parts in movies.

John F. Kennedy – April 1961: The Bay of Pigs fiasco. He had just been inaugurated president, and went along with the Cuban invasion plan (inherited from the previous administration) with heavy misgivings. When the invasion failed and U.S. aggression was assailed world-wide, Kennedy was angry and sick at heart. It was the worst defeat of his career, but according to Theodore Sorensen, "In later months he would be grateful that he had learned so many major lessons – resulting in basic changes in personnel, policy, and procedures."

Progressed Elongations

At both of Mercury's progressed elongation points your own judgment may come into conflict with that of a partner or opponent; in any case, there arises some question about the balance between your own needs and those of someone else. Since you are mentally very clear now, your own view must prevail. The elongations are more relationship-oriented than the conjunctions or stations. The chief difference between the two elongations is that at GWE your involvement is intense and personal, whereas at GEE you are cool and brisk. GWE tends to be malefic and GEE benefic, but again much depends on concurrent transits and directions.

Progressed GWE: Powerful, uncontrollable emotions are let loose (usually in an intimate relationship) which play upon your deepest fears and insecurities. There is often a deep-felt need to tell someone to go to hell. There is a call here for objective self-examination instead of instinctive reaction based on fear. You must put some distance between yourself and the people who are trying to make you conform to their images of you. You must cut loose now and experiment with new attitudes which are more congruent with your own true feelings and needs.

Examples of Progressed Mercury Greatest Western Elongation:

Sir Richard Burton – October 1854: In Arab disguise he penetrated the forbidden city of Harar, Somaliland (a dress-rehearsal for his later penetration of Mecca). "I was under the roof of a bigoted prince whose least word was death; amongst a people who detest foreigners; the only European that had ever passed over their inhospitable threshold, and the fated instrument of their future downfall." The prince wouldn't permit him to leave, which caused Burton increasing concern, but at length he received word that he was free. "Suddenly my weakness and sickness left me, so potent a drug is joy! – and, as we passed the gates loudly saalaming to the warders, a weight of care and anxiety fell from me like a cloak of lead."

General George Patton – October 1943: Two months previously, talking with wounded soldiers during a hospital tour, Patton came across one soldier who was obviously unwounded, and asked what was wrong. "It's my nerves," the soldier replied, "I can't stand the shelling any more." Patton yelled at him, "Your nerves Hell, you are just a Goddamn coward, you yellow son of a bitch!" and slapped him. "Shut up that Goddamn crying. I won't have these brave men here who have been shot seeing a yellow bastard sitting there crying!" And he hit him again. When Patton's superiors learned of this incident, they were appalled, but they tried to hush it up. Nevertheless word got out, and by November the American press and congress were up in arms, demanding Patton's immediate ouster. He narrowly escaped being court-martialed and removed from command altogether; and this incident and the subsequent hullabaloo it aroused prevented Patton from participating in the allied invasion of France.

Timothy Leary – October-November 1962: He had just moved in to the first hippie commune in the world (with Richard Alpert – later Baba Ram Das, Ralph Metzner, and their families, lovers, and assorted camp followers). Their neighbors complained and filed suit with the city to have them evicted; and Harvard was scandalized by the direction Leary's research on psychedelic drugs was taking, and began to shun him and his coworkers in the psychology department. "We agreed that as much as we loved and respected the University, this finishing school for Fortune 500 executives was not the place for the philosophic activists bent on changing practically everything. The honorable thing to do was to dissociate from Harvard." – which he did, before Harvard could fire him outright.

Progressed GEE: After a frustrating or limiting period, you leave your problems with other people to simmer on the back burner and embark on new, exciting activities which engage all your enthusiasm and interest. You are thrust into a new role of greater responsibility or authority over others, and also a greater freedom and scope for yourself. It devolves upon you to make decisions that will affect the welfare of all.

There is an opportunity at this time to prove your mettle – to respond to the situation with calm, level- headed leadership.

Examples of Progressed Mercury Greatest Eastern Elongation:

Anne Morrow Lindbergh – May 1929: Her marriage. She and Charles honeymooned on a yacht to escape the press; then they took off on the inaugural flight (with Lindbergh piloting) of Transcontinental Air Transport (his airline). In addition to the adjustments demanded by being a newlywed, for her it meant adjusting herself to being a celebrity – dogged by the press; assailed by the same vapid questions from everyone she met; having to learn to deal with people in a constrained, unnatural way.

Richard Nixon – December 1972: He had just been reelected to a second term in a landslide, and immediately called for the resignation of all executive employees, to reassert control over the loyalty of his subordinates. He also ordered the massive bombing of Hanoi, which led to a breakthrough in the stalled Vietnam peace talks, and a ceasefire in January 1973. This period was the pinnacle of Nixon's power and influence as president (that same January the trial of the Watergate burglars opened and the Ervin committee hearings in the senate began).

Jacqueline Kennedy Onassis – March 1975: This month her husband Aristotle Onassis died, and she learned that he had secretly had a law passed by the Greek government which invalidated their pre-nuptial agreement, thus effectively disinheriting her (except for a modest bequest). She was insulted and depressed by the will and the publicity surrounding it. She became more withdrawn socially, more serious and intellectual in her interests. That fall she took a job with a publishing firm.

Progressed Stations

At Mercury's progressed stations a situation crops up in which you are forced to critically re-examine certain assumptions which you had heretofore taken for granted. You learn to go it alone; to take care of yourself; to be more independent. The difference between the two stations is that at SR your life becomes more personal, absorbing, and intense – it takes on a deeper meaning for you; whereas at SD you learn that you need not take things so personally – you can be casual and relaxed about life.

Progressed SD: There has been some onerous sense of obligation that has been weighing upon you, and now you make the decision to lighten up and not let your circumstances oppress you.   There's a need for a conscious reordering of your priorities, a broader perspective on your life. You pull yourself out of the rut you're in, and in doing so come to find that you can do just as well acting in a less intense and obsessive manner – you don't have to worry about what others might think of you as long as you're at peace within yourself.

Examples of Progressed Mercury Stationary Direct:
Sigmund Freud – October 1913:   His final break with Carl Jung, whom he had originally considered his good friend and heir apparent in psychoanalysis. For some time Jung's views had moved more towards mysticism and away from sexuality, and there had been flare-ups between the two men; but both tried to avoid an open break. The conflict broke into the open at the Congress of psychoanalysts in fall 1913, and led to Jung's resignation as president several months later.   The press and public were delighted by this apparent repudiation of Freud's theories on sex, but Freud said, "Naturally everything that tries to get away from our truths will find approbation among the general public. We possess the truth; I am as sure of it as fifteen years ago. I have never taken part in polemics. My habit is to repudiate in silence and go my own way."
Mohandas Gandhi – January 1897:   His return to South Africa from India, a pariah because of his previous anti-racist agitation in Natal. He was met by a mob scene, captured, and severely beaten until rescued by police, who held him in protective custody while the mob outside – bent on lynching him – threatened to burn down the house where he was held. Again he was spirited away to safety. Later, when asked to name his attackers (whom he had recognized) he refused, and

forgave them instead. Later that year the English government, shocked by this treatment of Gandhi, forced the Natal government to annul racial discrimination in voting (which had been Gandhi's goal all along). Tempers then cooled, and the tension eased.

Clarence Darrow – August 1912: He was tried for jury-bribing. It was a trumped-up case, staged by his political enemies (in vengeance for Darrow's having defended violent labor agitators), and climaxed by his pleading for himself: "What am I on trial for? I am not on trial for having sought to bribe a man named Lockwood. I am on trial because I have been a lover of the poor, a friend of the oppressed, because I have stood for labor all these years and have brought down upon my head the wrath of the criminal interests in this country." The jury deliberated just half an hour before giving a verdict of acquittal.

Progressed SR: There has been a need for a greater sense of direction and organization in your life. Suddenly some situation pops up which engages all your attention and interest, and releases your pent-up energy. It gives you a raison d'etre: a real sense of purpose in life that was lacking heretofore, and a deeper understanding of who you really are, and what you truly desire from life. A new enthusiasm and zest for life replace the frustration you felt before.

Examples of Progressed Mercury Stationary Retrograde:
Will Rogers – May 1905: He had been trying to break into vaudeville with his trick roping act, to get out of doing wild west shows. Now he got his big break, roping a running horse on the vaudeville stage. He was a big hit, as much for his dry comments (which cracked audiences up) as for his roping skill. At first he was puzzled and disconcerted by the audiences' laughter; but he soon began to studiously put together an act – project a role of himself as a comedian – instead of just silently perform rope tricks (as he'd done previously). He even hired a shill with a great guffaw to sit in the front row and laugh at everything he said.

Oscar Wilde – June 1878:   He graduated from Oxford with highest honors, and also won Oxford's most prestigious poetry prize, which showed up the dons who had earlier put him down: "It is too delightful altogether this display of fireworks at the end of my career. The dons are 'astonished' beyond words – the Bad Boy doing so well in the end! I am on the best of terms with everyone including Allen who I think is remorseful of his treatment of me!"

Albert Schweitzer – October 1911: "In October 1911, I took the state medical examination. The fee for it I had earned the previous month at the French Musical Festival at Munich, by playing the organ. When on December 17th, after my last examination, I strode out of the hospital into the darkness of the winter evening, I could not grasp the fact that the terrible strain of the medical course was now behind me. Again and again I had to assure myself that I was really awake and not dreaming."

Appendix 2: The Transiting Mercury Cycle

The system of transits is an astrological technique for predicting (or, conversely, electing) dates of important events. The actual movement of a planet in the sky (as measured in the zodiac) is observed; and the dates when that planet transits significant points in the birth horoscope (as measured in the zodiac) are considered to be likely dates of predictable events in the life.

While the transits of the slower planets (such as Saturn and Uranus) may spread their effects out over several months' time, the transits of the swifter bodies – such as the marking points of Mercury's synodic cycle – should produce their effects within two days of the exact time of the marking point.

The technique is simple enough to apply: with a copy of the birth horoscope in hand, one scans down the Tables of Mercury's Synodic Cycle in Appendix 3 for the current year to see if the zodiacal longitudes of any marking points fall within two degrees of conjunction or opposition with a planet or other significant point in the birth horoscope. For example, Uranus in Mohandas Gandhi's birth horoscope was located at 21CN46 (21 degrees and 46 minutes of the sign Cancer). On 1/13/1924 Mercury's Inferior Conjunction fell at 21CP43 (21 degrees and 43 minutes of Capricorn), and on 2/5/1924 Mercury's GWE fell at 20CP05 – both transits within two degrees of opposition to Gandhi's natal Uranus; therefore, on these two dates (or on the days before or after) liberating events (Uranus) might be expected to occur in Gandhi's life. Indeed, on 1/12/1924 Gandhi was rushed from prison (where he'd been held for two years) to a hospital for an emergency appendectomy. Largely because of his weakness and the growth of an abscess following this operation, the government thought it prudent to release him from prison lest he die there and become a cause célèbre – and this was done on 2/5/1924.

Now it must be pointed out that these transits can fail: astrology is not an alarm clock that unfailingly sounds the tocsin at the precise moment it's supposed to. On the other hand, these transits do work most of the time; and their chief use is in elections (selecting propitious times, or avoiding unpropitious times, for taking action). The beneficial transits favor making moves, journeys, and launching new projects generally, depending on the nature of the natal planet contacted.

A transiting marking point of Mercury's synodic cycle ("TMP" for short) symbolizes a moment of truth – a realization or inspiration; a rush of understanding, assurance, or certainty; a moment in which things become clear. New possibilities / opportunities open up, and you have to change your thinking or plans (get beyond something you had been taking for granted). You are open to new ideas, and you must make the decision to embark on a new course of action. This insight may be due to new information you receive now, or to hitherto subconscious information which suddenly becomes conscious. There may be powerful and revealing dream experiences which impress and reassure you; or some situation which has been in the background for some time may suddenly spring to the fore with naked clarity. You may feel a surge of confidence and self-certainty, and thus take a plunge, test new waters, or try new life roles.

The meaning is not always favorable (especially when malefics such as Mars, Saturn, or Uranus are the contact points). The TMP may bring disappointment or restriction. You may discover unpleasant truths about someone you had trusted; or long latent (but vaguely bothersome) illnesses may demand serious attention now. Even if unfavorable events occur, however, you do reach a deeper level of understanding and are able to see beneath the surface into the plain truth of the matter.

It is difficult to distinguish the different TMP's from one another insofar as their effects are concerned (that is, to distinguish transiting SC from transiting GWE, for example) – they all tend to act merely as triggers, and the specific interpretation depends more on the natal point contacted. In a general sort of way, though, the transiting (like the progressed) elongations seem to refer more to relationships than the conjunctions or stations. The conjunctions are more "Aha!"'s

– sudden bursts of insight when the truth becomes clear – whereas the elongations tend to be shifts in perspective (often because you now must take another person's point of view into account). With the conjunctions, something that was hidden comes into plain view, whereas with the elongations it's more a matter of having to see a larger picture. The stations are more dynamic – "thought in action" – than either conjunctions or oppositions; and the realizations you have at these times tend to move you past a blind spot (a sticking point or hang-up).

Where Venus symbolizes our sense of self-worth (appreciating and being appreciated by others), Mercury symbolizes our self-images (approval / validation / agreement) from others. These are not the same thing: for example, there are many very unhappy relationships which are nonetheless cordial, polite, and frictionless on the surface (Mercury level works but Venus level doesn't); and there are also relationships in which people truly love one another but find insuperable barriers to communication and acceptance (Venus level works but Mercury level doesn't). Mercury's transiting marking points show moments in time in which your self-images (Mercury level) work: you either receive the approval of others, or else you learn that you can do very well without it.

The TMP's symbolize internal rather than external events. Although there usually is some event in the outside world which you are responding to, nonetheless the important part is the change in your own attitude or outlook which occurs now. You are able to take a broader view because you are forced to; the new information you receive now necessitates a reexamination of your old images. Usually this time is exciting and challenging; but even when there are difficulties and disappointments you are able to surmount them with your can-do spirit and your ability to see things in a new light – to reach for understanding rather than vindication or self-justification.

In short, you have to figure things out for yourself; take responsibility for yourself; rearrange matters to suit your own convenience. These transits usually bring a sense of relief and release from pressure because of a decision which you make that results in a change in your way of looking at things.

Note that identical TMP's falling on the same point in the birth horoscope at different times in the life often produce similar events. For example, transiting Mercury GWE fell on Carl Jung's midheaven on 12/8/1900, two days before he began his career as a psychologist (started work at his first job in a mental hospital); and transiting Mercury GWE again fell on this point on 12/11/1913, the day before he invented active imagination: "It was during Advent of the year 1913 – December 12, to be exact – that I resolved upon the decisive step. I was sitting at my desk once more, thinking over my fears. Then I let myself drop. Suddenly it was as though the ground literally gave way beneath my feet, and I plunged into the dark depths … ."

Because the two elongation points and the Inferior Conjunction of a given cycle often occur very close together in the zodiac, it sometimes happens that the same planet (or neighboring planets) in the birth horoscope will be "hit" several times within the space of a few weeks. When this occurs, the subsequent hits often symbolize further developments along the same line, or an unfolding of potentials begun at the time of the first hit. An example of this is the IC and subsequent GWE opp Mohandas Gandhi's natal Uranus early in 1924, which (as mentioned above) symbolized his acute illness and consequent liberation from prison. Another example is Franklin D. Roosevelt GEE opp Mercury 7/25/1912 when he learned that Tammany and the "Interests" were trying to prevent his renomination as state senator; and IC opp Mercury 8/22/1912 when he beat Tammany and received renomination by a unanimous vote.

The TMP's are also useful in synastry (horoscope comparison) since they often point to developments in relationships when they activate points in common between the horoscopes of the people involved. For example, transiting GEE on 9/25/1869 opposed Ulysses S. Grant's natal Saturn and Jay Gould's natal Mars. Prior to this Gould had made president Grant's brother-in-law his business partner, and had sold Mrs. Grant shares in the enterprise, in return for influence and advance information. Acting on the information Gould started panic selling which collapsed the gold market on Friday 9/24/1869, which came to be known as Black Friday, and caused a huge scandal for the Grant administration.

Another example: transiting IC on 9/9/1911 fell on Pablo Picasso's natal Uranus and Guillaume Apollinaire's natal Venus. Shortly before this a disreputable art dealer – from whom both men had purchased sculptures – was arrested for stealing the art he sold from the Louvre museum. Picasso and Apollinaire were terrified of being implicated. Apollinaire was arrested, and two days later – on 9/9/1911 – Picasso was also arrested, and at the police station he was brought face-to-face with his good friend and defender Apollinaire, who desperately needed Picasso's corroboration to prove his innocence. Picasso denied knowing Apollinaire, claiming he had but the slightest acquaintance with this fellow. Apollinaire began to cry, and was sent back to Sante prison, while Picasso was discharged and went home.

Here are keywords for the significant points in the natal horoscope when contacted by TMP's:

Sun: Determination – need to stand up, stand out, and shine on your own account.
Examples:
SD opp sun 7/27/1960 – Richard Nixon – nominated Republican presidential candidate
SC opp sun 5/30/1900 – Winston Churchill – a fortunate escape from a Boer ambush

Moon: Assurance – need for emotional sensitivity; taking a positive, hopeful outlook. Examples:
SR opp moon 11/1/1861 – Robert E. Lee – return to Richmond after major disasters with greatly diminished public reputation; but accepted by Jefferson Davis
GEE conj moon 5/7/1936 – Benito Mussolini – victory in Abyssinian war – now decreed the second Roman empire

Mercury: Understanding – need for clear communication and objective discernment. Examples:

IC opp Mercury 9/27/1919 – Albert Einstein – learned that eclipse experiments had confirmed his theory of Relativity (assuring worldly success after years of obscurity).

SR opp Mercury 4/30/1937 – Pablo Picasso – began painting "Guernica" (picture of Spanish town destroyed by Germans the preceding week).

Venus: Intimacy – need to renew personal ties and find joy and fulfillment

Examples:

SR opp Venus 12/9/1918 – Harry S. Truman – on leave in Paris after World War I armistice – "three happy days."

SD conj Venus 8/9/1933 – Anne Lindbergh – on a dark, gloomy night she lost her murdered son's comb – "I can't be comforted."

Mars: Advancement – need to take decisive action and break through obstacles

Examples:

GEE opp Mars 2/21/1868 – Robert E. Lee – forced to make a rare defense of his besmirched honor before U.S. Senate

SD opp Mars 3/5/1869 – Ulysses S. Grant – inaugurated president

Jupiter: Fulfillment – need to be light, expansive, benevolent, forward-looking

Examples:

SC conj Jupiter 2/14/1959 – Fidel Castro – became premier of Cuba

GWE conj Jupiter 11/4/1902 – William Randolph Hearst – won congressional election (his first public office – a great victory)

Saturn: Discipline – need for patience, restraint, and tact. Examples:

SC conj Saturn 12/20/1895 – Nikolai Lenin – arrested by St. Petersburg police (who had been following him for months) and imprisoned for a year.

SD opp Saturn 1/19/1944 – George Patton – after slapping scandal, now learned that Bradley, not he, would command invasion of France. Relieved of command 3 days later.

Uranus: Liberation – need to take a new tack, open new doors, give yourself greater scope. Examples:

IC conj Uranus 12/27/1924 – Howard Hughes – judge removed his "disability as a minor" and need for guardian; now he could take control of his inheritance

GWE opp Uranus 5/14/1958 – Charles DeGaulle – height of Algeria crisis; he took dictatorial control of French government.

Neptune: Attunement – need to pay attention to your intuition and subtleties, not allow yourself to be fooled. Examples:

SR opp Neptune 1/27/1962 –Carlos Castaneda – found his special hilltop (place of predilection) by "seeing" (using psychic vision)

IC conj Neptune 4/8/1919 – Mohandas Gandhi – his first arrest in India (confirmed his commitment to non-violence)

Pluto: Clarity – need for objectivity rather than obsession, and detachment rather than vigor. Examples:

SC opp Pluto 12/4/1955 – George Meany – long-awaited merger of AFL and CIO labor organizations after years of bickering; Meany unanimously acclaimed first president

GEE conj Pluto 6/1/1961 – John F. Kennedy – first meeting with Russian premier Khrushchev – both were "unyielding but courteous" and "argued vigorously but civilly"

North Node: Guidance – a blessing which steers you in the right direction.

IC conj N.Node 12/23/1944 – Ernest Hemingway – war reporting, received surprise visit at the front from his wife, who demanded a divorce.

South Node: Gratification – an ego-boost which may steer you the wrong way
IC conj S. Node 11/7/1960 – Jacqueline Kennedy Onassis – her husband elected president

Part of Fortune: Novelty – you learn to laugh things off and just be happy
SR conj POF 2/14/1882 – Theodore Roosevelt – appointed to State Assembly committee and within 2 days introduced 4 bills

ASC: Reorientation – begin a new phase or epoch in life
SC conj ASC (and Uranus) 10/15/1918 – Adolf Hitler – overcome by gas during attack; hospitalized; depressed and full of hate – decided him to enter politics

MC: Hope – gives you something to set your sights on or shoot for
GEE conj MC 5/23/1922 – Walt Disney – quit his job to incorporate his own company

DESC: Cooperation – changes the tone or direction of a relationship
SD conj DESC 4/21/1919 – Harry Truman – the day he returned to US from service in World War I.

IC: Resolution – requires you to stand your ground and consolidate your power
GEE conj IC 11/3/1959 – Ernest Hemingway – happy return to his home in Cuba (after Cuban revolution) and affectionate reunion with his wife (with whom he'd been fighting)

Magical Almanac –
http://groups.yahoo.com/group/MagicalAlmanac

is Bob Makransky's free quarterly ezine of astrology and magic for thoughtful, intelligent people who are seeking something deeper than the usual New Age – astrological fluff.

To subscribe send an e-mail to:
MagicalAlmanac-subscribe@yahoogroups.com

*   *   *   *   *   *   *

Books by Bob Makransky

Bob Makransky's Four Volume **Introduction to Magic** Series:

People who say that "they don't believe in magic" just haven't yet encountered the Real McCoy!"

"In this series, not only do we get an author who knows his subject inside out, but also a directness of approach often not seen in works of this kind. Not for Makransky the wishy-washy approach that attempts to soothe and reassure the reader with false promises of magical success - something about which many customer complaints arise on the Amazon website - but, rather, an honest and uncompromising study of what Magic really entails. – James Lynn Page (author of *Celtic Magic*, *Everyday Tarot* and *The Christ Enigma*)

*   *   *   *   *   *   *

What is Magic?, the introductory book on witchcraft, can be purchased at:
paperback $19.95: http://www.amzn.com/1499279418
ebook $9.95:
https://www.smashwords.com/books/view/132491
Kindle Edition $9.99: https://www.amzn.com/B0079K8X9O

Contents: Spirits, Intent, The Nature of Reality, Spells, Charms & Rituals, Science Debunked, Demons, The Nature of the Self, Bewitching, Magic & Money, Death, Black

Magicians & Vampires, Power Places, The Magician's God, Magical Time, Magic and Morality, Dreaming & Stalking, Magic and Sex.

"Bob is daring, willing to be offensive with his truths, and wise in the ways of words and magic. ... Bob Makransky, I feel, has written a great treatise on magic. I urge you to enjoy it as much as I have." from the foreword by Michael Peter Langevin, publisher of *Magical Blend* magazine.

"There is a certain no-nonsensical feel to his presentation that is both refreshing and a bit disconcerting. Makransky's writing style is very different from other New Age authors, and that alone should appeal to readers looking for a bit more substance in their study of magic" – J Byrne, *Psychic Magic* magazine

*   *   *   *   *   *   *

Magical Living, the second volume about paganism, can be purchased at:
paperback $16.95: http://www.amzn.com/1499279337
ebook $9.95:
https://www.smashwords.com/books/view/22860
Kindle edition $9.99: https://www.amzn.com/B0041843ZU

Winner of the Reader Views Reviewer's Choice Award; the Sacramento Publishers' Association Awards for Best Nonfiction and Best Spiritual book; and Mind-Body-Spirit Finalist in the National Indie Excellence Awards and the USA Book News Best Books Awards.

Contents: How to channel spirit guides, communicate with plants and nature spirits, develop your psychic vision; together with inspirational essays on managing love relationships, handling oppressive people, and dealing with hurt.

"I love this little book! ... Carry this book with you, read and reread the essays, and connect with joy. " – Kathryn Lanier, *InnerChange* magazine

"He writes beautifully, clearly, elegantly ... he is incapable of an unoriginal thought." – Joseph Polansky, *Diamond Fire* magazine

"I could not get enough! I actually read some of the essays 2 to 3 times and discovered new insights each time. ... Magical Living *by Bob Makransky is an easy to read little book with a lot of surprises. A great book to revisit more than once!"* – Susan Violante, *Reader Views*

"If learning how to live magically appeals to you, you'll love this book. Bob Makransky is a well-known astrologer and teacher of psychic techniques such as channeling, regressions, and working with nature spirits. In Magical Living, *he shares how to communicate with spirit guides, communicate with plants and work with nature spirits, how to manage love relationships, change your luck and more. This is not only an interesting book with some different ideas, it's also a fun book that can be used to lighten the readers' hearts, minds, and spirits."* – Krysta Gibson, *New Spirit Journal*

"It's a beautiful little book to carry around for when you just want something to read at odd moments, but I suspect that, for some, it will be a book that's picked up over and over again. At times, I find myself ruminating over something I read or glance at the contents page to have something jump out at me that's relevant to the moment. I highly recommend this book to anyone with an open mind and a real willingness to look at themselves and their surroundings." – J Byrne, *Psychic-Magic* magazine

The Great Wheel – *a commentary on the System of W.B. Yeats'* **A Vision**, the fourth volume about reincarnation and the lunation cycle, can be sampled and purchased at:
paperback $24.95 from: http://www.amzn.com/154416355X
ebook $9.99 from:
http://www.smashwords.com/books/view/306020
Kindle Edition $9.99: https://www.amzn.com/B00CD958PS

Contents: connecting with your true purpose in this life; how to run past life regressions, probable reality progressions, and recapitulation of present life memories; interpretations for the 28 phases of the moon in the natal horoscope; Mind and Memory, Waking and Dreaming, Change, Familiarity, and the Akashic Records.

"This new work in Bob Makransky's excellent and thought provoking 'Introduction to Magic' series ... is a fascinating and illuminating take on the meaning of the Moon. It's truly a Moon book unlike any other and is guaranteed to alter your perception of yourself and the world." – Paul F. Newman, author *LUNA: The Astrological Moon*

"Bob Makransky ... is directing the reader to access the higher consciousness. He gives many wonderful techniques for it . ... This is not the kind of book you just read and it's finished. It's really a work book. You have to practice the exercises he gives. You have to apply the lunar phases to your own chart and to others. Many statements require thought and reflection. Not beach reading material. Be prepared to be educated and also shocked!" – Joseph Polansky, *Diamond Fire* magazine

"It is difficult to change thought patterns to find a new path, and that is the primary reason I read The Great Wheel *and encourage others to read it. ... To use a 1960's term, this is a heavy book. It is very deep, thorough and forces one to step back and start looking at the big picture. What picture of your life is in need of help? What aspect of your personality could use some help? This book has the tools to help you".*
– Peggy Mathias, *Psychic-Magic* magazine

Intermediate-level Astrology textbooks:

Topics in Astrology is a delightful smorgasbord of three dozen essays on a wide variety of astrological topics ranging from practical, hands-on advice to technical issues to humor and satire. *Topics in Astrology* is chock-full of original tips and guidelines for experienced practitioners (it may be a bit advanced for beginners; but even they will find parts of the book fascinating).

Contents: Natal Astrology, Relationships, Transits, Progressions and Directions, Horary and Electional Astrology, Mundane Astrology, Mayan Astrology, Theory.

"The sheer scope of the work is mind boggling. Bob Makransky has thought deeply and cogently on the subject and it shows. He is one of our most prolific of astrology writers. ... In typical Makransky fashion he takes an axe to some of our most cherished assumptions. After the shock wears off, we are forced to consider what he says and go deeper in our own understanding. .... He is a beautiful writer and as always, you get a good read regardless of whether or not you agree with him. He shows aspects of Astrology that are outside the current mainstream. A very recommendable book for the serious astrological student." – Joseph Polansky, *Diamond Fire* magazine

"Makransky expounds on numerous subjects of interest to astrologers in his anthology of published articles, Topics in Astrology. *Makransky's plainspoken writing style is direct and thought-provoking. Beginners will enjoy and frequently refer to many of the articles. With his wide-ranging interests, Makransky offers something for everyone."* – Chris Lorenz, *Dell Horoscope* magazine

Topics in Astrology – 312 pages – paperback – Price = $19.95
order from: http://www.amzn.com/1519765878
Kindle edition $9.99:
http://www.amazon.com/dp/B019NSBP4Y

Planetary Strength – *a commentary on Morinus* explains the differences between the strengths conferred upon planets by virtue of their sign placements (celestial state); house placements (terrestrial state); and aspects (aspectual state). An essential reference work which both neophyte and experienced practitioners will consult every time they read a horoscope.

"In the introduction, he advises readers to study Morinus, but clearly Makransky's efforts are the better source. ... Try them in practice and compare these interpretations to what you might otherwise think about a planet. It may just sharpen your ability to make accurate statements about character, a person's history, and even to make predictions. And what more do you ask of astrology?" – Chris Lorenz, *Dell Horoscope* magazine

"This is certainly an interesting addition to reading and interpreting the translations of Morinus' original work. It is detailed and considered, and the author's knowledge and experience are evident throughout." – Helen Stokes, *AA Journal*

"Presenting a mixture of discussion, detailed cookbook offerings and chart examples as well as keywords and tables, this fascinating book also addresses the fixed stars. ... This fascinating book assumes a fair knowledge of astrology as well as some experience in preparing charts." – Margaret Gray, *ISAR*

"This is a book that every beginner as well as advanced student of astrology would do well to possess. The author is extremely perceptive in his descriptions of the planets in their various strengths and weaknesses ... this book would be a helpful aid to the researcher, as it would point him in the right direction." – Wanda Sellar, *Correlation*

Planetary Strength – 130 pages – paperback –
Price = £ 11.99 – order from:
http://www.wessexastrologer.com/product/waps001/

*   *   *   *   *   *   *

Planetary Combination picks up where *Planetary Strength* left off, explaining how the planetary influences combine in aspects and configurations to paint a picture of a person and his or her life. Descriptions of planetary configurations such as Grand Trines, Grand Squares, T-Crosses, Wedges, Fans, Rectangles, Kites, and Trapezoids provide overall schematics of people's psychological dynamics. Then, detailed interpretations for the conjunctions, sextiles/trines, squares, oppositions, parallels/contraparallels, and Mutual Receptions between the individual planets enable the practitioner to see clearly how these dynamics work out in a particular horoscope. An illuminating chapter on planetary conjunctions with the moon's nodes reveals the underlying karmic influences at work. An indispensable reference you'll consult every time you read a chart.

"While this book is nominally a series of explanations about aspects between the traditional planets, the degree of character description for each planetary pair is extraordinarily precise. An entire personality is captured within these aspects. In the same way that the author provides highly detailed character sketches for each planetary duo, he gives the same attention to configurations. In addition to the most common shapes, he also provides several pages on shapes that are not found in any other astrology text. An unusually terse and bold reference, Planetary Combination *transcends psychological mumbo-jumbo to give you the bare-naked reality of the adult Western psyche."* - Chris Lorenz, *Dell Horoscope* magazine.

"You are entering a world of verbal complexity and conceptual subtlety. There will be plenty you have not seen anywhere else. You may find Makransky's approach to astrology insightful, delightfully unconventional, or just plain

weird. *I applaud Bob Makransky and his publisher Margaret Cahill at Wessex Astrologer for having produced a work of originality and complexity and befuddlement, astonishment and inspiration and irritation."* – Joseph Crane, *The Astrology Institute*

"Planetary   Combination   *is   an   excellent   and comprehensive summary of all the relevant chart factors. ... One has to search hard to find such material! But this is all presented, as is all of Makransky's work, with vigour, wisdom and accessibility. ... Much of the book is taken up – as we might expect – with a very generous coverage of the astrological aspects. I looked up a few of my own and they were spot on. ... Planetary Combination fills a gap in the current state of astrological literature. It manages to retain both a sense of firm tradition whilst feeling utterly new and fresh."* – James Lynn Page, author of *Everyday Tarot, Celtic Magic, The Christ Enigma* and *The New Positive Thinking.*

"This is one of the best books on aspects out there. He not only deals with aspects themselves, but goes deep into chart morphology. It is one thing to analyze aspects and quite another to look at the "pictures" - the forms - that the aspects make.   Most books on aspects deal with the aspects of longitude. But he also includes the parallels and contra-parallels. He has an interesting discussion of orbs, values (strengths of an aspect) and mutual receptions. A student would have to read many books from many authors to get the information that is given here. As always with Bob Makransky's work, the book is interesting and well written, not for a beginner or casual reader, but fascinating nevertheless - especially for a serious student." – Joseph Polansky, *Diamond Fire* magazine

Planetary Combination – 232 pages – paperback
Price = £ 17.50 – order from:
http://www.wessexastrologer.com/product/wapc001/

Planetary Hours are an ancient astrological system for selecting favorable times to act (and avoiding unfavorable times), by assigning planetary rulers to the twenty-four hours of the day. **Contents:** instructions for finding and interpreting your birthday and birth hour rulers; electional astrology – how to use the Planetary Hours to find lucky times to act (to ask for money; to ask someone on a date or to marry; to go on a journey; to begin a new business); how to cast spells; the Firdaria, an ancient astrological prediction system; Tables of Planetary Hours for any day of the year, and for anywhere on earth from the Equator to 58° North and South latitudes.

"Bob Makransky's new book ably taps the rising vogue for traditional astrology, though eschewing the fatalism often assigned to so-called 'magical' ancient approaches. He describes Planetary Hours (PH) as the "astrology of luck" and a method of finding empowering life moments for the proper exercise of freewill – to be yourself and not an enslaved cog of convention, Makransky explains in this admirably lucid guide book. ... As an introduction, this book is highly accessible." – *AA Journal*

"Usually the subject of planetary hours gets a chapter (and usually less) in a larger book. Usually the subject is dealt with very superficially. How refreshing to have a whole book on the subject and one that goes very deep! How refreshing to have someone who knows his subject inside out, explain it. ... Bob Makransky has written the definitive book on Planetary Hours. It's the best book on the subject out there. It will be read and studied by future generations of astrologers. Its not just something that you read and discard. You want it in your bookshelf to refer to again and again." – Joseph Polansky, *Diamond Fire* magazine

"The Planetary Hours are an ancient astrological system for choosing favorable times to act. This book explains how to use them. Note that this is an astrology of luck, not a psychological astrology. By using this information, you can increase your chances of getting what you want. There is even a chapter on how to cast spells that really work. The actual

Planetary Hours can be easily calculated using the handy tables in the back of the book. Worth looking at!" – Donna Van Toen, *ISAR*

Planetary Hours – 130 pages – paperback
Price = £ 11.00 – order from:
http://www.wessexastrologer.com/product/waph001/

*　　*　　*　　*　　*　　*　　*

Appendix 3: Instructions for Determining Birth Types

How to Determine Mercury Cycle Birth Types:

In the following tables, find the page listing the birth year, and scan down the dates (ignoring, for the moment, the universal times and longitudes) to locate the date immediately preceding and the date immediately following the birth date. The marking points corresponding to these dates are listed in the extreme left hand column.

If the birth occurred within 2 days on either side of the exact time of an IC, SD, or SR; or within 5 days on either side of the exact time of an SC, GWE, or GEE; then use the interpretation for the given marking point and ignore the interpretation for phase.

Example: Birth on December 31, 1950: Per the tables, Mercury conjoined the sun at Inferior Conjunction (at 20:33 Universal Time) the next day (1/1/51). This is within the 2-day orb of inexactitude permitted for the IC, so we use the interpretation for IC in preference to that for phase 6.

For birth dates prior to 1900 see:
   http://www.astro.com/swisseph/ae/mercury1600.pdf.

It is also possible to determine the days when Mercury reached its marking points from a standard astrological ephemeris, using the table given below. Three parameters must be considered: 1) Whether Mercury is in direct motion or retrograde motion; 2) Whether Mercury is ahead or behind the sun in zodiacal longitude; and 3) Whether Mercury's daily travel is greater or less than the sun's daily travel.

The first two criteria can be readily determined by inspection from the ephemeris. The third can be calculated mentally: the difference between Mercury's longitude (at midnight or noon UT, depending upon the ephemeris) on the day of birth and Mercury's longitude the day following is Mercury's daily travel. The sun's daily travel is computed in like fashion, and the two are compared.

To Determine Mercury's Marking Points from Ephemeris:

Phase	Marking Point	Mercury Direct / Retro	Mercury ahead / behind sun in zod long.	Merc travel greater / less than sun's	Page where interps are found
	SC	D	=	greater	 97
4		D	ahead	greater	... 114
	GEE	D	ahead	=	... 104
5		D	ahead	less	... 118
	SR	SR	ahead	less	... 108
6		R	ahead	less	...112
	IC	R	=	less	 94
1		R	behind	less	...111
	SD	SD	behind	less	... 107
2		D	behind	less	... 118
	GWE	D	behind	=	... 104
3		D	behind	greater	... 113

TABLES OF MERCURY'S SYNODIC CYCLE 1900 - 2050 A.D.

1900   1911

	DATE	UT	LONG		DATE	UT	LONG		DATE	UT	LONG
SC	2/9/00	@ 20:25	= 20AQ40	SC	11/21/03	@ 14:55	= 28SC07	SC	9/7/07	@ 4:18	= 13VI23
GEE	3/8/00	@ 6:17	= 19AQ25	GEE	1/1/04	@ 8:26	= 28CP58	GEE	10/23/07	@ 7:35	= 22SC54
SR	3/15/00	@ 13:23	= 9AR09	SR	1/8/04	@ 12:06	= 3AQ03	SR	11/3/07	@ 16:34	= 29SC37
IC	3/25/00	@ 3:19	= 4AR02	IC	1/17/04	@ 11:53	= 25CP57	IC	11/14/07	@ 12:25	= 20SC59
SD	4/7/00	@ 18:51	= 26PI32	SD	1/28/04	@ 23:52	= 17CP00	SD	11/23/07	@ 17:48	= 13SC32
GWE	4/21/00	@ 23:20	= 4AR10	GWE	2/10/04	@ 10:15	= 24CP24	GWE	12/1/07	@ 16:07	= 18SC07
SC	5/30/00	@ 6:59	= 8GE23	SC	3/26/04	@ 21:18	= 5AR47	SC	1/14/08	@ 11:41	= 22CP55
GEE	7/4/00	@ 11:54	= 8LE03	GEE	4/21/04	@ 18:56	= 21TA13	GEE	2/13/08	@ 12:17	= 11PI31
SR	7/18/00	@ 12:52	= 15LE14	SR	5/2/04	@ 9:36	= 26TA23	SR	2/20/08	@ 2:23	= 15PI04
IC	8/1/00	@ 8:27	= 8LE36	IC	5/13/04	@ 11:24	= 22TA15	IC	2/29/08	@ 4:31	= 9PI12
SD	8/11/00	@ 15:13	= 3LE49	SD	5/26/04	@ 5:56	= 17TA23	SD	3/13/08	@ 9:34	= 0PI37
GWE	8/19/00	@ 18:13	= 7LE46	GWE	6/9/04	@ 1:41	= 24TA15	GWE	3/27/08	@ 6:17	= 8PI23
SC	9/13/00	@ 16:51	= 20VI24	SC	7/9/04	@ 23:32	= 17CN15	SC	5/7/08	@ 18:15	= 16TA45
GEE	10/30/00	@ 3:28	= 29SC52	GEE	8/19/04	@ 23:03	= 23VI49	GEE	6/8/08	@ 4:30	= 10CN54
SR	11/9/00	@ 23:34	= 6SG17	SR	9/2/04	@ 18:39	= 1LI20	SR	6/21/08	@ 19:47	= 17CN42
IC	11/20/00	@ 12:35	= 27SC45	IC	9/16/04	@ 2:27	= 22VI46	IC	7/4/08	@ 22:02	= 12CN28
SD	11/29/00	@ 21:28	= 20SC07	SD	9/25/04	@ 6:38	= 16VI53	SD	7/16/08	@ 0:22	= 8CN10
GWE	12/8/00	@ 6:53	= 25SC02	GWE	10/1/04	@ 17:09	= 20VI14	GWE	7/26/08	@ 4:24	= 13CN01
SC	1/22/01	@ 2:43	= 1AQ25	SC	10/31/04	@ 10:26	= 7SC34	SC	8/20/08	@ 14:56	= 27LE08
GEE	2/19/01	@ 19:24	= 18PI33	GEE	12/14/04	@ 12:22	= 12CP30	GEE	10/4/08	@ 18:00	= 6SC30
SR	2/26/01	@ 12:23	= 22PI05	SR	12/22/04	@ 9:39	= 17CP06	SR	10/17/08	@ 3:12	= 13SC42
IC	3/7/01	@ 17:08	= 16PI27	IC	12/31/04	@ 15:44	= 9CP34	IC	10/28/08	@ 16:20	= 4SC51
SD	3/21/01	@ 2:29	= 8PI07	SD	1/11/05	@ 10:21	= 0CP53	SD	11/6/08	@ 16:43	= 27LI52
GWE	4/4/01	@ 5:36	= 16PI00	GWE	1/22/05	@ 21:28	= 7CP46	GWE	11/13/08	@ 18:50	= 1SC51
SC	5/14/01	@ 17:21	= 23TA11	SC	3/10/05	@ 4:44	= 18PI57	SC	12/24/08	@ 4:51	= 2CP00
GEE	6/16/01	@ 7:13	= 19CN03	GEE	4/4/05	@ 10:35	= 2TA59	GEE	1/27/09	@ 3:17	= 25AQ01
SR	6/30/01	@ 2:52	= 26CN00	SR	4/13/05	@ 11:37	= 7TA26	SR	2/2/09	@ 16:01	= 28AQ35
IC	7/13/01	@ 11:59	= 20CN21	IC	4/23/05	@ 21:30	= 3TA02	IC	2/11/09	@ 14:05	= 22AQ14
SD	7/24/01	@ 8:14	= 15CN57	SD	5/7/05	@ 5:34	= 12AR13	SD	2/24/09	@ 4:56	= 13AQ17
GWE	8/2/01	@ 19:58	= 20CN30	GWE	5/21/05	@ 10:58	= 4TA30	GWE	3/9/09	@ 17:32	= 21AQ05
SC	8/27/01	@ 21:48	= 3VI53	SC	6/24/05	@ 9:51	= 2CN11	SC	4/21/09	@ 23:40	= 1TA12
GEE	10/12/01	@ 12:39	= 13SC22	GEE	8/2/05	@ 8:15	= 6VI37	GEE	5/20/09	@ 19:30	= 21GE22
SR	10/24/01	@ 12:14	= 20SC23	SR	8/16/05	@ 8:24	= 14VI03	SR	6/2/09	@ 16:03	= 27GE41
IC	11/4/01	@ 17:48	= 11SC37	IC	8/30/05	@ 2:35	= 6VI02	IC	6/14/09	@ 23:20	= 23GE12
SD	11/13/01	@ 19:53	= 4SC26	SD	9/8/05	@ 15:00	= 0VI35	SD	6/26/09	@ 16:23	= 19GE01
GWE	11/21/01	@ 5:48	= 8SC39	GWE	9/15/05	@ 10:07	= 4VI00	GWE	7/8/09	@ 14:15	= 24GE45
SC	1/2/02	@ 6:06	= 10CP55	SC	10/12/05	@ 8:43	= 18LI21	SC	8/4/09	@ 12:01	= 11LE25
GEE	2/3/02	@ 10:24	= 1PI56	GEE	11/27/05	@ 8:20	= 25SG59	GEE	9/17/09	@ 4:58	= 20LI06
SR	2/9/02	@ 22:27	= 5PI28	SR	12/6/05	@ 7:05	= 1CP14	SR	9/30/09	@ 8:38	= 27LI33
IC	2/18/02	@ 21:39	= 29AQ19	IC	12/15/05	@ 22:22	= 23SG18	IC	10/12/09	@ 15:40	= 18LI40
SD	3/3/02	@ 18:54	= 20AQ29	SD	12/26/05	@ 1:39	= 14SG59	SD	10/21/09	@ 14:12	= 12LI07
GWE	3/17/02	@ 10:52	= 28AQ16	GWE	1/5/06	@ 7:41	= 21SG08	GWE	10/28/09	@ 4:47	= 15LI42
SC	4/29/02	@ 0:42	= 7TA46	SC	2/20/06	@ 20:58	= 1PI19	SC	12/3/09	@ 6:47	= 10SG28
GEE	5/28/02	@ 21:39	= 29GE34	GEE	3/18/06	@ 13:02	= 15AR23	GEE	1/10/10	@ 15:05	= 8AQ30
SR	6/11/02	@ 4:41	= 6CN09	SR	3/26/06	@ 8:02	= 19AR18	SR	1/17/10	@ 10:42	= 12AQ22
IC	6/23/02	@ 20:04	= 1CN23	IC	4/5/06	@ 4:26	= 14AR28	IC	1/26/10	@ 9:02	= 5AQ33
SD	7/5/02	@ 6:23	= 27GE11	SD	4/18/06	@ 19:31	= 7AR33	SD	2/7/10	@ 6:55	= 26CP32
GWE	7/16/02	@ 10:41	= 2CN32	GWE	5/3/06	@ 1:52	= 15AR05	GWE	2/20/10	@ 5:03	= 4AQ08
SC	8/11/02	@ 14:58	= 18LE58	SC	6/8/06	@ 21:33	= 17GE08	SC	4/5/10	@ 22:51	= 15AR15
GEE	9/24/02	@ 22:52	= 26LI58	GEE	7/15/06	@ 13:13	= 18LE45	GEE	5/2/10	@ 16:07	= 2GE06
SR	10/7/02	@ 20:03	= 4SC22	SR	7/29/06	@ 14:36	= 26LE03	SR	5/14/10	@ 5:28	= 7GE43
IC	10/19/02	@ 19:20	= 25LI28	IC	8/12/06	@ 11:59	= 18LE50	IC	5/25/10	@ 17:07	= 3GE35
SD	10/28/02	@ 17:58	= 18LI44	SD	8/22/06	@ 11:16	= 13LE49	SD	6/7/10	@ 1:49	= 29TA05
GWE	11/4/02	@ 13:02	= 22LI29	GWE	8/29/06	@ 23:43	= 17LE30	GWE	6/20/10	@ 9:45	= 5GE38
SC	12/12/02	@ 12:18	= 19SG33	SC	9/24/06	@ 8:25	= 0LI22	SC	7/19/10	@ 16:13	= 26CN05
GEE	1/17/03	@ 11:15	= 14AQ53	GEE	11/9/06	@ 22:02	= 9SG24	GEE	8/30/10	@ 16:18	= 3LI32
SR	1/24/03	@ 15:06	= 19AQ09	SR	11/20/06	@ 1:33	= 15SG28	SR	9/13/10	@ 8:39	= 11LI05
IC	2/2/03	@ 12:57	= 12AQ31	IC	11/30/06	@ 5:52	= 7SG07	IC	9/26/10	@ 8:10	= 2LI21
SD	2/14/03	@ 18:24	= 3AQ30	SD	12/9/06	@ 20:38	= 29SC13	SD	10/5/10	@ 9:22	= 26VI14
GWE	2/27/03	@ 23:15	= 11AQ13	GWE	12/18/06	@ 21:28	= 4SG35	GWE	10/11/10	@ 19:24	= 29VI38
SC	4/13/03	@ 2:50	= 22AR00	SC	2/2/07	@ 16:55	= 12AQ42	SC	11/12/10	@ 14:33	= 19SC20
GEE	5/10/03	@ 15:33	= 10GE09	GEE	3/1/07	@ 22:58	= 28PI20	GEE	12/24/10	@ 22:07	= 22CP05
SR	5/22/03	@ 19:42	= 16GE06	SR	3/8/07	@ 22:19	= 1AR55	SR	1/1/11	@ 8:36	= 26CP22
IC	6/3/03	@ 15:24	= 11GE51	IC	3/18/07	@ 7:57	= 26PI34	IC	1/10/11	@ 10:22	= 19CP04
SD	6/15/03	@ 17:26	= 7GE33	SD	3/31/07	@ 21:53	= 18PI41	SD	1/21/11	@ 14:49	= 10CP13
GWE	6/23/03	@ 12:17	= 13GE45	GWE	4/15/07	@ 0:45	= 26PI23	GWE	2/1/11	@ 16:07	= 17CP26
SC	7/26/03	@ 16:30	= 2LE29	SC	5/24/07	@ 8:55	= 2GE02	SC	3/20/11	@ 13:03	= 28PI48
GEE	9/7/03	@ 9:50	= 10LI29	GEE	6/27/07	@ 12:16	= 0LE10	GEE	4/15/11	@ 0:39	= 13TA28
SR	9/20/03	@ 22:23	= 18LI13	SR	7/11/07	@ 11:18	= 7LE14	SR	4/24/11	@ 23:11	= 18TA20
IC	10/3/03	@ 15:03	= 9LI13	IC	7/25/07	@ 3:07	= 1LE01	IC	5/5/11	@ 17:49	= 14TA06
SD	10/12/03	@ 14:48	= 2LI55	SD	8/4/07	@ 15:16	= 26CN25	SD	5/18/11	@ 18:37	= 8TA51
GWE	10/19/03	@ 1:18	= 6LI20	GWE	8/13/07	@ 6:45	= 0LE34	GWE	6/1/11	@ 20:20	= 15TA58

TABLES OF MERCURY'S SYNODIC CYCLE: 1800 - 2060 A.D.

	DATE	UT	LONG		DATE	UT	LONG		DATE	UT	LONG
SC	7/4/11	@ 0:54	= 10CN56		5/1/15	@ 18:27	= 10TA17		2/23/19	@ 21:23	= 4PI13
GEE	8/13/11	@ 3:45	= 16VI39		6/1/15	@ 1:30	= 2CN43		3/21/19	@ 9:28	= 18PI09
SR	8/27/11	@ 2:26	= 24VI10		6/14/15	@ 10:38	= 9CN20		3/29/19	@ 9:02	= 22AR10
IC	9/9/11	@ 15:08	= 15VI48		6/27/15	@ 4:51	= 4CN27		4/8/19	@ 7:17	= 17AR24
SD	9/18/11	@ 22:26	= 10VI05		7/8/15	@ 13:06	= 0CN15		4/21/19	@ 22:00	= 10AR38
GWE	9/25/11	@ 11:20	= 13VI26		7/19/15	@ 11:20	= 5CN29		5/6/19	@ 4:47	= 18AR10
SC	10/23/11	@ 20:57	= 29LI20		8/14/15	@ 9:59	= 20LE31		6/11/19	@ 14:19	= 19GE35
GEE	12/7/11	@ 22:35	= 5CP35		9/27/15	@ 22:52	= 29LI38		7/18/19	@ 14:54	= 21LE41
SR	12/16/11	@ 5:59	= 10CP29		10/10/15	@ 17:19	= 6SC58		8/1/19	@ 16:04	= 29LE00
IC	12/25/11	@ 15:39	= 2CP45		10/22/15	@ 14:01	= 28LI05		8/15/19	@ 13:20	= 21LE39
SD	1/5/12	@ 3:28	= 24SG11		10/31/15	@ 13:11	= 21LI17		8/25/19	@ 10:47	= 16LE34
GWE	1/16/12	@ 2:09	= 0CP46		11/7/15	@ 9:45	= 25LI05		9/1/19	@ 19:58	= 20LE13
SC	3/2/12	@ 14:41	= 11PI40		12/16/15	@ 0:39	= 22SG58		9/27/19	@ 8:44	= 3LI11
GEE	3/27/12	@ 21:05	= 25AR30		1/20/16	@ 19:30	= 18AQ05		11/12/19	@ 22:13	= 12SG05
SR	4/5/12	@ 8:24	= 29AR44		1/27/16	@ 10:38	= 21AQ45		11/22/19	@ 21:08	= 18SG02
IC	4/15/12	@ 12:28	= 25AR09		2/5/16	@ 8:14	= 15AQ12		12/2/19	@ 23:19	= 9SG44
SD	4/29/12	@ 0:53	= 18AR52		2/17/16	@ 16:08	= 6AQ12		12/19/19	@ 15:31	= 1SG47
GWE	5/13/12	@ 7:18	= 26AR17		3/1/16	@ 23:43	= 13AQ58		12/21/19	@ 20:48	= 7SG15
SC	6/17/12	@ 12:03	= 25GE53		4/14/16	@ 21:30	= 24AR35		2/5/20	@ 20:44	= 15AQ46
GEE	7/25/12	@ 12:50	= 29LE15		5/12/16	@ 18:05	= 13GE15		3/3/20	@ 18:45	= 0AR59
SR	8/8/12	@ 12:57	= 6VI35		5/25/16	@ 2:34	= 19GE17		3/10/20	@ 20:55	= 4AR41
IC	8/22/12	@ 9:26	= 28LE53		6/6/16	@ 1:19	= 14GE59		3/20/20	@ 7:57	= 29PI25
SD	9/1/12	@ 2:08	= 23LE36		6/18/16	@ 1:02	= 10GE43		4/2/20	@ 22:39	= 21PI39
GWE	9/8/12	@ 3:05	= 27LE06		6/30/16	@ 13:47	= 16GE48		4/17/20	@ 1:30	= 29PI18
SC	10/4/12	@ 6:31	= 10LI39		7/28/16	@ 10:26	= 4LE58		5/26/20	@ 1:53	= 4GE30
GEE	11/19/12	@ 15:45	= 19SG02		9/9/16	@ 11:09	= 13LI12		6/29/20	@ 14:20	= 3LE11
SR	11/29/12	@ 2:19	= 24SG39		9/22/16	@ 20:26	= 20LI43		7/13/20	@ 14:04	= 10LE18
IC	12/8/12	@ 22:49	= 16SG31		10/5/16	@ 10:44	= 11LI51		7/27/20	@ 7:22	= 3LE55
SD	12/18/12	@ 20:18	= 8SG22		10/14/16	@ 9:51	= 5LI29		8/6/20	@ 17:40	= 29CN15
GWE	2/12/13	@ 13:41	= 14SG10		10/20/16	@ 21:22	= 8LI59		8/15/20	@ 4:52	= 3LE20
SC	2/12/13	@ 22:58	= 23AQ39		11/24/16	@ 2:18	= 1SG29		9/9/20	@ 1:55	= 16VI04
GEE	3/11/13	@ 3:28	= 8AR11		1/3/17	@ 6:11	= 1AQ39		10/25/20	@ 9:28	= 25SC38
SR	3/18/13	@ 12:57	= 11AR57		1/10/17	@ 6:38	= 5AQ40		11/5/20	@ 12:53	= 2SG11
IC	3/28/13	@ 4:27	= 6AR53		1/19/17	@ 6:14	= 28CP37		11/16/20	@ 6:10	= 23SC36
SD	4/10/13	@ 20:07	= 29PI32		1/30/17	@ 20:40	= 19CP39		11/25/20	@ 13:01	= 16SC06
GWE	4/25/13	@ 0:39	= 7AR07		2/12/17	@ 11:32	= 27CP09		12/3/20	@ 15:05	= 20SC47
SC	6/1/13	@ 23:48	= 10GE50		3/29/17	@ 17:14	= 8AR26		1/16/21	@ 19:31	= 26CP10
GEE	7/7/13	@ 14:54	= 11LE04		4/24/17	@ 19:18	= 24TA11		2/15/21	@ 8:37	= 14PI14
SR	7/21/13	@ 15:05	= 18LE15		5/5/17	@ 15:46	= 29TA29		2/21/21	@ 23:20	= 17PI45
IC	8/4/13	@ 11:28	= 11LE27		5/16/17	@ 20:07	= 25TA21		3/3/21	@ 2:15	= 11PI58
SD	8/14/13	@ 16:13	= 6LE36		5/29/17	@ 12:11	= 20TA36		3/16/21	@ 8:54	= 3PI29
GWE	8/22/13	@ 14:54	= 10LE29		6/12/17	@ 5:43	= 27TA24		3/30/21	@ 6:11	= 11PI13
SC	9/16/13	@ 15:34	= 23VI08		7/12/17	@ 16:45	= 19CN43		5/10/21	@ 11:37	= 19TA15
GEE	11/2/13	@ 3:22	= 2SG31		8/22/17	@ 22:24	= 26VI31		6/11/21	@ 7:52	= 14CN01
SR	11/12/13	@ 19:33	= 8SG51		9/5/17	@ 17:36	= 4LI04		6/25/21	@ 0:26	= 20CN51
IC	11/23/13	@ 6:07	= 0SG21		9/18/17	@ 23:31	= 25VI27		7/8/21	@ 5:17	= 15CN29
SD	12/2/13	@ 16:36	= 22SC40		9/28/17	@ 2:59	= 19VI30		7/19/21	@ 5:30	= 11CN09
GWE	12/11/13	@ 5:20	= 27SC40		10/4/17	@ 13:24	= 22VI52		7/29/21	@ 4:13	= 15CN54
SC	1/25/14	@ 8:36	= 4AQ33		11/3/17	@ 18:18	= 10SC45		8/23/21	@ 10:45	= 29LE44
GEE	2/22/14	@ 15:17	= 21PI12		12/17/17	@ 10:07	= 15CP10		10/7/21	@ 18:00	= 9SC08
SR	3/1/14	@ 9:45	= 24PI47		12/25/17	@ 4:51	= 19CP42		10/20/21	@ 0:17	= 16SC18
IC	3/10/14	@ 15:43	= 19PI14		1/3/18	@ 9:29	= 12CP12		10/31/21	@ 10:35	= 7SC28
SD	3/24/14	@ 2:25	= 11PI00		1/14/18	@ 6:38	= 3CP28		11/9/21	@ 11:06	= 0SC26
GWE	4/7/14	@ 3:22	= 18PI45		1/25/18	@ 21:45	= 10CP27		11/16/21	@ 16:41	= 4SC30
SC	5/17/14	@ 10:31	= 25TA39		3/13/18	@ 2:35	= 21PI42		12/27/21	@ 16:07	= 5CP23
GEE	6/19/14	@ 10:07	= 22CN07		4/7/18	@ 9:00	= 5TA51		1/29/22	@ 23:15	= 27AQ42
SR	7/3/14	@ 6:57	= 29CN07		4/16/18	@ 15:27	= 10TA25		2/5/22	@ 11:28	= 1PI13
IC	7/16/14	@ 18:01	= 23CN19		4/27/18	@ 3:31=	= 6TA03		2/14/22	@ 10:07	= 24AQ56
SD	7/27/14	@ 12:13	= 18CN53		5/10/18	@ 9:46	= 0TA24		2/27/22	@ 3:10	= 16AQ02
GWE	8/5/14	@ 18:33	= 23CN20		5/24/18	@ 15:45	= 7TA42		3/12/22	@ 16:30	= 23AQ49
SC	8/30/14	@ 18:23	= 6VI30		6/27/18	@ 2:43	= 4CN38		4/24/22	@ 17:43	= 3TA44
GEE	10/15/14	@ 13:46	= 16SC03		8/5/18	@ 8:49	= 9VI26		5/23/22	@ 21:56	= 24GE28
SR	10/27/14	@ 8:41	= 22SC58		8/19/18	@ 8:30	= 16VI53		6/5/22	@ 22:40	= 0CN53
IC	11/7/14	@ 11:48	= 14SC13		9/2/18	@ 1:32	= 8VI46		6/18/22	@ 8:46	= 26GE18
SD	11/16/14	@ 14:18	= 6SC59		9/11/18	@ 12:32	= 3VI16		6/29/22	@ 23:30	= 22GE08
GWE	11/24/14	@ 3:56	= 11SC19		9/18/18	@ 5:20	= 6VI37		7/11/22	@ 14:26	= 27GE42
SC	1/5/15	@ 16:00	= 14CP14		10/15/18	@ 12:31	= 21LI20		8/7/22	@ 6:29	= 13LE57
GEE	2/6/15	@ 5:32	= 4PI34		11/30/18	@ 7:41	= 28SG40		9/20/22	@ 4:58	= 22LI45
SR	2/12/15	@ 18:19	= 8PI07		12/9/18	@ 1:56	= 3CP51		10/3/22	@ 6:13	= 0SC12
IC	2/21/15	@ 18:18	= 2PI03		12/18/18	@ 15:49	= 25SG56		10/15/22	@ 10:41	= 21LI17
SD	3/6/15	@ 17:39	= 23AQ16		12/28/18	@ 21:18	= 17SG32		10/24/22	@ 9:27	= 14LI41
GWE	3/20/15	@ 11:15	= 1PI04		1/8/19	@ 7:41	= 23SG49		10/31/22	@ 0:50	= 18LI17

1922   1934

	DATE	UT	LONG	DATE	UT	LONG	DATE	UT	LONG
SC	12/6/22	@ 19:07	= 13SG53	9/19/26	@ 14:44	= 25VI53	7/15/30	@ 10:03	= 2CN10
GEE	1/13/23	@ 11:37	= 11AQ11	11/5/26	@ 3:50	= 5SG11	8/25/30	@ 22:52	= 9VI16
SR	1/20/23	@ 6:06	= 15AQ00	11/15/26	@ 15:12	= 11SG23	9/8/30	@ 16:35	= 6LI47
IC	1/29/23	@ 3:53	= 8AQ13	11/25/26	@ 23:39	= 2SG57	9/21/30	@ 20:20	= 28VI06
SD	2/10/23	@ 4:17	= 29CP12	12/5/26	@ 11:13	= 25SC12	9/30/30	@ 22:58	= 22VI04
GWE	2/23/23	@ 4:35	= 6AQ50	12/14/26	@ 4:02	= 0SG18	10/7/30	@ 8:32	= 25VI26
SC	4/8/23	@ 18:01	= 17AR52	1/28/27	@ 14:00	= 7AQ39	11/7/30	@ 2:49	= 13SC58
GEE	5/5/23	@ 17:43	= 5GE09	2/25/27	@ 11:20	= 23PI55	12/20/30	@ 8:03	= 17CP50
SR	5/17/23	@ 12:32	= 10GE53	3/4/27	@ 7:35	= 27PI30	12/27/30	@ 23:45	= 22CP17
IC	5/29/23	@ 2:52	= 6GE43	3/13/27	@ 14:40	= 22PI01	1/6/31	@ 3:19	= 14CP50
SD	6/10/23	@ 9:10	= 2GE18	3/27/27	@ 2:31	= 13PI54	1/17/31	@ 2:48	= 6CP03
GWE	6/23/23	@ 12:45	= 8GE44	4/10/27	@ 4:13	= 21PI38	1/28/31	@ 21:50	= 13CP09
SC	7/22/23	@ 9:48	= 28CN33	5/20/27	@ 3:39	= 28TA08	3/16/31	@ 0:08	= 24PI26
GEE	9/2/23	@ 15:33	= 6LI11	6/22/27	@ 13:07	= 25CN12	4/10/31	@ 7:41	= 8TA44
SR	9/16/23	@ 7:06	= 13LI47	7/6/27	@ 10:51	= 2LE12	4/19/31	@ 19:54	= 13TA25
IC	9/29/23	@ 4:19	= 4LI59	7/19/27	@ 23:41	= 26CN16	4/30/31	@ 10:07	= 9TA06
SD	10/8/23	@ 4:37	= 28VI48	7/30/27	@ 15:40	= 21CN46	5/13/31	@ 14:32	= 3TA35
GWE	10/14/23	@ 14:26	= 2LI11	8/8/27	@ 16:47	= 26CN08	5/27/31	@ 18:56	= 10TA49
SC	11/16/23	@ 0:33	= 22SC37	9/2/27	@ 15:13	= 9VI08	6/29/31	@ 19:38	= 7CN04
GEE	12/27/23	@ 19:35	= 24CP44	10/18/27	@ 13:58	= 18SC42	8/8/31	@ 9:22	= 12VI13
SR	1/4/24	@ 3:04	= 28CP57	10/30/27	@ 5:23	= 25SC33	8/22/31	@ 8:35	= 19VI40
IC	1/13/24	@ 4:23	= 21CP43	11/10/27	@ 5:43	= 16SC49	9/5/31	@ 0:08	= 11VI28
SD	1/24/24	@ 11:20	= 12CP50	11/19/27	@ 9:27	= 9SC31	9/14/31	@ 9:39	= 5VI54
GWE	2/5/24	@ 15:50	= 20CP05	11/27/27	@ 1:47	= 13SC55	9/21/31	@ 1:13	= 9VI15
SC	3/22/24	@ 9:46	= 1AR30	1/9/28	@ 1:27	= 17CP32	10/18/31	@ 16:54	= 24LI20
GEE	4/17/24	@ 0:11	= 16TA24	2/9/28	@ 1:52	= 7PI15	12/3/31	@ 6:22	= 1CP19
SR	4/27/24	@ 4:29	= 21TA23	2/15/28	@ 14:43	= 10PI44	12/11/31	@ 21:05	= 6CP24
IC	5/8/24	@ 1:37	= 17TA11	2/24/28	@ 15:13	= 4PI46	12/21/31	@ 9:20	= 28SG33
SD	5/21/24	@ 0:20	= 12TA04	3/8/28	@ 16:47	= 26AQ04	12/31/31	@ 16:49	= 20SG06
GWE	6/4/24	@ 0:45	= 19TA06	3/22/28	@ 12:22	= 3PI53	1/11/32	@ 7:35	= 29SG29
SC	7/5/24	@ 17:58	= 13CN23	5/3/28	@ 12:04	= 12TA47	2/26/32	@ 21:24	= 7PI04
GEE	8/15/24	@ 3:56	= 19VI24	6/3/28	@ 4:19	= 5CN49	3/23/32	@ 7:41	= 20AR59
SR	8/29/24	@ 1:47	= 26VI56	6/16/28	@ 16:11	= 12CN30	3/31/32	@ 10:25	= 25AR02
IC	9/11/24	@ 12:56	= 18VI29	6/29/28	@ 13:14	= 7CN30	4/10/32	@ 10:41	= 20AR20
SD	9/20/24	@ 19:01	= 12VI43	7/10/28	@ 19:20	= 3CN16	4/24/32	@ 0:45	= 13AR45
GWE	9/27/24	@ 7:07	= 16VI03	7/21/28	@ 11:03	= 8CN22	5/8/32	@ 7:30	= 21AR14
SC	10/26/24	@ 2:59	= 2SC25	8/16/28	@ 5:06	= 23LE04	6/13/32	@ 7:09	= 22GE02
GEE	12/9/24	@ 21:28	= 8CP17	9/29/28	@ 23:20	= 2SC16	7/20/32	@ 15:39	= 24LE33
SR	12/18/24	@ 1:05	= 13CP03	10/12/28	@ 14:35	= 9SC33	8/3/32	@ 17:12	= 1VI54
IC	12/27/24	@ 9:12	= 5CP22	10/24/28	@ 8:33	= 0SC41	8/17/32	@ 14:18	= 24LE25
SD	1/6/25	@ 23:24	= 26SG46	11/2/28	@ 7:40	= 23LI49	8/27/32	@ 10:02	= 19LE16
GWE	1/18/25	@ 3:00	= 3CP29	11/9/28	@ 6:28	= 27LI41	9/3/32	@ 16:13	= 22LE52
SC	3/5/25	@ 13:30	= 14PI28	12/18/28	@ 12:46	= 26SG22	9/29/32	@ 9:32	= 6LI01
GEE	3/30/25	@ 19:24	= 28AR22	1/22/29	@ 16:13	= 20AQ43	11/14/32	@ 22:41	= 14SG50
SR	4/8/25	@ 11:05	= 2TA39	1/29/29	@ 5:39	= 24AQ23	11/24/32	@ 16:46	= 20SG35
IC	4/18/25	@ 17:09	= 28AR08	2/7/29	@ 3:41	= 17AQ53	12/4/32	@ 16:47	= 12SG21
SD	5/2/25	@ 4:14	= 22AR01	2/19/29	@ 14:10	= 8AQ54	12/14/32	@ 11:03	= 4SG20
GWE	5/16/25	@ 10:35	= 29AR24	3/4/29	@ 22:47	= 16AQ40	12/23/32	@ 20:09	= 9SG55
SC	6/20/25	@ 4:51	= 28GE19	4/17/29	@ 15:58	= 27AR08	2/8/33	@ 0:04	= 18AQ47
GEE	7/28/25	@ 12:22	= 2VI02	5/15/29	@ 20:20	= 16GE18	3/6/33	@ 15:39	= 3AR44
SR	8/11/25	@ 13:30	= 9VI27	5/28/29	@ 9:16	= 22GE26	3/13/33	@ 19:44	= 7AR27
IC	8/25/25	@ 9:21	= 1VI38	6/9/29	@ 11:03	= 18GE06	3/23/33	@ 8:21	= 2AR15
SD	9/4/25	@ 0:33	= 26LE17	6/21/29	@ 8:26	= 13GE52	4/5/33	@ 23:37	= 24PI38
GWE	9/10/25	@ 23:09	= 29LE46	7/3/29	@ 15:56	= 19GE48	4/20/33	@ 3:22	= 2AR16
SC	10/7/25	@ 8:45	= 13LI33	7/31/29	@ 4:25	= 7LE28	5/28/33	@ 18:48	= 6GE57
GEE	11/22/25	@ 15:05	= 21SG41	9/12/29	@ 10:13	= 15LI50	7/2/33	@ 16:47	= 6LE12
SR	12/1/25	@ 21:36	= 27SG12	9/25/29	@ 18:26	= 23LI22	7/16/33	@ 16:39	= 13LE20
IC	12/11/25	@ 16:13	= 19SG07	10/8/29	@ 6:14	= 14LI29	7/30/33	@ 11:12	= 6LE48
SD	12/21/25	@ 15:52	= 10SG55	10/17/29	@ 5:22	= 8LI02	8/9/33	@ 19:31	= 2LE04
GWE	12/31/25	@ 12:45	= 16SG48	10/23/29	@ 17:54	= 11LI35	8/18/33	@ 1:52	= 6LE04
SC	2/16/26	@ 0:41	= 26AQ35	11/27/29	@ 14:03	= 4SG51	9/11/33	@ 23:55	= 18VI45
GEE	3/14/26	@ 0:00	= 10AR56	1/6/30	@ 2:43	= 4AQ17	10/28/33	@ 9:28	= 28SC17
SR	3/21/26	@ 12:55	= 14AR45	1/13/30	@ 1:50	= 8AQ15	11/8/33	@ 8:41	= 4SG46
IC	3/31/26	@ 6:02	= 9AR46	1/22/30	@ 0:39	= 1AQ16	11/18/33	@ 23:47	= 26SC12
SD	4/13/26	@ 21:34	= 2AR34	2/2/30	@ 17:48	= 22CP17	11/28/33	@ 7:32	= 18SC38
GWE	4/28/26	@ 2:54	= 10AR08	2/15/30	@ 10:47	= 29CP48	12/6/33	@ 13:47	= 23SC26
SC	6/4/26	@ 16:39	= 13GE17	4/1/30	@ 12:57	= 11AR04	1/20/34	@ 2:38	= 29CP21
GEE	7/10/26	@ 16:18	= 14LE00	4/27/30	@ 19:58	= 27TA11	2/18/34	@ 4:24	= 16PI55
SR	7/24/26	@ 17:04	= 21LE13	5/8/30	@ 22:21	= 2GE36	2/24/34	@ 20:15	= 20PI27
IC	8/7/26	@ 14:04	= 14LE17	5/20/30	@ 5:08	= 28TA27	3/6/34	@ 0:15	= 14PI44
SD	8/17/26	@ 16:57	= 9LE23	6/1/30	@ 18:40	= 23TA48	3/19/34	@ 8:27	= 6PI20
GWE	8/25/26	@ 11:32	= 13LE11	6/15/30	@ 8:43	= 0GE30	4/2/34	@ 8:03	= 14PI07

	DATE	UT	LONG	DATE	UT	LONG	DATE	UT	LONG
SC	5/13/34	@ 4:55	= 21TA44	3/ 8/38	@ 11:59	= 17PI16	12/22/41	@ 0:37	= 29SG46
GEE	6/14/34	@ 11:15	= 17CN08	4/ 2/38	@ 16:58	= 1TA11	1/25/42	@ 11:45	= 23AQ22
SR	6/28/34	@ 4:56	= 24CN00	4/11/38	@ 14:10	= 5TA36	2/ 1/42	@ 1:19	= 27AQ01
IC	7/11/34	@ 12:12	= 18CN29	4/21/38	@ 22:20	= 1TA08	2/ 9/42	@ 23:19	= 20AQ35
SD	7/22/34	@ 10:24	= 14CN07	5/ 5/38	@ 7:53	= 25AR11	2/22/42	@ 12:05	= 11AQ38
GWE	8/ 1/34	@ 2:48	= 18CN44	5/19/38	@ 14:32	= 2TA33	3/ 7/42	@ 22:48	= 19AQ25
SC	8/26/34	@ 6:45	= 2VI20	6/22/38	@ 21:41	= 0CN46	4/20/42	@ 10:17	= 29AR42
GEE	10/10/34	@ 19:01	= 11SC50	7/31/38	@ 13:35	= 4VI54	5/18/42	@ 22:57	= 19GE25
SR	10/22/34	@ 20:41	= 18SC53	8/14/38	@ 13:50	= 12VI19	5/31/42	@ 16:04	= 25GE38
IC	11/ 3/34	@ 4:40	= 10SC04	8/28/38	@ 8:58	= 4VI23	6/12/42	@ 20:49	= 21GE13
SD	11/12/34	@ 6:07	= 2SC57	9/ 6/38	@ 22:40	= 28LE59	6/24/42	@ 15:56	= 17GE01
GWE	11/19/34	@ 13:58	= 7SC06	9/13/38	@ 18:50	= 2VI27	7/ 6/42	@ 17:57	= 22GE50
SC	12/31/34	@ 2:52	= 8CP44	10/10/38	@ 11:36	= 16LI30	8/ 2/42	@ 22:35	= 9LE58
GEE	2/ 1/35	@ 19:02	= 0PI16	11/25/38	@ 14:31	= 24SG22	9/15/42	@ 11:13	= 18LI32
SR	2/ 8/35	@ 7:31	= 3PI52	12/ 4/38	@ 16:38	= 29SG46	9/28/42	@ 16:10	= 26LI00
IC	2/17/35	@ 6:20	= 27AQ40	12/14/38	@ 9:42	= 21SG44	10/11/42	@ 1:30	= 17LI06
SD	3/ 2/35	@ 1:38	= 18AQ47	12/24/38	@ 11:03	= 13SG29	10/20/42	@ 0:12	= 10LI36
GWE	3/15/35	@ 16:52	= 26AQ34	1/ 3/39	@ 13:52	= 19SG32	10/26/42	@ 13:25	= 14LI09
SC	4/27/35	@ 11:39	= 6TA16	2/19/39	@ 1:57	= 29AQ31	12/ 1/42	@ 1:57	= 8SG14
GEE	5/27/35	@ 1:01	= 27GE36	3/16/39	@ 20:26	= 13AR38	1/ 8/43	@ 23:36	= 6AQ57
SR	6/ 9/35	@ 5:06	= 4CN05	3/24/39	@ 13:19	= 17AR35	1/15/43	@ 20:57	= 10AQ50
IC	6/21/35	@ 18:03	= 29GE25	4/ 3/39	@ 8:05	= 12AR40	1/24/43	@ 19:14	= 3AQ56
SD	7/ 3/35	@ 6:25	= 25GE14	4/16/39	@ 23:28	= 5AR37	2/ 5/43	@ 14:47	= 24CP56
GWE	7/14/35	@ 16:02	= 0CN41	5/ 1/39	@ 5:03	= 13AR10	2/18/43	@ 10:06	= 2AQ28
SC	8/10/35	@ 1:05	= 16LE29	6/ 7/39	@ 9:29	= 15GE44	4/ 4/43	@ 8:32	= 13AR42
GEE	9/23/35	@ 4:30	= 25LI23	7/13/39	@ 18:05	= 16LE57	4/30/43	@ 20:49	= 0GE11
SR	10/ 6/35	@ 3:56	= 2SC49	7/27/39	@ 18:56	= 24LE13	5/12/43	@ 5:14	= 5GE44
IC	10/18/35	@ 5:33	= 23LI54	8/10/39	@ 16:10	= 17LE07	5/23/43	@ 14:34	= 1GE54
SD	10/27/35	@ 4:00	= 17LI13	8/20/39	@ 17:06	= 12LE09	6/ 5/43	@ 1:29	= 27TA01
GWE	11/ 2/35	@ 21:22	= 20LI55	8/28/39	@ 8:20	= 15LE53	6/18/43	@ 12:17	= 3GE38
SC	12/10/35	@ 7:28	= 17SG18	9/22/39	@ 14:14	= 28VI40	7/18/43	@ 3:31	= 24CN39
GEE	1/16/36	@ 7:58	= 13AQ50	11/ 8/39	@ 4:13	= 7SG51	8/28/43	@ 21:56	= 1LI54
SR	1/23/36	@ 0:57	= 17AQ37	11/18/39	@ 11:11	= 13SG56	9/11/43	@ 15:21	= 9LI29
IC	1/31/36	@ 22:50	= 10AQ54	11/28/39	@ 17:09	= 5SG34	9/24/43	@ 16:58	= 0LI45
SD	2/13/36	@ 1:59	= 1AQ52	12/ 8/39	@ 6:31	= 27SC44	10/ 3/43	@ 18:37	= 24VI41
GWE	2/26/36	@ 4:52	= 9AQ34	12/17/39	@ 3:16	= 2SG54	10/10/43	@ 4:20	= 28VI02
SC	4/10/36	@ 12:58	= 20AR28	1/31/40	@ 18:51	= 10AQ45	11/10/43	@ 11:58	= 17SC13
GEE	5/ 7/36	@ 19:47	= 8GE13	2/28/40	@ 7:46	= 26PI39	12/23/43	@ 5:56	= 20CP29
SR	5/19/36	@ 19:25	= 14GE03	3/ 6/40	@ 5:30	= 0AR15	12/30/43	@ 18:24	= 24CP50
IC	5/31/36	@ 12:37	= 9GE51	3/15/40	@ 13:56	= 24PI50	1/ 8/44	@ 21:13	= 17CP29
SD	6/12/36	@ 16:36	= 5GE30	3/29/40	@ 2:58	= 16PI50	1/19/44	@ 23:18	= 8CP39
GWE	6/25/36	@ 15:05	= 11GE48	4/12/40	@ 5:23	= 24PI34	1/31/44	@ 21:50	= 15CP48
SC	7/24/36	@ 3:30	= 1LE02	5/21/40	@ 20:39	= 0GE36	3/17/44	@ 21:23	= 27PI10
GEE	9/ 4/36	@ 15:56	= 8LI53	6/24/40	@ 15:36	= 28CN15	4/12/44	@ 6:37	= 11TA38
SR	9/18/36	@ 5:35	= 16LI28	7/ 8/40	@ 14:17	= 5LE18	4/22/44	@ 0:35	= 16TA25
IC	10/ 1/36	@ 0:18	= 7LI38	7/22/40	@ 4:47	= 29CN12	5/ 2/44	@ 17:08	= 12TA09
SD	10/10/36	@ 0:20	= 1LI22	8/ 1/40	@ 18:45	= 24CN38	5/15/44	@ 19:41	= 6TA47
GWE	10/16/36	@ 11:09	= 4LI49	8/10/40	@ 14:58	= 28CN55	5/29/44	@ 23:15	= 13TA57
SC	11/18/36	@ 11:08	= 25SC56	9/ 4/40	@ 12:16	= 11VI47	7/ 1/44	@ 12:38	= 9CN31
GEE	12/29/36	@ 17:26	= 27CP23	10/20/40	@ 13:11	= 21SC19	8/10/44	@ 8:52	= 14VI57
SR	1/ 5/37	@ 21:57	= 1AQ32	11/ 1/40	@ 1:34	= 28SC07	8/24/44	@ 8:23	= 22VI28
IC	1/14/37	@ 22:31	= 24CP22	11/11/40	@ 23:29	= 19SC26	9/ 6/44	@ 22:30	= 14VI10
SD	1/26/37	@ 8:14	= 15CP27	11/21/40	@ 3:55	= 12SC03	9/16/44	@ 6:49	= 8VI31
GWE	2/ 7/37	@ 17:15	= 22CP50	11/28/40	@ 23:49	= 16SC34	9/22/44	@ 20:59	= 11VI53
SC	3/25/37	@ 6:13	= 4AR11	1/11/41	@ 10:16	= 20CP49	10/20/44	@ 21:53	= 27LI23
GEE	4/20/37	@ 0:22	= 19TA22	2/10/41	@ 21:47	= 9PI57	12/ 5/44	@ 5:21	= 3CP59
SR	4/30/37	@ 10:01	= 24TA25	2/17/41	@ 10:52	= 13PI26	12/16/44	@ 16:20	= 8CP57
IC	5/11/37	@ 9:43	= 20TA16	2/26/41	@ 12:22	= 7PI31	12/23/40	@ 2:53	= 1CP10
SD	5/24/37	@ 6:16	= 15TA17	3/11/41	@ 15:50	= 28AQ53	1/ 2/45	@ 12:52	= 22SG40
GWE	6/ 7/37	@ 4:46	= 22TA16	3/25/41	@ 11:19	= 6PI38	1/13/45	@ 8:16	= 29SG10
SC	7/ 8/37	@ 11:05	= 15CN50	5/ 6/41	@ 5:35	= 15TA17	2/28/45	@ 21:00	= 9PI55
GEE	8/18/37	@ 3:56	= 22VI08	6/ 6/41	@ 7:23	= 8CN55	3/26/45	@ 4:48	= 23AR47
SR	9/ 1/37	@ 1:09	= 29VI41	6/19/41	@ 21:19	= 15CN40	4/ 3/45	@ 12:15	= 27AR55
IC	9/14/37	@ 10:31	= 21VI10	7/ 2/41	@ 21:11	= 10CN33	4/13/45	@ 14:29	= 23AR17
SD	9/23/37	@ 15:42	= 15VI20	7/14/41	@ 1:13	= 6CN17	4/27/45	@ 3:45	= 16AR51
GWE	10/ 3/37	@ 2:43	= 18VI40	7/24/41	@ 11:17	= 11CN17	5/11/45	@ 10:59	= 24AR20
SC	10/29/37	@ 9:51	= 5SC33	8/19/41	@ 0:24	= 25LE37	6/15/45	@ 23:55	= 24GE28
GEE	12/12/37	@ 19:18	= 10CP55	10/ 2/41	@ 23:31	= 4SC56	7/23/45	@ 17:00	= 27LE27
SR	12/20/37	@ 20:03	= 15CP37	10/15/41	@ 11:26	= 12SC09	8/ 6/45	@ 18:12	= 4VI48
IC	12/30/37	@ 2:52	= 8CP00	10/27/41	@ 2:56	= 3SC18	8/20/45	@ 14:57	= 27LE12
SD	1/ 9/38	@ 19:36	= 29SG21	11/ 5/41	@ 2:47	= 26LI21	8/30/45	@ 9:01	= 21LE59
GWE	1/21/38	@ 3:11	= 6CP10	11/12/41	@ 3:05	= 0SC13	9/ 6/45	@ 12:05	= 25LE31

	DATE	UT	LONG		DATE	UT	LONG		DATE	UT	LONG
SC	10/ 2/45	@ 10:48	= 8LI52		7/26/49	@ 21:18	= 3LE31		5/24/53	@ 13:37	= 3GE04
GEE	11/17/45	@ 21:58	= 17SG28		9/ 7/49	@ 16:18	= 11LI34		6/27/53	@ 17:54	= 1LE16
SR	11/27/45	@ 11:52	= 23SG07		9/21/49	@ 3:46	= 19LI07		7/11/53	@ 17:27	= 8LE22
IC	12/ 7/45	@ 10:12	= 14SG57		10/ 3/49	@ 20:10	= 10LI16		7/25/53	@ 9:28	= 2LE07
SD	12/17/45	@ 6:04	= 6SG52		10/12/49	@ 19:52	= 3LI57		8/ 4/53	@ 21:20	= 27CN30
GWE	12/26/45	@ 19:35	= 12SG35		10/19/49	@ 6:25	= 7LI23		8/13/53	@ 12:29	= 1LE41
SC	2/11/46	@ 2:43	= 21AQ46		11/21/49	@ 22:10	= 29SC16		9/ 7/53	@ 9:38	= 14VI27
GEE	3/ 9/46	@ 11:27	= 6AR27		1/ 1/50	@ 14:10	= 0AQ01		10/23/53	@ 13:15	= 23SC58
SR	3/16/46	@ 18:58	= 10AR13		1/ 8/50	@ 17:05	= 4AQ07		11/ 3/53	@ 21:47	= 0SG41
IC	3/26/46	@ 9:04	= 5AR06		1/17/50	@ 16:46	= 27CP01		11/14/53	@ 17:14	= 22SC03
SD	4/ 9/46	@ 0:37	= 27PI37		1/29/50	@ 4:59	= 18CP04		11/23/53	@ 22:50	= 14SC35
GWE	4/23/46	@ 4:55	= 5AR14		2/10/50	@ 16:32	= 25CP30		12/ 1/53	@ 21:50	= 19SC12
SC	5/31/46	@ 11:39	= 9GE24		3/28/50	@ 2:27	= 6AR51		1/14/54	@ 18:32	= 24CP04
GEE	7/ 5/46	@ 18:06	= 9LE09		4/23/50	@ 0:26	= 22TA19		2/13/54	@ 17:17	= 12PI36
SR	7/19/46	@ 18:56	= 16LE21		5/ 3/50	@ 16:09	= 27TA31		2/20/54	@ 7:38	= 16PI07
IC	8/ 2/46	@ 14:37	= 9LE40		5/14/50	@ 18:17	= 23TA22		3/ 1/54	@ 9:49	= 10PI16
SD	8/12/46	@ 21:06	= 4LE53		5/27/50	@ 12:29	= 18TA31		3/14/54	@ 15:09	= 1PI43
GWE	8/20/46	@ 22:57	= 8LE48		6/10/50	@ 8:30	= 25TA24		3/28/54	@ 11:17	= 9PI27
SC	9/14/46	@ 22:19	= 21VI28		7/11/50	@ 4:18	= 18CN18		5/ 8/54	@ 23:02	= 17TA47
GEE	10/31/46	@ 9:28	= 0SG55		8/21/50	@ 4:11	= 24VI52		6/ 9/54	@ 10:12	= 12CN01
SR	11/11/46	@ 4:48	= 7SG19		9/ 4/50	@ 0:12	= 2LI25		6/23/54	@ 2:09	= 18CN50
IC	11/21/46	@ 17:22	= 28SC48		9/17/50	@ 7:49	= 23VI51		7/ 6/54	@ 4:49	= 13CN35
SD	12/ 1/46	@ 2:38	= 21SC09		9/26/50	@ 11:52	= 17VI58		7/17/54	@ 6:52	= 9CN17
GWE	12/ 9/46	@ 12:10	= 26SC05		10/ 2/50	@ 22:20	= 21VI17		7/27/54	@ 10:32	= 14CN09
SC	1/23/47	@ 9:10	= 2AQ31		11/ 1/50	@ 17:13	= 8SC42		8/21/54	@ 20:01	= 28LE12
GEE	2/21/47	@ 4:11	= 19PI46		12/15/50	@ 17:40	= 13CP35		10/ 5/54	@ 23:50	= 7SC36
SR	2/27/47	@ 17:41	= 23PI09		12/23/50	@ 14:38	= 18CP10		10/18/54	@ 8:29	= 14SC44
IC	3/ 8/47	@ 22:33	= 17PI31		1/ 1/51	@ 20:33	= 10CP37		10/29/54	@ 21:14	= 5SC55
SD	3/22/47	@ 8:03	= 9PI12		1/12/51	@ 15:29	= 1CP55		11/ 7/54	@ 21:41	= 28LI54
GWE	4/ 5/47	@ 8:14	= 16PI57		1/24/51	@ 3:20	= 8CP50		11/15/54	@ 0:42	= 2SC55
SC	5/15/47	@ 22:07	= 24TA13		3/11/51	@ 10:07	= 20PI01		12/25/54	@ 12:04	= 3CP10
GEE	6/17/47	@ 13:25	= 20CN10		4/ 5/51	@ 15:29	= 4TA02		1/28/55	@ 8:28	= 26AQ04
SR	7/ 1/47	@ 9:13	= 27CN06		4/14/51	@ 17:53	= 8TA33		2/ 3/55	@ 21:05	= 29AQ39
IC	7/14/47	@ 18:36	= 21CN27		4/25/51	@ 4:01	= 4TA09		2/12/55	@ 19:10	= 23AQ18
SD	7/25/47	@ 14:35	= 17CN03		5/ 8/51	@ 11:49	= 28AR21		2/25/55	@ 10:19	= 14AQ22
GWE	8/ 4/47	@ 1:34	= 21CN33		5/22/51	@ 18:21	= 5TA42		3/10/55	@ 22:22	= 22AQ08
SC	8/29/47	@ 3:01	= 4VI56		6/25/51	@ 14:33	= 3CN13		4/23/55	@ 4:32	= 2TA15
GEE	10/13/47	@ 18:49	= 14SC26		8/ 3/51	@ 14:07	= 7VI42		5/22/55	@ 1:20	= 22GE30
SR	10/25/47	@ 17:29	= 21SC27		8/17/51	@ 14:08	= 15VI08		6/ 3/55	@ 22:47	= 28GE51
IC	11/ 5/47	@ 22:40	= 12SC40		8/31/51	@ 8:10	= 7VI07		6/16/55	@ 6:27	= 24GE20
SD	11/15/47	@ 0:32	= 5SC28		9/ 9/51	@ 20:22	= 1VI39		6/27/55	@ 23:11	= 20GE09
GWE	11/22/47	@ 11:33	= 9SC43		9/16/51	@ 14:47	= 5VI04		7/ 9/55	@ 19:50	= 25GE51
SC	1/ 3/48	@ 13:11	= 12CP04		10/13/51	@ 14:54	= 19LI27		8/ 5/55	@ 16:58	= 12LE29
GEE	2/ 4/48	@ 15:20	= 2PI57		11/28/51	@ 13:27	= 27SG01		9/18/55	@ 11:23	= 21LI11
SR	2/11/48	@ 3:18	= 6PI31		12/ 7/51	@ 12:05	= 2CP18		10/ 1/55	@ 14:02	= 28LI37
IC	2/20/48	@ 2:49	= 0PI23		12/17/51	@ 3:08	= 24SG21		10/13/55	@ 20:40	= 19LI43
SD	3/ 4/48	@ 0:17	= 21AQ33		12/27/51	@ 6:44	= 16SG02		10/22/55	@ 19:16	= 13LI10
GWE	3/17/48	@ 16:59	= 29AQ21		1/ 6/52	@ 12:56	= 22SG10		10/29/55	@ 10:03	= 16LI46
SC	4/29/48	@ 5:30	= 8TA48		2/22/52	@ 2:45	= 2PI25		12/ 4/55	@ 14:08	= 11SG38
GEE	5/29/48	@ 3:44	= 0CN41		3/18/52	@ 18:10	= 16AR27		1/11/56	@ 20:16	= 9AQ37
SR	6/11/48	@ 11:15	= 7CN15		3/26/52	@ 13:54	= 20AR24		1/18/56	@ 15:43	= 13AQ26
IC	6/24/48	@ 3:01	= 2CN29		4/ 5/52	@ 10:31	= 15AR35		1/27/56	@ 13:57	= 6AQ36
SD	7/ 5/48	@ 13:02	= 28GE18		4/19/52	@ 1:33	= 8AR41		2/ 8/56	@ 12:14	= 27CP36
GWE	7/16/48	@ 16:30	= 3CN36		5/ 3/52	@ 8:31	= 16AR15		2/21/56	@ 11:35	= 5AQ15
SC	9/11/48	@ 19:57	= 19LE01		6/ 9/52	@ 2:14	= 18GE10		4/ 6/56	@ 3:52	= 16AR19
GEE	9/25/48	@ 4:50	= 28LI02		7/15/52	@ 18:48	= 19LE51		5/ 2/56	@ 22:16	= 3GE14
SR	10/ 8/48	@ 1:18	= 5SC25		7/29/52	@ 20:31	= 27LE10		5/14/56	@ 12:11	= 8GE52
IC	10/20/48	@ 0:19	= 26LI31		8/12/52	@ 17:52	= 19LE55		5/26/56	@ 0:11	= 4GE43
SD	10/28/48	@ 23:02	= 19LI46		8/22/52	@ 16:56	= 14LE53		6/ 7/56	@ 8:33	= 0GE14
GWE	11/ 4/48	@ 18:08	= 23LI31		8/30/52	@ 4:36	= 18LE33		6/20/56	@ 15:50	= 6GE45
SC	12/12/48	@ 19:50	= 20SG43		9/24/52	@ 14:05	= 1LI27		7/19/56	@ 21:02	= 27CN07
GEE	1/18/49	@ 4:16	= 16AQ29		11/10/52	@ 3:42	= 10SG30		8/30/56	@ 22:32	= 4LI37
SR	1/24/49	@ 20:11	= 20AQ13		11/20/52	@ 6:35	= 16SG31		9/13/56	@ 14:10	= 12LI11
IC	2/ 2/49	@ 17:58	= 13AQ35		11/30/52	@ 10:37	= 8SG10		9/26/56	@ 13:21	= 3LI25
SD	2/14/49	@ 23:48	= 4AQ33		12/10/52	@ 1:23	= 0SG16		10/ 5/56	@ 14:28	= 27VI17
GWE	2/28/49	@ 1:17	= 12AQ08		12/19/52	@ 2:45	= 5SG38		10/12/56	@ 0:06	= 0LI39
SC	4/13/49	@ 7:47	= 23AR03		2/ 2/53	@ 23:08	= 13AQ49		11/12/56	@ 21:35	= 20SC29
GEE	5/10/49	@ 21:24	= 11GE16		3/ 2/53	@ 3:34	= 29PI21		12/25/56	@ 3:17	= 23CP08
SR	5/23/49	@ 2:14	= 17GE13		3/ 9/53	@ 3:44	= 3AR00		1/ 1/57	@ 13:33	= 27CP24
IC	6/ 3/49	@ 22:28	= 12GE58		3/18/53	@ 13:34	= 27PI39		1/10/57	@ 15:11	= 20CP08
SD	6/16/49	@ 0:07	= 8GE40		4/ 1/53	@ 3:34	= 19PI47		1/21/57	@ 20:01	= 11CP15
GWE	6/28/49	@ 18:28	= 14GE52		4/15/53	@ 6:25	= 27PI29		2/ 2/57	@ 21:12	= 18CP29

1957 | | | | | | | 1968

	DATE	UT	LONG		DATE	UT	LONG		DATE	UT	LONG
SC	3/20/57	@ 18:16	= 29PI52		1/ 5/61	@ 23:04	= 15CP23		10/15/64	@ 18:46	= 22LI26
GEE	4/15/57	@ 6:38	= 14TA35		2/ 6/61	@ 10:48	= 5PI37		11/30/64	@ 12:30	= 29SG41
SR	4/25/57	@ 5:29	= 19TA27		2/12/61	@ 23:30	= 9PI10		12/ 9/64	@ 6:54	= 4CP53
IC	5/ 6/57	@ 0:33	= 15TA13		2/21/61	@ 23:33	= 3PI07		12/18/64	@ 20:35	= 26SG58
SD	5/19/57	@ 1:04	= 9TA59		3/ 6/61	@ 23:14	= 24AQ20		12/29/64	@ 2:10	= 18SG34
GWE	6/ 2/57	@ 3:25	= 17TA06		3/20/61	@ 17:19	= 2PI09		1/ 8/65	@ 13:51	= 24SG53
SC	7/ 4/57	@ 5:38	= 11CN58		5/ 1/61	@ 23:16	= 11TA19		2/24/65	@ 3:04	= 5PI17
GEE	8/13/57	@ 10:26	= 17VI46		6/ 1/61	@ 7:09	= 3CN49		3/21/65	@ 15:02	= 19AR13
SR	8/27/57	@ 8:06	= 25VI15		6/14/61	@ 17:07	= 10CN27		3/29/65	@ 14:55	= 23AR15
IC	9/ 9/57	@ 20:33	= 16VI52		6/27/61	@ 11:43	= 5CN34		4/ 8/65	@ 13:25	= 18AR29
SD	9/19/57	@ 3:30	= 11VI09		7/ 8/61	@ 19:39	= 1CN21		4/22/65	@ 3:59	= 11AR45
GWE	9/25/57	@ 16:09	= 14VI29		7/19/61	@ 17:01	= 6CN35		5/ 6/65	@ 11:13	= 19AR17
SC	10/24/57	@ 3:30	= 0SC27		8/14/61	@ 14:58	= 21LE33		6/11/65	@ 19:01	= 20GE37
GEE	12/ 8/57	@ 4:15	= 6CP40		9/28/61	@ 4:42	= 0SC40		7/18/65	@ 20:12	= 22LE44
SR	12/16/57	@ 10:55	= 11CP31		10/10/61	@ 22:40	= 8SC01		8/ 1/65	@ 21:57	= 0VI05
IC	12/25/57	@ 20:24	= 3CP48		10/22/61	@ 18:58	= 29LI08		8/15/65	@ 19:11	= 22LE43
SD	1/ 5/58	@ 8:33	= 25SG15		10/31/61	@ 18:12	= 22LI19		8/25/65	@ 16:24	= 17LE37
GWE	1/16/58	@ 7:54	= 1CP50		11/ 7/61	@ 14:54	= 26LI08		9/ 2/65	@ 1:02	= 21LE14
SC	3/ 3/58	@ 20:10	= 12PI45		12/16/61	@ 8:03	= 24SG08		9/27/65	@ 14:29	= 4LI15
GEE	3/29/58	@ 2:36	= 26AR37		1/21/62	@ 0:57	= 19AQ09		11/13/65	@ 3:40	= 13SG10
SR	4/ 6/58	@ 14:23	= 0TA50		1/27/62	@ 15:42	= 22AQ49		11/23/65	@ 2:20	= 19SG04
IC	4/18/58	@ 18:43	= 26AR15		2/ 5/62	@ 13:16	= 16AQ16		12/ 3/65	@ 4:05	= 10SG47
SD	4/30/58	@ 6:57	= 20AR00		2/17/62	@ 21:34	= 7AQ15		12/12/65	@ 20:34	= 2SG48
GWE	5/14/58	@ 13:20	= 27AR25		3/ 3/62	@ 4:24	= 14AQ59		12/22/65	@ 1:56	= 8SG17
SC	6/18/58	@ 16:44	= 26GE55		4/16/62	@ 2:27	= 25AR37		2/ 6/66	@ 2:52	= 16AQ52
GEE	7/26/58	@ 18:23	= 0VI20		5/13/62	@ 23:36	= 14GE21		3/ 5/66	@ 0:16	= 2AR05
SR	8/ 9/58	@ 18:47	= 7VI41		5/26/62	@ 9:10	= 20GE24		3/12/66	@ 2:18	= 5AR45
IC	8/23/58	@ 15:11	= 29LE58		6/ 7/62	@ 8:22	= 16GE06		3/21/66	@ 13:36	= 0AR29
SD	9/ 2/58	@ 7:40	= 24LE41		6/19/62	@ 7:46	= 11GE51		4/ 4/66	@ 4:25	= 22PI44
GWE	9/ 9/58	@ 8:25	= 28LE11		7/ 1/62	@ 20:00	= 17GE54		4/18/66	@ 7:19	= 0AR23
SC	10/ 5/58	@ 12:34	= 11LI45		7/29/62	@ 15:16	= 6LE00		5/27/66	@ 6:37	= 5GE31
GEE	11/20/58	@ 21:30	= 20SG08		9/10/62	@ 15:40	= 14LI13		6/30/66	@ 20:22	= 4LE17
SR	11/30/58	@ 7:23	= 25SG42		9/24/62	@ 1:54	= 21LI47		7/14/66	@ 20:15	= 11LE25
IC	12/10/58	@ 3:35	= 17SG34		10/ 6/62	@ 15:50	= 12LI54		7/28/66	@ 13:44	= 5LE01
SD	12/20/58	@ 1:31	= 9SG25		10/15/62	@ 14:56	= 6LI32		8/ 7/66	@ 23:45	= 0LE20
GWE	12/29/58	@ 18:59	= 15SG14		10/22/62	@ 2:42	= 10LI00		8/16/66	@ 10:09	= 4LE25
SC	2/14/59	@ 4:51	= 24AQ45		11/25/62	@ 9:37	= 2SG38		9/10/66	@ 7:24	= 17VI08
GEE	3/12/59	@ 8:44	= 9AR14		1/ 4/63	@ 11:38	= 2AQ42		10/26/56	@ 14:18	= 26SC38
SR	3/19/59	@ 18:35	= 13AR01		1/11/63	@ 11:36	= 6AQ41		11/ 6/66	@ 18:00	= 3SG15
IC	3/29/59	@ 10:16	= 7AR58		1/20/63	@ 11:06	= 29CP40		11/17/66	@ 10:58	= 24SC38
SD	4/12/59	@ 1:51	= 0AR38		2/ 1/63	@ 2:00	= 20CP41		11/26/66	@ 18:00	= 17SC07
GWE	4/26/59	@ 6:52	= 8AR14		2/13/63	@ 16:40	= 28CP11		12/ 4/66	@ 20:05	= 21SC50
SC	6/ 3/59	@ 4:29	= 11GE52		3/30/63	@ 22:23	= 9AR29		1/18/67	@ 2:09	= 27CP17
GEE	7/ 8/59	@ 20:58	= 12LE10		4/26/63	@ 0:57	= 25TA18		2/16/67	@ 13:52	= 15PI16
SR	7/22/59	@ 21:04	= 19LE22		5/ 6/63	@ 22:30	= 0GE37		2/23/67	@ 4:22	= 18PI48
IC	8/ 5/59	@ 17:34	= 12LE32		5/18/63	@ 3:10	= 26TA28		3/ 4/67	@ 7:34	= 13PI01
SD	8/15/59	@ 22:04	= 7LE41		5/30/63	@ 18:52	= 21TA44		3/17/67	@ 14:25	= 4PI33
GWE	8/23/59	@ 19:41	= 11LE33		6/13/63	@ 11:24	= 28TA31		3/31/67	@ 12:12	= 12PI18
SC	9/17/59	@ 21:06	= 24VI13		7/13/63	@ 21:31	= 20CN45		5/11/67	@ 16:23	= 20TA17
GEE	11/ 3/59	@ 8:38	= 3SG33		8/24/63	@ 4:36	= 27VI36		6/12/67	@ 13:43	= 15CN08
SR	11/14/59	@ 0:30	= 9SG54		9/ 6/63	@ 23:08	= 5LI08		6/26/67	@ 6:50	= 21CN59
IC	11/24/59	@ 10:56	= 1SG24		9/20/63	@ 4:48	= 26VI30		7/ 9/67	@ 12:03	= 16CN35
SD	12/ 3/59	@ 21:35	= 23SC42		9/29/63	@ 8:09	= 20VI33		7/20/67	@ 11:59	= 12CN16
GWE	12/12/59	@ 11:13	= 28SC44		10/ 5/63	@ 18:08	= 23VI54		7/30/67	@ 9:49	= 17CN00
SC	1/26/60	@ 15:06	= 5AQ40		11/ 5/63	@ 1:09	= 11SC53		8/24/67	@ 15:54	= 0VI47
GEE	2/23/60	@ 20:51	= 22PI20		12/18/63	@ 15:51	= 16CP12		10/ 9/67	@ 0:07	= 10SC14
SR	3/ 1/60	@ 15:08	= 25PI52		12/26/63	@ 9:50	= 20CP43		10/21/67	@ 5:11	= 17SC20
IC	3/10/60	@ 21:14	= 20PI18		1/ 4/64	@ 14:16	= 13CP15		11/ 1/67	@ 20:58	= 8SC31
SD	3/24/60	@ 8:07	= 12PI06		1/15/64	@ 11:48	= 4CP31		11/10/67	@ 16:07	= 1SC27
GWE	4/ 7/60	@ 9:05	= 19PI51		1/27/64	@ 2:59	= 11CP29		11/17/67	@ 21:52	= 5SC32
SC	5/17/60	@ 15:15	= 26TA41		3/13/64	@ 7:54	= 22PI46		12/28/67	@ 23:17	= 6CP32
GEE	6/19/60	@ 15:46	= 23CN14		4/ 7/64	@ 13:56	= 6TA54		1/31/68	@ 3:53	= 28AQ42
SR	7/ 3/60	@ 13:15	= 0LE14		4/16/64	@ 21:50	= 11TA31		2/ 6/68	@ 16:34	= 2PI17
IC	7/17/60	@ 0:34	= 24CN25		4/27/64	@ 0:09	= 7TA10		2/15/68	@ 15:14	= 26AQ00
SD	7/27/60	@ 18:27	= 19CN58		5/10/64	@ 16:10	= 1TA31		2/28/68	@ 8:33	= 17AQ06
GWE	8/ 6/60	@ 23:50	= 24CN22		5/24/64	@ 21:33	= 8TA47		3/12/68	@ 22:56	= 24AQ55
SC	8/30/60	@ 23:33	= 7VI33		6/27/64	@ 7:25	= 5CN39		4/24/68	@ 22:34	= 4TA47
GEE	10/15/60	@ 18:58	= 17SC05		8/ 5/64	@ 14:30	= 10VI30		5/24/68	@ 4:26	= 25GE37
SR	10/27/60	@ 13:57	= 24SC01		8/19/64	@ 14:13	= 17VI57		6/ 6/68	@ 5:15	= 2CN01
IC	11/ 7/60	@ 16:39	= 15SC16		9/ 2/64	@ 7:03	= 9VI49		6/18/68	@ 15:48	= 27GE26
SD	11/16/60	@ 19:19	= 8SC01		9/11/64	@ 17:51	= 4VI18		6/30/68	@ 6:08	= 23GE15
GWE	11/24/60	@ 8:52	= 12SC20		9/18/64	@ 10:09	= 7VI40		7/11/68	@ 21:00	= 28GE51

	DATE	UT	LONG	DATE	UT	LONG	DATE	UT	LONG
SC	8/ 7/68	@ 11:27	= 14LE59	6/ 4/72	@ 21:22	= 14GE19	4/ 1/76	@ 18:04	= 12AR08
GEE	9/20/68	@ 10:30	= 23LI48	7/10/72	@ 21:45	= 15LE05	4/28/76	@ 1:47	= 28TA18
SR	10/ 3/68	@ 11:36	= 1SC14	7/24/72	@ 23:02	= 22LE19	5/ 9/76	@ 5:03	= 3GE44
IC	10/15/68	@ 15:41	= 22LI20	8/ 7/72	@ 20:03	= 15LE22	5/20/76	@ 12:14	= 29TA35
SD	10/24/61	@ 14:28	= 15LI43	8/17/72	@ 22:41	= 10LE31	6/ 2/76	@ 1:18	= 24TA57
GWE	10/31/68	@ 6:05	= 19LI21	8/25/72	@ 16:47	= 14LE15	6/15/76	@ 15:05	= 1GE38
SC	12/ 7/68	@ 2:31	= 15SG03	9/19/72	@ 20:15	= 26VI58	7/15/76	@ 14:51	= 23CN13
GEE	1/13/69	@ 16:18	= 12AQ11	11/ 5/72	@ 9:50	= 6SG15	8/26/76	@ 3:56	= 0LI17
SR	1/20/69	@ 11:07	= 16AQ01	11/15/72	@ 20:22	= 12SG24	9/ 8/76	@ 22:06	= 7LI51
IC	1/29/69	@ 8:48	= 9AQ17	11/26/72	@ 4:28	= 4SG01	9/22/76	@ 1:34	= 29VI10
SD	2/10/69	@ 9:35	= 0AQ15	12/ 5/72	@ 16:15	= 25SG17	10/ 1/76	@ 3:51	= 23VI09
GWE	2/23/69	@ 9:50	= 7AQ53	12/14/72	@ 9:33	= 1SG23	10/ 7/76	@ 13:35	= 26VI30
SC	4/ 8/69	@ 23:00	= 18AR55	1/28/73	@ 20:30	= 8AQ47	11/ 7/76	@ 9:47	= 15SC07
GEE	5/ 5/69	@ 23:37	= 6GE16	2/25/73	@ 16:18	= 24PI59	12/20/76	@ 13:30	= 18CP53
SR	5/17/69	@ 19:08	= 12GE01	3/ 4/73	@ 13:02	= 28PI34	12/28/76	@ 4:23	= 23CP19
IC	5/29/69	@ 9:49	= 7GE50	3/13/73	@ 20:15	= 23PI07	1/ 6/77	@ 8:07	= 15CP54
SD	6/10/69	@ 15:49	= 3GE26	3/27/73	@ 8:17	= 15PI01	1/17/77	@ 7:57	= 7CP06
GWE	6/23/69	@ 18:50	= 9GE52	4/10/73	@ 9:11	= 22PI43	1/29/77	@ 3:22	= 14CP12
SC	7/22/69	@ 14:36	= 29CN35	5/20/73	@ 8:23	= 29TA10	3/16/77	@ 5:24	= 25PI30
GEE	9/ 2/69	@ 21:56	= 7LI17	6/22/73	@ 18:56	= 26CN18	4/10/77	@ 13:18	= 9TA49
SR	9/16/69	@ 12:39	= 14LI51	7/ 6/73	@ 17:01	= 3LE20	4/20/77	@ 2:06	= 14TA31
IC	9/29/69	@ 9:30	= 6LI03	7/20/73	@ 6:06	= 27CN22	4/30/77	@ 16:43	= 10TA12
SD	10/ 8/69	@ 9:44	= 29VI52	7/30/73	@ 21:46	= 22CN54	5/13/77	@ 20:52	= 4TA43
GWE	10/14/69	@ 20:03	= 3LI16	8/ 8/73	@ 22:13	= 27CN11	5/28/77	@ 1:35	= 11TA55
SC	11/16/69	@ 7:49	= 23SC47	9/ 2/73	@ 20:26	= 10VI12	6/30/77	@ 0:22	= 8CN06
GEE	12/28/69	@ 1:01	= 25CP49	10/18/73	@ 18:16	= 19SC43	8/ 8/77	@ 14:15	= 13VI15
SR	1/ 4/70	@ 7:58	= 29CP59	10/30/73	@ 10:34	= 26SC35	8/22/77	@ 14:21	= 20VI46
IC	1/13/70	@ 9:13	= 22CP46	11/10/73	@ 10:32	= 17SC53	9/ 5/77	@ 5:42	= 12VI33
SD	1/24/70	@ 16:34	= 13CP54	11/19/73	@ 14:25	= 10SC34	9/14/77	@ 15:02	= 6VI58
GWE	2/ 5/70	@ 21:56	= 21CP11	11/27/73	@ 7:13	= 15SC00	9/21/77	@ 6:39	= 10VI20
SC	3/23/70	@ 14:55	= 2AR33	1/ 9/74	@ 8:21	= 18CP41	10/18/77	@ 23:17	= 25LI28
GEE	4/18/70	@ 6:00	= 17TA30	2/ 9/74	@ 7:13	= 8PI20	12/ 3/77	@ 11:48	= 2CP22
SR	4/28/70	@ 10:55	= 22TA29	2/15/74	@ 19:54	= 11PI50	12/12/77	@ 2:16	= 7CP27
IC	5/ 9/70	@ 8:21	= 18TA17	2/24/74	@ 20:29	= 5PI51	12/21/77	@ 14:07	= 29SG36
SD	5/22/70	@ 6:46	= 13TA12	3/ 9/74	@ 22:19	= 27AQ08	12/31/77	@ 21:58	= 21SG09
GWE	6/ 5/70	@ 7:07	= 20TA15	3/23/74	@ 17:32	= 4PI57	1/11/78	@ 13:31	= 27SG33
SC	7/ 6/70	@ 22:38	= 14CN25	5/ 4/74	@ 16:53	= 13TA50	2/27/78	@ 3:02	= 8PI09
GEE	8/16/70	@ 10:02	= 20VI29	6/ 4/74	@ 10:41	= 6CN57	3/24/78	@ 12:39	= 22AR02
SR	8/30/70	@ 7:25	= 28VI00	6/17/74	@ 22:38	= 13CN39	4/ 1/78	@ 16:17	= 26AR07
IC	9/12/70	@ 18:19	= 19VI33	6/30/74	@ 20:06	= 8CN38	4/11/78	@ 16:47	= 21AR26
SD	9/22/70	@ 0:19	= 13VI46	7/12/74	@ 1:57	= 4CN24	4/25/78	@ 6:49	= 14AR51
GWE	9/28/70	@ 12:22	= 17VI08	7/22/74	@ 17:03	= 9CN28	5/ 9/78	@ 13:41	= 22AR21
SC	10/27/70	@ 9:42	= 3SC33	8/17/74	@ 10:09	= 24LE07	6/14/78	@ 11:51	= 23GE04
GEE	12/11/70	@ 2:43	= 9CP20	10/ 1/74	@ 5:03	= 3SC20	7/21/78	@ 21:50	= 25LE39
SR	12/19/70	@ 6:07	= 14CP05	10/13/74	@ 19:51	= 10SC38	8/ 4/78	@ 23:08	= 3VI01
IC	12/28/70	@ 14:00	= 6CP25	10/25/74	@ 13:28	= 1SC45	8/18/78	@ 20:11	= 25LE31
SD	1/ 8/71	@ 4:40	= 27SG49	11/ 3/74	@ 12:41	= 24LI53	8/28/78	@ 15:42	= 20LE21
GWE	1/19/71	@ 8:15	= 4CP32	11/10/74	@ 11:31	= 28LI45	9/ 4/78	@ 21:45	= 23LE56
SC	3/ 6/71	@ 19:02	= 15PI33	12/19/74	@ 20:00	= 27SG32	9/30/78	@ 15:24	= 7LI06
GEE	4/ 1/71	@ 0:28	= 29AR27	1/23/75	@ 21:11	= 21AQ48	11/16/78	@ 3:39	= 15SG51
SR	4/ 9/71	@ 17:14	= 3TA44	1/30/75	@ 10:39	= 25AQ25	11/25/78	@ 21:47	= 21SG38
IC	4/19/71	@ 23:34	= 29AR15	2/ 8/75	@ 8:42	= 18AQ57	12/ 5/78	@ 21:32	= 13SG24
SD	5/ 3/71	@ 10:24	= 23AR09	2/20/75	@ 19:31	= 9AQ58	12/15/78	@ 16:06	= 5SG22
GWE	5/17/71	@ 17:20	= 0TA33	3/ 6/75	@ 3:45	= 17AQ41	12/25/78	@ 1:13	= 10SG57
SC	6/21/71	@ 9:32	= 29GE22	4/18/75	@ 20:54	= 28AR12	2/ 9/79	@ 6:03	= 19AQ53
GEE	7/29/71	@ 18:22	= 3VI08	5/17/75	@ 2:32	= 17GE27	7/ 7/79	@ 20:54	= 4AR50
SR	8/12/71	@ 19:15	= 10VI32	5/29/75	@ 16:00	= 23GE36	3/15/79	@ 1:14	= 8AR31
IC	8/26/71	@ 15:02	= 2VI43	6/10/75	@ 18:14	= 19GE14	3/24/79	@ 14:04	= 3AR20
SD	9/ 5/71	@ 6:03	= 27LE22	6/22/75	@ 15:18	= 15GE01	4/ 7/79	@ 5:19	= 25PI44
GWE	9/12/71	@ 3:56	= 0VI49	7/ 4/75	@ 22:18	= 20GE56	4/21/79	@ 9:22	= 3AR23
SC	10/ 8/71	@ 14:47	= 14LI39	8/ 1/75	@ 9:19	= 8LE31	5/29/79	@ 23:31	= 7GE59
GEE	11/23/71	@ 21:16	= 22SG48	9/13/75	@ 16:52	= 16LI56	7/ 3/79	@ 22:18	= 7LE17
SR	12/ 3/71	@ 2:24	= 28SG16	9/26/75	@ 23:48	= 24LI26	7/17/79	@ 22:43	= 14LE27
IC	12/12/71	@ 21:01	= 20SG11	10/ 9/75	@ 11:16	= 15LI32	7/31/79	@ 17:28	= 7LE54
SD	12/22/71	@ 20:55	= 12SG01	10/18/75	@ 10:24	= 9LI06	8/11/79	@ 1:32	= 3LE09
GWE	1/ 1/72	@ 19:18	= 17SG55	10/24/75	@ 22:46	= 1LI36	8/19/79	@ 7:02	= 7LE38
SC	2/17/72	@ 6:36	= 27AQ42	11/28/75	@ 21:19	= 6SG01	9/13/79	@ 5:26	= 19VI50
GEE	3/14/72	@ 4:58	= 11AR59	1/ 7/76	@ 7:47	= 5AQ20	10/29/79	@ 14:26	= 29SC18
SR	3/21/72	@ 18:40	= 15AR48	1/14/76	@ 6:51	= 9AQ18	11/ 9/79	@ 13:49	= 5SG48
IC	3/31/72	@ 11:58	= 10AR52	1/23/76	@ 5:32	= 2AQ20	11/20/79	@ 4:36	= 27SC15
SD	4/14/72	@ 3:30	= 3AR41	2/ 3/76	@ 23:01	= 23CP20	11/29/79	@ 12:31	= 19SC41
GWE	4/28/72	@ 9:28	= 11AR17	2/16/76	@ 15:56	= 0AQ51	12/ 7/79	@ 19:07	= 24SC30

1980   1991

	DATE	UT	LONG
SC	1/21/80	@ 9:12	= 0AQ29
GEE	2/19/80	@ 9:22	= 17PI57
SR	2/26/80	@ 1:33	= 21PI30
IC	3/ 6/80	@ 5:38	= 15PI48
SD	3/19/80	@ 14:02	= 7PI25
GWE	4/ 2/80	@ 13:07	= 15PI10
SC	5/13/80	@ 9:38	= 22TA46
GEE	6/14/80	@ 15:50	= 18CN10
SR	6/28/80	@ 11:12	= 25CN07
IC	7/11/80	@ 18:46	= 19CN35
SD	7/22/80	@ 16:40	= 15CN12
GWE	8/ 1/80	@ 8:20	= 19CN49
SC	8/26/80	@ 11:54	= 3VI23
GEE	10/11/80	@ 0:11	= 12SC52
SR	10/23/80	@ 2:02	= 19SC55
IC	11/ 3/80	@ 9:33	= 11SC07
SD	11/12/80	@ 11:07	= 4SC00
GWE	11/19/80	@ 18:45	= 8SC08
SC	12/31/80	@ 10:03	= 9CP53
GEE	2/ 2/81	@ 0:17	= 1PI23
SR	2/ 8/81	@ 12:40	= 4PI54
IC	2/17/81	@ 11:29	= 28AQ43
SD	3/ 2/81	@ 7:08	= 19AQ51
GWE	3/15/81	@ 22:52	= 27AQ39
SC	4/27/81	@ 16:28	= 7TA18
GEE	5/27/81	@ 6:39	= 28GE41
SR	6/ 9/81	@ 11:36	= 5CN12
IC	6/22/81	@ 0:57	= 0CN31
SD	7/ 3/81	@ 13:01	= 26GE20
GWE	7/14/81	@ 21:45	= 1CN46
SC	8/10/81	@ 6:02	= 17LE31
GEE	9/23/81	@ 10:41	= 26LI27
SR	10/ 6/81	@ 9:19	= 3SC51
IC	10/18/81	@ 10:32	= 24LI57
SD	10/27/81	@ 8:59	= 18LI16
GWE	11/ 3/81	@ 2:37	= 21LI57
SC	12/10/81	@ 14:52	= 18SG28
GEE	1/16/82	@ 13:47	= 14AQ54
SR	1/23/82	@ 5:53	= 18AQ38
IC	2/ 1/82	@ 3:48	= 11AQ57
SD	2/13/82	@ 7:21	= 2AQ55
GWE	2/26/82	@ 11:20	= 10AQ40
SC	4/11/82	@ 17:55	= 21AR30
GEE	5/ 9/82	@ 1:13	= 9GE18
SR	5/21/82	@ 2:06	= 15GE11
IC	6/ 1/82	@ 19:42	= 10GE58
SD	6/13/82	@ 23:21	= 6GE37
GWE	6/26/82	@ 21:33	= 12GE54
SC	7/25/82	@ 8:18	= 2LE04
GEE	9/ 5/82	@ 21:39	= 9LI56
SR	9/19/82	@ 11:06	= 17LI31
IC	10/ 2/82	@ 5:29	= 8LI41
SD	10/11/82	@ 5:27	= 2LI25
GWE	10/17/82	@ 15:56	= 5LI52
SC	11/19/82	@ 18:23	= 27SC05
GEE	12/30/82	@ 22:07	= 28CP27
SR	1/ 7/83	@ 3:06	= 2AQ34
IC	1/16/83	@ 3:24	= 25CP25
SD	1/27/83	@ 13:30	= 16CP29
GWE	2/ 8/83	@ 22:07	= 23CP52
SC	3/26/83	@ 11:23	= 5AR14
GEE	4/21/83	@ 6:05	= 20TA28
SR	5/ 1/83	@ 16:35	= 25TA33
IC	5/12/83	@ 16:36	= 21TA23
SD	5/25/83	@ 12:49	= 16TA25
GWE	6/ 8/83	@ 14:03	= 23TA22
SC	7/ 9/83	@ 15:49	= 16CN52
GEE	8/19/83	@ 10:18	= 23VI13
SR	9/ 2/83	@ 6:42	= 0LI45
IC	9/15/83	@ 15:50	= 22VI14
SD	9/24/83	@ 20:54	= 16VI23
GWE	10/ 1/83	@ 7:18	= 19VI42

	DATE	UT	LONG
SC	10/30/83	@ 16:30	= 6SC40
GEE	12/14/83	@ 0:39	= 11CP58
SR	12/22/83	@ 0:44	= 16CP39
IC	12/31/83	@ 7:40	= 9CP03
SD	1/11/84	@ 0:34	= 0CP23
GWE	1/22/84	@ 7:58	= 7CP11
SC	3/ 8/84	@ 17:30	= 18PI20
GEE	4/ 2/84	@ 22:47	= 2TA17
SR	4/11/84	@ 20:23	= 6TA42
IC	4/22/84	@ 4:49	= 2TA14
SD	5/ 5/84	@ 14:08	= 26AR18
GWE	5/19/84	@ 20:37	= 3TA39
SC	6/23/84	@ 2:23	= 1CN48
GEE	7/31/84	@ 19:18	= 5VI57
SR	8/14/84	@ 19:33	= 13VI24
IC	8/28/84	@ 14:33	= 5VI27
SD	9/ 7/84	@ 3:58	= 0VI02
GWE	9/14/84	@ 0:05	= 3VI27
SC	10/10/84	@ 17:38	= 17LI35
GEE	11/25/84	@ 20:43	= 25SG28
SR	12/ 4/84	@ 21:42	= 0CP49
IC	12/14/84	@ 14:27	= 22SG47
SD	12/24/84	@ 16:05	= 14SG31
GWE	1/ 3/85	@ 18:50	= 20SG34
SC	2/19/85	@ 7:46	= 0PI36
GEE	3/17/85	@ 2:31	= 14AR46
SR	3/24/85	@ 19:02	= 18AR39
IC	4/ 3/85	@ 14:03	= 13AR45
SD	4/17/85	@ 5:22	= 6AR44
GWE	5/ 1/85	@ 11:09	= 14AR16
SC	6/ 7/85	@ 14:08	= 16GE45
GEE	7/13/85	@ 23:50	= 18LE02
SR	7/28/85	@ 0:51	= 25LE19
IC	8/10/85	@ 22:08	= 18LE11
SD	8/20/85	@ 22:48	= 13LE13
GWE	8/28/85	@ 13:35	= 16LE57
SC	9/22/85	@ 19:51	= 29VI44
GEE	11/ 8/85	@ 10:18	= 8SG56
SR	11/18/81	@ 16:16	= 15SG00
IC	11/28/85	@ 21:56	= 6SG37
SD	12/ 8/85	@ 11:33	= 28SC47
GWE	12/17/85	@ 9:17	= 4SG03
SC	2/ 1/86	@ 1:10	= 11AQ52
GEE	2/28/86	@ 13:07	= 27PI43
SR	3/ 7/86	@ 10:55	= 1AR18
IC	3/16/86	@ 19:33	= 25PI55
SD	3/30/86	@ 8:44	= 17PI56
GWE	4/13/86	@ 10:24	= 25PI37
SC	5/23/86	@ 1:23	= 1GE38
GEE	6/25/86	@ 21:33	= 29CN20
SR	7/ 9/86	@ 20:28	= 6LE25
IC	7/23/86	@ 11:11	= 0LE18
SD	8/ 3/86	@ 0:46	= 25CN44
GWE	8/11/86	@ 20:15	= 29CN58
SC	9/ 5/86	@ 17:33	= 12VI51
GEE	10/21/86	@ 19:24	= 22SC24
SR	11/ 2/86	@ 6:41	= 29SC09
IC	11/13/86	@ 4:19	= 20SC29
SD	11/22/86	@ 8:52	= 13SC06
GWE	11/30/86	@ 5:09	= 17SC37
SC	1/12/87	@ 17:02	= 21CP57
GEE	2/12/87	@ 2:43	= 10PI59
SR	2/18/87	@ 16:03	= 14PI30
IC	2/27/87	@ 17:39	= 8PI35
SD	3/12/87	@ 21:21	= 29AQ57
GWE	3/26/87	@ 17:32	= 7PI45
SC	5/ 7/87	@ 10:23	= 16TA20
GEE	6/ 7/87	@ 14:09	= 10CN04
SR	6/21/87	@ 3:43	= 16CN51
IC	7/ 4/87	@ 4:03	= 11CN40
SD	7/15/87	@ 7:50	= 7CN24
GWE	7/25/87	@ 16:35	= 12CN21

DATE	UT	LONG
8/20/87	@ 5:31	= 26LE40
10/ 4/87	@ 5:09	= 5SC58
10/16/87	@ 16:43	= 13SC12
10/28/87	@ 7:51	= 4SC21
11/ 6/87	@ 7:49	= 27LI25
11/13/87	@ 8:48	= 1SC22
12/23/87	@ 7:51	= 0CP56
1/26/88	@ 17:15	= 24AQ27
2/ 2/88	@ 6:24	= 28AQ01
2/11/88	@ 4:22	= 21AQ39
2/23/88	@ 17:27	= 12AQ41
3/ 8/88	@ 4:47	= 20AQ28
4/20/88	@ 15:11	= 0TA45
5/19/88	@ 4:35	= 20GE31
5/31/88	@ 22:45	= 26GE47
6/13/88	@ 3:56	= 22GE21
6/24/88	@ 22:43	= 18GE09
7/ 7/88	@ 0:11	= 23GE57
8/ 3/88	@ 3:30	= 11LE00
9/15/88	@ 15:50	= 19LI32
9/28/88	@ 21:35	= 27LI04
10/11/88	@ 6:34	= 18LI09
10/20/88	@ 5:11	= 11LI39
10/26/88	@ 18:33	= 15LI12
12/ 1/88	@ 9:24	= 9SG24
1/ 9/89	@ 4:52	= 8AQ00
1/16/89	@ 1:36	= 11AQ54
1/25/89	@ 0:10	= 5AQ00
2/ 5/89	@ 20:05	= 25CP59
2/18/89	@ 16:24	= 3AQ34
4/ 4/89	@ 13:33	= 14AR45
5/ 1/89	@ 3:05	= 1GE19
5/12/89	@ 11:54	= 6GE51
5/23/89	@ 21:36	= 2GE42
6/ 5/89	@ 8:07	= 28TA09
6/18/89	@ 18:33	= 4GE45
7/18/89	@ 8:18	= 25CN41
8/29/89	@ 4:07	= 2LI59
9/11/89	@ 20:56	= 10LI34
9/24/89	@ 22:11	= 1LI49
10/ 3/89	@ 23:47	= 25VI44
10/10/89	@ 9:56	= 29VI08
11/10/89	@ 18:56	= 18SC21
12/23/89	@ 11:03	= 21CP32
12/30/89	@ 23:25	= 25CP54
1/ 9/90	@ 2:03	= 18CP32
1/20/90	@ 4:35	= 9CP42
2/ 1/90	@ 3:56	= 16CP54
3/19/90	@ 2:38	= 28PI13
4/13/90	@ 12:33	= 12TA44
4/23/90	@ 6:57	= 17TA31
5/ 3/90	@ 23:50	= 13TA16
5/17/90	@ 2:01	= 7TA55
5/31/90	@ 5:43	= 15TA05
7/ 2/90	@ 17:22	= 10CN36
8/11/90	@ 15:05	= 16VI03
8/25/90	@ 14:06	= 23VI34
9/ 8/90	@ 4:01	= 15VI16
9/17/90	@ 12:09	= 9VI36
9/24/90	@ 1:47	= 12VI56
10/22/90	@ 4:22	= 28LI31
12/ 6/90	@ 11:03	= 5CP03
12/14/90	@ 21:16	= 10CP01
12/24/90	@ 7:40	= 2CP13
1/ 3/91	@ 17:59	= 23SG43
1/14/91	@ 12:50	= 0CP12
3/ 2/91	@ 2:36	= 11PI00
3/27/91	@ 10:02	= 24AR51
4/ 4/91	@ 18:12	= 29AR01
4/14/91	@ 20:43	= 24AR25
4/28/91	@ 9:48	= 17AR59
5/12/91	@ 16:24	= 25AR26

DATE	UT	LONG	DATE	UT	LONG	DATE	UT	LONG
SC 6/17/91	@ 4:38	= 25GE32	4/14/95	@ 12:49	= 24AR06	2/ 4/99	@ 5:21	= 14AQ55
GEE 7/24/91	@ 22:58	= 28LE32	5/12/95	@ 3:56	= 12GE25	3/ 3/99	@ 8:43	= 0AR24
SR 8/ 7/91	@ 23:59	= 5VI55	5/24/95	@ 9:01	= 18GE21	3/10/99	@ 9:12	= 4AR03
IC 8/21/91	@ 20:43	= 28LE20	6/ 5/95	@ 5:39	= 14GE07	3/19/99	@ 19:15	= 28PI44
SD 8/31/91	@ 14:35	= 23LE04	6/17/95	@ 6:57	= 9GE49	4/ 2/99	@ 9:17	= 20PI53
GWE 9/ 7/91	@ 17:03	= 26LE34	6/30/95	@ 0:17	= 15GE58	4/16/99	@ 11:26	= 28PI32
SC 10/ 3/91	@ 16:41	= 9LI59	7/28/95	@ 2:10	= 4LE33	5/25/99	@ 18:23	= 4GE06
GEE 11/19/91	@ 3:28	= 18SG31	9/ 8/95	@ 22:02	= 12LI38	6/28/99	@ 23:48	= 2LE23
SR 11/28/91	@ 16:54	= 24SG11	9/22/95	@ 9:12	= 20LI11	7/12/99	@ 23:34	= 9LE29
IC 12/ 8/91	@ 14:59	= 16SG00	10/5/95	@ 1:18	= 11LI20	7/26/99	@ 15:50	= 3LE13
SD 12/18/91	@ 11:05	= 7SG55	10/14/95	@ 0:38	= 5LI00	8/ 6/99	@ 3:27	= 28CN35
GWE 12/28/91	@ 1:01	= 13SG37	10/20/95	@ 11:15	= 8LI26	8/14/99	@ 17:48	= 2LE46
SC 2/12/92	@ 8:45	= 22AQ53	11/23/95	@ 5:27	= 0SG26	9/ 8/99	@ 14:59	= 15VI31
GEE 3/ 9/92	@ 16:52	= 7AR33	1/ 2/96	@ 19:02	= 1AQ06	10/24/99	@ 20:20	= 25SC04
SR 3/17/92	@ 0:32	= 11AR19	1/ 9/96	@ 22:01	= 5AQ10	11/ 5/99	@ 3:03	= 1SG44
IC 3/26/92	@ 14:57	= 6AR13	1/18/96	@ 21:41	= 28CP04	11/15/99	@ 22:06	= 23SC05
SD 4/ 9/92	@ 6:28	= 28PI44	1/30/96	@ 10:13	= 19CP07	11/25/99	@ 4:02	= 15SC37
GWE 4/23/92	@ 10:58	= 6AR21	2/11/96	@ 22:41	= 26CP35	12/ 3/99	@ 3:15	= 20SC14
SC 5/31/92	@ 16:22	= 10GE29	3/28/96	@ 7:38	= 7AR54	1/16/00	@ 1:20	= 25CP12
GEE 7/ 6/92	@ 0:17	= 10LE16	4/23/96	@ 6:45	= 23TA27	2/14/00	@ 22:41	= 13PI40
SR 7/20/92	@ 0:54	= 17LE29	5/ 3/96	@ 22:43	= 28TA39	2/21/00	@ 12:53	= 17PI09
IC 8/ 2/92	@ 20:44	= 10LE49	5/15/96	@ 1:14	= 24TA29	3/ 1/00	@ 15:12	= 11PI20
SD 8/13/92	@ 2:51	= 5LE58	5/27/96	@ 19:02	= 19TA39	3/14/00	@ 20:42	= 2PI47
GWE 8/21/92	@ 4:18	= 9LE53	6/10/96	@ 14:32	= 26TA32	3/28/00	@ 18:16	= 10PI35
SC 9/15/92	@ 3:48	= 22VI34	7/11/96	@ 9:02	= 19CN19	5/ 9/00	@ 3:51	= 18TA49
GEE 10/31/92	@ 15:11	= 2SG00	8/21/96	@ 10:35	= 25VI58	6/ 9/00	@ 16:52	= 13CN08
SR 11/11/92	@ 9:55	= 8SG22	9/ 4/96	@ 5:45	= 3LI29	6/23/00	@ 8:32	= 19CN58
IC 11/21/92	@ 22:11	= 29SC51	9/17/96	@ 13:06	= 24VI54	7/ 6/00	@ 11:37	= 14CN41
SD 12/ 1/92	@ 7:39	= 22SC13	9/26/96	@ 17:05	= 19VI00	7/17/00	@ 13:23	= 10CN23
GWE 12/ 9/92	@ 17:54	= 27SC09	10/ 3/96	@ 3:39	= 22VI20	7/27/00	@ 15:45	= 15CN14
SC 1/23/93	@ 15:43	= 3AQ39	11/ 1/96	@ 23:57	= 9SC50	8/22/00	@ 1:06	= 29LE14
GEE 2/21/93	@ 5:26	= 20PI39	12/15/96	@ 23:15	= 14CP39	10/ 6/00	@ 5:20	= 8SC37
SR 2/27/93	@ 23:00	= 24PI13	12/23/96	@ 19:39	= 19CP13	10/18/00	@ 13:45	= 15SC47
IC 3/ 9/93	@ 4:03	= 18PI36	1/ 2/97	@ 1:23	= 11CP41	10/30/00	@ 2:10	= 6SC57
SD 3/22/93	@ 13:42	= 10PI18	1/12/97	@ 20:30	= 2CP58	11/ 8/00	@ 2:18	= 29LI56
GWE 4/ 5/93	@ 13:02	= 18PI00	1/24/97	@ 9:33	= 9CP55	11/15/00	@ 5:48	= 3SC57
SC 5/16/93	@ 2:52	= 25TA16	3/11/97	@ 15:35	= 21PI06	12/25/00	@ 19:25	= 4CP19
GEE 6/17/93	@ 19:52	= 21CN18	4/ 5/97	@ 21:33	= 5TA10	1/28/01	@ 13:18	= 27AQ05
SR 7/ 1/93	@ 15:30	= 28CN14	4/15/97	@ 0:11	= 9TA39	2/ 4/01	@ 1:56	= 0PI42
IC 7/15/93	@ 1:10	= 22CN35	4/25/97	@ 10:34	= 5TA15	2/13/01	@ 0:18	= 24AQ21
SD 7/25/93	@ 20:49	= 18CN09	5/ 8/97	@ 18:06	= 29AR28	2/25/01	@ 15:43	= 15AQ25
GWE 8/ 4/93	@ 7:24	= 22CN40	5/23/97	@ 0:28	= 6TA47	3/11/01	@ 3:45	= 23AQ10
SC 8/29/93	@ 8:13	= 6VI01	6/25/97	@ 19:15	= 4CN14	4/23/01	@ 9:23	= 3TA17
GEE 10/14/93	@ 0:11	= 15SC30	8/ 3/97	@ 19:52	= 8VI47	5/22/01	@ 7:52	= 23GE39
SR 10/25/93	@ 22:42	= 22SC31	8/17/97	@ 19:51	= 16VI14	6/ 4/01	@ 5:23	= 29GE58
IC 11/ 6/93	@ 3:34	= 13SC44	8/31/97	@ 13:44	= 8VI11	6/16/01	@ 13:28	= 25GE27
SD 11/15/93	@ 5:20	= 6SC32	9/10/97	@ 1:43	= 2VI42	6/28/01	@ 5:50	= 21GE16
GWE 11/22/93	@ 17:09	= 10SC49	9/16/97	@ 20:15	= 6VI07	7/10/01	@ 1:35	= 26GE56
SC 1/ 3/94	@ 20:21	= 13CP13	10/13/97	@ 21:03	= 20LI33	8/ 5/01	@ 21:53	= 13LE37
GEE 2/ 4/94	@ 20:15	= 4PI03	11/28/97	@ 19:13	= 28SG04	9/18/01	@ 15:50	= 22LI11
SR 2/11/94	@ 8:23	= 7PI34	12/ 7/97	@ 17:04	= 3CP22	10/ 1/01	@ 19:25	= 29LI41
IC 2/20/94	@ 8:02	= 1PI27	12/17/97	@ 7:54	= 25SG24	10/14/01	@ 1:44	= 20LI46
SD 3/ 5/94	@ 5:46	= 22AQ38	12/27/97	@ 11:49	= 17SG05	10/23/01	@ 0:22	= 14LI12
GWE 3/18/94	@ 23:15	= 0PI27	1/ 6/98	@ 19:47	= 23SG18	10/29/01	@ 15:28	= 17LI50
SC 4/30/94	@ 10:02	= 9TA51	2/22/98	@ 8:30	= 3PI30	12/ 4/01	@ 21:36	= 12SG48
GEE 5/30/94	@ 10:02	= 1CN49	3/19/98	@ 23:31	= 17AR34	1/12/02	@ 1:41	= 10AQ39
SR 6/12/94	@ 17:49	= 8CN25	3/27/98	@ 19:43	= 21AR30	1/18/02	@ 20:53	= 14AQ29
IC 6/25/94	@ 9:59	= 3CN38	4/ 6/98	@ 16:36	= 16AR40	1/27/02	@ 18:54	= 7AQ39
SD 7/ 6/94	@ 19:42	= 29GE25	4/20/98	@ 7:33	= 9AR48	2/ 8/02	@ 17:29	= 28CP38
GWE 7/17/94	@ 22:13	= 4CN43	5/ 4/98	@ 13:52	= 17AR20	2/21/02	@ 15:51	= 6AQ14
SC 8/13/94	@ 0:56	= 20LE04	6/10/98	@ 6:58	= 19GE12	4/ 7/02	@ 8:54	= 17AR21
GEE 9/26/94	@ 11:09	= 29LI07	7/17/98	@ 1:46	= 20LE59	5/ 4/02	@ 4:13	= 4GE20
SR 10/9/94	@ 6:40	= 6SC29	7/31/98	@ 2:28	= 28LE16	5/15/02	@ 18:52	= 9GE59
IC 10/21/94	@ 7:20	= 27LI35	8/13/98	@ 23:49	= 21LE00	5/27/02	@ 7:10	= 5GE49
SD 10/30/94	@ 4:13	= 20LI49	8/23/98	@ 22:38	= 15LE58	6/ 8/02	@ 15:13	= 1GE21
GWE 11/5/94	@ 23:26	= 24LI35	8/31/98	@ 9:39	= 19LE37	6/21/02	@ 21:34	= 7GE50
SC 12/14/94	@ 3:17	= 21SG53	9/25/98	@ 19:51	= 2LI32	7/21/02	@ 1:49	= 28CN09
GEE 1/19/95	@ 9:45	= 17AQ33	11/11/98	@ 9:56	= 11SG34	9/ 1/02	@ 3:28	= 5LI39
SR 1/26/95	@ 1:19	= 21AQ16	11/21/98	@ 11:38	= 17SG32	9/14/02	@ 19:40	= 13LI15
IC 2/ 3/95	@ 23:01	= 14AQ38	12/ 1/98	@ 15:24	= 9SG13	9/27/02	@ 18:33	= 4LI28
SD 2/16/95	@ 5:04	= 5AQ37	12/11/98	@ 6:22	= 1SG18	10/ 6/02	@ 19:29	= 28VI19
GWE 3/ 1/95	@ 10:20	= 13AQ21	12/20/98	@ 8:37	= 6SG42	10/13/02	@ 5:21	= 1LI42

	2002								2014	
	DATE	UT	LONG	DATE	UT	LONG	DATE	UT	LONG
SC	11/14/02 @	4:42	= 21SC37	9/ 1/06 @	4:52	= 8VI37	6/28/10 @	12:09	= 6CN42
GEE	12/26/02 @	8:54	= 24CP11	10/17/06 @	0:45	= 18SC10	8/ 6/10 @	20:15	= 11VI35
SR	1/ 2/03 @	18:22	= 28CP27	10/28/06 @	19:18	= 25SC05	8/20/10 @	20:00	= 19VI04
IC	1/11/03 @	20:02	= 21CP10	11/ 8/06 @	21:31	= 16SC20	9/ 3/10 @	12:38	= 10VI54
SD	1/23/03 @	1:09	= 12CP18	11/18/06 @	0:25	= 9SC04	9/12/10 @	23:12	= 5VI22
GWE	2/ 4/03 @	3:45	= 19CP33	11/25/06 @	14:26	= 13SC24	9/19/10 @	15:50	= 8VI47
SC	3/21/03 @	23:36	= 0AR56	1/ 7/07 @	6:04	= 16CP32	10/17/10 @	1:06	= 23LI33
GEE	4/16/03 @	12:05	= 15TA39	2/ 7/07 @	15:50	= 6PI39	12/ 1/10 @	18:06	= 0CP46
SR	4/26/03 @	12:00	= 20TA32	2/14/07 @	4:37	= 10PI14	12/10/10 @	12:06	= 5CP55
IC	5/ 7/03 @	7:21	= 16TA20	2/23/07 @	4:46	= 4PI10	12/20/10 @	1:24	= 28SG02
SD	5/20/03 @	7:34	= 11TA07	3/ 8/07 @	4:45	= 25AQ25	12/30/10 @	7:22	= 19SG38
GWE	6/ 3/03 @	9:11	= 18TA13	3/21/07 @	22:35	= 3PI13	1/ 9/11 @	19:13	= 25SG56
SC	7/ 5/03 @	10:22	= 13CN00	5/ 3/07 @	4:05	= 12TA21	2/25/11 @	8:46	= 6PI23
GEE	8/14/03 @	15:39	= 18VI49	6/ 2/07 @	13:35	= 4CN58	3/22/11 @	20:43	= 20AR20
SR	8/28/03 @	13:42	= 26VI19	6/15/07 @	23:42	= 11CN36	3/30/11 @	20:50	= 24AR21
IC	9/11/03 @	1:58	= 17VI56	6/28/07 @	18:41	= 6CN41	4/ 9/11 @	19:36	= 19AR36
SD	9/20/03 @	8:53	= 12VI13	7/10/07 @	2:16	= 2CN28	4/23/11 @	10:05	= 12AR53
GWE	9/26/03 @	21:45	= 15VI34	7/20/07 @	22:41	= 7CN40	5/ 7/11 @	16:41	= 20AR25
SC	10/25/03 @	10:02	= 1SC34	8/15/07 @	19:59	= 22LE36	6/12/11 @	23:45	= 21GE39
GEE	12/ 9/03 @	9:05	= 7CP41	9/29/07 @	11:20	= 1SC46	7/20/11 @	2:54	= 23LE53
SR	12/17/03 @	16:03	= 12CP33	10/12/07 @	4:01	= 9SC05	8/ 3/11 @	3:50	= 1VI12
IC	12/27/03 @	1:12	= 4CP50	10/23/07 @	23:56	= 0SC11	8/17/11 @	1:06	= 23LE48
SD	1/ 6/04 @	13:45	= 26SG17	11/ 1/07 @	23:03	= 23LI21	8/26/11 @	22:06	= 18LE42
GWE	1/17/04 @	13:47	= 2CP53	11/ 8/07 @	20:03	= 27LI11	9/ 3/11 @	6:22	= 22LE19
SC	3/ 4/04 @	1:43	= 13PI49	12/17/07 @	15:26	= 25SG18	9/28/11 @	20:19	= 5LI21
GEE	3/29/04 @	8:04	= 27AR41	1/22/08 @	5:54	= 20AQ12	11/14/11 @	10:13	= 14SG15
SR	4/ 6/04 @	20:30	= 1TA55	1/28/08 @	20:34	= 23AQ53	11/24/11 @	7:20	= 20SG07
IC	4/17/04 @	1:05	= 27AR21	2/ 6/08 @	18:18	= 17AQ20	12/ 4/11 @	8:54	= 11SG50
SD	4/30/04 @	13:07	= 21AR07	2/19/08 @	2:58	= 8AQ19	12/14/11 @	1:43	= 3SG51
GWE	5/14/04 @	19:35	= 28AR33	3/ 3/08 @	10:52	= 16AQ05	12/23/11 @	7:35	= 9SG21
SC	6/18/04 @	21:26	= 27GE57	4/16/08 @	7:23	= 26AR40	2/ 7/12 @	9:00	= 17AQ58
GEE	7/27/04 @	0:06	= 1VI24	5/14/08 @	6:17	= 15GE29	3/ 5/12 @	5:26	= 3AR09
SR	8/10/04 @	0:33	= 8VI47	5/26/08 @	15:50	= 21GE32	3/12/12 @	7:49	= 6AR49
IC	8/23/04 @	20:52	= 1VI02	6/ 7/08 @	15:28	= 17GE14	3/21/12 @	19:20	= 1AR34
SD	9/ 2/04 @	13:11	= 25LE45	6/19/08 @	14:33	= 12GE59	4/ 4/12 @	10:13	= 23PI51
GWE	9/ 9/04 @	13:24	= 29LE15	7/ 2/08 @	2:04	= 19GE00	4/18/12 @	13:08	= 1AR30
SC	10/ 5/04 @	18:31	= 12LI50	7/29/08 @	20:06	= 7LE03	5/27/12 @	11:20	= 6GE34
GEE	11/21/03 @	2:54	= 21SG10	9/10/08 @	21:45	= 15LI18	7/ 1/12 @	2:09	= 5LE24
SR	11/30/04 @	12:18	= 26SG43	9/24/08 @	7:18	= 22LI50	7/15/12 @	2:16	= 12LE33
IC	12/10/04 @	8:23	= 18SG37	10/ 6/08 @	20:54	= 11LI13	7/28/12 @	19:59	= 6LE07
SD	12/20/04 @	6:29	= 10SG27	10/15/08 @	20:09	= 7LI34	8/ 8/12 @	5:41	= 1LE26
GWE	12/30/04 @	0:56	= 16SG18	10/22/08 @	7:36	= 11LI03	8/16/12 @	15:22	= 5LE31
SC	2/14/05 @	10:47	= 25AQ50	11/25/08 @	16:52	= 3SG47	9/10/12 @	12:48	= 18VI12
GEE	3/12/05 @	13:47	= 10AR17	1/ 4/09 @	16:07	= 3AQ43	10/26/12 @	20:20	= 27SC43
SR	3/20/05 @	0:14	= 14AR06	1/11/09 @	16:46	= 7AQ45	11/ 6/12 @	23:06	= 4SG18
IC	3/29/05 @	16:10	= 9AR03	1/20/09 @	15:59	= 0AQ44	11/17/12 @	15:47	= 25SC49
SD	4/12/05 @	7:47	= 1AR45	2/ 1/09 @	7:11	= 21CP45	11/26/12 @	22:51	= 18SC10
GWE	4/26/05 @	13:24	= 9AR22	2/13/09 @	22:02	= 29CP14	12/ 5/12 @	2:09	= 22SC55
SC	6/ 3/05 @	9:12	= 12GE53	3/31/09 @	3:29	= 10AR33	1/18/13 @	8:55	= 28CP25
GEE	7/ 9/05 @	2:37	= 13LE15	4/26/09 @	6:45	= 26TA25	2/16/13 @	18:50	= 16PI20
SR	7/23/05 @	3:01	= 20LE28	5/ 7/09 @	5:01	= 1GE44	2/23/13 @	9:42	= 19PI52
IC	8/ 5/05 @	23:37	= 13LE37	5/18/09 @	10:03	= 27TA36	3/ 4/13 @	12:57	= 14PI06
SD	8/16/05 @	3:51	= 8LE45	5/31/09 @	1:22	= 22TA52	3/17/13 @	20:05	= 5PI38
GWE	8/24/05 @	1:13	= 12LE35	6/13/09 @	17:26	= 29TA39	3/31/13 @	18:11	= 13PI24
SC	9/18/05 @	2:40	= 25VI17	7/14/09 @	2:16	= 21CN47	5/11/13 @	21:11	= 21TA19
GEE	11/ 3/05 @	15:06	= 4SG37	8/24/09 @	10:36	= 28VI41	6/12/13 @	19:41	= 16CN14
SR	11/14/05 @	5:43	= 10SG56	9/ 7/09 @	4:46	= 6LI13	6/26/13 @	13:10	= 23CN06
IC	11/24/05 @	15:44	= 2SG27	9/20/09 @	10:07	= 27VI35	7/ 9/13 @	18:43	= 17CN42
SD	12/ 4/05 @	2:24	= 24SC44	9/29/09 @	13:15	= 21VI37	7/20/13 @	18:24	= 13CN22
GWE	12/12/05 @	15:50	= 29SC45	10/ 5/09 @	23:15	= 24VI57	7/30/13 @	14:54	= 18CN05
SC	1/26/06 @	21:32	= 6AQ47	11/ 5/09 @	8:04	= 13SC02	8/24/13 @	20:58	= 1VI50
GEE	2/24/06 @	1:24	= 23PI21	12/18/09 @	21:11	= 17CP16	10/ 9/13 @	5:21	= 11SC16
SR	3/ 2/06 @	20:32	= 26PI55	12/26/09 @	14:40	= 21CP47	10/21/13 @	10:30	= 18SC23
IC	3/12/06 @	2:44	= 21PI23	1/ 4/10 @	19:06	= 14CP19	11/ 1/13 @	20:21	= 9SC34
SD	3/25/06 @	13:44	= 13PI11	1/15/10 @	16:53	= 5CP35	11/10/13 @	21:15	= 2SC30
GWE	4/14/06 @	14:54	= 20PI56	1/27/10 @	9:00	= 12CP34	11/18/13 @	3:11	= 6SC35
SC	5/18/06 @	20:03	= 27TA44	3/14/10 @	13:15	= 23PI50	12/29/13 @	6:27	= 7CP41
GEE	6/20/06 @	22:52	= 24CN23	4/ 8/10 @	19:47	= 8TA02	1/31/14 @	9:17	= 29AQ45
SR	7/ 4/06 @	19:35	= 1LE22	4/18/10 @	4:06	= 12TA38	2/ 6/14 @	21:47	= 3PI20
IC	7/18/06 @	7:10	= 25CN32	4/28/10 @	16:44	= 8TA17	2/15/14 @	20:21	= 27AQ04
SD	7/29/06 @	0:40	= 21CN04	5/11/10 @	22:29	= 2TA40	2/28/14 @	14:02	= 18AQ10
GWE	8/ 7/06 @	5:26	= 25CN28	5/26/10 @	4:02	= 9TA55	3/14/14 @	4:52	= 25AQ59

2014
2025

	DATE	UT	LONG
SC	4/26/14	@ 3:28	= 5TA49
GEE	5/25/14	@ 10:36	= 26GE45
SR	6/ 7/14	@ 11:59	= 3CN10
IC	6/19/14	@ 22:52	= 28GE34
SD	7/ 1/14	@ 12:51	= 24GE23
GWE	7/13/14	@ 2:54	= 29GE55
SC	8/ 8/14	@ 16:24	= 16LE03
GEE	9/21/14	@ 15:50	= 24LI50
SR	10/ 4/14	@ 17:04	= 2SC18
IC	10/16/14	@ 20:41	= 23LI24
SD	10/25/14	@ 19:20	= 16LI46
GWE	11/ 1/14	@ 11:37	= 20LI25
SC	12/ 8/14	@ 9:51	= 16SG12
GEE	1/14/15	@ 22:02	= 13AQ18
SR	1/21/15	@ 15:56	= 17AQ05
IC	1/30/15	@ 13:45	= 10AQ20
SD	2/11/15	@ 14:58	= 1AQ18
GWE	2/24/15	@ 16:13	= 8AQ58
SC	4/10/15	@ 3:59	= 19AR58
GEE	5/ 7/15	@ 5:32	= 7GE23
SR	5/19/15	@ 1:50	= 13GE09
IC	5/30/15	@ 16:56	= 8GE58
SD	6/11/15	@ 22:35	= 4GE34
GWE	6/25/15	@ 0:51	= 10GE56
SC	7/23/15	@ 19:25	= 0LE37
GEE	9/ 4/15	@ 3:45	= 8LI21
SR	9/17/15	@ 18:11	= 15LI55
IC	9/30/15	@ 14:40	= 7LI07
SD	10/ 9/15	@ 15:00	= 0LI55
GWE	10/16/15	@ 1:02	= 4LI18
SC	11/17/15	@ 14:56	= 24SC56
GEE	12/29/15	@ 6:17	= 26CP51
SR	1/ 5/16	@ 13:07	= 1AQ01
IC	1/14/16	@ 14:04	= 23CP49
SD	1/25/16	@ 21:52	= 14CP54
GWE	2/ 7/16	@ 3:06	= 22CP12
SC	3/23/16	@ 20:11	= 3AR37
GEE	4/18/16	@ 11:32	= 18TA35
SR	4/28/16	@ 17:22	= 23TA36
IC	5/ 9/16	@ 15:12	= 19TA24
SD	5/22/16	@ 13:21	= 14TA20
GWE	6/ 5/16	@ 13:02	= 21TA22
SC	7/ 7/16	@ 3:25	= 15CN27
GEE	8/16/16	@ 15:00	= 21VI32
SR	8/30/16	@ 13:05	= 29VI04
IC	9/12/16	@ 23:41	= 20VI37
SD	9/22/16	@ 5:31	= 14VI49
GWE	9/28/16	@ 17:09	= 18VI11
SC	10/27/16	@ 16:20	= 4SC40
GEE	12/11/16	@ 7:58	= 10CP22
SR	12/19/16	@ 10:56	= 15CP07
IC	12/28/16	@ 18:47	= 7CP28
SD	1/ 8/17	@ 9:44	= 28SG51
GWE	1/19/17	@ 14:15	= 5CP35
SC	3/ 7/17	@ 0:31	= 16PI37
GEE	4/ 1/17	@ 6:00	= 0TA31
SR	4/ 9/17	@ 23:17	= 4TA51
IC	4/20/17	@ 5:54	= 0TA20
SD	5/ 3/17	@ 16:35	= 24AR16
GWE	5/17/17	@ 23:03	= 1TA37
SC	6/21/17	@ 14:15	= 0CN23
GEE	7/30/17	@ 0:33	= 4VI14
SR	8/13/17	@ 1:01	= 11VI38
IC	8/26/17	@ 20:43	= 3VI47
SD	9/ 5/17	@ 11:31	= 28LE26
GWE	9/12/17	@ 9:22	= 1VI53
SC	10/ 8/17	@ 20:55	= 15LI45
GEE	11/24/17	@ 2:43	= 23SG51
SR	12/ 3/17	@ 7:35	= 29SG18
IC	12/13/17	@ 1:50	= 21SG14
SD	12/23/17	@ 1:51	= 13SG00
GWE	1/ 2/18	@ 0:50	= 18SG58

DATE	UT	LONG
2/17/18	@ 12:26	= 28AQ47
3/15/18	@ 10:18	= 13AR02
3/23/18	@ 0:18	= 16AR55
4/ 1/18	@ 17:53	= 11AR56
4/15/18	@ 9:22	= 4AR47
4/29/18	@ 15:50	= 12AR24
6/ 6/18	@ 2:03	= 15GE20
7/12/18	@ 4:58	= 16LE14
7/26/18	@ 5:03	= 23LE27
8/ 9/18	@ 2:08	= 16LE27
8/19/18	@ 4:26	= 11LE32
8/26/18	@ 22:13	= 15LE19
9/21/18	@ 1:55	= 28VI02
11/ 6/18	@ 15:22	= 7SG17
11/17/18	@ 1:33	= 13SG30
11/27/18	@ 9:17	= 5SG03
12/ 6/18	@ 21:25	= 27SC16
12/15/18	@ 15:50	= 2SG27
1/30/19	@ 2:53	= 9AQ54
2/26/19	@ 21:39	= 26PI04
3/ 5/19	@ 18:21	= 29PI39
3/15/19	@ 1:48	= 24PI11
3/28/19	@ 14:00	= 16PI06
4/11/19	@ 15:05	= 23PI48
5/21/19	@ 13:07	= 0GE12
6/24/19	@ 1:07	= 27CN25
7/ 7/19	@ 23:17	= 4LE28
7/21/19	@ 12:37	= 28CN28
8/ 1/19	@ 3:59	= 23CN57
8/10/19	@ 3:28	= 28CN15
9/ 4/19	@ 1:41	= 11VI15
10/20/19	@ 1:18	= 20SC49
10/31/19	@ 15:43	= 27SC38
11/11/19	@ 15:23	= 18SC55
11/20/19	@ 19:15	= 11SC35
11/28/19	@ 12:45	= 16SC02
1/10/20	@ 15:19	= 19CP49
2/10/20	@ 12:05	= 9PI22
2/17/20	@ 0:53	= 12PI53
2/26/20	@ 1:46	= 6PI55
3/10/20	@ 3:49	= 28AQ13
3/23/20	@ 23:09	= 6PI01
5/ 4/20	@ 21:41	= 14TA52
6/ 4/20	@ 16:30	= 8CN03
6/18/20	@ 5:00	= 14CN46
7/ 1/20	@ 2:54	= 9CN44
7/12/20	@ 8:28	= 5CN30
7/22/20	@ 22:41	= 10CN34
8/17/20	@ 15:11	= 25LE09
10/ 1/20	@ 11:26	= 4SC24
10/14/20	@ 1:06	= 11SC40
10/25/20	@ 18:25	= 2SC47
11/ 3/20	@ 17:53	= 25LI54
11/10/20	@ 16:58	= 29LI46
12/20/20	@ 3:26	= 28SG42
1/24/21	@ 2:20	= 22AQ52
1/30/21	@ 15:54	= 26AQ29
2/ 8/21	@ 13:47	= 20AQ01
2/21/21	@ 0:53	= 11AQ01
3/ 6/21	@ 9:56	= 18AQ46
4/19/21	@ 1:50	= 29AR14
5/17/21	@ 7:52	= 18GE32
5/29/21	@ 22:36	= 24GE43
6/11/21	@ 1:14	= 20GE21
6/22/21	@ 22:02	= 16GE08
7/ 5/21	@ 4:02	= 22GE01
8/ 1/21	@ 14:10	= 9LE32
9/13/21	@ 22:13	= 17LI58
9/27/21	@ 5:11	= 25LI28
10/ 9/21	@ 16:20	= 16LI35
10/18/21	@ 15:19	= 10LI08
10/25/21	@ 3:45	= 13LI38

DATE	UT	LONG
11/29/21	@ 4:39	= 7SG10
1/ 7/22	@ 13:35	= 6AQ23
1/14/22	@ 11:43	= 10AQ18
1/23/22	@ 10:28	= 3AQ22
2/ 4/22	@ 4:14	= 24CP23
2/16/22	@ 22:07	= 1AQ55
4/ 2/22	@ 23:12	= 13AR11
4/29/22	@ 8:09	= 29TA26
5/10/22	@ 11:49	= 4GE50
5/21/22	@ 19:19	= 0GE43
6/ 3/22	@ 8:02	= 26TA05
6/16/22	@ 21:33	= 2GE47
7/16/22	@ 19:39	= 24CN15
8/27/22	@ 9:56	= 1LI22
9/10/22	@ 3:39	= 8LI55
9/23/22	@ 6:52	= 0LI14
10/ 2/22	@ 9:08	= 24VI12
10/ 8/22	@ 18:50	= 27VI32
11/ 8/22	@ 16:47	= 16SC15
12/21/22	@ 19:07	= 19CP57
12/29/22	@ 9:33	= 24CP21
1/ 7/23	@ 12:57	= 16CP56
1/18/23	@ 13:13	= 8CP09
1/30/23	@ 8:37	= 15CP13
3/17/23	@ 10:43	= 26PI34
4/11/23	@ 19:02	= 10TA54
4/21/23	@ 8:36	= 15TA36
5/ 1/23	@ 23:29	= 11TA19
5/15/23	@ 3:18	= 5TA51
5/29/23	@ 7:24	= 13TA03
7/ 1/23	@ 5:08	= 9CN08
8/ 9/23	@ 20:26	= 14VI21
8/23/23	@ 20:01	= 21VI51
9/ 6/23	@ 11:12	= 13VI36
9/15/23	@ 20:24	= 8VI00
9/22/23	@ 11:37	= 11VI23
10/20/23	@ 5:41	= 26LI34
12/ 4/23	@ 17:48	= 3CP28
12/13/23	@ 7:09	= 0CP29
12/22/23	@ 18:54	= 0CP39
1/ 2/24	@ 3:08	= 22SG11
1/12/24	@ 19:13	= 28SG37
2/28/24	@ 8:41	= 9PI14
3/24/24	@ 17:54	= 23AR07
4/ 1/24	@ 22:17	= 27AR13
4/11/24	@ 23:04	= 22AR32
4/25/24	@ 12:56	= 15AR59
5/ 9/24	@ 19:58	= 23AR29
6/14/24	@ 16:33	= 24GE06
7/22/24	@ 3:51	= 26LE46
8/ 5/24	@ 4:57	= 4VI06
8/19/24	@ 2:00	= 26LE35
8/28/24	@ 21:17	= 21LE24
9/ 5/24	@ 2:32	= 24LE58
9/30/24	@ 21:11	= 8LI11
11/16/24	@ 9:45	= 16SG55
11/26/24	@ 2:43	= 22SG40
12/ 6/24	@ 2:19	= 14SG27
12/15/24	@ 20:59	= 6SG24
12/25/24	@ 7:13	= 12SG01
2/ 9/25	@ 12:07	= 20AQ59
3/ 8/25	@ 1:41	= 5AR53
3/15/25	@ 6:47	= 9AR35
3/24/25	@ 19:49	= 4AR24
4/ 7/25	@ 11:09	= 26PI50
4/21/25	@ 14:54	= 4AR28
5/30/25	@ 4:13	= 9GE01
7/ 4/25	@ 5:20	= 8LE26
7/18/25	@ 4:46	= 15LE34
7/31/25	@ 23:43	= 9LE00
8/11/25	@ 7:31	= 4LE15
8/19/25	@ 12:33	= 8LE15

	DATE	UT	LONG
SC	9/13/25	@ 10:56	= 20VI54
GEE	10/29/25	@ 20:15	= 0SG22
SR	11/ 9/25	@ 19:04	= 6SG51
IC	11/20/25	@ 9:25	= 28SC18
SD	11/29/25	@ 17:41	= 20SC43
GWE	12/ 8/25	@ 0:06	= 25SC32
SC	1/21/26	@ 15:47	= 1AQ36
GEE	2/19/26	@ 14:37	= 19PI00
SR	2/26/26	@ 6:48	= 22PI34
IC	3/ 7/26	@ 11:01	= 16PI52
SD	3/20/26	@ 19:35	= 8PI29
GWE	4/ 3/26	@ 18:56	= 16PI16
SC	5/14/26	@ 14:24	= 23TA48
GEE	6/15/26	@ 22:13	= 19CN19
SR	6/29/26	@ 17:38	= 26CN15
IC	7/13/26	@ 1:27	= 20CN42
SD	7/23/26	@ 23:01	= 16CN19
GWE	8/ 2/26	@ 14:09	= 20CN57
SC	8/27/26	@ 17:07	= 4VI27
GEE	10/12/26	@ 6:11	= 13SC56
SR	10/24/26	@ 7:14	= 20SC58
IC	11/ 4/26	@ 14:26	= 12SC10
SD	11/13/26	@ 15:56	= 5SC02
GWE	11/21/26	@ 0:39	= 9SC13
SC	1/ 1/27	@ 17:07	= 11CP02
GEE	2/ 3/27	@ 5:15	= 2PI26
SR	2/ 9/27	@ 17:39	= 5PI59
IC	2/18/27	@ 16:38	= 29AQ47
SD	3/ 3/27	@ 12:33	= 20AQ56
GWE	3/17/27	@ 4:30	= 28AQ44
SC	4/28/27	@ 21:21	= 8TA21
GEE	5/28/27	@ 12:39	= 29GE49
SR	6/10/27	@ 18:18	= 6CN22
IC	6/23/27	@ 8:02	= 1CN39
SD	7/ 4/27	@ 19:42	= 27GE28
GWE	7/16/27	@ 3:17	= 2CN52
SC	8/11/27	@ 11:05	= 18LE34
GEE	9/24/27	@ 16:07	= 27LI30
SR	10/ 7/27	@ 14:39	= 4SC55
IC	10/19/27	@ 15:32	= 26LI01
SD	10/28/27	@ 14:13	= 19LI19
GWE	11/ 4/27	@ 7:58	= 23LI01
SC	12/11/27	@ 22:16	= 19SG38
GEE	1/17/28	@ 18:22	= 15AQ57
SR	1/24/28	@ 11:03	= 19AQ41
IC	2/ 2/28	@ 8:47	= 13AQ01
SD	2/14/28	@ 12:39	= 4AQ00
GWE	2/27/28	@ 15:33	= 11AQ40
SC	4/11/28	@ 22:57	= 22AR34
GEE	5/ 9/28	@ 7:24	= 10GE26
SR	5/21/28	@ 8:45	= 16GE19
IC	6/ 2/28	@ 2:47	= 12GE06
SD	6/14/28	@ 6:07	= 7GE45
GWE	6/27/28	@ 3:56	= 14GE02
SC	7/25/28	@ 13:10	= 3LE06
GEE	9/ 6/28	@ 4:07	= 11LI03
SR	9/19/28	@ 16:36	= 18LI35
IC	10/ 2/28	@ 10:40	= 9LI46
SD	10/11/28	@ 10:29	= 3LI30
GWE	10/11/28	@ 21:05	= 6LI56
SC	11/20/28	@ 1:40	= 28SC15
GEE	12/31/28	@ 3:45	= 29CP31
SR	1/ 7/29	@ 7:56	= 3AQ37
IC	1/16/29	@ 8:17	= 26CP29
SD	1/27/29	@ 18:42	= 17CP33
GWE	2/ 9/29	@ 4:13	= 24CP56
SC	3/26/29	@ 16:32	= 6AR18
GEE	4/21/29	@ 11:26	= 21TA33
SR	5/ 1/29	@ 23:08	= 26TA40
IC	5/12/29	@ 23:28	= 22TA30
SD	5/25/29	@ 19:23	= 17TA34
GWE	6/ 8/29	@ 16:52	= 24TA31

DATE	UT	LONG
7/ 9/29	@ 20:32	= 17CN54
8/19/29	@ 16:13	= 24VI18
9/ 2/29	@ 12:20	= 1LI49
9/15/29	@ 21:13	= 23VI18
9/25/29	@ 2:01	= 17VI27
10/ 1/29	@ 12:56	= 20VI47
10/30/29	@ 23:15	= 7SC49
12/14/29	@ 6:22	= 13CP02
12/22/29	@ 5:51	= 17CP42
12/31/29	@ 12:28	= 10CP06
1/11/30	@ 5:47	= 1CP26
1/22/30	@ 13:41	= 8CP14
3/ 9/30	@ 22:55	= 19PI24
4/ 4/30	@ 4:24	= 3TA23
4/13/30	@ 2:34	= 7TA48
4/23/30	@ 11:14	= 3TA21
5/ 6/30	@ 20:17	= 27AR26
5/21/30	@ 2:32	= 4TA46
6/24/30	@ 7:06	= 2CN50
8/ 2/30	@ 1:24	= 7VI04
8/16/30	@ 1:21	= 14VI30
8/29/30	@ 20:12	= 6VI32
9/ 8/30	@ 9:29	= 1VI07
9/15/30	@ 5:15	= 4VI32
10/11/30	@ 23:48	= 18LI42
11/27/30	@ 1:52	= 26SG31
12/ 6/30	@ 2:47	= 1CP52
12/15/30	@ 19:14	= 23SG51
12/25/30	@ 21:17	= 15SG33
1/ 5/31	@ 0:50	= 21SG39
2/20/31	@ 13:34	= 1PI42
3/18/31	@ 7:35	= 15AR50
3/26/31	@ 0:44	= 19AR45
4/ 4/31	@ 20:02	= 14AR51
4/18/31	@ 11:17	= 7AR51
5/ 2/31	@ 17:43	= 15AR26
6/ 8/31	@ 18:51	= 17GE47
7/15/31	@ 6:16	= 19LE10
7/29/31	@ 6:48	= 26LE25
8/12/31	@ 4:07	= 19LE17
8/22/31	@ 4:29	= 14LE18
8/29/31	@ 18:33	= 17LE59
9/24/31	@ 12:29	= 0LI49
11/ 9/31	@ 14:37	= 9SG55
11/19/31	@ 21:18	= 16SG03
11/30/31	@ 2:44	= 7SG40
12/ 9/31	@ 16:26	= 29SC49
12/18/31	@ 14:54	= 5SG06
2/ 8/32	@ 7:30	= 12AQ59
2/29/32	@ 17:37	= 28PI47
3/ 7/32	@ 16:24	= 2AR23
3/17/32	@ 1:11	= 27PI00
3/30/32	@ 14:31	= 19PI02
4/13/32	@ 17:15	= 26PI46
5/23/32	@ 6:07	= 2GE40
6/26/32	@ 3:17	= 0LE27
7/10/32	@ 2:34	= 7LE33
7/23/32	@ 17:33	= 1LE24
8/ 3/32	@ 6:53	= 26CN49
8/12/32	@ 1:30	= 1LE02
9/ 5/32	@ 22:50	= 13VI54
10/22/32	@ 1:13	= 23SC28
11/ 2/32	@ 11:58	= 0SG12
11/13/32	@ 9:10	= 21SC32
11/22/32	@ 14:03	= 14SC08
11/30/32	@ 10:24	= 18SC39
1/13/33	@ 0:00	= 23CP06
2/12/33	@ 7:41	= 12PI02
2/18/33	@ 21:23	= 15PI34
2/27/33	@ 23:00	= 9PI39
3/13/33	@ 2:58	= 1PI02
3/26/33	@ 22:52	= 8PI49

DATE	UT	LONG
5/ 7/33	@ 15:11	= 17TA22
6/ 7/33	@ 20:09	= 11CN11
6/21/33	@ 10:07	= 17CN55
7/ 4/33	@ 10:50	= 12CN47
7/15/33	@ 14:21	= 8CN31
7/25/33	@ 22:35	= 13CN26
8/20/33	@ 10:37	= 27LE44
10/ 4/33	@ 10:35	= 7SC01
10/16/33	@ 22:05	= 14SC16
10/28/33	@ 12:47	= 5SC24
11/ 6/33	@ 12:41	= 28LI28
11/13/33	@ 13:52	= 2SC24
12/23/33	@ 15:09	= 2CP05
1/26/34	@ 22:24	= 25AQ32
2/ 2/34	@ 11:23	= 29AQ06
2/11/34	@ 9:29	= 22AQ42
2/23/34	@ 22:57	= 13AQ45
3/ 9/34	@ 10:07	= 21AQ31
4/21/34	@ 20:07	= 1TA47
5/20/34	@ 11:03	= 21GE40
6/ 2/34	@ 5:25	= 27GE55
6/14/34	@ 11:01	= 23GE28
6/26/34	@ 5:24	= 19GE17
7/ 8/34	@ 6:11	= 25GE04
8/ 4/34	@ 8:27	= 12LE03
9/16/34	@ 21:56	= 20LI38
9/30/34	@ 3:01	= 28LI07
10/12/34	@ 11:38	= 19LI13
10/21/34	@ 10:24	= 12LI43
10/28/34	@ 0:00	= 16LI16
12/ 2/34	@ 16:46	= 10SG33
1/10/35	@ 9:51	= 9AQ02
1/17/35	@ 6:44	= 12AQ56
1/26/35	@ 5:06	= 6AQ03
2/ 7/35	@ 1:26	= 27CP02
2/19/35	@ 22:30	= 4AQ40
4/ 5/35	@ 18:41	= 15AR48
5/ 2/35	@ 8:21	= 2GE25
5/13/35	@ 18:42	= 7GE59
5/25/35	@ 4:46	= 3GE50
6/ 6/35	@ 14:56	= 29TA18
6/20/35	@ 1:02	= 5GE53
7/19/35	@ 13:07	= 26CN43
8/30/35	@ 9:22	= 4LI02
9/13/35	@ 2:29	= 11LI37
9/26/35	@ 3:24	= 2LI53
10/ 5/35	@ 4:53	= 26VI47
10/11/35	@ 14:37	= 0LI10
11/12/35	@ 1:59	= 19SC30
12/24/35	@ 16:30	= 22CP35
1/ 1/36	@ 4:24	= 26CP56
1/10/36	@ 6:53	= 19CP35
1/21/36	@ 9:43	= 10CP45
2/ 2/36	@ 9:22	= 17CP55
3/19/36	@ 7:53	= 29PI17
4/13/36	@ 18:28	= 13TA51
4/23/36	@ 13:20	= 18TA37
5/ 4/36	@ 6:34	= 14TA23
5/17/36	@ 8:31	= 9TA03
5/31/36	@ 11:26	= 16TA12
7/ 2/36	@ 22:05	= 11CN35
8/11/36	@ 20:43	= 17VI07
8/25/36	@ 19:50	= 24VI38
9/ 8/36	@ 9:29	= 16VI18
9/17/36	@ 17:23	= 10VI38
9/24/36	@ 6:56	= 13VI59
10/22/36	@ 10:51	= 29LI37
12/ 6/36	@ 16:13	= 6CP05
12/15/36	@ 2:06	= 11CP03
12/24/36	@ 12:25	= 3CP16
1/ 3/37	@ 23:00	= 24SG45
1/14/37	@ 19:18	= 1CP18

	DATE	UT	LONG	DATE	UT	LONG	DATE	UT	LONG
SC	3/ 2/37	@ 8:08	= 12PI04	12/14/40	@ 10:40	= 23SG03	9/26/44	@ 1:33	= 3LI37
GEE	3/27/37	@ 15:50	= 25AR56	1/19/41	@ 15:00	= 18AQ34	11/11/44	@ 14:54	= 12SG36
SR	4/ 5/37	@ 0:06	= 0TA06	1/26/41	@ 6:14	= 22AQ18	11/21/44	@ 16:53	= 18SG36
IC	4/15/37	@ 2:57	= 25AR29	2/ 4/41	@ 4:00	= 15AQ41	12/ 1/44	@ 20:11	= 10SG17
SD	4/28/37	@ 15:58	= 19AR06	2/16/41	@ 10:28	= 6AQ41	12/11/44	@ 11:32	= 2SG22
GWE	5/12/37	@ 22:58	= 26AR34	3/ 1/41	@ 15:50	= 14AQ24	12/20/44	@ 13:58	= 7SG45
SC	6/17/37	@ 9:19	= 26GE32	4/14/41	@ 17:42	= 25AR08	2/ 4/45	@ 11:35	= 16AQ03
GEE	7/25/37	@ 4:52	= 29LE38	5/12/41	@ 9:51	= 13GE31	3/ 3/45	@ 13:58	= 1AR28
SR	8/ 8/37	@ 5:47	= 6VI59	5/24/41	@ 15:39	= 19GE29	3/10/45	@ 14:44	= 5AR07
IC	8/22/37	@ 2:29	= 29LE21	6/ 5/41	@ 12:40	= 15GE13	3/20/45	@ 0:57	= 29PI49
SD	8/31/37	@ 20:10	= 24LE07	6/17/41	@ 13:43	= 10GE56	4/ 2/45	@ 15:11	= 21PI59
GWE	9/ 7/37	@ 22:30	= 27LE38	6/30/41	@ 5:54	= 17GE04	4/16/45	@ 18:00	= 29PI40
SC	10/ 3/37	@ 22:36	= 11LI03	7/28/41	@ 7:01	= 5LE35	5/25/45	@ 23:08	= 5GE08
GEE	11/19/37	@ 9:17	= 19SG34	9/ 9/41	@ 4:24	= 13LI43	6/29/45	@ 6:22	= 3LE31
SR	11/28/37	@ 22:03	= 25SG13	9/22/41	@ 14:46	= 21LI14	7/13/45	@ 5:39	= 10LE36
IC	12/ 8/37	@ 19:43	= 17SG03	10/ 5/41	@ 6:27	= 12LI23	7/26/45	@ 22:07	= 4LE19
SD	12/18/37	@ 16:14	= 8SG57	10/14/41	@ 5:52	= 6LI03	8/ 6/45	@ 9:29	= 29CN41
GWE	12/28/37	@ 7:13	= 14SG41	10/20/41	@ 16:58	= 9LI31	8/14/45	@ 23:09	= 3LE48
SC	2/12/38	@ 14:37	= 23AQ58	11/23/41	@ 12:51	= 1SG36	9/ 8/45	@ 20:23	= 16VI35
GEE	3/10/38	@ 22:13	= 8AR37	1/ 3/42	@ 0:39	= 2AQ10	10/25/45	@ 1:41	= 26SC08
SR	3/18/38	@ 6:08	= 12AR22	1/10/42	@ 2:47	= 6AQ13	11/ 5/45	@ 8:09	= 2SG46
IC	3/27/38	@ 20:41	= 7AR16	1/19/42	@ 2:33	= 29CP07	11/16/45	@ 2:55	= 24SC09
SD	4/10/38	@ 12:13	= 29PI50	1/30/42	@ 15:33	= 20AQ11	11/25/45	@ 8:55	= 16SC41
GWE	4/24/38	@ 17:20	= 7AR29	2/12/42	@ 3:39	= 27CP36	12/ 3/45	@ 9:00	= 21SC19
SC	6/ 1/38	@ 21:05	= 11GE28	3/29/42	@ 12:41	= 8AR57	1/16/46	@ 8:00	= 26CP20
GEE	7/ 7/38	@ 6:34	= 11LE23	4/24/42	@ 12:11	= 24TA32	2/15/46	@ 3:45	= 14PI43
SR	7/21/38	@ 7:00	= 18LE35	5/ 5/42	@ 5:14	= 29TA45	2/21/46	@ 18:03	= 18PI14
IC	8/ 4/38	@ 2:58	= 11LE52	5/16/42	@ 8:05	= 25TA36	3/ 2/46	@ 20:31	= 12PI25
SD	8/14/38	@ 8:50	= 7LE03	5/29/42	@ 1:32	= 20TA47	3/16/46	@ 2:13	= 3PI52
GWE	8/22/38	@ 9:30	= 10LE57	6/11/42	@ 21:11	= 27TA42	3/29/46	@ 23:26	= 11PI39
SC	9/16/38	@ 9:27	= 23VI37	7/12/42	@ 13:46	= 20CN21	5/10/46	@ 8:39	= 19TA52
GEE	11/ 1/38	@ 20:54	= 3SG03	8/22/42	@ 15:45	= 27VI01	6/10/46	@ 23:03	= 14CN17
SR	11/12/38	@ 14:58	= 9SG24	9/ 5/42	@ 11:23	= 4LI33	6/24/46	@ 15:00	= 21CN06
IC	11/23/38	@ 2:59	= 0SG54	9/18/42	@ 18:24	= 25VI58	7/ 7/46	@ 18:24	= 15CN49
SD	12/ 2/38	@ 12:31	= 23SC15	9/27/42	@ 22:22	= 20VI03	7/18/46	@ 19:53	= 11CN31
GWE	12/10/38	@ 23:26	= 28SC12	10/ 4/42	@ 9:00	= 23VI24	7/28/46	@ 21:28	= 16CN19
SC	1/24/39	@ 22:09	= 4AQ46	11/ 3/42	@ 6:48	= 10SC58	8/23/46	@ 6:17	= 0VI18
GEE	2/22/39	@ 10:35	= 21PI42	12/17/42	@ 4:13	= 15CP41	10/ 7/46	@ 11:26	= 9SC42
SR	3/ 1/39	@ 4:11	= 25PI16	12/25/42	@ 0:43	= 20CP16	10/19/46	@ 18:58	= 16SC51
IC	3/10/39	@ 9:27	= 19PI39	1/ 3/43	@ 6:11	= 12CP44	10/31/46	@ 7:05	= 8SC11
SD	3/23/39	@ 19:21	= 11PI22	1/14/43	@ 1:50	= 4CP01	11/ 9/46	@ 7:27	= 1SC00
GWE	4/ 6/39	@ 18:56	= 19PI05	1/25/43	@ 14:20	= 10PI45	11/16/46	@ 11:09	= 5SC01
SC	5/17/39	@ 7:37	= 26TA17	3/12/43	@ 20:59	= 22PI10	12/27/46	@ 2:34	= 5CP28
GEE	6/19/39	@ 1:30	= 22CN24	4/ 7/43	@ 2:32	= 6TA14	1/29/47	@ 18:11	= 28AQ09
SR	7/ 2/39	@ 21:50	= 29CN23	4/16/43	@ 6:19	= 10TA45	2/ 5/47	@ 7:01	= 1PI45
IC	7/16/39	@ 7:45	= 23CN40	4/26/43	@ 17:05	= 6TA22	2/14/47	@ 5:22	= 25AQ25
SD	7/27/39	@ 3:08	= 19CN14	5/10/43	@ 0:20	= 0TA37	2/26/47	@ 21:06	= 16AQ29
GWE	8/ 5/39	@ 12:34	= 23CN44	5/24/43	@ 6:34	= 7TA55	3/12/47	@ 10:02	= 24AQ16
SC	8/30/39	@ 13:30	= 7VI03	6/26/43	@ 23:56	= 5CN16	4/24/47	@ 14:17	= 4TA20
GEE	10/15/39	@ 6:22	= 16SC34	8/ 5/43	@ 1:41	= 9VI52	5/23/47	@ 13:47	= 24GE46
SR	10/27/39	@ 3:55	= 23SC33	8/19/43	@ 1:34	= 17VI19	6/ 5/47	@ 12:07	= 1CN07
IC	11/ 7/39	@ 8:28	= 14SC46	9/ 1/43	@ 19:18	= 9VI15	6/17/47	@ 20:35	= 26GE35
SD	11/16/39	@ 10:39	= 7SC35	9/11/43	@ 7:04	= 3VI46	6/29/47	@ 12:37	= 22GE25
GWE	11/23/39	@ 22:13	= 11SC50	9/18/43	@ 1:19	= 7VI10	7/11/47	@ 7:19	= 28GE03
SC	1/ 5/40	@ 3:24	= 14CP22	10/15/43	@ 3:17	= 21LI39	8/ 7/47	@ 2:47	= 14LE34
GEE	2/ 6/40	@ 1:13	= 5PI05	11/30/43	@ 1:02	= 29SG10	9/19/47	@ 22:07	= 23LI17
SR	2/12/40	@ 13:40	= 8PI36	12/ 8/43	@ 22:00	= 4CP25	10/ 3/47	@ 0:46	= 0SC45
IC	2/21/40	@ 13:13	= 2PI30	12/18/43	@ 12:41	= 26SG26	10/15/47	@ 6:45	= 21LI50
SD	3/ 5/40	@ 11:21	= 23AQ42	12/28/43	@ 16:48	= 18SG07	10/24/47	@ 5:20	= 15LI15
GWE	3/19/40	@ 4:41	= 1PI30	1/ 8/44	@ 1:19	= 24SG20	10/30/47	@ 20:31	= 18LI52
SC	4/30/40	@ 15:11	= 10TA52	2/23/44	@ 14:14	= 4PI36	12/ 6/47	@ 5:01	= 13SG58
GEE	5/30/40	@ 16:18	= 2CN56	3/20/44	@ 4:24	= 18AR36	1/13/48	@ 6:56	= 11AQ43
SR	6/13/40	@ 0:20	= 9CN32	3/28/44	@ 1:31	= 22AR35	1/20/48	@ 1:46	= 15AQ32
IC	6/25/40	@ 16:54	= 4CN43	4/ 6/44	@ 22:41	= 17AR46	1/28/48	@ 23:51	= 8AQ43
SD	7/ 7/40	@ 2:22	= 0CN32	4/20/44	@ 13:36	= 10AR55	2/ 9/48	@ 22:47	= 29CP42
GWE	7/18/40	@ 4:30	= 5CN50	5/ 4/44	@ 20:04	= 18AR27	2/22/48	@ 21:39	= 7AQ20
SC	8/13/40	@ 5:57	= 21LE06	6/10/44	@ 11:39	= 20GE14	4/ 7/48	@ 13:54	= 18AR35
GEE	9/26/40	@ 16:30	= 0SC09	7/17/44	@ 6:56	= 22LE06	5/ 4/48	@ 10:19	= 5GE28
SR	10/ 9/40	@ 12:07	= 7SC31	7/31/44	@ 8:24	= 29LE22	5/16/48	@ 1:32	= 11GE08
IC	10/21/40	@ 10:18	= 28LI37	8/14/44	@ 5:44	= 22LE05	5/27/48	@ 14:16	= 6GE58
SD	10/30/40	@ 9:07	= 21LI52	8/24/44	@ 4:12	= 17LE02	6/ 8/48	@ 22:00	= 2GE30
GWE	11/ 6/40	@ 4:35	= 25LI37	8/31/44	@ 14:48	= 20LE42	6/22/48	@ 4:24	= 9GE00

	DATE	UT	LONG		DATE	UT	LONG		DATE	UT	LONG
SC	7/21/48	@ 6:37	= 29CN11		7/ 5/49	@ 15:06	= 14CN02		6/20/50	@ 2:07	= 28GE59
GEE	9/ 1/48	@ 9:45	= 6LI45		8/14/49	@ 20:20	= 19VI51		7/28/50	@ 5:20	= 2VI29
SR	9/15/48	@ 1:10	= 14LI19		8/28/49	@ 19:23	= 27VI25		8/11/50	@ 6:24	= 9VI53
IC	9/27/48	@ 23:42	= 5LI32		9/11/49	@ 7:26	= 19VI01		8/25/50	@ 2:38	= 2VI07
SD	10/ 7/48	@ 0:29	= 29VI22		9/20/49	@ 14:12	= 13VI17		9/ 3/50	@ 18:45	= 26LE49
GWE	10/13/48	@ 10:18	= 2LI46		9/27/49	@ 2:37	= 16VI36		9/10/50	@ 18:34	= 0VI18
SC	11/14/48	@ 11:46	= 22SC46		10/25/49	@ 16:36	= 2SC42		10/ 7/50	@ 0:31	= 13LI57
GEE	12/26/48	@ 13:58	= 25CP13		12/ 9/49	@ 14:43	= 8CP44		11/22/50	@ 8:54	= 22SG15
SR	1/ 2/49	@ 23:17	= 29CP31		12/17/49	@ 21:02	= 13CP37		12/ 1/50	@ 17:21	= 27SG47
IC	1/12/49	@ 0:51	= 22CP14		12/27/49	@ 5:59	= 5CP54		12/11/50	@ 13:10	= 19SG40
SD	1/23/49	@ 6:20	= 13CP21		1/ 6/50	@ 18:54	= 27SG19		12/21/50	@ 11:34	= 11SG31
GWE	2/ 4/49	@ 9:00	= 20CP36		1/17/50	@ 19:13	= 3CP58		12/31/50	@ 6:17	= 17SG20
SC	3/22/49	@ 4:45	= 1AR59		3/ 5/50	@ 7:13	= 14PI54				
GEE	4/16/49	@ 17:37	= 16TA46		3/30/50	@ 13:07	= 28AR44				
SR	4/26/49	@ 18:22	= 21TA40		4/ 8/50	@ 2:29	= 3TA01				
IC	5/ 7/49	@ 14:03	= 17TA27		4/18/50	@ 7:22	= 28AR27				
SD	5/20/49	@ 13:59	= 12TA16		5/ 1/50	@ 19:12	= 22AR14				
GWE	6/ 3/49	@ 15:22	= 19TA22		5/16/50	@ 1:24	= 29AR38